JOYCE, BAKHTIN, AND POPULAR LITERATURE

JOYCE, BAKHTIN, AND POPULAR LITERATURE

Chronicles of Disorder

BY R. B. KERSHNER

The University of North Carolina Press

CHAPEL HILL AND LONDON

© 1989 The University of North Carolina Press

Library of Congress Cataloging-in-Publication Data
Kershner, R. B., 1944–

Joyce, Bakhtin, and popular literature:
chronicles of disorder /
by R. B. Kershner, Jr.

p.   cm.
Bibliography: p.
Includes index.
ISBN 0-8078-1833-X (alk. paper)
ISBN 0-8078-4387-3 (pbk.: alk. paper)
1. Joyce, James, 1882–1941—Knowledge—Literature.
2. Bakhtin, M. M. (Mikhail Mikhaïlovich), 1895–1975.
3. Popular literature—History and
criticism—Theory, etc.   4. Books and reading in
literature.   5. Popular culture in literature.
6. Dialectic.   I. Title.
PR6019.09Z674   1989   88-22711
823'.912—dc19   CIP

The paper in this book meets the guidelines for
permanence and durability of the Committee on
Production Guidelines for Book Longevity of the
Council on Library Resources.

Printed in the United States of America

96   95   94   93   92   6   5   4   3   2

FOR
RHONDA,
DANIEL,
AND
RACHEL

CONTENTS

ACKNOWLEDGMENTS

During the past fifteen years the subject of Joyce's use of popular literature has intrigued me. The path toward this book has been anything but
straightforward, marked by wide detours and extravagances, blind alleys
and dead ends, but along the way I have been given generous assistance
by more sources than I can name. The Graduate School of the University
of Florida twice supported me with summer research grants, and the
National Endowment for the Humanities did so once. I was especially
fortunate to be given the opportunity of teaching at University College
Dublin during a semester in 1984, and I want to express my gratitude to
the faculty in the department of English and Anglo-Irish literature there
for the warm welcome I received. In particular I want to thank J. C. C.
Mays, Declan Kiberd, Seamus Deane, and Augustine Martin for their
substantial help in my research and for their unstinting encouragement
and personal kindness. An early version of my discusion of "The Sisters"
was delivered under the auspices of the department's Staff Seminars. The
staff of the National Library was helpful and efficient, and several of
Dublin's nonacademic Joyceans gave me more of their time and attention than I had any right to expect. I especially want to thank Gerry
O'Flaherty and Hugh Oram—who shared with me his vast knowledge of
Irish newspapers—and to express my gratitude to the late John Garvin.

I have been unusually fortunate in my colleagues at Florida, many of
whom have helped clarify my thinking, suggested useful references, or
simply lent informed moral support during this project. Academic work
often hinges on happy accidents; it was a graduate student, Carlos
Valdes, who suggested at the right time that Bakhtin's writings might be
useful to me. Among my colleagues, I would like to express my gratitude
to Jim Twitchell, Robert Ray, Alistair Duckworth, Jack Perlette, Anne G.
Jones, Ronald Carpenter, Al and Judy Shoaf, Robert Thomson, Ellie
Ragland-Sullivan, and Greg Ulmer. Ruth Baldwin of the Baldwin Library was helpful in providing rare copies of nineteenth-century children's literature. As always, my students have been a source of inspiration; in particular I would like to thank my senior English Honors
seminar in Joyce and Bakhtin for providing the most exciting class of my
teaching experience and for suggesting many readings and ideas that

have undoubtedly made their way into this book, but that I can no longer distinguish from my own thoughts.

Among my colleagues elsewhere, Weldon Thornton, to whom all contemporary Joyceans are greatly indebted, encouraged me in the early stages of my research, as did Leslie Fiedler. Zack Bowen kindly sent me opera libretti. Suzette Henke has made valuable suggestions in the course of the book's writing, and Cheryl Herr, whose work in some ways has paralleled mine, has been a helpful and insightful critic. Her ground-breaking work in the study of Irish popular culture has been a stimulus and an example. During the writing of this book, Bob Fuhrel loaned me his Joyce library. I am grateful for this, and for his friendship. I would also like to acknowledge two of my teachers, Ian Watt and J. Hillis Miller. Although neither may recognize his trace in any part of this book, both are powerful voices in it, in however distorted or inadequate a form.

I am indebted to the editors of *ELH*, where a portion of chapter 4 appeared in different form, for permission to reprint parts of my essay. I am also indebted to the editors of the *James Joyce Quarterly* for permission to reprint a portion of chapter 5.

Finally, I would like to express my gratitude to Rhonda Riley. If, as Bakhtin says, "the self is the gift of the other," mine is most nearly hers.

ABBREVIATIONS IN THE TEXT

References to Joyce's and to Bakhtin's works are cited parenthetically in the text and are to the following editions:

James Joyce:

CW *The Critical Writings of James Joyce.* Ed. Ellsworth Mason and Richard Ellmann. New York: Viking Press, 1959.

D *"Dubliners": Text, Criticism, and Notes.* Ed. Robert Scholes and A. Walton Litz. New York: Viking Press, 1968.

E *"Exiles": A Play in Three Acts, Including Hitherto Unpublished Notes by the Author, Discovered after his Death, and an Introduction by Padraic Colum.* New York: Viking Press, 1951.

P *"A Portrait of the Artist as a Young Man": Text, Criticism, and Notes.* Ed. Chester G. Anderson. New York: Viking Press, 1968.

SH *Stephen Hero.* Ed. John J. Slocum and Herbert Cahoon. New York: New Directions, 1963.

U *"Ulysses": The Corrected Text.* Ed. Hans Walter Gabler, with Wolfhard Steppe and Claus Melchior. New York: Random House, 1986. Parenthetical references following the slash are to *Ulysses* (New York: Random House, 1961). Quotations follow Gabler's text.

Mikhail Bakhtin:

DI *The Dialogic Imagination: Four Essays.* Ed. Michael Holquist; trans. Caryl Emerson and Michael Holquist. Austin: University of Texas Press, 1981.

FMLS *The Formal Method in Literary Scholarship.* As by Bakhtin/P. N. Medvedev. Trans. Albert J. Werle. 1978. Reprint. Cambridge: Harvard University Press, 1985.

MPL *Marxism and the Philosophy of Language.* As by V. N. Volosinov. Trans. Ladislav Matejka and I. R. Titunik. 1973. Reprint. Cambridge: Harvard University Press, 1986.

PDP *Problems of Dostoevsky's Poetics.* Trans. Caryl Emerson. Minneapolis: University of Minnesota Press, 1984.

RW *Rabelais and His World.* Trans. Helene Iswolsky. Bloomington: Indiana University Press, 1984.

SG *Speech Genres and Other Late Essays.* Ed. Michael Holquist; trans. Vern McGee. Austin: University of Texas Press, 1986.

JOYCE, BAKHTIN, AND POPULAR LITERATURE

· 1 ·

JOYCE, BAKHTIN, AND

THE CANON

Joyce and Popular Literature

Toward the middle of the "Nighttown" episode of *Ulysses*, Leopold Bloom has become both Messiah and Ruler, but his hegemony is threatened by jeers from the Man in the Macintosh. Fearing that the populace will be alienated, Bloom and his bodyguard take immediate countermeasures: they distribute to the crowd "Maundy money, commemoration medals, loaves and fishes, temperance badges . . . , 40 days' indulgences, spurious coins," and a host of similar items, all either cheap, useless, or counterfeit. But the climactic gift is a set of "cheap reprints of the World's Twelve Worst Books: Froggy and Fritz (politic), Care of the Baby (infantilic), 50 Meals for 7/6 (culinic), Was Jesus a Sun Myth? (historic), Expel That Pain (medic), Infant's Compendium of the Universe (cosmic), Let's All Chortle (hilaric), Canvasser's Vade Mecum (journalic), Loveletters of Mother Assistant (erotic), Who's Who in Space (astric), Songs that Reached Our Heart (melodic), Pennywise's Way to Wealth (parsimonic)" (*U*, 396/485–86). The Women spontaneously hail Bloom as "Little father!" and even the Citizen is moved to tearful praise. In the context of his other efforts to entertain the multitudes, Bloom's gesture is clearly in the nature of an opiate; a cynical leader, he manipulates public opinion with bread and circuses.[1] "Loveletters of Mother Assistant" and the other titles prove to be a particularly effective variety of circus.

But Joyce's attitude toward popular literature was not as simply scornful or dismissive as this episode might imply. Gerty MacDowell's apparent possession in the "Nausicaa" episode by the guiding consciousness
of *The Lamplighter* and *The Princess Novelette* certainly has its comic
side, but it has a tragic aspect as well; like a cut-rate Madame Bovary or
Julien Sorel, she has been painfully misled by her reading, indeed lamed
by it. And all of the major characters in *Ulysses* have, to greater or lesser
extents, been affected by the reading that Joyce painstakingly specifies—
the newspapers, magazines, romances, "self-improvement" guides, and
casual works of fiction that lie scattered throughout the text, giving the
book so much of its period flavor. The sheer mass of allusion to popular
literature and other aspects of popular culture in *Ulysses* is daunting and
often dismissed as either random bits of period "furniture" thrown in to
add historical verisimilitude or as evidence of an encyclopedic technique
run amok. But, as Cheryl Herr argues in her ground-breaking study of
popular culture in Joyce, Joyce's allusions are both structural and functional. In their broadest implications, they testify to "the force of culture
on the writer, the extent to which what we conceive to be a continuous
individual consciousness is composed of materials derived from sources
outside the mind."[2] Long before his writing career began, Joyce was
fascinated by the use of words in the popular culture of his time and
convinced of the resonance of popular literature within any consciousness—his own included. That his fascination was at times horrified is
undeniable; but as he aged, in this respect—as in most others—his attitude became increasingly complex and ambivalent. And from the beginning of his writing, shop signs, newspapers, playbills, magazines, and
popular novels crop up with striking frequency.

Adolescent Attitudes

In the draft version of *A Portrait of the Artist as a Young Man* published
as *Stephen Hero*, Stephen readily propounds an aesthetic in which the
socio-literary context of words determines their value. "Words," he
claims, "have a certain value in the literary tradition and a certain value
in the market-place—a debased value" (*SH*, 27). Yet he is "often hypno-
tised by the most commonplace conversation," and finds words for his
"treasure-house" not only in Skeat's dictionary but "in the shops, on

advertisements, in the mouths of the plodding public" (*SH*, 26, 30). He reads street ballads in shop windows and racing forms outside tobacco shops and pours over bookstalls selling literary rubbish (*SH*, 145). Stephen may believe that the aspiring artist is capable of a rescue operation, saving words from their debasing circumstances, yet this still fails to explain the peculiar hypnotic power over his mind held by words from the popular domain. Stephen's fellows are more likely to be intrigued by his absorption in serious modern literature, since they share the popular confusion between serious literature and risqué books. He finds their misapprehension both amusing and annoying, as when Wells expresses the hope that his friend will someday be author of "a second *Trilby* or something of that sort" (*SH*, 72). Stephen himself finds no difficulty in identifying a cone-shaped model of writing, with poetry at the apex and the "chaos of unremembered writing" at the base (*SH*, 78).

But for Joyce, even at this early stage, the situation may not be so clear-cut. It is immediately after these passages that Stephen becomes the target of rather crude authorial irony: he is characterized as "the fiery-hearted revolutionary" and "this heaven-ascending essayist" (*SH*, 80). For Stephen is involved already in contradictions and ambivalences; he believes that art is not an escape from life, but "the very central expression of life" (*SH*, 86), and in most analyses popular literature is undeniably an aspect of that. Indeed, one of the sources of the "sudden spiritual manifestation" that he terms *epiphany* is a "vulgarity of speech" of the sort codified in popular writing (*SH*, 211). Like the president with whom Stephen argues over Ibsen, a man who quotes journalistic opinion on that playwright despite his own low opinion of the newspapers, Stephen may be less programmatic in his opposition than he believes himself to be.

He is fascinated by popular writing in much the way he is fascinated by Cranly. His friend's willed facade of what Stephen calls "impossible prosiness" must, he feels, conceal a "mysterious purpose" (*SH*, 220). On several occasions in *Stephen Hero* Cranly stands, apparently mesmerized, before a posted newspaper; on one such, he reads out the items "in his flattest accent," from "Nationalist Meeting at Ballinrobe" and "Important Speeches" down through "Mad Cow at Cabra" and "Literature &" (*SH*, 221). In the ensuing elliptical conversation Cranly is quick to challenge Stephen's assumption that literature is actually the most important item on the list—a challenge Stephen believes, but cannot be sure, is made out of "sheer perversity." Stephen interprets the newspaper—a series of unrelated items and categories united, as McLuhan said, only by their dateline—as a horrible example of the degradation of art by subordinating it to a mad cow; but Cranly's world-weary recitation implies that all the items are equally valueless.

The final appearance of popular literature in the fragmentary manuscript of *Stephen Hero* is more disturbing than inscrutably banal. Walking with a group of young men, Stephen comes upon a crowd gathered at a canal bank, where a woman has drowned. Stephen remains behind, "gazing into the canal near the feet of the body, looking at a fragment of paper on which was printed: The Lamp a magazine for . . . the rest was torn away and several other pieces of paper were floating about in the water" (*SH*, 252–53). Certainly we are meant to see the woman's corpse and the fragment of magazine as parallel in their pitiable vulgarity; probably we are also meant to realize the weakness of the light shed by popular religious periodicals like *The Lamp*. The scene is powerful, at least in part because it is narrated with scrupulous objectivity. Stephen, both repelled and fascinated, unable to walk away from the sad tableau, cuts a more attractive figure here than in most of the manuscript. Uncharacteristically and mercifully, he is silent. The scene suggests similar but less dramatic incidents in *Portrait* where Stephen Dedalus stands as if hypnotized before shop signs and billboards, or where he walks off into the least attractive byways of Dublin, breathing "horse piss and rotted straw" in order to calm his heart (*P*, 86). There is an element of self-mortification in these episodes, but there is also an element of willed "grounding" of a self overly inclined to spirituality and abstraction. Stephen, and probably Joyce as well, is something of an aesthetic Antaeus; he weakens if he goes too long without touching the earth.

Joyce, the Press, and Popular Writing

For Joyce, as for many modern writers, the "earth" of popular experience is already text. Joyce grew up in a household where, as with most middle-class Dublin households around the turn of the century, popular novels and magazines and the popular press were a constant presence. A favorite hobby of Joyce's father was studying the picture puzzles in *Tit-Bits* and *Answers to Correspondents* magazines, for the solution of which substantial prizes were offered weekly; Joyce told Eugene Sheehy that on his university admissions form he described his father's occupation as "going in for competitions."[3] Through puzzles and quizzes, extensive letters columns, and even the provision of free life insurance to subscribers, popular magazines in Great Britain spared no efforts to involve themselves directly in the lives of their readers. In this early avatar of what Hans Magnus Enzensberger has termed the "consciousness industry," publishers were responding to an unprecedented growth and diversity in the genres of popular periodicals and popular fiction and to the concomitant unprecedented increase in competition for a limited readership. By 1904 magazines addressed specifically to homemakers included *Home*, *Home Chat*, *Home Circle*, *Home Companion*, *Home Fashions*, *Home Friend*, *Home Life*, *Home Links*, *Home Messenger*, *Home Notes*, *Home Stories*, and *Home Words*; if the reader's interests were less purely domestic, she might prefer the *Ladies' Review*, *Lady of the House*, *Lady's Companion*, *Lady's Home Herald*, *Lady's Home Magazine*, *Lady's Magazine*, *Lady's-Own Novelette*, *Lady's Realm*, or *Lady's World*. An audience less concerned with social station might receive the *Woman at Home*, *Woman's World*, *Woman's Life*, *Woman's Work*, or *Womanhood*.[4]

But if competition was intense, the rewards for a successful publisher were also remarkable. The Dublin-born Alfred Harmsworth, later Lord Northcliffe, was as responsible as any one man for the invention of modern journalism. He founded his publishing empire upon magazines for boys and girls that attacked, emulated, competed with, and soon displaced the old "penny dreadfuls"; as a writer he contributed to *Tit-Bits*, then founded the competing *Answers to Correspondents*. Conundrum magazines like *Tit-Bits* and *Answers*, which offered a potpourri of faintly spicy stories for gentlemen, quizzes, puzzles, games, jokes, oddities and curiosities, and contests, helped Harmsworth realize that his semiliterate readership demanded above all else brevity and clarity in the "bits" making up its magazines. He applied the same principles successfully in the newspapers he founded, notably the *Daily Mail* (in 1896) and the *Daily Mirror* (1903); among his other innovations, Harmsworth gave new emphasis, informality, and brevity to newspaper headlines, a feat Joyce reflects and parodies in "Aeolus." By 1908 he had bought out the *Observer* and the *Times* and saw himself as an immense influence in the political life of Great Britain. Perhaps unsurprisingly, he died a megalomaniac. Commentators who feared the erosion of artistic standards in an industrialized world—and they were certainly a majority—saw in Harmsworth a focus of contagion. Shane Leslie, an Edwardian man of letters characterizing the Edwardian age, writes, "the influences which corroded literature worked with tenfold corruption through the press. The *Daily Mail*, ochre offspring of the yellow nineties, reached its zenith in Edwardian days, when its proprietor became proprietor of the *Times*. . . . Journalism and literature became as indistinguishable as republicanism and Empery under Napoleon."[5]

Joyce grew up reading Harmsworth's magazines for boys, as "An Encounter" attests, and while a student at Belvedere wrote a story he intended to submit to *Tit-Bits*. "In it a man who has attended a masked ball dressed as a prominent Russian diplomat is walking by the Russian Embassy on his way home, thinking about the 'laughing witch,' his fiancée, when a Nihilist tries to assassinate him. The police arrest him as well as his assailant, but his fiancée, hearing of the attempt, realizes what has happened and comes to the police station to explain and release him. . . . Three or four years later [Joyce] rewrote the story simply as a burlesque . . . and he refers to it jocularly in *Ulysses* as 'Matcham's Masterstroke.' "[6] The notion of earning ready cash through popular publication may have died hard; in 1905 Joyce informed his brother that he had read Marie Corelli's *Sorrows of Satan* (1895) and *Ziska, The Problem of a Wicked Soul* (1897), Mrs. Lovett Cameron's *A Difficult Matter* (1898), *Good Mrs. Hypocrite* (1899) by "Rita" (Mrs. Desmond Humphreys), Sir Max Pemberton's *The Sea Wolves* (1894), Conan Doyle's *The Tragedy of Korosko* (1898), and Elinor Glyn's *Visits of Elizabeth* (1900). "If I had a phonograph or a clever stenographist," Joyce laments, "I could *certainly* write any of the novels I have read lately in seven or eight hours."[7] On the other hand, he had a certain respect for the craft of a well-made popular novel, at least to the extent that he would use it to deflate literary pretension. The following month, he tells Stanislaus that he has just read James's *Confidence*, Anatole France's *Monsieur Bergeret à Paris*, and Captain Marryat's *Peter Simple*, "and I prefer the last of the three. It seems to me much better than most of the modern scamped adventure-stories."[8]

Literary and journalistic worlds interpenetrated at the turn of the century far more than they do now; most of the weeklies and a number of the daily newspapers ran serial fiction and occasional verse. Indeed,

"The Sisters," "Eveline," and "After the Race" were first published in A. E.'s agricultural and literary weekly *The Irish Homestead*, which Joyce ungratefully called "the pig's paper." A major theme of Joyce's work is the confrontation of the literary with the journalistic. In *Dubliners* "A Little Cloud" opposes the poetaster Chandler to the popular journalist Gallaher, while in "A Painful Case" the litterateur Duffy confronts life in a newspaper story. *Ulysses* features an aspiring literary artist and an advertising canvasser with popular literary ambitions, and in the "Aeolus" section Stephen, urged by Myles Crawford to write something for the paper, replies indirectly with a hyper-naturalistic narrative whose main point is its utter unsuitability as newspaper fiction. Even in the *Wake*, the self-obsessed artist figure Shem is offset by Shaun, a figure both popular and in a sense journalistic. While much Joycean criticism has presented these oppositions as Manichaean, it is more fruitful to regard them as dialectical; each extreme, the hyper-literary and the popular-literary, brings forth and requires its opposite.[9] In *Ulysses*, for example, when Stephen wonders why restaurants stack chairs on the tables overnight, Bloom replies immediately, "To sweep the floor in the morning" (*U*, 539/660). If one is to write a novel, this is the sort of thing one must know.

Joyce by no means spent his reading life closeted with Flaubert, Ibsen, Bruno, and Vico. In his early years in Europe he read with some regularity *Sinn Fein* and the *United Irishman*, the *Daily Mail*, and *Figaro*; Aunt Josephine sent him the *Irish Catholic* and *Dialogues of the Day*; and occasionally he saw *The Republic*, which was a Belfast nationalist weekly, *The Leprechaun*, a general-interest Irish weekly, and *Dublin Opinion*, a comic paper.[10] He followed a popular fiction supplement in the *Daily Mail* and even emulated his father by entering a missing-letter puzzle contest in *Ideas*, though with more seriousness than John Joyce ever brought to the enterprise: he planned to mail Stanislaus a registered letter with his solutions in order to take legal action against the paper if they failed to award him the prize. Joyce and Nora both followed *T. P.'s Weekly*, a London paper edited by the Irishman T. P. O'Connor, about whom Joyce felt warmly.[11] Of course, Joyce was a contributor to the popular press as well as a consumer; he published reviews of both serious and popular novels in the *Daily Express* and essays in the Triestine *Il Piccolo della Serra*. He even published a long letter on cattle disease in the *Evening Telegraph*, an undertaking he later parodied in *Ulysses*.

Joyce's exposure to popular and journalistic writing was extensive and, by the time he had begun to write *Ulysses*, consciously directed. His *Letters* include a barrage of appeals to friends, especially Frank Budgen, for specific popular texts, from the anonymous *My Three Husbands* to Cleland's *Fanny Hill*. From the frequency and kind of allusions to popular books, magazines, and newspapers in *Ulysses*, it is clear that Joyce was attempting a sketch of the textual contribution to popular consciousness in Dublin in 1904. A full investigation of popular literature in *Ulysses* is beyond the scope of this volume, but Joyce's readily apparent practice in *Ulysses* is at least indirect evidence that he was already aware of the issue in *Dubliners*, *Portrait*, and *Exiles*.

It should be noted that in these early works there is a socially determined anachronism in the constellation of popular works to which Joyce alludes. While newspapers and periodicals, including magazines for children, were strenuously up-to-the-minute and strove to engage their readers in a continuous and immediate interchange, the same cannot be said of popular novels. Certainly there were novels that addressed current social questions, whose popularity was tied to the currency of those problems, such as *The Woman Who Did*, *Trilby*, or the spate of "invasion scare" novels shortly after the turn of the century. But the preferred reading of most middle-class houses also included old favorites like Dickens and Scott, or perhaps Bulwer-Lytton and Eugène Sue. In the course of the century, the audience for the romantic narratives of a "radical" artist like Byron had shifted downward socially, so that they too might be said to have become popular literature. And among the young, like Stephen Dedalus and the first five protagonists of *Dubliners*, the idea of a current best-selling novel did not arise. Their fiction of choice was serialized by Harmsworth and his competitors or else was one of the acknowledged "standards" like *Robinson Crusoe*, *The Three Musketeers*, or *The Count of Monte Cristo*. The machinery of the twentieth-century culture industry was not yet fully engaged.

The Problematics of Popularity

Several recent books have altered the direction of Joyce scholarship through an investigation of Richard Ellmann's compilation and reconstruction of Joyce's Trieste library in the appendix to *The Consciousness of Joyce*. Among these are Ellmann himself, Dominic Manganiello in *Joyce's Politics*, and Richard Brown in *James Joyce and Sexuality*. Especially these latter two attempt to place Joyce within the social and intellectual context of his time, to present him as a participant in the heated dialogue regarding, respectively, politics and sex. Implicit in all three books is the assumption that Joyce's reading, no matter how trivial, is reflected in his work; his stories, novels, and play are related intertextually not merely to the work of his acknowledged "masters," such as Ibsen and Flaubert, but to the mass of public writing that surrounded him. Such an approach threatens the New Critical ideology that presents Joyce as an autonomous artist *sui generis*, uninterested in and divorced from political and social context. In contrast, Brown's and Manganiello's criticism foregrounds theme and presumes that Joyce's work responds, if only negatively, to the mass of relevant material with which he was familiar. Often such an approach involves some historical reconstruction; the late Victorian and Edwardian debate over marriage and sexuality, for example, which is treated by both Brown and the present study, is far less familiar than is Stephen Dedalus's stance on the subject—a stance he is at pains to present as radical and self-generated.

Included in Ellmann's list are some fifty works that might reasonably be regarded as popular literature. Here, of course, the problem of definition and discrimination arises. Where the distinction between "folk" culture and "high" culture may appear perfectly clear-cut, the hallmark of bourgeois popular culture in the nineteenth century is that its relation to high culture, particularly high literary culture, is both close and ambiguous; in fact, that relationship cannot even be characterized without making some ideological commitment. Thus popular culture may be seen as parasitic upon high culture, as an archaic and fossilized form of it, as a relatively independent phenomenon whose development parallels that of high culture, as a repertoire of texts and images whose basic structure is unchanging within industrial society, or even as the vital seedbed from which the higher arts spring.[12] Current critical theory tends to deny that there is any substantive distinction whatever to be made between "high" and "low" literary art. To identify popular literature simply by measuring the popularity of a given work is notoriously unreliable, as the examples of Dickens and Thackeray in the nineteenth century and Fitzgerald or Hemingway in the twentieth demonstrate; a major writer may produce a best-seller, just as a work designed and tailored for the popular market may be a marketing failure. Instead, most approaches to popular literature rely on some sort of analysis and evaluation of the text itself, and the majority of these approaches invoke the notion of genre in doing so. Within contemporary industrial culture so great a proportion of the marketing of popular fiction is devoted to the well-known genres of espionage and suspense, westerns, mysteries, romances, and gothic horror tales that a work's generic identity has become a reliable key to its status: the more closely it conforms to the generic description, the more confident we may be in assigning it to the broad category of popular literature.

Unfortunately, in the late nineteenth and early twentieth centuries even this criterion is difficult to apply. Many of the modern popular genres, such as the mystery, were in their formative stages, so that a figure like Wilkie Collins now appears to be a peculiar hybrid of mystery-writer and Victorian novelist. The few surveys of the field, such as Amy Cruse's *After the Victorians* (London: George Allen & Unwin, 1938) or Margaret Dalziel's *Popular Fiction 100 Years Ago* (London: Cohen & West, 1957), are informal and thematic in approach. But if contemporary genre classifications are not appropriate for the period, many historians of popular literature see the late Victorian and early Edwardian periods as crucial because of the new pervasiveness of the print medium. Malcolm Bradbury claims that the "expansion of cultural expression and interaction through the media" continued throughout the nineteenth century, "but a special distillation occurs with print in the late nineteenth century and with other media in the 1950s."[13] Victor Neuburg ends his history of popular literature at the year 1897, arguing that in that year the circulation of *Pearson's Weekly* reached one and a quarter million—which was also roughly the circulation of *Tit-Bits* and *Answers*—thus marking the beginning of "the age of mass-produced literature" and of "mass culture" generally.[14] Neuburg's implication, one accepted by many commentators, is that with the twentieth century proper we may begin to speak of the "mass media" and of a coherent industry of popular literature; before this point, we are in a transitional period, in which the folk roots of popular literature are still discernable and in which the literature is, relatively speaking, "innocent." By 1905 Victoria was dead and the word "best-seller" entered the language, pejoratively, in an article in the *Atheneum*. The debate over popular culture in general, most forcefully inaugurated by Arnold in "Culture and Anarchy," became widespread, so that serious writers such as Wells and Gissing were encouraged to explore aspects of it such as advertisement in *Tono-Bungay* (1909) and popular journalism in *New Grub Street* (1891). Perhaps, as Harry Levin has suggested, this tendency began on the day Flaubert decided to immerse himself in *Keepsakes* magazine as preparation for *Madame Bovary*; but by the turn of the century there was no doubt that popular literature had become a subject of serious literature.

If the lack of rigid popular genres in the modern sense makes the evaluation of nineteenth-century popular literature more difficult, the emergence of a nineteenth-century canon during the past century has made it easier. The work of Dickens, Thackeray, Austen, and Eliot now appears quite distinct from that of Marryat, Disraeli, Bulwer-Lytton, and Charlotte Yonge, even while we strenuously question the value of that distinction. The problem of Marie Corelli's literary importance no longer seems debatable, nor do we, like some responsible critics in the 1890s, regard the poet Stephen Phillips as the heir to Dante and Milton.[15] Here the implicit discrimination the contemporary reader makes is not one of authorial intent, or of intended audience, but of the work's "literary quality"—an aspect of texts that now appears both ideologically coded and also dependent upon historical perspective. What may have once appeared to most readers to be a serious and skillful undertaking of important themes, such as the work of Hall Caine, James Lane Allen, or Grant Allen, in retrospect may appear sensational, incompetent, middlebrow, or even kitsch. The work of the Frankfurt School, especially Theodor Adorno, Max Horkheimer, and Leo Lowenthal, in analyzing the paradigms of bourgeois culture has sensitized the modern reader to the varieties of social rationalization that permeate these strata of literature.[16] Even more important in the process of canon formation has been the heritage of F. R. Leavis, a figure considerably to the right of the Frankfurt School, who has also stressed the necessity for the artist to occupy a position of opposition to modern mass culture. Outside the "Great Tradition," he implied, lay outer darkness, and Q. D. Leavis made the implications of this view for popular literature explicit in *Fiction and the Reading Public* (1932). From a literary rather than a social perspective, both critiques stem from the oppositionist, elitist ideology of modernism itself that, uniquely among literary movements, defined itself against the social norm of the literary. No one could be more stringent in narrowing the canon than Joyce, who appalled his brother by deriving Meredith's novels from Disraeli's, was bored by James, and delighted in picking apart the works of George Moore or Maupassant.

The canon that allows such discriminations has, of course, been attacked recently from various quarters. Feminist critics have argued convincingly that major women writers have been slighted because their writing concerned or addressed a world of women, or because their implicit attacks on patriarchy disquieted male critics. Leslie Fiedler and a number of critics who came to prominence in the 1960s have attacked the canon in the name of an antielitist counterideology that might foreground a work's explicit social content, its mythic resonance, or its radical technique, regardless of its literary sophistication or the situation of the author or intended audience. Both of these are overtly revisionist programs; perhaps more subtly influential has been the influence of literary structuralism, a school that on the whole ignores the social status of a text and stresses the conventionally "coded" nature of both classical literary texts and the phenomena of popular culture. Roland Barthes announced "the death of the author," whose role was supplanted by a multitude of texts, endlessly proliferating and mutating in a fashion that made authorial intervention appear beside the point.[17] When they are not engaged in distinguishing between "readerly" and "writerly" texts, or "classic" and "modern," structuralist and semiotic approaches are, almost by definition, nonevaluative, and the same can be said for poststructuralist and deconstructive strategies. Meanwhile, such strategies have proved surprisingly powerful as analytical tools applied to texts of any provenance; the present study, while it relies fundamentally on Bakhtin, also calls upon other structuralist and poststructuralist methodologies where they seem appropriate.

One contemporary critical approach that might offer hope in distinguishing between serious literature and popular entertainment is that of revisionist Marxists such as Fredric Jameson or Louis Althusser. Althusser, in his essay "Ideology and Ideological State Apparatuses," argues that the spheres of communications, including the press, radio, and television, and the sphere of the cultural, including the arts, literature, and sports, both belong to what he terms the "ideological state apparatus." Unlike the directly repressive state apparatus—institutions like the army, courts, police, and prisons—the ideological state apparatus works through ideology, in disguised, even symbolic forms, to buttress the prevailing power structure.[18] For Althusser, "genuine" art, on the other hand, is not merely an example of ideology; in fact, true artists "give us a 'view' of the ideology to which their work alludes and with which it is constantly fed, a view which presupposes a *retreat*, an *internal distantiation* from the very ideology from which their novels emerged. They make us 'perceive' (but not know) in some sense *from the inside*, by an *internal distance*, the very ideology in which they are held."[19]

Clearly, Althusser wants to save art from ideology; equally clearly, he would see popular literature as wholly ideological, and thus consciously or not at the service of the ruling classes. Part of his implicit program is to avoid the crudity of "naive" Marxism, which views literature as simply a reflection of the economic base and values literary works purely on the basis of the expressed political orientation of the author. Fredric Jameson goes further in this direction, proposing three distinct stages in the analysis of a literary work. In the first, the text is explicated, but only as a symbolic act on the author's part; in the second, in which the semantic horizon widens to include the social order, the text is seen as a single utterance within "the great collective and class discourses" of the time; in the third, the "ideology of form" within the work is examined. At each of these steps the ideological import of the work may change utterly.[20] Jameson here uses the term "ideology" in a more universal, more potentially positive sense than does Althusser; art does not escape it, but "mystifies" it; all narrative, for Jameson, is allegorical, and betrays, in some form, the workings of the "political unconscious."

Neither Althusser's nor Jameson's formulations have direct relevance to a distinction between popular literature and high art, but both can contribute something to it. Althusser's description of the function of art is a useful characterization of Joyce's texts; in the present work, *Dubliners*, *Portrait*, and *Exiles* are examined with an eye to their presentation of prevailing ideologies as embodied in popular discourse, whether that discourse is conversational or subliterary. Jameson sees the "structural breakdown of the older realisms" at the end of the nineteenth century as resulting in the emergence not of modernism alone, "but rather two literary and cultural structures, dialectically interrelated and necessarily presupposing each other for any adequate analysis," that is, high literature and popular literature.[21] In one respect, this observation underlies the present study, in that the participation of various examples of popular literature in Joyce's works is seen as genuinely *intertextual*: Joyce's fictions may "enclose" the works to which he alludes, but those works are not present simply as social documents or inert illustrations. Like high art, popular literature is not ideologically "transparent," a direct reflector of the value systems, fantasies, and mythical narratives of the society that produces it. But it is far less mediated—from a politically analytic point of view one might say less mystified—than the work of important writers. It is also more closely bound to the specific social conventions of reading of its era. This means that our experience of the popular literature of a century ago is inevitably ironic and distanced. The text seems stylized, mannered, or even obsessive, and is liable to lead to unintended merriment. Perhaps more to the point—since all this can be true of literary texts as well—the stylization seems to be un-motivated, or externally motivated, a requirement of the genre rather than of the specific book's ostensible concerns.

Some of the works treated in this study are "popular classics," like *The Three Musketeers*, *The Count of Monte Cristo*, and *Tom Brown's School-Days*, and when a work has such enduring popularity we may assume that there is some continuity between its ideologies and our own; others, like *Eric, or Little by Little* or *A Modern Daedalus*, must have appeared badly dated within decades of their appearance. Appar-ent seriousness of intent is no guarantee of cultural longevity, and some of the novels dealing with the "Marriage Question" at the turn of the century, such as Grant Allen's *The Woman Who Did* and Filson Young's *The Sands of Pleasure*, now appear more strongly structured by uncon-scious cultural assumptions than by their explicit concerns. But the dis-tinction between high and popular art, however clear-cut at the ex-tremes, becomes extremely murky with works like Edouard Dujardin's *L'Initiation au péché et à l'amour*, Marcelle Tinayre's *The House of Sin*, or Karin Michaëlis's *The Dangerous Age*. All three novels had a brief period of popularity, or even notoriety, before lapsing into obscurity, but all three were the work of highly competent and "original" writers who, knowingly or not, refused the temptations of straightforward genre writ-ing. Thanks to Joyce, Dujardin is already a minor literary figure, while it is quite possible that a feminist rediscovery of Michaëlis could result in her entry into the canon as a secondary writer of some importance. These three books are nonetheless included in this study because of their presence in Joyce's library, because they are unknown to most readers of Joyce, and because they present such interesting possibilities for inter-textual interpretation.

Bakhtin's Dialogism

In order to deal with the contribution of literary and subliterary texts to Joyce's writing, what is needed is a theoretical approach that, although oriented to genre, allows for the stylistic and ideological analysis of texts of any social level. The most useful, flexible, and suggestive theory is provided in the works of M. M. Bakhtin. Over the past fifteen years Bakhtin's work has become increasingly influential in the West; indeed, although much of it was produced in the late 1920s, it is only since the 1960s that it has achieved any recognition in the Soviet Union. Part of the reason for Bakhtin's current popularity is no doubt the ambitious and ambiguous nature of his work. His writing touches on linguistics, psychology, theology, sociology, and poetics; he has been variously treated as a formalist, a structuralist, a poststructuralist, a Buberian theologian, a democratic humanist, and a Marxist of any stripe from relative orthodoxy to essential heresy. No doubt he would be delighted with this critical polyphony. The book originally written for his doctoral examination, *Rabelais and His World*, has been a major force in Renaissance studies and has evoked at least one book-length rebuttal; the four essays collected by Michael Holquist under the title of *The Dialogic Imagination* has, as Gary Saul Morson observes, "begun to appear in footnotes almost as often and inevitably as works by Northrop Frye, Roman Jakobson, or Jacques Derrida once did (or still do)."[22] Tzvetan Todorov asserts "without too many qualms" that Bakhtin is "the most important Soviet thinker in the human sciences and the greatest theoretician of literature in the twentieth century."[23]

Bakhtin's importance rests on two key concepts, *dialogism* (which in some contexts Bakhtin terms "polyphony" and which is closely related to *heteroglossia*) and *carnivalization* (which Bakhtin often explores through the idea of the *chronotope*). For Bakhtin, both written and spoken language and inner monologue are made up of a great variety of conflicting variants—"languages" of officialdom, vernaculars, occupational jargons, technical, literary, and subliterary languages, all polyphonically resounding. Language variants often are undetectable simply through diction and semantics, but rely upon *intonation* and upon context; thus Bakhtin in his attack on formalism stresses the need for a "translinguistics" to represent the reality of communication through utterance.[24] The condition of our existence is thus heteroglossia, a conflicting multiplicity of languages; dialogism is the necessary mode of knowledge in such a world, a form of relationship between or among different languages that, like dialectics, defines a sort of logic.[25] Because for Bakhtin consciousness is always language, and thus unavoidably ideological, the linked processes of perception and interaction with the human world are always dialogical.[26]

Although Bakhtin asserts that dialogism is a universal and necessary condition, he often speaks less formally of dialogism as a realization or embodiment of this truth. Thus in *Rabelais and His World* he represents the "official" culture of the Middle Ages as *monological* and stresses the way in which Rabelais dialogizes that culture by confronting it with an opposing voice. The opposing voice—really a sort of super-voice, in that it is linked with folk-consciousness and is capable of overturning any other language—is carnival. As a "theater without footlights" in which all are participants, the carnival festival undermines the concept of au-thoritative utterance, and through its characteristic rituals of mockery, crowning and decrowning of fools, billingsgate, nonsense, and the de-grading of everything held noble or holy, carnival presents a "contradic-tory and double-faced fullness of life" (*RW*, 61). Rabelais embodies the spirit of carnival in his works through the use of grotesque realism, which regularly reduces "higher" issues to the "material bodily lower stratum," and through parody. Thematically, Rabelais places an empha-sis on feasting and elimination, sexuality and death, which helps estab-lish the characteristic time and space complex, or chronotope, of carni-val. But most importantly, it is Rabelais's shattering, life-affirming laughter that Bakhtin sees as an "essential form of truth concerning the world as a whole," through which "the world is seen anew, no less (and perhaps more) profoundly than when seen from the serious standpoint" (*RW*, 66).

Throughout his literary work, Bakhtin is concerned to establish a ge-nealogy of the carnivalesque and of the dialogical impulse in writing. Unsurprisingly, the two are often linked, and each can be reformulated in terms of the other; Dominick LaCapra asserts that "carnivalization is for Bakhtin the most creative form of dialogized heteroglossia."[27] If Ra-belais is the culmination of carnival in literature, he has antecedents in Socratic dialogue and in Menippean satire, the diatribe and the sympo-sium.[28] Similarly, Dostoevsky, who represents the culmination of novel-istic heteroglossia—and thus, in Bakhtin's reformulation of the genre, the culmination of the potentiality of the novel itself—has antecedents in the lesser-known byways of classical fiction and anticipations in the work of Cervantes, Defoe, Goethe, Pushkin, Smollett, Sterne, Dickens, and so forth.[29] The novel, a metagenre that overtakes (or "novelizes") such other genres as romantic poetic narrative, because it is dialogical can take no final shape, but is in a process of continuous metamorphosis. Nonetheless, Bakhtin makes it clear that its development is most to be celebrated when it most emphatically embraces heteroglossia. Clark and Holquist argue that the two stylistic lines of development Bakhtin traces in the novel might be termed the "monoglot" and the "heteroglot," of which the heteroglot novel is a later development and has far fewer exemplars. Its line "runs from Rabelais in the sixteenth century to the picaresques of the seventeenth century and through virtually all the great novels of the modern period, including many Bakhtin does not list, such as Joyce and Proust."[30]

Joyce is the striking absence in Bakhtin's work; a number of critics have puzzled over his omission, since all of Bakhtin's major concepts seem best and most obviously illustrated by *Ulysses* and *Finnegans Wake*. Reviewing *The Dialogic Imagination* in *TLS* in 1981, George Steiner called Bakhtin's silence regarding Kafka and Joyce his "drastic lacunae," while Bakhtin's French admirers, such as Julia Kristeva and much of the *Tel Quel* school, inevitably invoke Joyce.[31] Clark and Holquist believe the omission is politically motivated:

> One of the many enigmas about Bakhtin is that he makes no mention in *Rabelais* of James Joyce's *Ulysses*, a book that might be described as a celebration of heteroglossia and of the body as well. This is especially surprising since Joyce was known to several of Bakhtin's associates. Pumpiansky was at work on a book on Joyce in 1932, and V. O. Stenich . . . translated Joyce. . . . [But as] of at least the First Writers' Congress in 1934, *Ulysses* could no longer be praised in print, and this was still true in 1965 when the dissertation was published as a book. Thus, Bakhtin effectively had two choices as regards Joyce, to attack him or not to mention him.[32]

There may be an anachronistic sensibility operating in this chorus; Bakhtin, after all, was notoriously disheartened with the modern world and spent far less time with the novels of his contemporaries than with classical fiction. Nevertheless, given his predispositions and methodology, there is an undeniable sense in which, if Bakhtin did not celebrate Joyce, he should have.

Certainly Joyce's last two books are outstanding illustrations of heteroglossia and of carnivalization, but the same concerns and techniques
that animate those works are present in embryonic form in *Dubliners*
and *Portrait* as well. Admittedly, carnivalization is not apparent in most
of Joyce's early work; there is only a single scene in *Portrait* wherein
Stephen seems briefly to be visited by the carnival muse:

> His fellowstudent's rude humour ran like a gust through the clois-
> ter of Stephen's mind, shaking into gay life priestly vestments that
> hung upon the walls, setting them to sway and caper in a sabbath
> of misrule. The forms of the community emerged from the gust-
> blown vestments, the dean of studies, the portly florid bursar with
> his cap of grey hair . . . , the tall form of the young professor of
> mental science discussing on the landing a case of conscience with
> his class like a giraffe cropping high leafage among a herd of ante-
> lopes. . . . They came ambling and stumbling, tumbling and caper-
> ing, kilting their gowns for leap frog, holding one another back,
> shaken with deep fast laughter, smacking one another behind and
> laughing at their rude malice, calling to one another by familiar
> nicknames. (*P,* 192)

There is humor in the stories of *Dubliners* and even in *Portrait*, but aside
from this brief vision of Stephen's it is generally ironic, even embittered
humor; Lynch deflates Stephen's aesthetic pronouncements with a crude
commentary, but he hardly can be said to epitomize a dominant voice in
the novel. What does emerge in Joyce's early writing, though, is his
powerfully dialogical imagination. Paul de Man explains dialogism as a
"principle of radical otherness"; "the function of dialogism is to sustain
and think through the radical exteriority or heterogeneity of one voice
with regard to any other, including that of the novelist himself."[33] The
more intensive our examination of *Dubliners* and *Portrait*, the more we
are struck by the fully realized, wholly distinctive qualities of the characters' voices, each of them held in dialogical tension with the narrative
voice of the author. In the case of *Portrait*, Joyce's exploration of voice
goes even further, in the direction of an analysis of the competing elements within Stephen's own inner monologue and of his indebtedness to
the voices of his society.

In the essay "Discourse in the Novel" and in the chapter "Discourse
in Dostoevsky" from *Problems of Dostoevsky's Poetics*, Bakhtin establishes three broad applications of dialogism in a literary text: (1) be-

tween authorial language and protagonist's language; (2) between protagonist's language and the languages of other characters in a text; and (3) between the language of a text or a protagonist taken as a whole and the language of other relevant texts to which implicit or explicit allusion is made. This third area of dialogism immediately suggests the notion of *intertextuality* as it has been developed by various contemporary critics, notably Kristeva, Michael Riffaterre, and Jonathan Culler. Bakhtin's dialogism does not wholly coincide with structuralist and poststructuralist intertextuality, because for Bakhtin the model of language is spoken, rather than written, a distinction to which Derrida lends great force; but in practice, because Bakhtin avoids all implications of origin, "presence," and authority in his characterization of voice, the play of voices in his work resembles the play of text in Derrida's. Bakhtin is somewhat inconsistent in his classifications of novelistic dialogism, but his interest is clearly in "double-voiced" discourse, that is, discourse oriented toward the discourse of another. This may take the form of parody, stylization, irony, internal polemic, discourse "with a sideward glance" at another's discourse, hidden dialogue, or any of various intermediate forms for which no good terminology is available. Dialogical relationships may exist between narrator and characters, where the speech of the characters in not simply "objectified" (that is, used as a characterizing or typifying technique) but has sufficient force and integrity to compete with the narration; or it may exist among characters in the novel. Bakhtin's special interest is in the area of interpenetration of authorial voice and character's voice, such as is found in the quasi-internal monologue of *style indirect libre* or in what he terms "character zones," areas of linguistic influence surrounding characters in a novel even when they do not explicitly interrupt the authorial narration.

This sort of analysis is of course useful in Joyce's early fiction, and indeed has been practiced—without the accompanying theoretical structure—by Hugh Kenner, among others. But there are other correspondences between Bakhtin's thought and Joyce's practice that should engage our interest. Bakhtin stresses that the formation of the self is a linguistic process; consciousness, for him, is a matter of self-articulation in an inner monologue that depends upon and responds to the surrounding environment of speech. "The logic of consciousness is the logic of ideological communication, of the semiotic interaction of a social group. If we deprive consciousness of its semiotic, ideological content, it would have absolutely nothing left" (*MPL*, 13). Indeed, consciousness is for him a boundary phenomenon, located midway between an unguessable core of self and the surrounding otherness that gives definition and even existence to the self. Joyce's portrayal of consciousness in the inner monologues of *Ulysses* and, as we shall see, in *Dubliners* and *Portrait* as well, is equally language-dependent, not simply because as a writer he had no alternative but to use language to represent consciousness, but because his conception of selfhood relied on language as its dominant component. More than those of other novelists, Joyce's characters speak themselves into existence, are seduced, appeased, threatened, annoyed, and shaped by the languages around them. These may be the banalities of lower-middle-class adults, the sonorities of the pulpit, the coded jargon of schoolboys, the rich rhetoric of boys' magazines, or the flat pseudo-factualities of the newspaper; they may belong to any of an infinite variety of what Bakhtin terms "speech genres," from familial intimacy to corruptly sophisticated, man-of-the-world bonhomie. Like Bakhtin, Joyce experienced censorship and formed a passionate attachment to "the language of the outlaw," the voice that sets itself in opposition to the dominant voice of the culture. But throughout his work, he gives the most scrupulous attention to intonation, accent, gesture, all of the exactitudes of language interaction in the social dynamics of speech.

Bakhtin is not, except in patches, systematic. The thrust of his ideas is generally to deny the desirability or even the possibility of erecting totalizing systems. For him, there is no "last word." His examples of speech genres, like his examples of social "languages," are suggestive rather than exhaustive, and it is likely that he would view any catalogue of his basic analytical units (such as *ideolegeme*, language, or speech genre) as provisory. In the following chapters, no attempt has been made to develop such an analytic catalogue; languages are characterized by their function, intonation, source, or context, as seems most appropriate. Similarly, the term *ideology* is employed with a stronger subjective component and has far more "play" than in the work of many contemporary Marxist critics.[34] In his early work Bakhtin uses the term almost interchangeably with "language," and, in a note to "The Problem of Speech Genres," Clark and Holquist observe that "ideology as it is used here is essentially any system of ideas," with the proviso that ideology is semiotic; "every speaker is thus an ideologue and every utterance an ideologeme" (*SG*, 101).

Actually, Bakhtin's thought cuts across the grain of many current debates, since he allows no opposition between language and conceptual structures of an authentic, naked "self" and the surrounding society; the self "always already" finds language appropriated and ideologically dense. But, aside from his portrayal of the Medieval period, Bakhtin does not imply that the "dominant voice" of the culture is univocal; at least in recent centuries there may be a prevailing discourse that is authorized by and in turn legitimates the dominant class, but there is also a polyphony of voices of opposition, voices of local dominance and local opposition, voices inserted at odd angles to the major debates, and so forth. In this respect Peter Berger and Thomas Luckman's *The Social Construction of Reality* (New York: Doubleday, 1966) offers a useful parallel from a nonlinguistic perspective: Berger and Luckmann argue for the coexistence of various and conflicting phenomenological "worlds," each of them socially constructed, within any consciousness. Discourse is a sort of palimpsest in which languages arise and falter through time, generate their own opposition, triumph or fall, but are never wholly lost. Bakhtin's vision of the human world, like Joyce's, is filled with conflict and opposition, but there is a joy and affirmation in its energy, dynamism, and continuity in the heart of change. As he wrote in a fragment soon before his death, "There is neither a first nor a last word and there are no limits to the dialogic context. . . . Nothing is absolutely dead: every meaning will have its homecoming festival" (*SG*, 170).

· 2 ·

YOUNG DUBLINERS:

POPULAR IDEOLOGIES

"The Sisters": Breaking the Silence

Quietude and *silence* (the absence of the word). The pause and the beginning of the word. The disturbance of quietude by sound is mechanical and physiological (as a condition of perception); the disturbance of silence by the word is personalistic and intelligible: it is an entirely different world. In quietude nobody makes a sound (or somebody does not speak). Silence is possible only in the human world (and only for man). Of course, both quietude and silence are always relative. . . . Silence—intelligible sound (a word)— and the pause constitute a special logosphere, a unified and continuous structure, an open (unfinalized) totality. (*SG*, 133–34)

Dubliners records the breaking of the silence: the silence before Joyce's first mature work and the silence given to the child-protagonist in response to the multitude of passionate questions that he already knows he must refuse to ask. Certainly this is a book about the confrontation with languages at the most fundamental level. In each of the first three stories the child encounters an adult or group of adults who speak a different language, what might be termed a "language of the initiate" that refers perpetually to something always unstated but always implied in their speech. Through silences and gestures of exclusion the adults enact—almost ritually—an insistence that the child remain incommunicado; but of course the child, frustrated and alienated by this barrage of exclusive language, refuses to admit his situation. He adopts a disguise, refuses to respond as expected, and retaliates with silences of his own or with a disguised speech that will not betray his position.

Virtually all interpretations of "The Sisters," the first and strangest of the stories, note its peculiar foregrounding of language. Several have noted the silences, suppressions, and ellipses as well; Jean-Michel Rabaté notes, "What strikes one from the first page is the deliberate suspension of a number of terms: the identity of the dead priest is disclosed through a series of hesitating, unfinished sentences, and even the 'now' of the initial paragraph is not related to a precise chronology."[1] But the hesitations, suspensions, and silences are indissolubly linked to an explicit interrogation of language. The boy begins by speculating upon the priest's statement, "I am not long for this world," which he had thought to be "idle words" but now believes may have been something more. He then recites to himself the word *paralysis*, which had always "sounded strangely" in his ears, like the words *gnomon* and *simony*. At the conclusion of the first paragraph, the boy imagines *paralysis* to be the name of "some maleficent and sinful being" (D, 9) whom he fears yet whom he also wishes to approach, and this allegorical embodiment of the word exemplifies the importance language has for him. He is unduly fascinated by the written word. It seems to him significant that the priest's house has a sign with the "vague name of *Drapery*" (D, 11) and ordinarily boasts a second sign saying "*Umbrellas Re-covered*" (D, 12). After reading the memorial card, he occupies his mind by reading all the theatrical advertisements in the shop windows along Great Britain Street. The importance the adults seem to attach to language is shown throughout by their scrupulous refusal to complete their sentences, to reveal the focus of their conversation to the boy by naming it. Indeed, the play of silence and speech itself becomes almost theatrical at times: during the visit the boy and his aunt pay to the sisters, deaf Nannie never speaks, except for the incoherent muttering of her prayer, while Eliza, after the long opening pause, is virtually never silent.

Throughout, the boy is interrogating signs: the sign/signal of the window and the more ambiguous signs of language. In the first paragraph alone, this interrogation is highlighted. But most striking in this interrogation is the fact that the boy is either mystified or mistaken in each instance—just as, at the beginning of *Dubliners*'s last story, Gabriel Conroy's speeches and actions are consistently lies and mistakes. In "The Sisters" the priest's words were not "idle," although at the story's end his chalice is. As the boy repeats the word "simony," he stares at the lighted square of window, in search of a sign—the "reflection of candles on the darkened blind"—that would mean the priest had died. But the priest dies before the boy sees the "sign," and he learns that fact first from his uncle, whom he distrusts, and then from a wholly different (and literal) sign. The famous three words *paralysis, gnomon,* and *simony* are unfamiliar to him, and much of their portentousness is due to their unfamiliarity. Finally, it should be noted that the narrator makes a very curious slip in describing the sign he expects when he terms it the "reflection" of candles on the blind. What he might expect to see would be the blurred image of the candle flames *through* the blind; a reflection would originate outside the window, as, later in the story, the windowpanes of the houses "reflected the tawny gold of a great bank of clouds" (*D,* 14). This confusion of reflection and refraction, internal and external, is thematically embodied in the remainder of the text as well, as the boy investigates the priest's identity and meaning both internally, through dream, and externally, through the overheard conversations.[2] It also anticipates one of Bloom's famous confusions in "Calypso": "Black conducts, reflects, (refracts is it?), the heat" (*U,* 46/57).

In "The Sisters," as in all of Joyce's stories, direct dialogical interchange takes place on two planes: between the presumed authorial voice and the voice of the protagonist and between the protagonist and other characters. Hugh Kenner's definition of "character" in *Ulysses* applies equally well, though less obviously, in *Dubliners*: "an interference phenomenon between 'his' language and language not his, sometimes other characters', sometimes the author's."[3] Because of Joyce's notorious self-effacement in his narratives it is always difficult to isolate an authorial voice, and in "The Sisters" any such distinction is further complicated by the ambiguous quality of the protagonist's voice. There are in the narrative the conventional two mingled voices of the narrator-protagonist—the voice of immediate (child's) experience and the voice of retrospection (from some indeterminate distance in time). These are oddly mixed in "The Sisters," in part because the boy seems in some respects to be a disguised adult—he is almost preternaturally sensitive, suspicious, and evasive. To what extent are we to attribute the boy's expressions of suspicion, hostility, and general free-floating anxiety to a later retrospection, and to what extent may they be directly attributed to the child's immediate experience? If there is an authorial narrative element, where are we to look for it? Tacitly, criticism has avoided such questions and addressed the fiction as a form of autobiography, conflating the retrospection of the boy grown older with "Joyce's own language." And indeed such questions, which for Bakhtin are unavoidable in the novel, may be unapproachable in such a minimal text as this.

Examining the second plane of dialogical interaction is more fruitful. Here we encounter a third voice, the massed chorus of Old Cotter, the uncle, the aunt, and Eliza, all of whom share a vocabulary, a syntax, and, in a specialized sense, an ideology. Far more than half of the text is devoted to a literal recording of their inane comments, as if it were an expanded version of the naturalistic epiphanies scattered throughout *Portrait*. This language, with its "hum and buzz of implication," in Trilling's phrase, is the boy's real environment, with which he must come to terms. Bakhtin comments,

> Social man is surrounded by ideological phenomena, by objects-signs . . . of various types and categories: by words in the multifarious forms of their realization (sounds, writing, and the others), by scientific statements, religious symbols and beliefs, works of art, and so on. All of these things in their totality comprise the ideological environment, which forms a solid ring around man. And man's consciousness develops and lives in this environment. Human consciousness does not come into contact with existence directly, but through the medium of the surrounding ideological world.
>
> The ideological environment is the realized, materialized, externally expressed social consciousness of a given collective. . . . In fact, the individual consciousness can only become a consciousness by being realized in the forms of the ideological environment proper to it: in language, in conventionalized gesture, in artistic image, in myth, and so on. (*FMLS*, 14)

The language of the "others" does not seem to us overtly ideological because we share in so much of it; it may be banal, but it is relatively transparent to the reader. Joyce's achievement is to dull this transparency by setting a literal recording of it against the resistant consciousness of the boy, to whom every casual statement by the adults seems an attack or an obfuscation.

The communal voice is difficult to characterize. It is Irish, lower-middle-class, turn-of-the-century, ill-educated. But Joyce underlines several aspects for us. It is a generalizing, defining, typifying voice that is eager to subsume the unique experience under the heading of common wisdom: the priest was "one of those . . . peculiar cases" (D, 10), the boy is a "Rosicrucian" (D, 11), the minds of children are "impressionable" (D, 11). The voice is prescriptive and proscriptive: "let a young lad run about and play with young lads" (D, 10), "Let him learn to box his corner" (D, 11), "I wouldn't like children of mine . . . to have too much to say to a man like that" (D, 10). Rabaté characterizes the voice as *orthodoxy* and associates the truncated sentences with a submerged image of cutting: "For the orthodoxy divides in order to anathematize through the particular injunction of lacerated sentences, in a series of performative utterances which stop abruptly before the end."[4] The voice vacillates between a cynical and an idealizing extreme, so that experience is reduced either to a reassuring platitude—"You did all you could for him" (D, 15), "He looked that peaceful and resigned" (D, 15), "He's gone to a better world" (D, 15), "There's no friends like the old friends" (D, 16)—or to the assertion that things are not what they seem, and the speaker has always been aware of the fact: "but there was something queer . . . there was something uncanny about him" (D, 9–10), "Mind you, I noticed there was something queer coming over him latterly" (D, 16). Proverbs and folk wisdom are ladled out like the stirabout with which the boy crams his mouth shut.

But the most frustrating aspect of this popular speech for the boy is the *rhetoric of ellipsis*, in which sentences typically trail off, unfinished, and may even begin as if in response to an ongoing dialogue of which the boy is ignorant. Old Cotter's first speech begins in medias res, "as if returning to some former remark of his" (D, 9), while Eliza's last speech, the final sentence of the story, is unfinished. Indeed, the majority of Cotter's sentences and a great part of Eliza's end in ellipsis. Even the aunt is unable to speak of something as obvious as the priest's death, asking, "Did he . . . peacefully?" and then inquiring, "And everything . . . ?" (D, 15). The boy's comment about Old Cotter, "I puzzled my head to extract meaning from his unfinished sentences" (D, 11), could be taken as emblem for his entire experience of the adult world. Wherever he turns he confronts a puzzling, imperative *tacebimus* that is difficult to distinguish from banal, elliptical, or evasive speech. For these are not the silences to which Bakhtin alludes, which indicate that one speaker has finished and another may start, but appropriative silences that signify that the speaker is not ready to relinquish the floor—is, in fact, never ready, because the world must be filled with banalities lest something unspoken break to the surface. Like Cotter's stories about the distillery, these utterances are "endless." In the context of "The Sisters" the shared language of Old Cotter, the uncle, and Eliza is the socially dominant discourse, and as Richard Terdiman remarks, "the apparatus of dominant discourse, unlike the text, has no final sentence and never concludes. The clichés run along endlessly under their own power." Indeed, silence is a way of continuing this hegemonic speech, for the "inherent tendency of a dominant discourse is to 'go without saying.' " [5]

But there is another sort of authoritative discourse implied (though never directly embodied) in the story, and this is the particular genre of theological discourse represented by the priest. Silenced by his death, this "fourth voice" of the priest echoes all the more powerfully through the narrative. Where popular discourse attempts to level events and decisions toward banality or tautology—what Phillip Herring neatly terms a "tyranny of triteness" [6]—the intellectual rhetoric of the priest has a precisely opposite aim: to show "how complex and mysterious were certain institutions of the Church which I had always regarded as the simplest acts." He shows the boy "books as thick as the *Post Office Directory* and as closely printed as the law notices in the newspaper" (D, 13) that treat the questions he poses to the baffled boy. The technique is the inverse of Cotter's—catechism, a mock-dialogue instead of an endless monologue—but the result is much the same. Where the boy is excluded from popular adult dialogue through silence and omissions, he is excluded from theological dialogue by the very weight of words. When the opportunity for his response is offered, he is forced into silence: "Often . . . I could make no answer or only a very foolish and halting one" (D, 13). Just as he consciously puzzles over Cotter's unfinished sentences, he unconsciously broods on the unstated message of the priest, but hears only a vaguely murmuring voice that wishes to confess something. No wonder he feels that his dream has been set in a foreign land; he does not speak the language.

Fredric Jameson has observed that ordinarily "a ruling class ideology will explore various strategies of the *legitimation* of its own power position, while an oppositional culture or ideology will, often in covert and disguised strategies, seek to contest and to undermine the dominant 'value system.' " He further notes, following Bakhtin, that the relevant discourse here is dialogical, and that "the normal form of the dialogical is essentially an *antagonistic* one."[7] While Jameson has in mind far larger battles of discourse, his comments are entirely appropriate to the situation of the boy in "The Sisters." Within the horizon of the story, ellipsis is clearly a strategy of legitimation of the ruling, bourgeois discourse; the priest's discourse, in disguised fashion, lessens the transparency of the ruling discourse through a strategy of complication (or obfuscation, from another viewpoint); and the boy finds his own language, and his ability to participate in the dialogue, under attack by both. Among the strategies he adopts, in turn, is disguise. He will withhold his own language—his inner speech—and give no clue to his thoughts and feelings. As much as possible, he refuses to participate in the discourse of social ritual. At times the boy appears nearly paranoid: when told the priest is dead, he says, "I knew that I was under observation so I continued eating as if the news had not interested me" (*D*, 10). He acts as if he were some sort of spy in the enemy camp—as indeed he is, in the Victorian cliché, "heaven's spy." He finds his safety in disguise and silence. After the boy's aunt has said, "God have mercy on his soul" (*D*, 10), Cotter stares at the boy as if to tell him that a response is expected of him. Only when the boy remains silent does the old man spit into the grate and air his views on the proper raising of children. When Cotter refers to him as an impressionable child, he crams stirabout into his mouth to keep from saying anything, and then when pressed to partake of the mock-communion at the sisters's house, refuses. He pretends to pray over the corpse and goes to taste his sherry only when everyone is wrapped in silence and he can move "under cover of it" (*D*, 17). During the entire story he speaks only three words, a phatic interrogative: "Is he dead?" (*D*, 10). Surely this child is the earliest exemplar of silence and cunning, if not yet of exile.

But apart from presenting the conflicts of separate discourses, the story also suggests that there is something inherently dangerous or mystifying about language itself. This is most directly implied by the boy's image of the word *paralysis* frighteningly personified, but throughout the text it is indicated by a series of faults, slippages, contradictions, and blunders of language. Most obviously, there are Eliza's malapropisms—*rheumatic* for *pneumatic* (*D*, 17), *Freeman's General* for *Freeman's Journal* (*D*, 16). The discourse of Old Cotter and the uncle is mined with ideological contradictions that are rooted in language: religious education is a good thing, but it's not good for a boy to be exposed to too much of it; the priest is "uncanny," unique, but he's one of a number of cases with which we are all familiar. Old Cotter "has his own idea" about things, but justifies it by appealing to Uncle Jack—and, by implication, to common proverbial wisdom. The entire conversation of Eliza with the boy's aunt is the simultaneous assertion that everything went as it should with the priest's death and that something mysterious went very wrong.

The same failure of language is implied in the priest's lessons, which seem to begin with simple catechistic questions and end with more and more complex ones, in a spiralling infinite regress of language. Joyce may have in mind a specific source here, the Latin tome by M.-M. Matharan entitled *Casus de matrimonio* . . . (Parissis: Victor Retaux et Filius, 1893) which remained a part of Joyce's library until his death. The book is a compendium of difficult cases in canon law bearing on matrimony with the accompanying judgments, many portions of which Joyce underlined. A typical case, number 400, reads in English translation:

> Albertina requests a disposition from the Holy See that she may be able to marry a relative in the second degree; she alleges delicate health, the danger of a bad reputation because of excessive intimacy with the betrothed, the smallness of the place, her late age [i.e., verging on permanent spinsterhood], and the insufficiency of her dower. —Physical infirmity and the danger of a bad reputation because of intimacy with the betrothed are not of themselves impelling causes; if the betrothed woman is not able easily to find another man for herself, the three other causes can be sufficient although they must be applied separately. A place is considered small if it does not have more than three hundred hearths or fifteen hundred inhabitants, although in a whole parish many more may live; —generally, late age is considered to be that which passes 24 years and in certain regions 20 or even 18; —moreover dowry is insufficient which is not enough for marrying a man of her own station. *S. Congr. Conc., 16 Dec. 1876. —Congr. de Prop. Fide, 9 maii 1877. —Bucc., ench. t. 2. n. 866. Sanch., 1. 8. d. 19. n. 12 et seqq. —Gobat, exp. th. tr. 9. 642 et seqq. —Corradus, 1. 7. c. 2. n. 6. et seqq. —Krimer, n. 2071 et seqq. —Joder, p. 63 et seqq.*[8]

The ecclesiastical logic here is simultaneously reassuring and discomfiting, suggesting both that there is a precedent, however obscure, for deciding all cases—such as that a woman may plead the extenuation of age if she is older than twenty-four—and that circumstances may alter these rules, so that "in certain regions" (which regions? why?) that age may be twenty or eighteen. Two of the causes are not in themselves "impelling," although the other three may be, if "applied separately": is any one sufficient, or must all three causes be judged acceptable? The priest of "The Sisters," capable of evaluating the recursive mystifications of such discussions, falls back on asking the boy to "patter" the responses of the Mass, smiling lewdly all the while as if in anticipation of his soft, nihilistic laughter in the confession-box. The priest has made the discovery of a vacancy at the heart of his language; he is confessor to the infinite regress of ecclesiastical discourse, and he is not resigned.

He was, in Eliza's characterization, "too scrupulous always" (D, 17). This is another instance of linguistic slippage—a wholly unlikely word for a semi-literate woman to employ, especially one who confuses *pneumatic* and *rheumatic*. As Brian Bremen has pointed out, the word is theologically exact; scrupulosity, a mental disorder recognized by the Catholic church, "causes ordinary, everyday questions to be viewed as impenetrable and insoluble."[9] But to regard Eliza's use of the word as an authorial intrusion calling attention to a thematic strand really solves nothing; in the text of the story it is primarily operative as a term from one discourse transposed into the context of another. Someone else—the priest, the boy—is speaking through the boy's memory of Eliza's utterance. The unlikely term is balanced by the narrator's misuse of "reflection" in the first paragraph: he is, without noticing the fact, mimicking Eliza's malapropisms in a slightly more sophisticated way, just as she unconsciously or accidentally mimics his usual precision. Both instances of slippage point to the inevitably dialogistic quality of discourses. However careful the speaker of a given language may be to keep it private and inviolate, it will be overheard and "corrupted" by other speakers outside the social group.

This, indeed, is what is happening to the boy. As Bakhtin insists, the languages that surround him, with their concomitant ideological structures, are the only means of thought and speech available to the boy; he cannot escape them, however alien he feels them to be. They are the world, and they articulate his consciousness. This fact, more than any vacancy at the center of languages, is responsible for the tone of inescapable menace that pervades the story and hovers around the theme of language. Whether he will or not, the boy must speak with the over-scrupulous priest's voice and with the voices of the unscrupulous adults he despises. Unwittingly, he falls prey to their infectious silences: his dream, his major effort at interpretation, is cut short, or at least he claims that he cannot remember the conclusion, and registers that omission by appropriating one of the adults' ellipses: "I felt that I had been very far away, in some land where the customs were strange—in Persia, I thought. . . . But I could not remember the end of the dream" (D, 13–14). But the crowning irony of the story is its first line, in which the boy begins his narration with an unconscious tribute to Old Cotter, his uncle and aunt, and Eliza: "There was no hope for him this time: it was the third stroke." Admittedly, the narrator, unlike the adults, would be aware of the paranomasia of "stroke," but apart from this rather awkward literary gesture the utterance is pure, fatidic, proverbial wisdom. As speech-act, the sentence is parallel to the final statement of the boy in the following story, who welcomes the return of his despised friend Mahony. He has run to the priest to escape the adults in his house, only to be "find himself at check" there as well. In the end the banalities of his guardians are no more menacing than the sophistries of the disappointed priest; without either wishing or desiring to do so he finds himself returning to them at the beginning.

"An Encounter": Boys' Magazines and the Pseudo-Literary

The explicit themes of "An Encounter" are familiar enough: perverse sexuality, transgression, the disappointment of romantic expectations. But, neatly enough, the second story of the collection is also the first of the *Dubliners* tales to be framed intertextually by popular literature. Unlike the boy of "The Sisters," this protagonist exists in a social context of his peers—a context structured through the ideologies of genres of popular literature, among other elements—and has come to define himself with respect to that context. He sees himself as both one of them and distinct from them; he shares in their ideology, but with a sense of distance that leaves him with the impression that most of his actions are inauthentic: he is play-acting, dramatizing, or impersonating the boy he appears to be. He shares this motif of disguise with the boy of the previous story, but without that boy's pervasive sense of the menace surrounding him. This is ironic, for in fact the protagonist of "An Encounter" is much more directly menaced than is the priest's protégé. Naturally, he shares the younger boy's sense of alienation from adults, but he has the advantage of a social subgroup with whom to share that sense. His playacting is thus less dangerous, because it is less of a private ritual and more of a social one. Acting, in this story, is one of the modes through which the boy attempts to discover his identity, an identity that is posited upon his social situation. He is in the process of determining his individuality and paradoxically finds he must inevitably do so in terms of the ideological formations surrounding him.

The most highly structured source of these ideological formations is the group of boys' magazines shared by the protagonist's peers. Joe Dillon, the future priest, has cemented the bonds among the group of schoolfellows with a library of old numbers of *The Union Jack*, *Pluck*, and *The Halfpenny Marvel* (D, 19). The heyday of magazines for children was the late nineteenth and early twentieth century; Sheila Egoff argues that their two main sources were the magazines inspired by the Sunday School movement, whose publication began in the early years of the nineteenth century and continued throughout it, and the boys' "blood and thunder" magazines (or "bloods"), which were inaugurated in *The Boys of England* (1866), a magazine of "Sport, Sensation, Fun and Instruction," and continued to increase in number and popularity until the first World War.[10] The latter group had its origin in the "penny parts" or "penny dreadfuls" ostensibly intended for adults and incorporating a strong pseudo-Gothic element and a less literary, more streamlined and repetitive style. The publisher of *Boys of England*, E. J. Brett, can lay some claim to inventing modern mass-market publication practices, in that his magazine was produced cheaply and sold for a penny weekly, while its only competitors sold for sixpence and catered to the "classes." In 1869 he issued a halfpenny magazine, *Boys of the World*, thus anticipating the successes of the magazines of the 1890s. Brett also inaugurated the practice of presenting contests with substantial prizes, a promotion scheme that would be crucial to the success of Alfred C. Harmsworth's publications for both children and adults.

The Irish-born Harmsworth's fortune, like that of his rival of the 1890s, George Newnes, was founded on his boys' magazines, of which his Amalgamated Press published more than all other publishers combined.[11] His first effort in this line was *Comic Cuts*, in 1890. *The Halfpenny Marvel Library* began publication in 1893, changed its title to *The Halfpenny Marvel* after three issues, and continued under this title until 1898, when it became simply *The Marvel* (1898–1922).[12] Ironically for a magazine generally regarded as cheaply sensational, it claimed the intent of counteracting the influence of unhealthy sensationalism aimed at children, announcing in the first issue, "No more penny dreadfuls! These healthy stories of mystery, adventure, etc., will kill them."[13] Soon *The Marvel* began printing testimonials such as that of the Reverend C. N. Barham expressing pleasure that the magazine was so "pure and wholesome in tone." On the front cover of that issue was a man being tortured, with the caption, "The gaoler screwed up the horrible machine until the brigand's bones were nearly broken and he shrieked aloud for mercy, though none was shown."[14] The sadomasochistic element in boys' periodicals was far less visible to the adults of the late nineteenth century than to ourselves; as will become apparent in the discussion of school stories below, it was an accepted, relatively transparent aspect of the ideology of bourgeois schooling.

The *Union Jack Library of High-Class Fiction* lasted from 1894 to 1933, succeeding an earlier, unrelated magazine entitled *The Union Jack*, which was founded in 1880 and ran for three years. Its inaugural issue opened with "The Silver Arrow"; early issues featured redskins, explorers, prospectors, sailors, and so forth, with only an occasional appearance by the detectives who would later be its mainstay.[15] *Pluck* appeared in 1895, for the first two issues as *Stories of Pluck*, and continued until 1916. It was self-characterized as "Stories of Pluck—being the daring deeds of plucky sailors, plucky soldiers, plucky railwaymen, plucky boys and plucky girls and all sorts and conditions of British heroes," and asserted unconvincingly that it would contain "true stories," although sometimes the names of the protagonists would be thinly disguised.[16] Self-characterized as "a high class weekly library of adventure at home and abroad, on land and sea,"[17] one of its favorite themes concerned the adventures of three boys in foreign lands.[18] These were "Jack, a brave British boy with the adventurous spirit; Sam, a skilled hunter; and Pete, a Negro ventriloquist, who was the real life of the party."[19] Rather than the straight blood-and-thunder formula, the popular Jack, Sam, and Pete series featured overseas escapades with a strong element of farce. The three boys of "An Encounter" no doubt imagine themselves such a lucky trio, a miniature paradigm of Empire. They are also, of course, a degenerate version of the Three Musketeers. The protagonist will furnish pluck and inspiration, Mahony the warrior's skills, and Leo Dillon comic relief. Unfortunately, they are Irish and thus awkward representatives of Empire. The protagonist is enough a literalist of the imagination to believe that, as in the magazines, "real adventures . . . must be sought abroad" (D, 21), and so is skeptical even before the expedition starts. As coup de grace to this early exercise in reader-identification, Leo Dillon fails to show up for the adventure.

All three Harmsworth magazines participated in the new upsurge of romanticism modified by realistic detail that characterized popular literature of the 1880s and 1890s, when Stevenson, Macdonald, Verne, and Barrie blurred the distinction between children's and adults' fiction. All three also were unusual in featuring a heroine, whose part in the stories was negligible—usually consisting in blundering into the clutches of the nearest villain—but who was often, at least in *The Marvel*, given a head-and-shoulders illustration of her own.[20] Thus the girl hovered like a mysterious icon above the male adventures, intimately connected with them in wholly unspecified ways. The "old josser" quizzing the two boys about their "totties" at the climax of their day must seem oddly appropriate to the children. They know from their reading that their "adventure" is about sexuality, although they—like their culture—have no idea why. In both these boys' magazines and the monologue of the old man, the young girl with beautiful hair serves as putative goal and justification for a narrative that in fact demonstrates her irrelevance.

Cheaper variants of more respectable publications such as the famous "B.O.P.," or *Boys' Own Paper* (1879–1946), *Young England* (1880–1935?), and *Boys of the Empire* (1888–89), these adventure magazines of the nineties occupied a dubious middle ground between the penny dreadfuls and truly innocent children's magazines such as *Chatterbox*, whose readers came in time to refer to Harmsworth's magazines as themselves penny dreadfuls. In turn, by the time Joyce was composing the stories of *Dubliners*, Leo Dillon's library was to be supplanted by Amalgamated Press's own *Gem* and *Magnet*, papers whose public-school stories Orwell analyzed politically to such devastating effect.[21] Even at the time of the story Dillon's magazines were regarded by adventurous boys as tame, so that even a reader as sheltered as the protagonist-narrator, who attends a Catholic school in Dublin, has a taste for racier American imports such as the "detective stories which were traversed from time to time by unkempt fierce and beautiful girls" (D, 20). These would have been easily available to him: E. S. Turner observes that "the setting up of private detectives was a major literary industry in the 'nineties," and that the Aldine Company alone produced over 250 detective titles, many of them American imports.[22]

Still, *The Halfpenny Marvel* with its green jacket and Wild West stories would be better than nothing; virtuous on the whole, it would nevertheless have the allure of priestly proscription. Perhaps more important, it was among the first thoroughly modern mass-market publications for children, one of the wave of magazines of the 1880s and 1890s that nearly equalled in volume the sum total of those published during the previous eighty years. Harmsworth's magazines helped solidify the genres of story—detective, exploration, sea adventure, science fiction, school story, Wild West—into categories that persist today. The popularity of Wild West stories in cultures such as that of middle-class Dublin deserves some analysis in itself.[23] Clearly, the narrator of "An Encounter" feels it to be somewhat artificial: "The adventures related in the literature of the Wild West were remote from my nature but, at least, they opened doors of escape." He is a reluctant participant in the communal fantasy and joins the cowboy-and-Indian games of his fellows out of social fear, because he is "afraid to seem studious or lacking in robustness" (D, 20). Appropriately, this fear would be instilled most directly by the ideology of the "school stories" of those very magazines, stories whose ethics and typologies descended lineally from *Tom Brown's School-Days*.

The boy's fear of appearing overly studious to his classmates is of central significance in the ideological framework of this story. Both of the adults in the story—Father Butler and the "old josser"—immediately invoke a culturally reified distinction between boys who are active, unthinking, and lower-class and those who are studious, responsible, and upper-middle class. The priest, on discovering Leo Dillon reading "The Apache Chief" instead of his Roman History, exclaims, "I'm surprised at boys like you, educated, reading such stuff. I could understand it if you were . . . National School boys" (D, 20). Father Butler's pause indicates that he has trouble finding a suitable circumlocution for "lower-class," preferably a term that will immediately instill shame in the boys' hearts. During the protagonist's "miching" expedition, the old man, discovering the protagonist's professed taste for "literature," says, "—Ah, I can see you are a bookworm like myself. Now, he added, pointing to Mahony who was regarding us with open eyes, he is different; he goes in for games" (D, 25). The distinction goes back to medieval typologies of the "active" and "contemplative" lives, but during the late nineteenth century had begun to take on new social implications.

Raymond Williams points out that the word *culture*, in its modern sense of arts and letters, is seldom encountered before the nineteenth century, and acquires an aura of hostility only in the closing years of that century, partly as a result of the debate surrounding Arnold's *Culture and Anarchy*.[24] When Old Cotter asserts that a young lad should run about and play with lads of his own age rather than study with a priest (D, 10), he is articulating this relatively new, class-based hostility to "culture"—an antagonism exacerbated by the popular Irish identification of "culture" with the ruling Protestants. The boy of "An Encounter" finds himself in a situation of ideological contradiction, or perhaps at a locus of conflicting ideologies. He does not want to be thought an unmanly "swot," or a pretender to cultural (and thus class) distinction, and yet he has also internalized the public value system represented by the priest. He is thoroughly aware of the social distinction between himself and his friends on the one hand and children educated at public expense on the other. He immediately identifies the boys and girls he and Mahoney encounter as "ragged girls" and "ragged boys" (D, 22), tags which signify that they attend one of the "Ragged Schools" of Dublin slum areas.[25] Judging from the appearance of the narrator and Mahony, the "ragged" children identify them as better off, and thus Protestants. The narrator feels mingled pride and shame in the status to which his Jesuit education entitles him and the further status accrued from his personal identification with "culture." The priest's rebuke of Dillon affects him greatly, and the protagonist believes that "the confused puffy face of Leo Dillon awakened one of my consciences" (D, 20); but then, in reaction, he is drawn to the "active" life and hungers for the "escape which those chronicles of disorder alone seemed to offer me" (D, 21).

"Chronicles of disorder" is the key term here. The two boys who skip school are both enacting popular literary plots, but each has a different conception of the genre. Mahony is playing Wild West: he brings a catapult for weapon and "began to play the Indian as soon as we were out of public sight" (D, 22). If, as John Cawelti has argued, the Wild West dime novel characteristically engages themes of disguise that include sexual ambiguity, then Mahony's game is disturbingly appropriate for the story.[26] Indeed, the Western's divided allegiance between civilization and pastoral freedom is mirrored in the fact that Joe Dillon, the source of the boys' anarchic fictions, later becomes a priest. Compared to Mahony, the narrator has a vaguer and more complex idea of the drama he is engaged in, but it is probably a romance of the sea. Travel is a necessity, because "real adventures . . . do not happen to people who remain at home: they must be sought abroad" (D, 21). This rather odd elision of schoolboy drama and sea story in the protagonist's mind was in fact perfectly anticipated by boys' magazines; Jack Harkaway, whose original home was *Boys of England*, immediately leaves for the sea following his school adventures; in fact, he goes on to the Wild West, China, and to various wars, so that the same protagonist could slide easily among genres that later would be strictly segregated.[27]

Watching the ship unloading, the boy "examined the foreign sailors to see had any of them green eyes for I had some confused notion . . . " (D, 23). The narrator's use of ellipsis here, as in the boy's narration of his dream in "The Sisters," suggests a turning aside from a realization best left unconscious, because to put it into words would be to denude it of the mystery upon which the image feeds. More specifically, he is looking for the young, red-haired, green-eyed sailor who is the hero of picaresque adventures in the diluted tradition of Marryat. Mahony has the opportunity to enact his fantasy first, since opportunities for warfare were easily come by; the two boys impersonate Protestants more or less accidentally, and when Mahony chases a crowd of Catholic girls a couple of boys, "out of chivalry" (D, 22), decide to retaliate. Mahony and the protagonist then arrange a "siege," which is a failure because two boys is not enough. The protagonist's fantasy is even more of a failure, since the only green-eyed sailor he can spot is the tall man "who amused the crowd on the quay by calling out cheerfully every time the planks fell: —All right! All right!" (D, 23). Far from the folkloric hero who embodies the principles of imagination, sexual regeneration, and anarchy in a necessary opposition to social norms, this quotidian sailor plays to the crowd and gives them back their banal nonsense. Both boys identify with the figure who appears to represent an alternative to the hierarchical, highly ordered aspect of bourgeois ideology: Mahony with the savage Indian, the protagonist with the picaresque sailor. They fail not merely because reality cannot satisfy the desires of the imagination, but also because the "imagination" they have invoked is as ordered, structured, and predictable as the "reality" they are attempting to escape. What appear to be "chronicles of disorder" are merely rituals of a different order, in which the savage Indian and the adventurous sailor must play their endless, assigned roles.

The appearance of the "queer old josser" marks the division between the boys' pretended adventures and their real one. Instead of an opposing gang of cowboys representing society's order, Mahony meets a sinister figure who invokes an entirely different "us-them" distinction: the cultured bookworms versus the ignorant game-players. Instead of a green-eyed sailor, the protagonist meets a man dressed in "greenish-black" (D, 24) with "bottle-green eyes" (D, 27) who walks and speaks in slow, continuous circles, and who takes him on a disturbing voyage of the mind. Unlike Eveline's Frank, who woos her with *The Bohemian Girl* and popular fantasies of a sailor's adventurous life, this seducer invokes Thomas Moore, Sir Walter Scott, and Lord Lytton. It is nonetheless clearly an attempted seduction, as most commentators have noted: the boy is sitting, holding "one of those green stems on which girls tell fortunes" (D, 24), while the man wields a phallic stick; the boy, repulsed by his advances, pretends to adjust his shoe in a classic ingenue's gesture. For reasons that are not specified, the boy claims to have read every book the old man mentions. Certainly he is proud of the extent of his reading, and he also feels he must choose sides in the dichotomy both the old man and Father Butler have drawn. Rather than be identified with the simple Mahony he risks identification with the literary stranger. He is unaware that the figures the old man mentions were at the time a sort of lowest common denominator of literature, writers who might be more readily identified as popular than as serious. Moore's reputation as poet had been declining since his death in 1852, and by the nineties he survived almost exclusively as a "parlour poet" and as precursor of sentimentally patriotic versifiers in the tradition of Young Ireland. Less than a decade later even the philistine Bloom feels it to be appropriate that his statue is erected over a urinal (U, 133/162). Scott's reputation was near its nadir among literati, although his popularity continued, especially among the older generation. He seems to have been Joyce's particular bête noir, since a taste for him is also assigned to both the dead priest in "Araby" and to the dwarfish, monkey-faced old "captain" in *Portrait*.

Edward George Earle Lytton (1803–73), who styled himself Bulwer-Lytton after he was created a baronet, is a more interesting case, especially in the context of "An Encounter." By the 1890s his reputation had also plummeted in critical opinion, although his elevation to the peerage and the self-consciously "cultured" tone of his books hid their essential vulgarity from many readers. Bulwer-Lytton's ambition, energy, intellect, and ability were disproportionate to the quality of his literary production, so that he came to be regarded as the greatest Victorian example of "talent betrayed by character." Disraeli is said to have invoked him as a standard of egotism; the statesman once is supposed to have called Charles Greville "the most conceited man I ever met, though I have read Cicero and known Bulwer-Lytton." Perhaps the best-known British inheritor of the romantic tradition of Byron and Goethe in its novelistic form, he was also a successful playwright whose *Lady of Lyons* still played frequently in Dublin during Stephen Dedalus's boyhood. He was even better known for his novels in the "Silver Fork" tradition of social melodrama in a high-society setting, such as *Pelham*. In books such as these he was able to satisfy the bourgeois taste for images of decadent luxury while simultaneously expressing a bourgeois moral disapprobation of the scene. But despite the explicit moralizing of his novels several of them were generally regarded as dangerous, the sort of book you would not want to fall into the hands of women and children—much like some of the classics whose aura he appropriated. The most notorious of these was *The Last Days of Pompeii* (1834), an interminable melodrama of decadent Roman Empire society. Like *Rienzi* (1835), *The Last of the Barons* (1843), and *Harold* (1848), *The Last Days of Pompeii* is packed with carefully researched archaeological information, sometimes integrated into the narrative and sometimes relegated to intrusive footnotes or narrative essays; the Victorian reader would have no doubt that he was receiving valuable instruction even as he was being titillated by the racy story or the extensive descriptions of banquets and decadent entertainments. The style of both dialogue and narrative is mock-classical and slides between the Biblical and the euphuistic. It is a language intended to bear the undeniable signifiers of cultural and social elevation:

The two friends, seated on a small crag which rose amidst the smooth pebbles, inhaled the voluptuous and cooling breeze, which dancing over the waters, kept music with its invisible feet. There was, perhaps, something in the scene that invited them to silence and reverie. Clodius, shading his eyes from the burning sky, was calculating the gains of the last week; and the Greek, leaning upon his hands, and shrinking not from that sun,—his nation's tutelary deity,—with whose fluent light of poesy, and joy, and love, his own veins were filled, gazed upon the broad expanse, and envied, perhaps, every wind that bent its pinions towards the shores of Greece.

"Tell me, Clodius," said the Greek at last, "hast thou ever been in love?"

"Yes, very often."

"He who hath loved often," answered Glaucus, "has loved never. There is but one Eros, though there are many counterfeits of him."[28]

Insofar as the novel can be said to have themes, they are a banal potpourri of Christian admonition and romantic cliché. Like the novels of Marie Corelli sixty years later, the book has simple, melodramatic action sequences culminating in tableaus intended to inspire the reader with awe and pity. Lest the inattentive reader fail to recognize these moments of frozen passion, at one such tableau the narrator announces, "And never, perhaps, since Lucifer and the Archangel contended for the body of the mighty Lawgiver, was there a more striking subject for the painter's genius than that scene exhibited."[29] The leisurely narrative is frequently interspersed with Bulwer-Lytton's poetry, usually in the guise of a song performed by one of the characters. The elevated diction, Roman milieu, and archaeological references all conspire to suggest to the reader that he is experiencing the classical Sublime.

Certainly this would be the primary book the "old josser" has in mind when he observes that there are some of Lord Lytton's works that boys could not read (D, 25). Marvin Magalaner has observed of Joyce's early reading of Bulwer-Lytton that "he appropriated those characters and situations within the general story which might serve as analogues and surrogates, literary substitutes for the people and scenes of his own projected narratives."[30] *The Last Days of Pompeii* was the only one of Bulwer-Lytton's novels in Joyce's Trieste library and has considerable significance for "An Encounter." In Bulwer-Lytton's novel the first major plot movement is parallel to that in *The Lady of Lyons*: an old, wealthy suitor of a beautiful young girl is displaced by a young pseudo-prince, and the older man attempts revenge through the younger. Here the romantic lead is Glaucus, a Greek-born aristocrat of Pompeii who has good instincts but has been leading a life of mild dissolution. The older man is Arbaces, an enormously wealthy and powerful Egyptian who is also known to the initiated as Hermes; he is also a priest of Isis, a dark goddess with a large number of followers in Pompeii. Arbaces is given to dark rites and orgies that are dimly known in the city, but he has such a plausible manner and powerful intellect that his reputation hardly suffers. He has been made guardian of the beautiful singer Ione and her brother Apaecides, orphans of Greek extraction also. Although he stands in loco parentis to the adolescents, he has begun the seduction of both: Apaecides, a highly impressionable, religious-minded boy, he has begun to induct into the mysteries of the temple of Isis in order to bind him to his will; Ione, whom he desires, but who regards him as a father, he wishes to seduce by means of the hold he has over her brother.

Arbaces is a sort of emotional vampire who draws the youth from his victims; furthermore, he believes himself genuinely in love for the first time. But Ione has met Glaucus, and the two noble youngsters are fated for each other. Enraged, Arbaces calumniates Glaucus, accusing him of toying with Ione's affection, and takes advantage of her wounded pride to entice her to his house. Meanwhile, her brother, discovering that Isis is a sham and the temple miracles tricks, has been brought near nervous breakdown. Arbaces takes advantage of his instability to bring the boy into the inner sanctum of the priest's house, where he is made drunk and given slave-girls to entertain him while Arbaces looks on delightedly. At first, he is flattered that the priest "had deigned to rank him with himself, to set him apart from the laws which bound the vulgar."[31] Transposed into a melodramatic key, the situation is exactly parallel to that in "The Sisters" and "An Encounter": a boy is tempted by an old, somehow disreputable priest-figure who offers initiation into mysteries that combine arcane learning and an undefined element of dark sensuality and that are not accessible to ordinary humanity. Afterward, filled with self-disgust and lassitude, Apaecides encounters a group of early Christians who help him to escape from the evil influence, just in time to join Glaucus in rescuing Ione from the Egyptian's clutches.

Once the girl is in his home, Arbaces presses his suit in slightly disguised form. He urges a sort of Platonic love, although he certainly does not mean to imply that their relationship should not be physical: "There is a love, beautiful Greek, which is not the love only of the thoughtless and the young—there is a love which sees not with the eyes, which hears not with the ears but in which soul is enamoured of soul. The countryman of thy ancestors, the cave-nursed Plato, dreamed of such a love—his followers have sought to imitate it; but it is a love that is not for the herd to echo. . . . Wrinkles do not revolt it—homeliness of feature does not deter; it asks youth, it is true, but it asks it only in the freshness of the emotions."[32] The narrator stresses Ione's bewilderment and Arbaces's caution: "He knew that he uttered a language which, if at this day of affected platonisms it would speak unequivocally to the ears of beauty, was at that time strange and unfamiliar."[33] Like the old josser, Arbaces cannot afford to articulate his desires except through indirection; he also must entice the young with a language they are not ready to understand. But Arbaces eventually makes his intentions clear, while as dramatic counterpoint huge banquets, fountains, and luxurious displays appear before them. When Ione confesses her love for Glaucus, he is overcome with rage and seizes her; she emulates Victorian heroines by fainting away, just as Glaucus and Apaecides burst in to the rescue. Aided by a preparatory tremor from the volcano, the heroes are able to defeat Arbaces and bring the first cycle of the plot—and the only one relevant to "An Encounter"—to a close.

The coincidence of themes in Bulwer-Lytton's novel and Joyce's story is apparent simply from an outline of the action, but in fact it goes considerably deeper than this. The actual scenes of orgy and seduction in the melodrama are rather mild and go no further than a stolen kiss or a man's head upon a woman's lap; but mingled strains of pedophilia, sodomy, and sadomasochism run just below the surface. Most prominent is the seduction of Ione through her brother, an action barely justified in terms of the plot—there is little evidence that Arbaces's hold over Apaecides gives him any leverage with Ione.

Indeed, far more of the book is devoted to the more elaborate and successful seduction of the boy than to the relatively perfunctory (and unsuccessful) seduction of the girl. Several of the subplots and minor characters encourage such a reading as well. One of Glaucus's companions is described as a man "in whom Nature seemed twisted and perverted from every natural impulse, and curdled into one dubious thing of effeminacy and art," who spends his happiest hours patting and stroking the shoulders of gladiators with a "blanched and girlish hand."[34] Perhaps the book's most shocking scene involves the wife of a retired gladiator, herself a sort of ambiguously sexed monster of brutality, who brawls with young gladiators in her tavern. Glaucus enters to discover her passionately beating a blind young slave-girl with a cord "already dabbled with blood."[35] The narrative regularly circles around to such scenes, as if in peripheral and periphrastic commentary upon the relatively straightforward heterosexual romance of the main plot.

The old josser's monologue is a simplified, repetitive version of what might be termed an "ideology of perversion" couched, like Bulwer-Lytton's narrative, within a framing context of moral disapproval and, curiously enough, within an additional assumed context of superior social status. Steven Marcus has observed that the "literature of flagellation in Victorian England assumes that its audience had both interest in and connection with the higher gentry and the nobility—that this assumption may itself be laden with fantasies is not at this moment to the point. It further assumes that its audience had the common experience of education at a public school. . . . Indeed, for this literature perversity and social privilege are inseparable marks of distinction.[36] This linkage between high social status and perversity is directly invoked by the old man in "An Encounter," and in fact helps tie together the story's themes. Further, Marcus notes that although there are two basic scenarios of flagellation, in one of which a boy is beaten by a mother-figure and in the other of which a girl is beaten by an older woman, "in fact no such distinctions really obtain, on either side of the transaction. In this literature, anybody can be or become anybody else, and the differences between the sexes are blurred and confused."[37]

The sexual confusion is apparent in *The Last Days of Pompeii*, where it functions as part of the disguise of the underlying perverse narrative. It is also apparent in the old man's narrative, where it functions similarly, as an attempt to disarm his young auditor. Joyce's josser is clearly attracted to boys but disguises this unsuccessfully by continual reference to girls:

> There was nothing he liked, he said, so much as looking at a nice young girl, at her nice white hands and her beautiful soft hair. He

gave me the impression that he was repeating something which he had learned by heart or that, magnetised by some words of his own speech, his mind was slowly circling round and round in the same orbit. (D, 26)

And if a boy had a girl for a sweetheart and told lies about it then he would give him such a whipping as no boy ever got in this world. . . . He described to me how he would whip such a boy as if he were unfolding some elaborate mystery. (D, 27)

The old man's confusion, repetitiousness, and mechanical speech are of course indices of his paralysis, but more specifically they point to the fact that he is a creature of his reading. He recites aloud not only the conventional erotic description of the Victorian girl (to whom he is not attracted) but also the description of a boy being whipped, in which he has considerable psychic investment. He is a male, pornographic counterpart to Gerty MacDowell; his consciousness is suffused by sadomasochistic, pedophilic narratives, until like some perverse Ancient Mariner he is condemned to recite them to unwilling ears. And like participants in those narratives, he is trapped in an endless, confused round of mechanical repetition of the same scenario: "His mind, as if magnetised again by his speech, seemed to circle slowly round and round its new centre" (D, 27).

Joyce's narrative, which dialogically embraces and interacts with the explicit and implied narratives of popular literature that are its subject, is remarkable in several regards. First it should be noted that the josser is given only two very brief speeches in direct discourse; the vast majority of his talk is presented in indirect discourse, so that it emerges as an amalgam of the boy's and the old man's language—or, more precisely, of the old man's language and the two languages of experience and retrospection embodied in the boy's narration. The major effect of this strange heteroglossia is to make the boy complicit in the old man's speech, to underline his ambivalence in the face of a language that he first accepts, then attempts to reject. The second and last example of direct reported speech of the man is his observation, "Every boy has a little sweetheart." The narrator admits that "In my heart I thought that what he said about boys and sweethearts was reasonable. But I disliked the words in his mouth" (D, 25). The old man works upon his listener much as the pornographic text works upon its reader, attempting to establish complicity through an appeal to commonly accepted values (lying merits punishment) and then wrenching the reader into an increasingly perverse realm of experience.

Marcus notes that flagellant literature typically is written from a split perspective: "The writers of this literature, like some propagandists for homosexuality, need to reassure themselves that their affliction is simultaneously exclusive and universal."[38] The relationship of the flagellant narrator with the reader of this genre is radically unstable. He is addressed both as one of an elite of sensibility and as a man who shares the unadmitted desires of all men. The old man employs the same unconscious tactic: "At times he spoke as if he were simply alluding to some fact that everybody knew, and at times he lowered his voice and spoke mysteriously as if he were telling something secret which he did not wish others to overhear" (D, 26). Even more than the general run of pornography, flagellant narrative is essentially anecdotal and repetitive; like Bulwer-Lytton's novel, it exists for the tableau. The indirect reportage of the old man's speech heightens this effect for the reader. Argument and narrative drop away, and we are left with an impression of monotonous, repetitive circularity. The words are subsumed by the voice: "He repeated his phrases over and over again, varying them and surrounding them with his monotonous voice" (D, 26). Before this assault the boy has no option but to invoke the strategies of his predecessor in "The Sisters," silence and disguise. Appropriately for a story that addresses popular fictions, he decides to play "spy" by plotting with Mahony to give an assumed name if questioned. But even there he does not escape the round of fictions surrounding him, for he assigns Mahony a lower-class, Irish name, "Murphy," and chooses for himself the higher-status Anglo-Irish name of "Smith." Both names, of course, are banal; but that merely emphasizes the poverty of the imaginative resources available to him.

Criticism of "An Encounter" has generally centered on the boy's final appeal to Mahony and his shame at having secretly despised his schoolfellow. Julian Kaye reads the story as the "symbolic history of the boy narrator's rejection of the authority of father, church, and state as perverted and degenerate and his despairing substitution of the friendship of a contemporary who, although mediocre, can assuage his loneliness."[39] Less forgivingly, Sidney Feshbach argues that the story is a formal elegy showing the spiritual death of a young boy, and that his "penitence serves society."⁴⁰ In the perspective of popular fictions, it seems clear that the social distinction the boy-narrator makes a gesture toward abandoning at the end is not his intuitive sense of superiority as artist, but a pernicious fiction enunciated first by the priest and then inadvertently deconstructed by the old josser. What the boy comes intuitively to realize is that fictions like the active/intellectual or the Church School/National School oppositions are not harmlessly free-floating distinctions, but part of complex, embedded ideologies whose ramifications may be baffling or dangerous. If you love Walter Scott you may have to assent to whipping; if you are a bookworm you may wind up mesmerized by a strange and simple text. "An Encounter" does not recount the defeat of imagination by reality, because the "imagination" that inspires the outing is mass-produced and the "reality" the boys encounter is merely another genre of popular fiction.

"Araby": Varieties of Popular Romance

Like "An Encounter," "Araby" is introduced by three titles. Instead of *The Union Jack*, *Pluck*, and *The Halfpenny Marvel*, they are Scott's *The Abbot*, *The Devout Communicant*, and *The Memoirs of Vidocq*; they belong not to the future priest Joe Dillon but to an anonymous dead priest. They are somewhat more literally a legacy to the boy-protagonist, and as in the preceding story they have ironic significance both for the situation of the original owner and for the experience of the boy. These old "paper-covered" books are found in the "waste room behind the kitchen" among "old useless papers" (D, 29), in a close, musty atmosphere that dampens and curls their pages. Set against this hothouse imagery is the wild garden behind the house with its symbolic central apple tree and marvelously inappropriate rusty bicycle pump. The abandoned, trashy library and the decayed Eden with its disintegrating snake or phallus are parallel, involuntary legacies to the boy from the "very charitable priest" who "had left all his money to institutions and the furniture of his house to his sister" (D, 29). Both reflect upon the boy's first, "innocent" infatuation with Mangan's sister and upon the way in which he willfully nurtures his childish, hothouse passion in solitude. The initial scene of the story also sets a strangely ambivalent tone. Where "The Sisters" opens with an increasingly intense sinister air and

"An Encounter" with a note of brisk cheeriness, "Araby" oddly mixes the sinister and the farcical. The boy's house is at the "blind end" of a "blind" street, set apart from the neighboring houses that gaze at one another "conscious of decent lives within them" (D, 29), as if to emphasize that no such decent life is lived in the boy's house. Yet this dead priest apparently harbored no disgraceful secret comparable to the paralysis, loss of faith, pedophilia, or syphilitic decay with which Nannie and Eliza's brother James might be charged. If his reading is any indication, he was not even an intellectual.

Apart from his bequests and the setting of his house, all we know of the priest who haunts this story is his reading, and the more closely this is examined the more problematic it appears. *The Devout Communicant* seems appropriate enough; it is generally identified as a work by the English Franciscan Friar Pacificus Baker, *The Devout Communicant; or, Pious meditations and aspirations, for three days before and three days after receiving the Holy Eucharist. To which is added, A Method of visiting the Blessed Sacrament. . . . As also, some pious hymns, &c. in honour of this Sacred Mystery* (1813). The work stretched to 215 pages, and Gifford quotes a nineteenth-century comment that Baker's books are "without much originality . . . remarkable for unction, solidity, and moderation; but we wish the style was less diffuse and redundant of words" [*sic*].[41] Baker apparently specialized in the Church calendar, as he also wrote *A Lenten Monitor, Sundays Kept Holy*, and *The Christian Advent*, all accompanied by pious thoughts for the occasion.[42] Certainly Baker's book gives a meaningful frame to the boy's chivalric infatuation; he takes communion from the image of Mangan's sister and devotes the time before and after his encounters to pious meditations, recitations, and ejaculations in the religion of love. As most critics have noted, the boy consciously conflates his secular passion with a religious one: "I imagined that I bore my chalice safely through a throng of foes. Her name sprang to my lips at moments in strange prayers and praises which I myself did not understand. . . . I pressed the palms of my hands together until they trembled, murmuring: *O love! O love!* many times" (D, 31).

But the irony is redoubled when we discover that there are several other books of the same title, reprints of which the priest might have owned. One of these is Abednego Seller's *The devout communicant, assisted with rules for the worthy receiving of the blessed Eucharist . . .*

printed in London in 1686 for R. Chiswell, a volume upon which Baker's is no doubt modeled. In an early essay Harry Stone assumed that this was the volume alluded to and pointed out that this author, whose name suggests simony, was "a Protestant clergyman . . . who had written tracts against 'Popish Priests,' engaged in published controversy with a Jesuit divine, and was eventually relieved of his office."[43] A third, equally disturbing alternative, is *The devout communicant, according to the Church of England, etc.*, attributed to James Ford and printed in Ipswich for J. Raw in 1815.[44] Certainly this is a most unlikely volume for a Catholic priest to have owned; but then, on reflection, so are *The Abbot* and *The Memoirs of Vidocq*.

Stone was among the first to point out the apposite oddity of Scott's novel in the context of "Araby": "That Scott's unblemished romantic heroine, an idolized Catholic queen by the name of Mary, should also be (though not to Scott) a 'harlot queen,' a passionate thrice-married woman who was regarded by many of her contemporaries as the 'Whore of Babylon,' as a murderess who murdered to satisfy her lust—this strange dissonance, muted and obscured by Scott's presentation, is a version of the boy's strikingly similar and equally muted dissonances."[45] Actually, there are plenty of admirable antipapist characters in *The Abbot* (1820) who characterize Mary Stuart as the Whore of Babylon; this element is "muted" only insofar as the book's protagonist is mainly associated with Catholics and himself conceives a chivalric passion for the deposed Queen. This protagonist, Roland Graeme, corresponds to the boy in "Araby" in a number of regards. First, he is without living parents and has been raised by his grandmother, Magdalen Graeme. At the opening of the book he is ten years old and is rescued from drowning by the dog of Lady Mary of Avenel, wife of Sir Halbert Glendinning. The book is set in the 1560s, when Mary Queen of Scots has become a desperate cause for persecuted Catholics; Sir Halbert, a knighted commoner and a Protestant who has the Regent's favor, is often absent from the castle. Having rescued the boy, Sir Halbert's childless and lonely wife decides to make him a page. From his appearance and manner it seems clear to Lady Mary and to others in the castle that he has "gentle blood."

On his return Sir Halbert finds Roland firmly established as a favorite. He has already been "spoiled," and he shows signs of a hot temper and, considering his low station, considerable pride. Sir Halbert is worried that his wife has made a great mistake in giving the boy ideas above his station and expectations, but he indulges her. Like the boy of "Araby," Roland is being raised by foster-parents from whom he feels distant; the mother-figure is his defender, but he is at the mercy of an absent and unpredictable father-figure who has no sympathy for his secret ambition. Hovering ambiguously in the background is a priest, or rather several priests. First is the Abbot Eustace, who rules a ruined abbey nearby, a situation that is barely tolerated by the government and the largely Protestant population. This priest dies before making an appearance in the novel. The second, larger figure, is the brother of Sir Halbert, Father Ambrose, who is elected Abbot after the death of the first. That Father Ambrose is a Catholic double of Sir Halbert is made clear by the friendly, guarded relations of the two—both are reasonable, brave, and committed men with military expertise—and by the comment of a retainer that, should Mary Stuart regain the crown, Father Ambrose would become Sir Edward and take Sir Halbert's place.

This, of course, never happens, and as Scott himself admits in his introduction, the book changed so from its original conception that "these retrenchments have rendered the title no longer applicable to the subject." Much of the original supernatural machinery that would have made the Abbot at least symbolically central has been removed; still, in retitling the work "I should have destroyed the necessary cohesion between the present history, and its predecessor THE MONASTERY, which I was unwilling to do."[46] This, despite the fact that *The Monastery* was a relative failure. The parallel to Joyce's world is unmistakable: a dead priest presiding over romantic adventures that really do not involve him, a figure whose time of authority is past, who symbolizes the memory and the possibility of power but who is paralyzed in the present. Both are stories of romantic, lost causes defended by boys. Scott's description of the Cell of Saint Cuthbert, over which the Abbot officially presides, suggests the priest's garden in "Araby": "The flowers, which had been trained with care against the walls, seemed to have been recently torn down, and trailed their dishonoured garlands on the earth; the latticed window was broken and dashed in. The garden, which the monk had maintained by his constant labour in the highest order and beauty, bore marks of having been lately trod down and destroyed by the hoofs of animals and the feet of men."[47] Indeed, Scott's position with regard to Catholicism is moot. Throughout he associates it with mildly gothic imagery suggesting that it is a religion in desuetude. Still, he allows it some admirable spokespersons such as the new Abbot. The narrator refers to Catholicism as "a decaying superstition," and says of the group dedicated to Mary's cause that "those who, with sincerity and generosity, fight and fall in an evil cause, posterity can only compassionate as victims of a generous but fatal error."[48] On the other hand, this group certainly has all the narrator's romantic sympathies; and Roland, who despite his religious ambivalence winds up a central actor in the rescue of Mary Stuart, is richly rewarded at the book's end. But in Roland, as in the boy of "Araby," the religious impulse is displaced by the chivalric, and it is chivalry that has Scott's full sympathy.

Apart from the priestly parallel, the most obvious correspondence between *The Abbot* and "Araby" is in the boy-protagonist's foster-parents and in the objects of his devotion. Roland has not only Lady Mary but Magdalen Graeme as a surrogate mother, and the latter makes explicit the tyranny that the former seldom exercises. After several years at the castle Roland's aggressive high spirits embroil him in disputes, and Sir Halbert feels he must send the boy away; no sooner is he free than he is met by Magdalen, whom he also calls "mother." She is a figure of uncanny power, thought by people in the neighborhood to be either a Protestant devotee, a Catholic in disguise, or perhaps a witch: at various times, she appears in each of these guises. At this point we learn that she is actually a fanatical Catholic dedicated to Mary Stuart's cause, who has ensured that while Roland was at the castle his Protestant instruction was offset by secret instruction from a priest. However, Roland is reluctant to commit himself to either creed. He is mollified, though, when he is brought to meet young Catherine Seyton who is in the care of the old Abbess of St. Catherine, a friend of Magdalen's and fellow fanatic. Catherine displaces Lady Mary as the object of his chivalric affections, and his first sight of her is as tantalizing as the sight of Mangan's half-lit sister: she is veiled and seated at a table, eyes averted, so that he only gradually comes to an idea of her appearance. Indeed, as later events make clear, he is at no time positive of her appearance. The two are left to "get acquainted," and after a good deal of pseudo-Shakespearean courtly dialogue it becomes evident that she is something of a tease who finds Roland attractive but does not take him seriously. As is later revealed, she is too nobly born for his aspiration.

He perseveres nonetheless and in his inexperience and vainglory becomes the butt of a succession of farcical scenes. His first heroic act is to attempt to protect her from a monster that appears suddenly and turns out to be a cow. Later, he is surprised to encounter her dressed as a young nobleman and on numerous occasions pays court to her in this guise; eventually he discovers that he has been romancing her hotheaded twin brother, while neither of the Seytons has trusted him sufficiently to clarify the misunderstanding for him. At one point, he finds the brother in a lady's attire and expostulates when the person does not acknowledge him: " 'Fair Catherine,' said the page, 'he were unworthy ever to have seen you, far less to have dwelt so long in the same service, and under the same roof with you, who could mistake your air, your gesture, your step in walking or in dancing, the turn of your neck, the symmetry of your form—none could be so dull as not to recognise you by so many proofs; but for me, I could swear even to that tress of hair that escapes from under your muffler.' "⁴⁹

With the exception of her "step," the inventory is precisely that partial and misleading list of attributes through which Mangan's sister is perceived by the boy: the figure, the neck, the tress. When the "damsel" attempts to adjust her veil and swears at it in manly fashion Roland is taken aback, and the "damsel" observes, "You are surprised . . . at what you see and hear—But the times which make females men, are least of all fitted for men to become women; yet you yourself are in danger of such a change." Seyton explains that it is womanly to risk losing your religion simply because "it is assailed on all sides by rebels, traitors, and heretics." The theme of a beleaguered, dying religion defended only by a few fanatics lends a romantic, even gothic air to Scott's novel, while in Joyce's story the imagery of dead priest and empty, dark church suggests only absence and betrayal. Seyton further accuses Roland of "pretending to a gentle name" while being "cowardly, silly, and self-interested"—in short, of being driven and derided by vanity, by aspiration above his station.⁵⁰ Much later, after he has learned the truth, while Catherine reads *La Cronique d'Amour* to the Queen, Roland sits wondering how he could possibly have mistaken brother for sister.⁵¹ Scott's implication is clear, and it applies to the boy of "Araby" as well: the youth's love is a literary product, itself a sort of blindness. At root Roland's infatuation, like the boy's in "Araby," is more conventional than sexual.

Throughout the book Roland is given to rash acts and statements that are literary in inspiration: he is "inconsiderate and headlong as we have described him, having no knowledge of real life but from the romances which he had read, and not an idea of checking himself in the midst of any eager impulse."[52] Almost magically, he manages to land on his feet each time, though he often appears laughably quixotic. His elders are perpetually reminding him that it is "no time to make a flourish of thy boyish chivalry,"[53] for he does have a "dreadful purpose," to help Catherine rescue the Queen from her imprisonment by the Lady of Lochleven. Magdalen has somehow managed to introduce Catherine among the Queen's ladies-in-waiting and arranged for Roland to be added to her attendants in his identity as a good Protestant serving Sir Halbert. There he is once again dogged by a preacher and infuriated by the irrelevance of religious doctrine to his real concerns: "He adhered to the forms of his religion rather because he felt it would be dishonourable to change that of his fathers, than from any rational conviction or sincere belief in its mysterious doctrines."[54]

He is also distrusted by both sides—the Protestants, who find him overly devoted to Queen Mary, and the Catholics, who are suspicious of his time at Avenel. Both suspect that, like the boy of "Araby," he might be a sort of spy. The Catholics need not worry; between his desire for Catherine and his total courtly devotion to Mary—the ultimate damsel in distress—he is no longer in doubt about his loyalties. But Roland's suspicious observers have a point: a romantically infatuated boy behaves much like one with a secret mission. He is distanced from everyone else by his fixation on the loved object and is accountable to no one.[55] From this point on, however, he becomes for the most part an observer of the historical personages whose conflicts are played out before him. He and Catherine manage to play small but significant roles in the drama of Mary's escape, but his courtly devotion to the Queen is displaced by that of her real suitors, the authors of her brief deliverance.

Roland visits a succession of "Araby's" in the course of the book, in each of which he plays a foolish part. One is the festival near the castle where Mary is sequestered, where during a costumed dance he meets Catherine's brother disguised as a girl, with the consequences described above. A more striking festival—a genuine carnival, in Bakhtin's terms—interrupts the Mass celebrating the election of Father Ambrose as Abbot of Kennaquhair. A group of townspeople burst into the Abbey in masquerade, led by a masked "Lord Abbot of Unreason," and proceed to enact a mocking parody of the Mass. Scott, in an extensive note, explains the historical background of this ritual, which at a former time was countenanced by the church itself but later became a ritualized form of anti-Catholic demonstration. The crowd itself is a study in inversions: men dressed as wild animals, peasants dressed as St. George, a man dressed as a dragon who menaces a boy dressed as a damsel in distress; "Men were disguised as women, and women as men—children wore the dress of aged people, and tottered with crutch-sticks in their hands . . . while grand-sires assumed the infantine tone as well as the dress of children."[56] The songs and acts of the revelers cross the highest liturgical ritual with obscenity and vileness, the elevated with the grossly mundane. Roland, naturally, fails to appreciate the parody. He is, almost literally, bearing his chalice through a throng of foes, although the chalice is not really his and the foes are friends in disguise since the revellers include friends from Avenel.

In fact, during the greater part of the action Roland is in a sort of Araby, a land of disguises and enchantments. A boy of apparently low birth, he is first catapulted among the nobility as Lady Mary of Avenel's servitor, then as a messenger to the Regent from Lord Halbert, and finally as the Queen's attendant. He attempts to play the good and faithful knight to Lady Mary, Catherine, and Queen Mary, but gradually realizes that his desires and postures are insignificant in the larger drama around him. Just as no one is certain of Roland's role in the greater action, so he finds himself faced with disguises and hidden motivations at every turn. Late in the book, in an anguished complaint and confession, he tells Magdalen, "I have been treated amongst you—even by yourself, my reverend parent, as well as by others—as one who lacked the common attributes of free-will and human reason, or was at least deemed unfit to exercise them. A land of enchantment have I been led into, and spells have been cast around me—every one has met me in disguise—every one has spoken to me in parables—I have been like one who walks in a weary and bewildering dream."[57] Of course, in Scott's romantic ideology, this disillusionment is not final; Roland perseveres and, despite his inexperience, manages to help the Queen escape. As if by magic, the political consequences of this act are nullified in a hasty summary during the denouement: Roland is revealed to be of noble birth—his parents were secretly married—and thus marries his Catherine. Even his Catholicism ceases to be a problem, because "to the true Gospel the heart of Roland had secretly long inclined,"[58] a fact the reader must find surprising. Roland is presented as a chastened, wiser man at the book's ending, although it is difficult to see why he should be chastened by the enormous rewards his impulsive self-indulgence and inordinate aspirations have won him. Scott's novel is peculiarly double-voiced; the ideology of nineteenth-century realism and Evangelical admonishment coexists uneasily with romantic ideology, so that Child Roland emerges as a figure both farcical and heroic, both chastened and victorious. The boy of "Araby," unfortunately, is trapped in a very different sort of narrative, where the idealism that is Roland's saving grace is exactly the quality responsible for the Irish boy's failure.

The last and strangest of the priest's inadvertent bequests to the boy is the *Memoirs of Vidocq*, a best-selling account of his life purportedly written by François Eugène Vidocq (1775–1857) himself but probably penned by hired hacks. If *The Abbot* relies heavily on the more positive aspects of romantic ideology, these largely spurious memoirs rely upon its darker side. Their structure is essentially episodic, like that of the *roman-feuilleton*; they begin as *Gil Blas* and end as *The Count of Monte Cristo*, with Vidocq playing the dark avenger. It is unlikely that the facts of Vidocq's life will ever be known with any precision, since he was an intensely secretive and self-romanticizing personality who manipulated the popular press of his day in order to keep his mysterious and powerful image before the public. Further, he was a friend of the major romantic authors of the *roman-feuilleton*, notably Dumas *père* and Eugène Sue; both used the tales Vidocq was fond of telling in their works. Dumas wrote a newspaper article about him in 1833 that was often reprinted, portraying him as a mastermind who only had to announce his identity in order for criminals to surrender, so great was their superstitious dread of the detective. Sue borrowed some of the man's tales for *Les Mystères de Paris* (1842–43) and wholeheartedly adopted Vidocq's liberal program for the rehabilitation of criminals. Returning the favor, Vidocq had published under his own name *Les Vrais Mystères de Paris* (1844). Balzac was among his intimates and modeled Inspector Vautrin upon him, while Hugo is thought to be responsible for some of the works attributed to the detective.[59] With the possible exception of Buffalo Bill Cody it is difficult to think of a historical figure in whose life fact and fiction were so inextricably intertwined; but Vidocq was far more sophisticated than Cody in his willing participation in the process.

As Oscar Wilde observed of himself with somewhat less justification, Vidocq's life and image were his greatest imaginative creation.

Vidocq's early life was putatively that of the classical picaresque knave. Bored in a provincial town, at an early age he became involved with local criminals; he enlisted in the army, was apparently trapped into marriage, served on board ship, and after several desertions and impostures, including the serious crime of impersonating an officer, he was sentenced to the galleys. On several occasions he escaped—a remarkable feat—and for brief periods led a life of bourgeois respectability. His erotic liaisons, however, were frequent and chaotic, and on several occasions he was betrayed to the police by a woman with whom he was involved; his wife, who had betrayed him with another man, eventually obtained a divorce. In a preface to his four-volume *Memoirs*, Vidocq complains to the reader that the entire first volume and part of the second were revised by a literary man who had been recommended to him, and because of an ill-timed indisposition he had not overseen the revision. He was, he claims, shocked and dismayed to find "that my compilation had been entirely altered; and that, instead of a narrative developing perpetually the sallies, vivacity, and energy of my character, another had been foisted in, totally deprived of all life, colouring, or promptitude. With few alterations, the facts were nearly the same; but all that was casual, involuntary, and spontaneous, in a turbulent career, was given as the long premeditation of evil intent. The necessity that impelled me was altogether passed over; I was made the scoundrel of the age, or rather a Compère Mathieu, without one redeeming point of sensibility, conscience, remorse, or repentance."[60] But because production was well advanced, contracts had been signed, and a pirated edition was already beginning to appear, Vidocq claims that he was unable to alter the *Memoirs*; he hints darkly at plots by the police, whose jealousy and hatred for him were unbounded once he had left the Sûreté.

Fairly early in his career Vidocq realized that he was not meant for a criminal life and offered his services to the Paris police as an informant, in exchange for immunity from prosecution for his current offenses. Eventually, his assistance bought him a pardon for his earlier ones as well, including his many escapes. By 1809 he had offered his services to the state and under Napoleon helped created the Sûreté, an agency he headed for many years and staffed largely with former prostitutes and criminals. The success of the new detective bureau was undeniable and well publicized by Vidocq; until late in his career he apparently kept several secret criminal "identities" current, in which he was accepted within the criminal subculture. A series of shady women assisted him in his exploits, some of whom, like the mysterious "Annette," themselves became subjects of popular dramas. His position throughout his life was precarious, owing to the jealousy of his administrative rivals and perhaps, if their accusations were correct, because of considerable corruption in his own adminsitration; he was accused of arranging a major crime in order to solve it with the maximum publicity and élan.

His secondary profession as a moneylender also brought him criticism, and he was reputed to use the personal services of the prostitutes he hired. After his resignation in 1832 he set up the first private detective bureau, which was eventually suppressed by the authorities. Late in his life he embarked on a series of lectures in London, where he displayed his own museum of criminology. An anonymous melodrama entitled *Vidocq! the French Police Spy* was produced in London in 1829, and another, *The Thief Taker of Paris, or Vidocq*, in 1860; both contributed to his legend and to the popularity of his translated *Memoirs*. Vidocq died in relative poverty despite the enormous income he had earned, the result of an extravagant and self-indulgent style of life. His genuine contributions to criminology included some of the first scientific use of fingerprints, blood typing, and ballistics, and of course the organization of a paid network of informants. His influence on modern criminology was considerable, and his influence on the detective story, through Poe and Conan Doyle, even greater.

Stone has remarked the inappropriateness of *The Memoirs of Vidocq* as reading for a priest and its incidental relevance to the boy: "That Vidocq should escape from a prison hospital disguised in the stolen habit of a nun, a veil over his face; that he should then assist a good-natured curé in celebrating mass, pretending to make the signs and genuflections prescribed for a nun—this is a version of what the boy will do."[61] In fact, Vidocq, who was educated by the Franciscans, generally embeds the blasphemous incidents in a moral context. Describing the inevitable corruption of life in "The Bagne," or galleys, he recalls: "Thus, at Anvers, an ex-bishop experienced, at first, all the outpourings of the riotous jokes of his companions; they always addressed him as monseigneur, and asked his blessing in all their obscenities; at every moment they constrained him to profane his former character by blasphemous words, and by dint of reiterating these impieties, he contrived to shake off their attacks; at a subsequent period he became the public-house keeper, at the Bagne, and was always styled monseigneur, but he was no longer asked for absolution, for he would have answered with the grossest blasphemies."[62] Although this incident scarcely presents the clergy in a favorable light, Vidocq's main point is that even the best men will become hardened in such a society. Certainly Vidocq has few illusions about the kindness of the clergy: the head of the guards at Anvers, one Father Mathieu, "had the eyes of a lynx, and such a knowledge of the men he had to deal with, that he could tell at the slightest glance if they were scheming to deceive him. . . . He never spoke without mentioning his cudgel; it was a never-ending theme of pleasurable recital to talk of the many bastinadoes he had inflicted personally."[63] Perhaps Father Mathieu prepared Stephen for Father Dolan and his accusations of idle scheming, or struck fear into the heart of the boy of "Araby" when the priest asks sternly whether he is "beginning to idle" (D, 32). Certainly Vidocq would have reinforced, and may have inspired, Joyce's tendency to associate the Irish clergy with the police.

But more than the occasional anticlerical motifs of the book, the continuing themes of disguise, secret missions, and the sense of *election* are Vidocq's dominants. On numerous occasions in his youth Vidocq escapes punishment because of his air of culture and intelligence, which is immediately recognized by one of his captors—or, more likely, by a woman who can intervene on his behalf. Among his most frequent protectors are ladies of the aristocracy. Vidocq lays heavy stress on this Byronic distinction, and as narrator often expresses surprise and offense when he is mistaken for a common criminal simply because he is among criminal associates, has a criminal record, and is engaged in a criminal enterprise. Like Roland, he bears his chalice among foes, but unlike him must genuinely do so "even in places the most hostile to romance." Like the boy of "Araby," Vidocq fears the contamination of his environment and is determined to hold himself above it. He says of the criminals in the galleys, "When, day and night, in my presence, they openly practised the most vile and demoralized actions, I was not so confident in the strength of my own character as not to fear that I might become but too much familiarised with such atrocious and dangerous conversation."[64] This fear of moral "infection" is ever-present, as the narrative continually juxtaposes the crudest slum-naturalism with the protagonist's elevated sentiments: his undefined aspiration for himself, his frequent infatuations—all portrayed as innocent and sincere on his part—and his eventual desire to contribute to the social order. Like the boy of "Araby," he lives among "the back doors of the dark dripping gardens where odours arose from the ashpits," running the gauntlet of "the rough tribes from the cottages" (D, 30), yet remains himself untouched by the corruption around him. In this personal aspect of romantic ideology, disguise is a key ploy. As Joyce's boy narrators realize, the true self may be expressed only in solitude or it will inevitably be corrupted by a corrupt environment.

The ultimate popular exemplar of this mode of being is the Count of Monte Cristo, upon whom Stephen Dedalus models himself (see chapter 4 below). Dumas himself asserted that his novel was inspired by Vidocq,[65] and indeed below the level of specific incidents, the motifs that help structure the ideology of the *Memoirs of Vidocq* and *Count of Monte Cristo* are identical. Both begin with an "innocent" involvement in a crime, are betrayed by associates and by their fiancées, are imprisoned, manage remarkable escapes, and finally return in a secret identity to wreak a slow and elaborate revenge. Both are essentially dramatists, elaborating scenarios in which the guilty parties will betray themselves while remaining ignorant of the author of their doom. Both are physical and mental supermen, using a grasp of science to foil their foes, and it is their extraordinary sufferings that have enabled them to transcend the powers of ordinary humanity. Both have a reputation for decadent luxury in their personal lives, assisted by their great wealth, but both preserve a highly correct, cool public demeanor.

Memoirs of Vidocq is the boy's favorite among the priest's books, if only because of its yellow pages, and the vision upon which he acts is as much a product of this text's ideology as of Scott's. He plays detective, at first with his friends: "If my uncle was seen turning the corner we hid in the shadow until we had seen him safely housed" (D, 30). Then he and his friends watch Mangan's sister from their hiding place, to see if she will persist in calling him in to tea. Finally he alone is "shadowing" the girl: "Every morning I lay on the floor in the front parlour watching her door. The blind was pulled down to within an inch of the sash so that I could not be seen. When she came out on the doorstep my heart leaped. I ran to the hall, seized my books and followed her. I kept her brown figure always in my eye and, when we came near the point at which our ways diverged, I quickened my pace and passed her" (D, 30). His secret identity is the Lover, and to betray it would put him in peril of general ridicule. Kept to himself, however, it elevates him above his surroundings; secure in his secret, he spends much time in the upper back room where the priest died, looking down on humanity. "The high cold empty gloomy rooms liberated me and I went from room to room singing" (D, 33). Just so did Vidocq often keep watch from an upper window for his prey, confident in his disguise and his superiority. Only the memory of his secret mission to Araby enables the boy to "endure the gossip of the tea-table," the corrupt concerns of common mortals.

But of course the boy is no Vidocq; even as Stephen Dedalus he will be dependent upon the image of the girl to transfigure him so that "weakness and timidity and inexperience would fall from him" (P, 65). Araby alone cuts him down to size, in two distinct ways. First, its tawdry glamour is stripped bare by closing time; the loud fall of coins, the silence, the empty spaces and darkness in the upper hall conspire to suggest the vacancy at the heart of his vision of Eastern luxury and chivalric romance. A crusader in the Holy Land, he finds only desert where he had anticipated a glorious token for his lady. Second, his own inadequacy is highlighted: instead of looking down on his playmates he now must look up at the young lady shopkeeper and even the "great jars that stood like eastern guards at either side of the dark entrance to the stall" (D, 35). He is too shy to buy even these diminished wares, or perhaps he realizes that he has barely enough money in his pocket to pay his fare home.

But most crucially, his ideal romance is destroyed through language. His uncle, who is for the boy the essence of vulgarity, can embrace his secret mission in the language of popular wisdom: "All work and no play makes Jack a dull boy" (D, 34). Worse, he demystifies Araby itself by enthusiastically participating in the image, reciting "The Arab's Farewell to his Steed." The horror of this is not that the popular poem is inappropriate to the boy's vision, but rather that it is entirely appropriate. Not, as Stone argues, because the theme of simony is suggested when the speaker imagines selling his horse to foreign masters,[66] but because the poem as a whole articulates fragments of the romantic ideologies of Scott and Vidocq upon which the boy depends to separate himself from his surroundings: at the poem's end the speaker asserts that he will *never* sell the horse ("my beautiful"), which embodies freedom and separation from earthly involvements. As the poem's courtly language makes apparent—the "proudly arched" neck, the "dark and fiery eye"—the mock-Arab's horse is a mock-lady who, in this degenerate popular version of neoplatonism, can transport her rider into a realm of perfect freedom, of pure superiority to the mundane, in the mysterious East. By a romantic fiat the poem's speaker declares himself above monetary considerations. But the boy at the bazaar with eight pennies in his pocket finds that the image of Mangan's sister has little power even to transport him home again. Once at the fair, the boy's language is again assaulted, this time from the rear, as he overhears the conversation between the young lady who keeps the stall and her "suitors":

—O, I never said such a thing!
—O, but you did!
—O, but I didn't!
—Didn't she say that?
—Yes. I heard her.
—O, there's a . . . fib! (*D*, 35)

The ugly banality of this interchange, so like Joyce's original collection of "negative epiphanies," completely demoralizes the boy. He realizes that he is listening to the genuine "language of romance," which bears no resemblance to the formalized courtly conversations in Scott and even in Vidocq. He ends the story in silence, his disguise stripped away, his language preempted by his uncle and demystified by the shopkeeper.

"Eveline": Bourgeois Drama and Pornography

The four stories of adolescence, "Eveline," "After the Race," "Two Gallants," and "The Boarding House," lack the power and density of reference of the stories of childhood. They each feature protagonists very much unlike the author, whereas for Joyce's technique to be most effective, the implicit dialogue between author and protagonist must be close and intense. The shift from first-person to third-person narration in "Eveline" need not preclude such a dialogue—it is present in "The Dead," for instance—but it does signal the increased distance between author and protagonist. Where "The Sisters," "An Encounter," and "Araby" all close with a moment of recognition—in the latter two signalled by a heightened rhetoric—these four stories involve characters who are far less conscious of their situations, and who have less hope of escaping the most banal of prevailing ideologies. The boys of "The Sisters," "An Encounter," and "Araby" are not precisely entrapped, but they have less room for maneuver than they think. The boy of "The Sisters" may oppose the dominant discourses with the ambiguous language of dream, with silence and disguise, but his language has already been infiltrated. The boy of "An Encounter" comes to recognize the inefficacy of his literary ideologies of adventure, and to rebel against the social disjunction between the culturally initiate and the mindlessly active; but he does not realize the extent to which his dreams of disorder and escape are themselves socially programmed. The boy of "Araby" comes to an explicit realization of his own "vanity," while the reader comes to realize the force of the ideological pressures that have sent him on his quest in the first place.

By contrast, the "adolescents" are less conscious of the nature of their bind, even at the conclusions of their stories. They are more purely the victims of a dominant discourse. Appropriately from the start, each is already enslaved by a figure representing authority. Eveline is literally paralyzed at story's end, unable to evaluate either her hopes or her fears and unable to act on either; Jimmy has a muffled, unarticulated recognition of the role he has played for his friends, but feels only a vague alarm in a situation that merits paroxysms of Dostoevskian *Schadenfreude*; Lenehan, a mock-adolescent and mock-protagonist, has a cynical understanding of his situation that is totally divorced from his actions. Instead of standing in Eveline's frozen immobility, he walks his pointless rounds, constantly circling what he takes to be experience. As for poor Polly Mooney, she plays as small a part in her story as does Lenehan in his, and at the end she retreats into "hopes and visions" of such intricacy— and irrelevancy—that until her mother calls her she is no longer consciously present.

At first glance, Eveline would appear to be an ordinary young woman who is simply unable to take the leap to freedom with her suitor Frank; she is caught in a situation that destroyed her mother and yet is so bound by habit that she cannot choose to free herself from it. It was Hugh Kenner who first explained forcefully that Eveline is refusing a fiction, not a genuine possibility: " 'He had fallen on his feet in Buenos Ayres (comma) he said (comma) and had come over to the old country just for a holiday.' Great issues may be said to hang on those commas, which stipulate not only that Eveline is quoting Frank, but that Frank has been quoting also: quoting from the kind of fiction Eveline will believe, the fiction in which ready lads 'fall on their feet.' . . . The hidden story of 'Eveline' is the story of Frank, a bounder with a glib line, who tried to pick himself up a piece of skirt. She will spend her life regretting the great refusal."[67] Kenner's ear for the cadences of popular literature is impeccable, but he fails to note that Eveline must also present her homely alternative to herself in terms of a set of irrelevancies that themselves create a popular fiction: the photograph of the priest (anonymous and departed), the harmonium (broken), the father making her toast and reading to her, or putting on his wife's bonnet to make the children laugh (*D*, 37, 39)—incidents she recalls mainly because they were unprecedented.

Similarly, when she feels she must "escape" with Frank, she assures herself, "Frank would take her in his arms, fold her in his arms" (*D*, 40), the latter clause—the formulation she settles on—coming closest to the language that resolves a popular melodrama. The story to which Joyce's story alludes, the abduction of an innocent girl by a disguised rake who promises marriage, has been a convention of the novel since Richardson. Eveline's choice is greatly a choice between languages of fiction; as Arnold Goldman observes from a somewhat different perspective, "the longer the story goes on, the more does the language bully the girl."[68] Yet Eveline is no Gerty MacDowell: she builds her fantasy of Victorian domesticity in the face of the facts that she fully acknowledges, such as her father's drunken brutality and pennypinching. As Kenner recognizes, she really has no choice but to fictionalize her choices. She realizes that she needs "shelter and food" (*D*, 37) and, increasingly, someone "to protect her" (*D*, 38); but she cannot live her imaginative life within the parameters of such a stark vision. Like the rest of humanity, she cannot live without ideology.

Formal popular fictions are indeed present in the story, providing a context and structure for her fruitless meditations, but whereas in the stories of childhood the protagonist consciously enters into some degree of complicity with them, in the stories of adolescence the protagonist is generally unaware of their presence. They hover below the text of the stories just as they hover below the threshhold of a character's awareness, sometimes surfacing as a brief allusion, sometimes only as a characteristic structure of imagery or—in Kenner's example, for instance—as an intonation. In "Eveline" the dominant popular fiction is represented by *The Bohemian Girl* (1843), the locally famous light opera by the Dubliner Michael William Balfe (1808–70). This is the entertainment Frank takes Eveline to see, in hopes that it will help make his argument convincing; but the opera, which mirrors all the major explicit themes of the story, probably contributes to her eventual paralysis.

Even in the opera's Argument, the opposing themes are apparent: the widowed Count Arnheim has arranged a hunt for which his retainers are preparing. Meanwhile the Outsider, Thaddeus, a Polish exile and fugitive from the Austrian troops, stumbles into the scene and meets a band of gypsies led by Devilshoof, who hide him from the army. When cries of dismay from the count's retainers announce that the count's young daughter, Arline, is in danger, Thaddeus impulsively seizes a rifle, runs off, and shoots the stag that is menacing her. He returns her, slightly wounded, to the arms of her distraught father. The grateful count insists that Thaddeus attend a feast of celebration, which turns ugly when the young man refuses to toast the Emperor. Devilshoof appears and defends his friend; he is seized while Thaddeus is allowed to depart, but soon afterward the gypsy escapes, taking the daughter with him. Even at the end of the first act, it is clear that the daughter will be torn between loyalty to her young rescuer, whom she believes to be a gypsy, and loyalty to her father, precisely as Eveline is torn between Frank and her father.[69]

The second act takes place twelve years later, on the outskirts of a nearby city where the gypsies are encamped. Florestein, the count's foppish nephew, meets Devilshoof, who robs him of a medallion. Back at the camp Arline, now a beautiful young woman, lives in the tent of the sinister queen of the gypsies. Thaddeus tells Arline the story of her rescue, but without revealing her noble birth. The two confess their love and are reluctantly joined by the gypsy queen, who lusts after Thaddeus. Arline then goes off to entertain the crowd in the city, including Florestein, who attempts to seduce her; the queen slips the medallion around the girl's neck, and when Florestein spots it he has her arrested. Protesting her innocence, she is brought before the count and in her humiliation attempts to stab herself. The count restrains her and then recognizes her by her old wound, and "the Act ends with an effective *tableau*."[70] In the final act Arline is restored to her home but still pines

for Thaddeus. Yet when he braves all dangers in order to see her and
tempt her with the gypsy life, she is reluctant to leave her father. The
count and retainers burst in on the lovers, and the gypsy queen enters to
give dire warnings, but when Thaddeus announces his noble birth, and
proves it by presenting his commission, the count declares that political
considerations should not hinder the love-match. The queen, enraged,
orders one of her tribe to fire at Thaddeus, but Devilshoof strikes the
man's arm so that the queen is killed instead.

The opera's libretto, by Alfred Bunn (1796–1860), conveniently and
conventionally foregrounds the major themes. The count's retainers chorus the imperial theme, associated with patriarchal authority: "Up with
the banner, and down with the slave / Who shall dare to dispute the
right, / Wherever its folds in their glory wave, / Of the Austrian eagle's
flight"; the band of gypsies chorus the rejoinder:

> In the gipsy's life you may read
> The life that all would like to lead.

> Through the wide world to rove,
>   Be it sunny or drear,
> With but little to love,
>   And still less to fear.

Anarchy and freedom from entanglements is the antithesis to the Father's imperial thesis. But Thaddeus, lamenting his exile, claims that the
root of loneliness is not the lack of a fatherland but of a person to love:

> Yet, hard as are such ills to bear,
>   And deeply though they smart,
> Their pangs are light to those who are
>   The orphans of the heart!

Thaddeus thus avoids choosing sides in the antinomy between authority
and freedom, hearth and vagary, by invoking romantic love, the master-
term in this ideology, which can resolve dilemmas by transcending them.
This, of course, is precisely Frank's strategy: he will "fold her in his
arms" and thereby resolve her doubts and, incidentally, the contradictions of bourgeois ideology. Unfortunately, Frank is no Thaddeus; although Irish-born, he is genuinely rootless, whereas Thaddeus is a gypsy
only for the duration of the drama—indeed, unless we are to assume

that he has fallen in love with a girl of about five and then waited twelve years for her to mature, from a psychological perspective it is very difficult to see why he remains among the gypsies for so long. He does so basically to satisfy bourgeois taste: he must be closely associated with their anarchic freedom in order to give the tang of danger to Arline's choice, but he must ultimately be revealed as belonging to the same order as the father's authority. Thaddeus consciously and Arline unconsciously play at being gypsies before returning to the serious business of nobility.

Another theme enunciated by various characters is nostalgia, Tennyson's "Tears, idle tears." Thaddeus sings, "The scenes and days to me, / Which seemed so blest to be, / No time can e'er restore," while the Count stresses the self-defeating nature of the emotional process:

Whate'er the scenes the present hour calls forth before the sight,
They lose their splendour when compared with scenes of past delight.
The heart bow'd down by weight of woe,
   To weakest hopes will cling,
To thought and impulse while they flow,
   That can no comfort bring.

This, of course, is what Eveline is doing at the opening of the story: conjuring up "past delights," however dubious. She muses on the changes in her neighborhood and thinks of the days she spent playing with the children of the avenue until her father appeared to "hunt them in out of the field with his blackthorn stick." Even this rather sinister note—in the light of his present threats of violence—becomes pleasing in retrospect, as she thinks, "Still they seemed to have been rather happy then" (D, 36). Among the things Eveline chooses as she stands immobile at the story's end is her childhood, gilded by retrospection.

As Eveline sits, dreaming of her past, she touches on another minor theme of the opera: the past as dream. While Arline is quizzing Thaddeus about her past, she performs the aria, "I dreamt that I dwelt in marble halls," the song Maria in "Clay" will unsuccessfully attempt to render. In "Eveline," the song functions neatly in two directions. When the song is rendered apart from the context of the opera, the singer appears to be telling the loved one that even when imagining herself a princess besieged with suitors, the important thing was that "you loved me still the same"; within the context of The Bohemian Girl, Arline is recounting a dream that is also a memory of the past and attempting to place Thaddeus within it. This is certainly dramatically effective, but it takes on a sinister implication later in the opera when Arline has been returned to her former state and soliloquizes, "The past appears to me but a dream from which I have at length aroused me. Yet my heart recalls enough to convince me it was all reality." We begin to suspect that for Arline—as, perhaps, for Eveline—all of life is a dream illumined only by the recollections of the heart. After all, Arline apparently managed to pass twelve years in happy ignorance of her own past, just as Eveline is surprised to realize that she has never learned the name of the priest whose picture presides over the sitting room. Yet we can excuse Arline her incuriosity because of the genre in which she exists; perhaps Eveline is attempting to join her there.

The twin themes of romantic love and paternal love, which provide the explicit conflict of the drama, are sounded repeatedly. When Thaddeus fears that explaining the secret of her birth will estrange Arline from him, she reassures him by asking, "Where is the spell hath yet effaced / The first fond lines that love hath traced?" But somewhat greater force is given the paternal tie when at the close of Act 2 the count "clasps Arline to his heart—kisses her head, hands, hair, and shed[s] tears of joy" while the chorus affirms,

> Praised be the will of heaven,
> > Whose light on them smiled,
> And whose bounty hath given
> > The father his child!

The conflict of the two ends in a paralysis strikingly similar to that of Eveline. When Devilshoof and Thaddeus secretly visit Arline in the castle, her suitor asks, "And will you then forsake your home, your kindred all! and follow me?" Arline waffles:

> Through the world I will fly
> > From the world with thee,
> Could I hush a father's sigh
> > That would heave for me.

Devilshoof warns the two that the count's retainers are about to arrive, and they must fly, but Arline rather ambiguously begs Thaddeus not to "snap the string / Of the fondest tie / In my memory / To which the heart can cling." Thaddeus announces, "I am chained by fate to the spot," and Devilshoof summarizes the situation: "Escape is hopeless." All three stand rooted to the spot, like Eveline before the gangplank.

Of course, escape is provided in this escapist drama by negating the need for it; Arline need not choose between the alternatives, and so she and Thaddeus are both freed from paralysis. The past is effectively negated in the play's final affirmation, sung by all three principals in turn:

> Ne'er should the soul over sorrows grieve,
> With which the bosom hath ceased to heave.
> Ne'er should we think of the tempest past,
> If we reach the haven at last.

Certainly this philosophy is requisite in the situation. Immediately before Thaddeus's revelation of his identity, the count had shouted at Arline, "False thing! beloved too long, too well, / Brave not the madness thou can'st not quell!" The violence of this paternal rejection is perhaps best simply ignored in the interests of a happy final tableau. Similarly, everyone has agreed to ignore the fact that Thaddeus is at least an accessory in Arline's kidnapping and has lived with the child for twelve years under the chaperonage of a murderous gypsy queen, not to mention the fact that he is her father's sworn political enemy. None of this is finally important, because at the climax patriarchy has been affirmed so resoundingly. As the curtain falls, "ARLINE rushes into the arms of THADDEUS, and then passes over to the COUNT." In some ways, she has never left the Count's paternal embrace. The play's major unconscious irony occurs when Arline is entertaining the townspeople as a fortuneteller. She warns one, "Pretty maiden, take care, take care, / What havoc love maketh there!" and, pointing to the wedding ring of another, sings, "And this token, from love you borrow, / Is the prelude of many a sorrow."

On reflection, Eveline might find in *The Bohemian Girl* a stronger argument for the paternal bond than for the romance of escape. A father, however threatening, is still a father, and in her dreams of the past she can partially rehabilitate him. The only security Frank offers is that of marriage: "Then she would be married—she, Eveline. People would treat her with respect then. She would not be treated as her mother had been" (*D*, 37). Perhaps not: Frank, she feels, echoing the descriptions of popular adventure heroes, is "very kind, manly, open-hearted" (*D*, 38).

But Kenner is surely correct to be suspicious of this ostensible marriage offer. After all, marriage in *The Bohemian Girl* is a chancy affair. Thaddeus and Arline are actually married by the gypsy queen in the second act. The queen declaims,

> Hand to hand, and heart to heart,
> Who shall these I have mated part
> By the spell of my sway,
> Part them who may!

And everyone, including the gypsy queen herself, then has considerable success in parting the two. Their dubious marriage, unblessed by the count, is negligible. Were it not for Thaddeus's hidden nobility, the opera would have ended in paralysis, or madness. If Roland Smith is correct in the way he construes Mrs. Hill's dying words, "Derevaun Seraun" is corrupt Irish for "The end of song is raving madness."[71] Frank has no hidden proofs of nobility. All he has is romantic song: "The Lass that Loves a Sailor," the Italian organ-grinder's song that her father abruptly terminated (of which "she knew the air"), and the melodic melange of *The Bohemian Girl*.[72] At the critical moment, "All the seas of the world tumbled about her heart. He was drawing her into them: he would drown her" (*D*, 41). Strapped to her own mast, Eveline has listened too closely to the libretto to succumb to her siren-sailor.

Her refusal to join Frank does not save her; there can be little doubt that the remainder of her life will be dominated by an increasingly abusive father and by the daily demands of her role as surrogate mother to the children still at home, even while she clerks in Pim's under Miss Gavan's vindictive eye. Given the social situation of the time, the chances are that, having refused one suitor, she will never marry.[73] Her only hope will be to continue the forceable transformation of her experience into an image of Victorian domesticity. With practice, she may come to view herself as does Gerty MacDowell: "A sterling good daughter was Gerty just like a second mother in the house, a ministering angel too with a little heart worth its weight in gold" (*U*, 291/355).

But Joyce suggests that there are several levels of reality here. There is the inescapable quotidian material world of food and shelter; balancing it, and in dialogical tension with one another, there are the narratives of the ideologically structured worlds of Eveline's alternatives as she perceives them. But there is also a half-lit world of sexual tensions whose images and essential structures are those of Victorian pornography. From the perspective of this world, the fight between her father and Frank is one for sexual possession: Frank needs her as the lass that loves a sailor, or at least the girl in his home port, while her father needs her as the replacement for his wife. The scene is ripe for incest, with her mother dead, her father both threatening physical abuse just as she attains marriageable age and reacting violently to the threat of a suitor for her.

Steven Marcus has noted the prevalence of incest motifs in Victorian pornography, indeed its literary conventionality: "Pornography exists in order to violate in fantasy that which has been tabooed; and incest occurs in it with about the same frequency as marriages occur at the end of English novels."[74] Numerically comparing categories of Victorian "pornotopias," Henry Miles finds incest fantasies to be third in relative frequency, following simple heterosexual and homosexual fantasies and ahead of flagellation, sado-masochism, and fetishism.[75] Given Joyce's considerable knowledge of the pornography of the period, it is quite possible that the story "Eveline" itself is an allusion to the anonymous novel *Eveline*, which Peter Gay characterizes as "a Victorian instance [of the pornography of incest] apparently revised more than once and very popular for decades."[76] This Eveline introduces herself by observing, "There are at least two families of high and ancient aristocratic pretensions, whose loud-tongued, drinking, gambling male descendents openly boast that they have never allowed a maiden of their noble line to pass, as such, out of the family and into the arms of her spouse. Ours is a third, only we are not so simple as to publish the fact."[77]

Like the rest of her family, Eveline is concerned for public propriety and indeed asserts, "I am pointed out by anxious mothers as an example of excellent training, combined with the advantages of a Continental finishing course."[78] Her private life, however, is one of unbridled license, unaffected by even the slightest moral misgivings. From early adolescence, her precocious intelligence and cynical understanding have made her the captain of her fate; unlike the heroines of most Victorian pornography, even Fanny Hill, she is never the passive victim of another's desires. In fact, throughout her narrative she assumes the role of omnipotent female sexual desire. The climax of the book's early sections is Eveline's seduction of her father, Sir Edward, who has returned from a seven years' absence in India. Although Eveline's mother is in the house, she is effectively absent, as she remains at all times in her bedroom, a dipsomaniac, and is ignored by both Eveline and her father. After the sexual consummation with Sir Edward, Eveline pricks herself with a pin to produce a bit of blood and thus spare her father's sensibilities—apparently he would have been disturbed to find his daughter was not virginal. She remarks with academic satisfaction, "The thing was done. I had gained my end. My theories were correct; nothing could ever equal the pleasure he had given me."[79]

It may also be of significance that just as Eveline Hill shares her given name with the heroine of the most notorious of Victorian pornographic novels, she shares her surname with another. Joyce of course was familiar with Cleland's book, and during the writing of "Penelope" asked Budgen to send him an unexpurgated copy.[80] Fanny Hill is a genuine innocent at the beginning of her narrative, unlike the pornographic Eveline. But by the end of her first letter in this epistolary novel she is an experienced courtesan who has lost her "true love," Charles, through mischance and her gentleman protector, "Mr. N . . . ," through his discovery of her dalliance with his own servant. A kindly madam helps Fanny seduce a new protector, an elderly and dissolute man named Mr. Norbert, with whom Fanny plays the part of an innocent virgin. Like Eveline, she arranges for a spurious proof that the nearly impotent suitor has captured her virginity: "The illusion was complete, no other conception entered his head but that of having been at work upon an unopened mine; which idea, upon so strong an evidence, redoubled at once his tenderness for me."[81] Thus both pornographic heroines are aware of the erotic and social value assigned to virginity and manipulate this aspect of sexual ideology to their advantage. The ruse succeeds, and Fanny moves into his apartments. But she soon tires of this fatherly lecher, and while walking to market is accosted by a sailor fresh from the sea. "I looked at him with a beginning of anger and indignation at his rudeness, that softened away into other sentiments as I viewed him: for he was tall, manly carriaged, handsome of body and face, so that I ended my stare with asking him, in a tone turned to tenderness, what he meant; at which, with the same frankness and vivacity as he had begun with me, he proposed treating me with a glass of wine."[82] The glass of wine leads immediately to fuller intimacies, which Fanny enjoys both for their own sake and perhaps also as a gesture of rebellion against Mr. Norbert. But, as will Joyce's Eveline, Fanny prudently returns home again, sacrificing her frank and manly sailor's charms for the sake of her protector's security.

Henry Miles has suggested that pornography with a theme of incest—and, to an extent, pornography in general—is "a form of protest literature, whether conscious or not, opposing the cosy artificial world of the Victorian family, presented by the penny novels and general fiction of the circulating libraries."[83] Certainly this aspect of pornography would have occurred to Joyce and appealed to him as well. Eveline's fantasies of domesticity and of romance are pernicious alternatives, beneath which, on the naturalistic level, lies a narrative of entrapment. But beneath that level as well, Joyce nastily implies, is an abortive narrative of triumphant incestuous desire. Ironically, it is on this narrative level that Eveline would have the most control over her fate—but only if she can cut through the mystifications of desire that bind the men around her. Thus Joyce's most scrupulously naturalistic story is flanked by "ghost narratives" of domesticity, of romantic light opera, and of pornography, all of which reflect intertextually upon the text of "Eveline." Indeed, they reflect upon the girl's experience as well, for her consciousness is to a degree an amalgam of the ideologies of popular literature. Her choices have already been written and, whether or not she is consciously aware of the fact, they provide her with highly structured allegories of the experience she refuses to contemplate.

"After the Race": Modern Musketeers

As Joyce recognized, "After the Race" is one of his least successful stories.[84] It has at times the feeling of being "worked up" from Joyce's brief experience of the racing world when, in the year of its composition, he interviewed a race driver. Here the *style indirect libre*, so effective in the simplicities of "Eveline," at times betrays an awkwardness not easily ascribable to the protagonist: "Ségouin was in good humour because he had unexpectedly received some orders in advance (he was about to start a motor establishment in Paris) and Rivière was in good humour because he was to be appointed manager of the establishment; these two young men (who were cousins) were also in good humour because of the success of the French cars" (D, 43). The story's ironies are both easy and relatively heavy-handed: "Now and again the clumps of people raised the cheer of the gratefully oppressed" (D, 42). Doyle's discomfiture evokes a fairly obvious moral without forcing on the reader the painful bleakness of Eveline's world. In part, of course, this simply reflects the difference in sex and social station of the two protagonists: because he is so much farther from the poorhouse, things simply count less for Jimmy Doyle. Nor does he have Eveline's impoverished, mute dignity. If she is a "helpless animal," he is a helpful one, who assists in his own embarrassment. Popular literature as such plays no direct role in the story of Jimmy Doyle's naive aspiration after fast society, but popular fictions in a more general sense do permeate the tale, to such an extent that at times "After the Race" itself begins to resemble a popular story of fashionable disillusionment. Indeed, Bernard Huppé has suggested that in it Joyce may have been attempting a parody of a turn-of-the-century gentleman's magazine story.[85] But the main thrust of the narrative is Jimmy Doyle's attempt to learn a language that is unfamiliar to him but that he aspires after: the language of sophisticated European society.

Throughout the story, Jimmy has difficulties in understanding and in speaking. In the car, "often Jimmy had to strain forward to catch the quick phrase," which is especially disconcerting for him because "he had nearly always to make a deft guess at the meaning and shout back a suitable answer in the teeth of a high wind." Presented to a French competitor, he manages only a "confused murmur of compliment" (D, 44). He is astonished at the dexterity with which Ségouin directs the conversation, but then, once his tongue has been loosened by drink, manages to spoil the general conversation by embroiling Routh, the Britisher, in a political argument about Ireland. Just as, that evening, "the city wore the mask of a capital" (D, 46), Jimmy wears the mask of a sophisticate, but he is less successful in his impersonation. After the encounter with Farley, the fat American, "a torrent of talk followed," although "no one knew very well what the talk was about" (D, 47)— most especially the protagonist, since the story is narrated almost entirely from his perspective. His final effort at the language, before lapsing into drunken speechlessness during the card game, is his long speech. He can remember not a word of it, and it is greeted by no doubt derisive applause. Notably, not a single word of Jimmy's is narrated directly: in his own story he is the mute.

He is not entirely speechless, though, since "After the Race" makes full use of what Bakhtin terms "character zones," specific locations in which the authorial language is interpenetrated by the natural speech of

the character. "Such a character zone is the field of action for a character's voice, encroaching in one way or another upon the author's voice"
(*DI*, 316). Jimmy's voice surfaces on numerous occasions, and it is primarily this effect that is responsible for the lingering feeling of parody in
the story. The narrator in the second paragraph describes the party in
the car as "almost hilarious" (*D*, 42), suggesting a degree of narrative
coolness, an analytical measuring of the precise degree of their exhilara-
tion. But then, following an extended description of Jimmy, during
which the reader is brought closer to the attitudes of the boy and his
father, the narrator continues breezily, "the car ran on merrily with its
cargo of hilarious youth" (*D*, 44). Such a sentence would not be out of
place in a gentleman's magazine; it is the sort of description Jimmy
himself might write. And of course the *style indirect libre* affords numerous instances of the characteristic cadences and vocabulary of the
protagonist's ordinary language: "In what style they had come careering
along the country roads!" (*D*, 45), "What merriment! . . . This was seeing life, at least! . . . What jovial fellows! What good company they
were!" (*D*, 47–48), or, finally, "They were devils of fellows but he
wished they would stop: it was getting late" (*D*, 48). Enthusiastic, colloquial, naive, and flatly banal, his language does not admit of subtleties
or gradations.

But Jimmy has another language as well, one he believes is appropriate to the sophisticated life after which he aspires: "Jimmy, whose imagination was kindling, conceived the lively youth of the Frenchman twined
elegantly upon the firm framework of the Englishman's manner. A
graceful image of his, he thought, and a just one" (*D*, 46). Jimmy's self-
congratulation is merited, although not in the way he means: his image's
grotesquerie, its implications of parasitism and suppressed homoeroti-
cism, nicely suggest the hidden dangers of this party at which he is a
sacrificial victim. But Jimmy is certainly unaware of the implications of
his own formulation. Even if he should learn to speak the sounds of a
new language, it is implied, he would not understand them. A similarly
baroque image occurs in the dialogized zone of interpenetration of authorial and protagonist's language: "The journey laid a magical finger
on the genuine pulse of life and gallantly the machinery of human nerves
strove to answer the bounding courses of the swift blue animal" (*D*, 45).
The enthusiastic tone and lyrical elevation belong to Jimmy, while the
precise rhetorical formulation is the author's. The multiple ironies of the

sentence certainly are borne of a perspective wider than the boy's: the real "pulse of life" is felt in an automobile ride, while the human turns mechanical in response to the animizing of a machine.

Parallel to these three voices—the authorial voice and Jimmy's two voices, all of which mingle throughout the story—there is a counterpoint of ideologies, or rather ideological fragments. Some of these, like the "advanced" Nationalism of Mr. Doyle, are little more than a conventional bundle of ideas and phrases, a mask or suit to be donned or doffed as the situation warrants. Thus Mr. Doyle modifies his views as soon as he is within sight of economic success, while Jimmy suddenly finds himself echoing his father's "buried zeal" (D, 46) during the party without any notion of why he does so, or, presumably, whether he actually believes in the ideas he is espousing. The enthusiastic tenor of Jimmy's association with Ségouin in the first place is an aspect of popular nationalism, since the crowd looks to "their friends, the French" (D, 42) for a political deliverance that failed to materialize in the 1690s and 1790s, and would again fail in the twentieth century. Quite unrelated, indeed opposed, to popular Irish Nationalism, is the haut-bourgeois veneration of wealth—or rather the insignia of wealth, for it is Ségouin's "unmistakeable air of wealth" (D, 45) that impresses Jimmy and his father. Mingled with this attitude is the conventional and ambivalent Anglo-Irish vision of Continentals, particularly the French, as inherently sophisticated, sexually and sensually experienced creatures. This myth has an irresistible attraction for Jimmy, but underlying his admiration for Ségouin and his companions is a puritan distrust that surfaces only in hints and disguised forms: the slight sinister note of "Ségouin had managed to give the impression that it was by a favour of friendship the mite of Irish money was to be included" (D, 44–45), or Jimmy's outburst of Nationalism, which is really an assertion of simple, unregenerate Irish values in the face of all the foreigners.

But the major fragment of ideology operative in the story is one lifted directly from popular literature. Jimmy's vision of youthful fellowship, the good life available to young sophisticates who are above the common herd, is rooted in Dumas's *Three Musketeers*. This popular vision is not restricted to the original formulation, of course; it continued, little changed, in Kipling's *Soldiers Three* (1888) and in numerous less famous avatars. But a number of details in Joyce's story suggest that Jimmy sees himself as living out Dumas's novel. After all, he is of the new nobility, son of a "merchant prince," and joins three men "whose spirits seemed to be at present well above the level of successful Gallicism" (D, 42). The huge Hungarian, whose main concern is his stomach, is clearly Porthos; the silent Rivière is Athos, the brooding; while Ségouin, the aristocratic arranger of the evening, is the courtly leader of the original three Musketeers, Aramis. Jimmy wishes to play d'Artagnan, the young man from the provinces who so impresses the famous trio that he is taken into their company, to join them in their fights, their gambling, their endless drinking, and their gargantuan banquets. Each of the images of fellowship in "After the Race" is thematized in Dumas's book. The public parade is first, because in Dumas's ideology accomplishment is equated with strutting performance: "Loose, deep drinkers, truculent, the King's Musketeers . . . swaggered about in the cabarets, the public walks, and at the public sports, shouting, twisting their moustaches, clanking their swords."[86] Gambling is their ordinary occupation when not actively fighting: "As to the rest, the life of our four young friends was joyous enough. Athos played, and that generally without luck. Nevertheless, he never borrowed a sou from his companions. . . . Porthos played by fits. On the days when he won he was insolent and ostentatious; if he lost, he disappeared for several days, after which he reappeared with a pale face and thinner person, but with money in his purse.[87]

Drinking and eating are not only thematized, but undergo a Rabelaisian expansion, so that even within this literature of excess the Musketeers's consumption verges on the superhuman. The three Musketeers and d'Artagnan gather regularly to dine at one or another of their houses, but their greatest gustatory feats occur during d'Artagnan's journey to England; each of the Musketeers in turn is left fighting a rearguard action, until only d'Artagnan is left to continue. On his return he discovers all of them wounded but displaying gigantic appetites, at the expense of the inns where they are lodged: "Porthos was in bed, and was playing a game of lansquenet with Mousqueton [his valet], to keep his hand in. A spit loaded with partridges was turning before the fire, and at each side of a large chimney-piece, over two chafing-dishes, were boiling two stew-pans, from which exhaled a double odor of *gibelotte* and *matelotte*, very grateful to the olfactory nerves. In addition to this, d'Artagnan perceived that the top of a wardrobe and the marble top of a commode were covered with empty bottles"[88] But the comic Porthos is no match for Athos, who generally plays a tragic romantic figure. Athos, attacked by a crowd directed by the inn's host, has barricaded himself in the cellar with his valet. Not only do they refuse to give their host access to the provisions, but they daily demand that more food and wine be brought them. Meanwhile, as d'Artagnan discovers, they have decimated the provisions:

> Beyond the fortifications through which Athos had made a breach in order to get out, and which were composed of faggots, planks, and empty casks, heaped up according to all the rules of the strategic art, they found, swimming in puddles of oil and wine, the bones and fragments of all the hams they had eaten. A heap of broken bottles filled the whole left-hand corner of the cellar, and a tun, the cock of which was left running, was yielding, by this means, the last drop of its blood. . . . Of sixty large sausages that had been suspended from the joists, scarcely any remained. . . . The host armed himself with a spit, and rushed into the chamber occupied by the two friends.
> "Some wine!" said Athos, on perceiving the host.
> "Some wine!" cried the stupefied host, "some wine! why, you have drunk more than a hundred pistoles' worth!—I am a ruined man, lost! destroyed!"
> "Bah!" said Athos; "why, we were always dry."[89]

The comic conflation of food and warfare, which dates back to Rabelais, is transferred directly to Joyce's modern Musketeers, where it is entirely appropriate. The Musketeers of "After the Race" are mounted upon the blue racing car instead of their extravagantly turned-out horses, and conquest in battle has been replaced by financial success, but the ideology remains essentially unchanged. Other elements of Dumas's novel resonate with Joyce's story as well. There is even a faint, mocking parallel between the original Musketeers' support of the British Duke of Buckingham, their King's enemy but the Queen's lover, and the entertainment of Routh, the Britisher, by Ségouin and his friends. But while chivalry is the excuse for the Musketeers' treason, Jimmmy's friends are motivated by strictly economic considerations.

Jimmy Doyle's problem in attempting to invoke the chivalric/militaristic ideology is twofold. First, he does not actually live in a world where the fellowship of youth, excitement, food, and drink—or even old college ties—can compete against financial considerations. The first sign of the decay of the evening is when the "Musketeers" are joined by the wealthy outsiders Routh, who is the traditional enemy of both Jimmy and Ségouin, and Farley, who rightfully should have no place at all in the European community, but who winds up hosting the drinking and gaming by virtue of his possession of a yacht. The second problem is that he has miscast himself. D'Artagnan may have been a young, enthusiastic, and naive provincial when he arrived in Paris with nothing but a noble name, but his bravery, swordsmanship, and native cunning soon make him the leader of the three companions he had so envied. Jimmy has arrived with his "sword"—his father's money—but is clearly out of his league both personally and financially.

He is more of an outsider than he realizes, even on a direct linguistic level, as he is doubtless the only member of the original group whose French is very limited. The best he can do is to join in singing "Cadet Roussel" as they swagger arm-in-arm through the streets. The Royalist marching song is perfectly appropriate for the Three Musketeers, although it arose nearly a century after their period; Dumas's creations are, after all, a nineteenth-century version of the seventeenth-century "gallant," and riddled with anachronisms. The song's mockery of Cadet Roussel, the "good guy" who has three of everything, surely suggests the contempt with which his companions view Jimmy.[90] Even in the original terms of the gallant ethic he fails: the Musketeers, whether gorged or dead drunk, were never incapable, while Jimmy "frequently mistook his cards and the other men had to calculate his I.O.U.'s for him" (D, 48). It is difficult to believe that this man has survived Cambridge, much less that he has accumulated a small reputation for dissipation. In terms of all the traditional popular signifiers of virility, Jimmy is unmanned; like the boy of "Araby," he does not have enough of the real, personal, capital to trade in this bazaar.

In the cold light of morning, the entire episode will appear tawdry, not gallant, courtly, or romantic; it has been an evening of excess, but not the sort of excess of which his family can be "covertly proud" (D, 43). Even in a straight thematic reading the Hungarian's final announcement, "Daybreak, gentlemen!" is ironic; Jimmy has just been realizing that he will "regret in the morning," and welcoming the "dark stupor that would cover up his folly" before that. There is no longer even time for a spell of stupor; the Hungarian is standing "in a shaft of grey light" (D, 48). But an additional irony is provided by our recognition that the story's ending is itself an extremely common device of popular literature. Among the books in Joyce's Trieste library, Filson Young's *The Sands of Pleasure* (1905) contains a similar scene: the protagonist, Richard Grey, has just spent the first night in his completed lighthouse while a storm rages outside and he agonizes internally over the Parisian prostitute with whom he had allowed himself to become involved. At the end of this dark night of the soul, the lightkeeper enters Grey's chamber: " 'Sunrise, sir,' said the lightkeeper, with his watch in his hand."[91] There follows a description of the clearing of the storm, from which the protagonist and his lighthouse have both emerged unscathed.

A second example, this one from a book Joyce reviewed in 1903 (*CW*, 130–31), occurs in A. E. W. Mason's *The Courtship of Morrice Buckler*.[92] Here the situation is far closer to that of Joyce's story, in that a group of men is playing cards and one of them is a heavy loser. The young protagonist has found his cousin near the end of an all-night card game in the course of which he has pledged all his property; after the protagonist's arrival his cousin's luck changes, and a sinister young man across the table from him, who will later emerge as the book's villain, begins to lose consistently. Mason is unstinting in his gothic detail:

> But with a sudden cry I stopped. For as I turned, I glanced across the table to his opponent, and I saw his face change all in a moment to a strangely grey and livid colour. And to make the sight yet more ghastly, he sat bolt upright in his chair, without a gesture. . . .
> "Great God!" I cried. "He is dying."
> "It is the morning," he said in a quiet voice, which had yet a very thrilling resonance, and it flashed across me with a singular uneasiness that this was the first time that he had spoken during all those hours.
> I turned towards the window, which was behind my cousin's chair. Through a chink of the curtains a pale beam of twilight streamed full onto the youth's face. So long as I had stood by Elmscott's side, my back had intercepted it; but as I moved away I had uncovered the window, and it was the grey light streaming from it which had given to him a complexion of so deathly an ashen colour. . . . The heavy gildings, the yellow glare of the candles, the gaudy hangings about the walls, seen in that pitiless light, appeared inexpressibly pretentious and vulgar; and the gentlemen with their leaden cheeks, their disordered perukes, and the soiled

finery of their laces and ruffles, no more than the room's fitting complement.[93]

Mason's grey morning light plays the same role as Joyce's daybreak: it unmasks, removes the aura of romance and good-fellowship from what is revealed as a pitiable or disgusting scene. Indeed, Mason's over-wrought, overwritten scene does a good deal more, with its suggestions of vampirism and the Rake's Progress. The major point here, however, is not that Joyce might have adapted the scene from Mason's book; it is that the dramatic arrival of daybreak after a night-long indulgence was a popular convention, and Joyce was well aware of that fact. Just as in *Ulysses* Joyce adapts the narrative voice of the domestic Victorian romance for his portrayal of Gerty MacDowell, here in *Dubliners* he was already experimenting with the formal—rather than substantial—allusion to popular literature. Like the boys of "An Encounter" and "Araby," Jimmy is another victim of the ideologies of popular literature, and it is only fitting that his minor epiphany of limited self-awareness should itself be drawn from those annals.

"Two Gallants": The Ideology of Gallantry

"Two Gallants" is perhaps Joyce's most aptly titled story, especially considering the widening rings of implication about the word. The French root of "gallant" denoted making merry and making a show; as an adjective, the word suggested "dashing, spirited, bold," but also "gay in appearance" or "fitted for the pleasures of society"—a divided connotation pointing in one sense to internal qualities and in the other to outer appearance or mere social seeming. Still further back, the word is thought to be adapted from an Old High German root meaning "to wander or go on pilgrimage," a sense retained in the modern verb form meaning to "go about idly" or "to escort or convey," both meanings that figure in Joyce's story. But the major implications of "gallant" are either amorous or military, reflecting the ideal identity of these two roles, which writers like Castiglione posited. Yet in contemporary usage, within each domain the word can have ironic connotations. "Gallant" is both a term of praise and a mere conventional epithet for a military officer; it may signify either "pertaining to romance, amatory" or "markedly polite and attentive to the female sex," indeed "flirtatious" or "dandy-like." A man's military followers are his "gallants," while a woman's suitors—serious or not—are hers. Generally, the word's original preponderantly positive connotations of noble birth and high personal qualities have been obscured with the rise of bourgeois culture, and the ironic or dismissive connotations of showiness, pretention, and fakery have come to the fore; but this is certainly not invariably the case, and nineteenth-century bourgeois culture retained a sentimental attachment to the unironic notion of gallantry, especially in its application to modes of address and forms of casual politeness. Usage, of course, reflects prevailing ideologies, and the bourgeois attitude toward the notion of gallantry is highly ambivalent.

Joyce's own attitude, far from ambivalent, was almost programmatic. The idea for "Two Gallants," he wrote Stanislaus, came from Guglielmo Ferrero, whom he had probably read during his phase of self-confessed socialism.[94] In a BBC broadcast, Stanislaus claimed that Joyce had told him the story was specifically suggested by Ferrero's discussion in *L'Europa giovane* (1897) of the relationship between the Musketeer Porthos and the wife of a tradesman.[95] Indeed, in a letter defending his story from the outrage of Grant Richards's printer, Joyce asks, "Is it the small gold coin . . . or the code of honour which the two gallants live by which shocks him? I see nothing which should shock him in either of these things. His idea of gallantry has grown up in him (probably) during the reading of the novels of the elder Dumas and during the performance of romantic plays which presented to him cavaliers and ladies in full dress. . . . I would strongly recommend to him the chapters wherein Ferrero examines the moral code of the soldier and (incidentally) of the gallant. But it would be useless, for I am sure that in his heart of hearts he is a militarist."[96] Unfortunately, there is no chapter of *L'Europa giovane* wherein Ferrero examines the moral code of the soldier and of the gallant, nor does Ferrero in any major work cite the incident from Dumas. Susan L. Humphries has convincingly argued that at the time of composition of "Two Gallants" Joyce had probably not yet read *L'Europa giovane*, but may well have read *Il Militarismo* (1898) and several articles by Ferrero in the European press.[97] It seems likely that this is the book to which Joyce is directing Richards's printer, and that the association between the moral code of the soldier and that of the gallant is Joyce's, rather than Ferrero's. Similarly, it is possible that Stanislaus mistook an illustration that struck his brother—Porthos's scene in *The Three Musketeers*—for one Joyce was citing from Ferrero. Equally likely, Joyce may have wanted to add Ferrero's authority to an idea substantially his own, as Stephen Dedalus does with Aquinas, for example.

Ferrero argued in *Militarism* that massive warfare, which had been necessary in the early history of mankind, had become an impossibility in the modern age, because it would be too destructive; as Humphries points out, Joyce echoed this sentiment in a 1906 letter to Stanislaus.[98] Ferrero has a loose and hopeful strain of Herbert Spencer's spiritual evolutionism running through his work, and believes strongly not only in national character, but in the spiritual development of the character of peoples through time. He begins by asserting that warfare has its origins in a thirst for emotion and sensation, which may be satisfied variously by base means, such as drunkenness; through more elevated means, such as love; through "the great collective passions, such as patriotism and religious ardor"; or through the still higher intellectual and aesthetic passions. The most "abstract" means of satisfying the passion for intenser life, though, is "to aim at superiority over men and things" through conquest. In a small proportion of men, this desire approaches an obsession for tyranny and for ostentation.[99]

In Ferrero's analysis, figures such as Caesar and Napoleon emerge not as national heroes, but as monomaniacal thugs, whose passions are in opposition to the general civilizing tendency of mankind. In opposing physical or military courage and moral courage Ferrero draws a distinction that must have appealed greatly to Joyce: "the habit of arms and the perils of war can be combined with great moral cowardice," so that "an army which can subdue entire unarmed populations may easily be subdued in its turn by a handful of more resolute ruffians."[100] Indeed, Ferrero analyzes Napoleon-worship as an element in popular romantic ideology, although not in those terms:

> May I be allowed to say it frankly: the Napoleon-worship is to the higher classes what brigand-worship is to the lower. . . . Thus the cultured classes in Europe read with avidity the history of Napoleon for the same reasons that the working classes devour brigand tales. One of the greatest intellectual pleasures, felt by men in all conditions, lies in the perusal of books of adventure, describing life free from all the laws which render ours so secure and monotonous. . . . The power of the great is much reduced nowadays, for

the conflict of interests tends to establish an equilibrium of power, and few possess sufficient energy to be able to support a life of adventure. Men, therefore, seek a personal satisfaction in the perusal of the histories of brigands and heroes.[101]

Not only works of popular literature from various social strata, but major social institutions are also complicit in purveying the ethic of militarism. In France, Ferrero argues, both the public schools and the Catholic church contribute to the "subtle and varying work of propaganda" that maintains a state of nationalist miliary agitation among the populace.[102] So powerful and insidious is the militarist ethic that the nation is inclined to ignore either danger or actual harm that results from it: "France may adore her soldier, and be happy to be ill-treated by him, like certain hysterical women who are fond of brutal lovers who beat them."[103]

This is about as close as Ferrero's book comes to associating militarism with any specific code of personal conduct toward women, but implicit in his argument is the notion that the soldier's mentality is essentially one of brutal conquest; women would fall either into the category of a person to be conquered or a thing to be displayed as conspicuous ornament. Dominic Manganiello argues from the presumption that Joyce did read *L'Europa giovane* early enough for it to have had an influence on "Two Gallants." In this book, according to Manganiello, Ferrero associates German cultural "brutality" with militarism and also with a mechanical approach to sexual liaison:

> Ferrero associates . . . militaristic activity, which he considered typical of the Germanic races, with the art of gallantry. In Berlin, for example, a casual encounter between a youth and a girl in the street will, after engaging in a brief conversation, easily result in an affair the next day; the girl will be a mistress without even knowing her lover's name. Such "brutal" encounters resemble the equally anonymous ones on the battlefield. The male lacks all patience regarding the art of "gallantry" because not love but biological need impels him to seek women. Ferrero's point is that sexual relations are adjusted to the brutality of the male rather than to the gallantry that the female might desire.[104]

There seem to be several problems with Manganiello's argument here, most notably the central question of the relationship between militarism and gallantry. Manganiello first claims that militarism and gallantry are associated by Ferrero, then contrasts the two impulses—perhaps because he fails to realize that for Joyce "gallantry" is itself a degraded and degrading concept. Further, there is the problem that Ferrero's discussion here refers to the Germanic races, which are quite different in his view from the Celtic races. It seems clear from the letter to Richards that Joyce, at least, felt that gallantry and militarism were different forms of the same impulse, whatever the cultural context. In illustrating Ferrero's ideas by invoking the world of Dumas, Joyce takes the historian's argument a step further, linking ostensibly courtly gallantry with the primitive rage to conquest and acquisition.

This is the metaphor that presides over "Two Gallants." The title is not, after all, ironic; the story of Corley and Lenehan simply lays bare the heart of gallantry without romantic mystifications. Here, and throughout *Dubliners*, Joyce's text destabilizes the ideological structures implicit in popular literature precisely through its intertextual participation in them. Paraphrasing Pierre Machéry, Terry Eagleton presents a possible model for the process: the "literary text throws ideology into disarray *by* fixing it. By endowing the ideological with a precise, specific configuration, it gives a certain 'foregrounding,' but thereby also begins to foreground its limits and lacunae, that of which it cannot at any cost speak, those significations that necessarily evade (but also covertly *invade*) it. By 'formalizing' ideology, the text begins to highlight its absences, expose its essential incompleteness, articulate the ghostly penumbra of absent signs that lurk within its pronouncements."[105] Manganiello's conservative formulation of Joyce's "intent" fails to do justice to the radical critique posed by the text.

And after all, the economic objectifications of the gallant ethic are only minimally mystified even in its original formulations. A glance at Dumas's *Three Musketeers* shows that, half-apologetically, Dumas was well aware of the mercenary aspects of his heroes' amatory dealings:

> We have observed that young cavaliers received presents from their King, without shame; let us add that, in these times of lax morality, they had no more delicacy with respect to their mistresses, and that the latter almost always left them valuable and durable remembrances, as if they endeavoured to conquer the fragility of their sentiments with the solidity of their gifts.
>
> Men then made their way in the world by the means of women

> without blushing. Such as were only beautiful gave only their
> beauty. . . . Such as were rich gave in addition a part of their
> money; and a vast number of heroes of that gallant period may be
> cited who would neither have won their spurs in the first place, nor
> their battles afterward, without the purse, more or less furnished,
> which their mistresses fastened to the saddlebow. . . . D'Artagnan,
> following the strange custom of the times, considered himself in
> Paris as on a campaign, and that neither more nor less than if he
> had been in Flanders—Spain yonder, women here. In each there
> was an enemy to contend with, and contributions to be levied.[106]

Here Dumas makes his apologies to nineteenth-century bourgeois morality on three fronts: first, he explains that the times were morally lax,
so that his heroes were only acting according to prevailing custom; second, he argues that the dubious means were justified by the glorious
ends; and third, he invokes the standard Renaissance equation between
battle and courtly love.

Yet for the sake of comedy and a bit of satire against the petite bourgeoisie Dumas is more than willing to strip away the mystifications from
these economic transactions. In the passages that so struck Joyce, in
which Porthos is equipping himself, the self-regarding motives of both
parties are made clear. Porthos has come to a romantic understanding
with the wife of M. Coquenard, a wealthy but tight-fisted merchant. But
her cupidity is constantly at war with her desire to sponsor a Musketeer
of her own, so that Porthos must play upon her jealousy to convince her
to equip him properly for the upcoming campaign. D'Artagnan observes
Porthos attending mass in a fashionable church attended by Mme. Coquenard; Porthos keeps sending meaningful glances toward a noble lady
—who is in fact a complete stranger to him—and arranges for his hand
to touch hers at the basin of holy water. When Mme. Coquenard, whom
he has been assiduously ignoring, confronts and reproaches him for this
"unfaithfulness," he makes it clear that she was not sufficiently generous
to him in the past, when he wrote to her for money:

> "Madame Coquenard, I gave you the preference. I had but to
> write to the Duchess de ——, but I won't repeat her name, for I am
> incapable of compromising a woman; but this I know, that I had
> but to write to her, and she would have sent me fifteen hundred."
> The procureuse let fall a tear.
> "Monsieur Porthos," she said, "I can assure you, you have se-

verely punished me; and if in the time to come you should find
yourself in a similar situation, you have but to apply to me."

"Fie, madame, fie!" said Porthos, as if disgusted. "Let us not
talk about money, if you please, it is humiliating."

"Then you no longer love me?" said the procureuse, slowly and
sadly.[107]

Porthos is successful, although not without further implied threats of
turning to his purported noble admirer; Mme. Coquenard at first outfits
him rather cheaply, and only under pressure does she relent and furnish
him with gear of the best quality. In return, Porthos visits her house in
the guise of a cousin and dines with her and the unsuspecting husband.
The entire interchange is sordid, and played for comedy; for example,
Porthos has to suffer through a very cheap meal *en famille* as a part of
his campaign and must further act so as to make it clear to Mme. Coquenard's friends that he is her beau, all the while concealing this from
M. Coquenard. He feels degraded by having to resort to a bourgeois
patroness while the other Musketeers have noble ladies to support them,
yet in some way realizes that despite his genetic connection to nobility
he is too clownish a figure to aspire so high.

This scenario of course represents a nineteenth-century vision of seventeenth-century gallantry, or rather half of that vision; the other half,
as in the discussion of d'Artagnan's solicitations, presents the "conquests" of the gallant in a perspective of mingled excuse and reluctant
admiration. But whether viewed as farce or as high romance, the gallant
ethic is one of straightforward appropriation. The patroness must be
married or otherwise inaccessible, so as to preclude the possibility of
public acknowledgment and therefore responsibility for the relationship,
and yet she must be known to the gallant's circle of intimates, so that she
may function as conquest and ornament. The element of performance is
central to gallantry; even the gallant's feats of arms must be as public as
possible and should be accomplished with style and grace rather than
dispatch. As noted in the discussion of "After the Race," the gallant is
essentially a conspicuous consumer whose public consumption of food,
drink, apparel, and ornaments validates his masculinity. He lives to parade. Dumas repeatedly insists that the true gallant is of noble birth, a
quality that licenses his behavior and invests him with a mystifying
virtu; thus he in turn can play the part of conquest or ornament for his
patroness. When the patroness is of lower social rank, as in the case of

Porthos and his "lady," the gallant needs no personal qualities to justify him. His cachet is sufficient.

Gallantry, in short, is a variety of objectification and depersonalization that is especially pernicious because it mimics and parodies romantic devotion, while replacing the interpersonal element with impersonal economic exchange. As the final scene of "Two Gallants" makes clear, it is a secular form of simony. In gallantry the relationship is oriented outward, toward spectators, rather than inward, toward the participants. The gallant, such as Porthos, plays his patroness like an instrument—like the harpist in Kildare Street—hoping for tangible reward. The patroness, unaware that like the harp she has been stripped bare to public examination, collaborates in her own exploitation. Corley, the first of Joyce's gallants, plays upon his slavey like Porthos upon Mme. Coquenard by invoking superior social status: "I told her I was in Pim's. . . . She thinks I'm a bit of class, you know" (D, 51). His ostensible status—and of course his gallantry—is underlined by his military bearing: "the son of an inspector of police," he "had inherited his father's frame and gait. He walked with his hands by his sides, holding himself erect and swaying his head from side to side." Like a soldier, he "always stared straight before him as if he were on parade" (D, 51); his "bulk, his easy pace and the solid sound of his boots had something of the conquerer in them" (D, 55). Apart from direct economic exploitation—the gold coin withheld until the story's last line—Corley's interest in the girl seems less a matter of sexual gratification than of display. He and Lenehan arrange an elaborate pantomime so that his "disciple" can witness the pair walking together, Corley can secretly acknowledge Lenehan's witnessing, and Lenehan can secretly acknowledge the acknowledgment.

But prior to becoming an item of visual display, the slavey's major role is in *linguistic display*: she is the center of Corley's narrative. Corley's speech is as essentially repetitive as pornographic narrative, consisting in endless reiterations of his conquests and seductions. His speech itself comes as close to pure display as possible for a dialogic medium: "He spoke without listening to the speech of his companions. His conversation was mainly about himself: what he had said to such a person and what such a person had said to him and what he had said to settle the matter" (D, 51–52). He appears to speak of himself in the third person during these performances, like Mr. Duffy, so as to give his narrative the further monologic authority of encompassing even its speaker as character: "When he reported these dialogues he aspirated the first letter of his name after the manner of the Florentines" (D, 52). Corley's narrative performances are dependent upon the simplest of popular literary patterns—the woman driven to prostitution by her seduction and betrayal, for example. Lenehan appreciates this, and his clichéd catechistic responses of "Base betrayer!" and "You're what I call a gay Lothario" are entirely appropriate (D, 53, 52). Corley's ultimate triumph is to perform a gallant seduction *as he is narrating it*, before Lenehan's eyes. The slavey is important to him in the degree to which she will play her part in the banal narrative that already encompasses and defines her.

The result of this sort of reduction of human relationships to repetitive patterns, this triumph of monologism, is a dehumanization of all the parties, which is literally reflected in the text. All the characters of "Two Gallants" appear to be mechanical dolls or marionettes, ambulatory masks with nothing behind their appearances. Corley is a sort of robot: "His head was large, globular and oily; it sweated in all weathers; and his large round hat, set upon it sideways, looked like a bulb which had grown out of another." So inflexible is this automaton that "when he wished to gaze after someone in the street, it was necessary for him to move his body from the hips" (D, 51). In times of necessity, though, Lenehan sees that the mechanism does display some cranial mobility: "He watched Corley's head which turned at every moment toward the young woman's face like a big ball revolving on a pivot" (D, 56). The slavey at first appears to have some life in her, with the "rude health" that "glowed in her face, on her fat red cheeks and in her unabashed blue eyes," but on second glance her features, dehumanized by analysis, appear rigidly fixed, with "broad nostrils, a straggling mouth which lay open in a contented leer, and two projecting front teeth" (D, 55, 56). Indeed, she herself is in the process of transformation into a military doll like Corley, with her sailor's hat and wide leather belt whose great silver buckle "seemed to depress the centre of her body" (D, 55). Corley's trophy pays him the dubious compliment of taking on her conquerer's appearance.

Lenehan, the second gallant, parodies the first, with the perverse variation that he pays court to Corley as he mimics him. He too aspires after a roguish military appearance, with his yachting cap worn rakishly, breeches, and the "light waterproof which he had slung over one shoulder in toreador fashion" (*D*, 50). He has a "brave manner" of confronting a "party" or a "company" in a bar, and is a "sporting" vagrant (*D*, 50). But as he literally dances attendance on Corley, skipping off and onto the sidewalk, it is clear that he wears a thin disguise as superficial as the "amused listening face" he has assumed (*D*, 49). He is an aging, exhausted actor, "and his face, when the waves of expression had passed over it, had a ravaged look" (*D*, 50). Part of his exhaustion is due to the fact that he has tired of the endless repetition of his part; he has probably elaborately courted Corleys for the sake of a coin many more times than Corley has courted his slaveys. He plays upon Corley as mechanically as the harpist plays upon the strings, as idly as own his fingers play upon the railings of the Duke's Lawn (*D*, 56). Still, he plays out the gallant scene, now assuming the role of the seductee; he hurries to his appointment with Corley just as had the slavey and, as she does, arrives too early, tormented by the suspicion that he has been betrayed.

He has not: Corley displays the only loyalty of which he is capable, loyalty to his chosen audience, although he first must flirtatiously withhold from Lenehan the story's climax. Corley needs Lenehan as much as Lenehan needs Corley, since the gallantry that defines him requires an audience. Meanwhile, Joyce has encouraged the reader's collaboration in the degrading ritual. Clive Hart observes that as Lenehan "whiles away the time during Corley's absence, we begin to share his prurient interest in Corley's affair, until at the end of the story we are as anxious as Lenehan to know the truth: 'Did it come off? . . . Did you try her?' "[108] Our anxiety is rewarded by a "trick ending" reminiscent of Maupassant or even O. Henry, through which the sexual conquest we had anticipated is revealed as an economic transaction. The gold coin in Corley's palm explicates the story's title—it is Joyce's commentary on the nature of gallantry—and it is also the token required to start this collection of mechanical dolls dancing. But beyond these significances, and the well-known Biblical allusion it also suggests, the coin is the price of admission we have paid, our investment as readers in what we took for a tawdry melodrama of seduction and revelation. Like "The Boarding House," "Eveline," "A Painful Case," and even "The Dead," "Two Gallants" is indeed a drama of seduction and revelation, but like all of the other stories its denouement averts or withholds the expected climax. As readers, we are seduced by the banal genre; but Joyce, the base betrayer, ends the story by holding before our eyes something very different from what we had hoped and feared to see.

"The Boarding House": The Rhetoric of Oxymoron

In light of the discussion of "Two Gallants" it should be apparent that all four stories of adolescence deal with aspects of courtship and, specifically, of gallantry. In "Eveline" the romantic suitor makes his ambiguous offer, and it is strongly suggested that in exchange for a night at the opera and a few songs Frank has demanded Eveline's virtue. "After the Race" highlights the dubious good-fellowship of a group of modern Musketeers and perversely places Jimmy Doyle in the roles of suitor and of seductee. Sex is not an explicit issue, although sexual currents run throughout the story; instead, the issue is money. "Two Gallants" plays on precisely this substitution; within the dialogic context of the texts of gallantry the story can be seen as a demystification of the gallant ethic, in which sexuality becomes a means to a monetary end. In "The Boarding House" the same substitution is explored from the opposite perspective. Here Bob Doran the "seducer" is equally the seduced; the gallant exploiter is himself exploited.[109]

This reversal is made possible by Doran's situation. He is caught at the point of intersection of two conflicting ideologies, that of gallantry and that of bourgeois Christianity, and he discovers that while playing the role of hunter in the first he has become the hunted in the second. Doran's situation at the borders of opposing ideologies can stand as metonym for the social milieu of the story as a whole, for "The Boarding House" is an exploration of the socially ambiguous, the transitional, the borderline, and the marginal. Mrs. Mooney's establishment is neither a home nor a hotel; and its "floating population" is made up of tourists and *artistes*, while its "resident population" consists of clerks, "young men" who are no longer clearly young (*D*, 62). Mrs. Mooney's firm matriarchal hand suggests that she is the mother of an extended family, while her daughter's titillating presence suggests that she is "*The Madam*" of a brothel (*D*, 62). The same sort of sinister conflict is apparent in the two institutions that symbolically stand behind her, the butcher's shop and the church. Doran's plight is that he is forced to interpret a situation of radical ambiguity, to read a text composed of conflicting messages, and he does not know how to do so. How should he react to Polly's advances? As romantic lover? As brother? As husband? As client in a brothel? In loco parentis? Because he does not know the genre of drama in which he is engaged, he has no clue as to his role.

Bob Doran is the apposite victim of Mrs. Mooney's stage-managing because his own identity is so ambiguous. For one thing, it never becomes clear whether he or Polly is the protagonist of the story. The placement of "The Boarding House" among the "stories of adolescence" suggests that this is Polly's story, but if so she is a curiously vacant center. Even Eveline is more in command of her own narrative. Doran sidles onto center stage more or less by default, an "adolescent" only in the metaphorical Italian sense of a "young adult." Mrs. Mooney first thinks of him as "one of the young men" (D, 63) but, once he responds to Polly, she observes that he "was thirty-four or thirty-five years of age, so that youth could not be pleaded as his excuse" (D, 64). Immediately afterward, she muses that he "was a serious young man" (D, 65). Evidently, he is young when considered as suitor, mature when assigned the role of seducer. Likewise, Doran's ethical stance is transitional or undecided; he "had boasted of his free-thinking and denied the existence of God" in his youth, but now "attended to his religious duties and for nine-tenths of the year lived a regular life." His conversion is hardly complete, though: he gives no evidence whatsoever of religious belief and indeed still buys a copy of the freethinking *Reynolds's Newspaper* every week (D, 66). He holds a minor job in a major industry, clerking in a "great Catholic wine-merchant's office" (D, 65)—a position with its own internal contradictions.

His most striking feature, though, is that he is virtually without point of view; he is at the mercy of any social pressures that can be brought to bear on him, so that after his discussion with the priest "he was almost thankful at being afforded a loophole of reparation." This is despite his realization that the priest has "drawn out every ridiculous detail of the affair" and unfairly "magnified his sin" (D, 65). He even understands that he is being grossly victimized: he "had a notion that he was being had" (D, 66). Yet his realizations seem to afford him no room to maneuver; as soon as he has established a possible point of view upon the affair, he is overwhelmed by the opinions he ascribes to Mrs. Mooney, the priest, and people in general. Their views periodically blind him to his own: "every two or three minutes a mist gathered on his glasses so that he had to take them off and polish them with his pocket-handkerchief" (D, 65). Bob Doran tragically exemplifies the realization that understanding will not free us from ideology; he can no more leave the boarding house than he can stand outside of culture or speak in a way his language disallows.

The horrific quality of Doran's particular dilemma is rooted in the ambiguity of the actions he tries to evaluate. Is Polly sincere when she weeps in his arms, confessing that she has confessed to her mother and threatening suicide? Sincerity is nearly meaningless in such a tableau; no doubt she threatens suicide because that is what the heroine of a popular melodrama would do, but then that is no doubt how she sees herself. After all, she later weeps alone, although those tears are succeeded quickly by a vacant calm. To speak of Polly as hypocritical, as many critics do, is to miss the point of her perfectly poised unconsciousness. As Warren Beck notes, hypocrisy in "The Boarding House" is difficult to identify clearly, in Polly or even in Mrs. Mooney: "in her way she is genuine, and she has her own formidable integrity."[110] Polly's song thematizes the impossibility of identifying sincerity here:

> I'm a . . . naughty girl.
> You needn't sham:
> You know I am

she sings, encapsulating multiple ambiguities of role. She is impersonating a "good girl" impersonating a harlot (or whatever the tantalizing ellipses signify) impersonating a "naughty girl," and she assures her auditors that they need not pretend to take her for anything better. Yet because this is a putatively ironic, "teasing" performance, she is of course asking her listeners to take her for nothing of the kind. The roles are all "sham," but what lies beneath?[111]

Doran's tenuous hold on identity and the milieu of contradiction in which he must operate are most subtly presented by means of language. First, Mrs. Mooney and her daughter share a tendency toward social slippage in their speech; their solid middle-class discourse frequently strays into lower-class locutions. Doran notes Polly's occasional *If I had've known*s and naively asks, "But what would grammar matter if he really loved her?" (*D*, 66). He might better ask where else does grammar matter more. Joyce's narration makes it clear that the confusion of social linguistic levels is absolutely characteristic of the Mooneys' consciousness. Mrs. Mooney, whose language dialogically permeates the narrative, strays among three levels of discourse: the colloquial, public level, rich with cliché ("Mr Mooney began to go to the devil. He drank, plundered the till, ran headlong into debt. It was no use making him take the pledge") (*D*, 61); the formal, prescriptive level, slightly archaic and heavily influenced by institutions ("For her only one reparation could make up for the loss of her daughter's honour: marriage") (D, 65); and the vulgar level ("She knew he had a good screw for one thing and she suspected he had a bit of the stuff put by") (D, 65). Both the confusion among social levels of speech and the conflict among levels of discourse can be seen as conflicting "primary" speech genres, in Bakhtin's terms—genres which "have high, strictly official, respectful forms as well as familiar ones" (SG, 79). What is so disconcerting for Doran in the slippage among speech levels is that "each speech genre in each area of speech communication has its own typical conception of the addressee, and this defines it as a genre" (SG, 95). When Mrs. Mooney speaks to him directly, her speech will betray the same shifting variety of genres. The effect of this is that Doran feels his own identity to be in question.

The sort of schizophrenic confusion of inner speech Mrs. Mooney betrays is more than characterizing detail in the story and has ramifications beyond the realm of any dialogical interchange between characters. It also represents a contradiction that permeates the narrative, in what might be termed the rhetoric of oxymoron. Thematically, "The Boarding House" juxtaposes ironically a widening series of oppositions: butchery/religion, hospitality/predation, family/brothel, mediation/violence, seducer/seduced, innocence/depravity. And the narrative itself, in some of the infrequent instances when its language cannot be ascribed to the "zone" of any of the characters, ascends to a pitch of pure linguistic oppositions: Polly's habit of glancing upwards when addressed "made her look like a little *perverse madonna*" (D, 62, my emphasis); her attitude during the Doran affair is characterized as a "*wise innocence*" (D, 64, my emphasis). The point of these emphatic oxymora is to destroy any essentialist reading by highlighting the radical ambivalence at the heart of the characters. Polly is both corrupt and pure; she both understands and does not understand her own role in Doran's entrapment. Similarly, Mrs. Mooney acts both from moral outrage and from economic calculation, and Doran is both eager participant and unwilling victim. There is no "essence" to these people. All are afloat in a sea of conflicting ideological currents and opposed rhetorical systems, all of which are socially affirmed. But where Doran has been caught in a dangerous eddy, Mrs. Mooney and Polly are comfortably afloat in the milieu of contradiction, the former through her schizophrenic ability to maintain opposed value systems simultaneously, the latter through habitual unconsciousness.

Cheryl Herr, in another context, has related Joyce's frequent use of binary oppositions to the ideological contradictions of his culture: "Certainly, the persistent binarism of Joyce's fictions grows out of historical patterns of power and subservience more than out of Joyce's conscious efforts either to build his texts from oppositions or to capture those intellectual operations that might be said to express the intrinsic nature of the human consciousness."[112] In one sense, "The Boarding House" presents a character enmeshed in the "historical patterns of power and subservience"; interpretations of the story that foreground the perverted religious symbolism can lead easily to this inference. But it is important to note that Doran's predicament is verbal and thus, in Bakhtin's formulation, escapes pure binarism.[113] The important question is what sort of narrative will reflect his relationship to Polly—or, more directly, how he will answer Mrs. Mooney's questions. And once our focus is upon the language of the story, Doran's situation is transformed all the way down to the ontological level of inquiry.

Certainly the rhetoric of the story, its tropological dimension, undermines any sense of transparency in language or even the delusion of interpretation; to this extent Paul de Man's "disjunction in language between the hermeneutic and the poetic" is effectively deconstructive here.[114] In "The Boarding House" as in "The Sisters" and in many of the following stories, linguistic play and slippage, coupled with conspicuous tropes, set up countermovements against the overdetermined ideological oppositions invoked within the stories. Of course, this is of little help to Bob Doran. Doran is trapped in the dialogic interplay of conflicting rhetorics, rhetorics that themselves dialogically permeate the narrative. Unsure of the voice of his own consciousness, he is easy prey when Mrs. Mooney and the priest adopt the monological voice of proper Dublin society. The insistent play of oxymoron may be of more help to the attentive reader, to whom it offers some escape—not, *pace* de Man, an escape from ideology, but perhaps a few steps beyond the boarding house of representation.[115]

· 3 ·

OLDER DUBLINERS:

REPETITION AND RHETORIC

Stories of Maturity

In most of the preceding stories, sexuality has played a leading role. Nascent and idealized in "Araby," perverse in "An Encounter," shackled to economics in "Two Gallants" and "The Boarding House," it has still maintained a kind of innocent integrity and force as primum mobile. But in the stories of "maturity" sexuality itself appears mediated, especially by power relationships. In "A Little Cloud" Chandler's sexuality is challenged by Gallaher's grossly "masculine" personality and by his reduction of Chandler's marriage to blind bondage, "put[ting] your head in the sack" (D, 81). Farrington's only sexual venture in "Counterparts" is frustrated, while his masculine role is systematically destroyed by his conquerors and oppressors. Maria in "Clay" and Mr. Duffy in "A Painful Case" are male and female variants of the celibate; if Chandler and Farrington have their sexual roles denied by their circumstances, Maria and Mr. Duffy have themselves attempted to uproot the sexual motive from their lives. Yet in all these cases, the repressed returns: Chandler and Farrington vent their sexual rage upon their children, while Maria and Mr. Duffy discover that their moribund sexuality has unexpectedly arisen to mock them.

Superficially, the backgrounding of sexuality in these stories might be seen as the effect of character and circumstance. Chandler is a childlike, "feminine" personality, Farrington an exaggeratedly "masculine" personality forced into a subordinate position and thus castrated; Maria is a secular nun whom romance has passed by, and Duffy an obsessive personality who forcefully denies his own erotic dimension. But from another perspective, these are ordinary characters in a world in which sexuality itself has become secondary, mediated by the language of economic and power relationships. Ignatius Gallaher puts the premise most forcefully when he insists, "I mean to marry money" (D, 81). Courtship and gallantry make faint, ghostly appearances in the stories, in the inebriated "gentleman" on the bus who probably takes Maria's cake, the woman in the bar Farrington admires, and the entire mock-courtship of Duffy and Mrs. Sinico. But these remnants only reinforce the notion that in mature life the dominant ideologies structure wholly different concerns.

The general movement of *Dubliners* is toward the hegemony of public rhetoric. While language is foregrounded throughout the volume, during the stories of "maturity" dialogue gradually supplants narration, until in the stories of "public life," especially "Ivy Day" and "Grace," little but dialogue remains. On the mimetic level, this may simply suggest that as Dubliners age life becomes increasingly a matter of conversations; but from a dialogical perspective the inference is unavoidable that the more "natural" categories of thought, perception, and action are yielding to the mediated category of public speech. Put another way, internality is giving way to externality. Increasingly, Joyce's Dubliners *are* what they *say*. The four stories of maturity represent a midpoint in this progression, featuring as they do two conscious, more or less intellectual protagonists—Chandler and Duffy—and two relatively unconscious ones—Farrington and Maria. Chandler and Duffy share a special relationship toward language, since they are both would-be writers, but clearly this aspiration does little to save them; for different reasons, the languages with which they hope to create identities are drowned out in the general buzz of speech surrounding them. And since both are failed writers, their self-creation must take place within the sphere of their interpersonal interactions, especially through dialogue.

Popular literature per se plays a decreasing role in the stories of *Dubliners* as the book progresses. Specific allusions are far fewer in the later stories, nor do the narratives themselves allude so directly to popular literature. What literary allusions do occur, as in Chandler's or Duffy's stories, point to examples of "high" culture—Byron, Nietzsche,

Hauptmann—and function more as characterizing detail than as truly dialogical narrative impulses. The allusions, and their accompanying discourses, are "objectified." Further, as the impressionable youths and adolescents of *Dubliners* age, most of them tend to abandon reading of any sort, with the exception of the newspaper. Newspapers do indeed play a significant role in the stories of maturity. Ignatius Gallaher is a walking example of yellow journalism, while the newspaper account of Mrs. Sinico's death brings Duffy close to a realization of the sort of story he has been living. But newspapers are a special case among the popular literary genres. In the lives of these older protagonists popular fictions abound, but they are no longer so directly linked to popular literature. The later stories tend instead to function through the dialogical clash of ideological contexts belonging to public discourse, contexts that have already assimilated a multitude of specific structures from the popular literary genres. Here Bakhtin's concept of *speech genres* is the most useful one:

> We speak only in definite speech genres, that is, all our utterances have definite and relatively stable typical *forms of construction of the whole*. Our repertoire of oral (and written) speech genres is rich. We use them confidently and skillfully *in practice*, and it is quite possible for us not even to suspect their existence *in theory*. . . . Even in the most free, the most unconstrained conversation, we cast our speech in definite generic forms, sometimes rigid and trite ones, sometimes more flexible, plastic, and creative ones (everyday communication also has creative genres at its disposal). . . . The forms of language and the typical forms of utterances, that is, speech genres, enter our experience and our consciousness together, and in close connection with one another. (*SG*, 78)

Although some of the discussion of "The Boarding House" revolved around speech genres, it is in the stories of maturity and of public life that Joyce highlights their action.

"A Little Cloud": Exclusion and Assimilation

Little Chandler's story, more than that of any other character, works upon a framework of massive oppositions. Of all the Dubliners he and his opposite number, Gallaher, are perhaps the closest to stock characters; the two seem to exist only in order to complement one another.

Indeed, the growing tension between the two suggests that each is growing annoyed at the extent to which his identity depends upon the dialogical opposition of the other. Their conversation is a symphony of dialogic
encounters: Gallaher attempts to preempt Chandler's claim to "culture"
by his frequent use of French tags (and even an occasional Irish one)
within his enveloping man-of-the-world discourse, while Chandler is finally driven to adopt Gallaher's language wholesale in an aggressive
conversational gesture: "You'll put your head in the sack, repeated Little
Chandler stoutly, like everyone else if you can find the girl" (D, 81).

Gallaher's goal is monologic performance, and Chandler at first appears to play to this by restricting his contributions to leading questions
and direct responses to Gallaher's queries. But soon, under the influence of drink, he begins his attempt to preempt Gallaher's role. While
throughout their conversation Gallaher has been forcing drinks on a
reluctant Chandler, Chandler's first aggressive gesture is uncharacteristically ordering a final drink, which Gallaher is reluctant to accept. So
successful is Chandler in destroying Gallaher's claim to monologism that
the latter's final long speech must adopt the rhetoric of the Underground
Man's "word with a sideward glance": "Why, man alive, said Ignatius
Gallaher, vehemently, do you know what it is? I've only to say the word
and to-morrow I can have the woman and the cash. You don't believe it?
Well, I know it. There are hundreds—what am I saying?—thousands of
rich Germans and Jews, rotten with money, that'd be only too glad. . . .
You wait a while, my boy. See if I don't play my cards properly. When I
go about a thing I mean business, I tell you. You just wait." (D, 81).
Ironically, Gallaher's declaration of independence is his weakest utterance. Like the Underground Man's speeches, it shows "extraordinary
dependence upon [the other's discourse] and at the same time extreme
hostility toward it and nonacceptance of its judgments" (PDP, 230).

The confrontation between Chandler and Gallaher is a battle between
two different sorts of banality. As Hugh Kenner observes regarding
Chandler's meditation on his projected literary career (D, 73–74),
"every phrase that passes through Chandler's mind, from 'temperament
on the point of maturity' to 'the Celtic note,' is reviewers' jargon; quotation is as close to reality as he gets."[1] Chandler's personal ideology is
degenerate romantic, with a strong infusion of the cult of sensibility. He
feels he is sensitive, which is to say artistic, because he is often sad:
"Melancholy was the dominant note of his temperament, he thought"

(*D*, 73). Central to his thoughts is the romantic figure of radical *transformation*. Most directly, this is visible in his hope of being himself transformed into a genuine artist through a sort of possession from without, as when "a poetic moment had touched him" (*D*, 73). But this is also a characteristic movement of his mind: he enjoys the idea that Gallaher "whom he had known under a shabby and necessitous guise had become a brilliant figure on the London Press" (*D*, 71). Even the city through which he walks undergoes startling transformations. At one moment the old men and children in a park are transfigured by the sun's "shower of kindly golden dust," at the next, playing children in a street appear as "minute vermin-like life" (*D*, 71). The act of evaluation for Chandler is a matter of exaltation or abasement; Paris must be the most beautiful city, or the most immoral, or both. The polarity of the judgment matters less than the extremity.

Extreme evaluations are useful to Chandler because he defines himself primarily through *exclusions*. He senses himself as separate from the world around him and is alert to the possibility of contamination. Like Duffy, he fancies himself an observer; he first appears staring out his office window at the urban scene, and when he must traverse Dublin he "picked his way deftly through" it (*D*, 71). Nor is this simply squeamishness, because he is equally reluctant to become involved with the high-class patrons of Corless's: "He had always passed without turning his head to look" (*D*, 72). He has a terrified fascination with the life of the city, high or low, with its intimations of immorality, to the point that he sometimes wanders "the darkest and narrowest streets," thrilling with fear at "the wandering silent figures" (*D*, 72). But as soon as he is confronted with "immorality" in a wider, European context, he is quick to exclude the entirety of "old jog-along Dublin where nothing is known of such things" (*D*, 78). The logic is identical: *I* have nothing to do with *it*; *we* have nothing to do with *them*.

Against Chandler's mythology of exclusion, Gallaher sets a mythology of inclusion. Where Chandler is "abstinent" (*D*, 80), Gallaher is self-indulgent; where Chandler is "shy" (*D*, 71), Gallaher is expansive. Like Whitman, he means to include multitudes. He asserts direct familiarity with circles of which his knowledge must be extremely indirect, such as "religious houses on the continent" and "high society" (*D*, 78). Yet he is all the quicker to insist on his Irish origins: "I'm deuced glad, I can tell you, to get back to the old country. . . . I feel a ton better since I landed in dear dirty Dublin." Even while expanding on his exciting new life, he is the first to toast "old times and old acquaintance" (D, 75). Gallaher wishes to be seen as both purely Irish and irrevocably cosmopolitan. He claims both the superior freedom of the single man and the increased status and potential he expects once he marries money.

If Chandler aims at the sort of distinction accrued from censorship of rejected qualities, Gallaher aims at an all-inclusive grandiosity. Naturally he feeds Chandler the popular myths that sustain the weekly press—the gaiety of Paris, the corruption of the continent, the sexual excesses of the upper classes, the erotic expertise of Europeans and Jews. No doubt he too believes these myths; allowing for the difference in form, there is little difference between his conversation and the yellow press he represents. But Gallaher's tactic is to insert himself into the very categories of scandal that he appears to decry. He is a cornucopia of cigars and whiskey, is leaving soon for a gambling party, and hints heavily at the immoral women waiting for him to harvest them. Indeed, his intention is to marry a wealthy German or Jew. The basic imagery he invokes is *ingestion*: "When they heard I was from Ireland they were ready to eat me, man," (D, 77) he asserts, and when criticizing Chandler's marriage he "imitated with his mouth the act of tasting" and comments, "Must get a bit stale" (D, 82). Gallaher eats the world, and thus both dominates and becomes it.

Chandler eats nothing, but he does swallow Gallaher's line. He knows the journalistic litany almost as well as his friend and is ready to feed Gallaher the proper cues. "Tell me, he said, is it true that Paris is so . . . immoral as they say?" (D, 77). "And is it really so beautiful as they say?" (D, 76). Gallaher earns a living codifying and permuting what "they say," but Chandler at heart is equally dedicated to the realm of *on dit*. "Those dark Oriental eyes, he thought, how full they are of passion, of voluptuous longing! . . . Why had he married the eyes in the photograph?" (D, 83). For all the vulgarity and banality of his friend's existence, which Chandler dimly recognizes, he still aspires to "live bravely, like Gallaher" (D, 83). He admires even Gallaher's crashing cliché about his "considering cap" (D, 73). And from his own socio-linguistic situation, Gallaher obviously aspires after the aesthetic and scholarly elevation with which he vaguely associates Chandler, who is better born and better educated. His gentlemanly journalistic locutions such as "a pleasure deferred" (D, 79) and "tasted the joys of connubial bliss" (D, 78), like his pretentious gallicism "*parole d'honneur*" (D, 80), testify to the man of letters he hopes his audience will detect behind his facade of vulgar language. Indeed, the crowning irony of their violent dialogic encounter is that both combatants, with their diametrically opposed phenomenologies of inclusion and exclusion, aspire after identical linguistic identities. Yet neither can recognize this, because the identity of each is founded on the tactic of self-definition through opposition to the other. Chandler's fury and anguish at the story's end betray his shame and jealousy, but they are equally markers of the double bind of identity formation in which he is trapped.

The conclusion of "A Little Cloud," following the asterisk break, is a sort of coda. Chandler carries his unwonted aggressiveness home with him, where he meets a wife and home that mirror his own fastidiousness: "mean," "prim," without "passion" or "rapture" (D, 82–83). But even as he accuses Annie of a lack of passion, in his own desperate circumstance Chandler feels only a "dull resentment." He tries to place Byron's juvenile rhetoric into dialogical relationship with the movement of his own thoughts so that he can become Byron, a myth that in Chandler's mind is probably little more complex than the myth of Gallaher. The attempt fails, interrupted by his child's cries. Again, he repeats his gestures of exclusion: he is reading a poem about a dead beloved woman —how romantically passionate he would feel about his wife if only she were dead!—and then imagines his son dying in his arms. When his wife bursts in, he hardly recognizes her: "a young woman ran in, panting" (D, 84).

Chandler simply cannot handle the guilt. He has tried to become Gallaher and, at least in his thoughts, has managed to betray his wife. He has tried to defeat Gallaher by brandishing his fatherhood, and now his infant son is rejecting him. Chandler shouts out his credo, "Stop!" He wants everything outside himself to go away, to stop challenging and defiling the "melancholy of his soul." When Annie takes the baby from him he sees only "hatred" in her eyes, and "his heart closed together" (D, 85). The hatred is his own, of course. Walled up in a selfhood that refuses to acknowledge its own debt to others, the only genuine emotion of which mild Chandler is capable is aggression. His heart perpetually closes, since love is as foreign to him as poetry. But however he misreads Annie's attitude, he is aware that he has finally arrived at a moment of passionate intensity, and it is at this point that the aspiring master of language makes his final statement: "—It's nothing. . . . He . . . he began to cry. . . . I couldn't . . . I didn't do anything. . . . What?"

"Counterparts": Obsessive Repetition

If the treatment of Chandler and Gallaher in "A Little Cloud" is a complex deployment of oppositions that collapse into identity, "Counterparts"—as the title suggests—is an equally complex exercise in repetitions.[2] Farrington is a copyist, whose official function is repetition, but who also "fails" through repetition and is "punished" through repetition: when he inadvertently writes "Bernard Bernard" in place of "Bernard Bodley" he must recopy the entire page (D, 90). He copes with failure by repeatedly slipping out for a drink and is detected in this transgression because of repetition: "I know that game, [the chief clerk] said. Five times in one day is a little bit . . ." (D, 89). This is despite the fact that Farrington has disguised his trip to the bar by leaving one hat on the rack and secreting another (actually a cap) in his pocket. He is twice threatened with dismissal. Farrington's oppressor, Mr. Alleyne, has a ghostly double, Mr. Crosbie, who doubles the threat to Farrington. Farrington's problems are multiplied by his failure to produce copies of two letters from the Delacour file. The witness to Mr. Alleyne's discomfiture, Miss Delacour of the "Jewish appearance" (D, 90), is doubled by the woman in the bar with the "large dark brown eyes" (D, 95). Of course the British Weathers who twice defeats Farrington at arm-wrestling doubles Alleyne with his Protestant, northern accent, while at the story's end Farrington browbeats his son precisely as Alleyne browbeats him. Meanwhile, his wife has gone to the chapel for solace just as Farrington had earlier visited his "curate" (D, 89).

But Joyce focuses the narrative specifically on verbal repetition with all its ramifications. Virtually nothing in the story is spoken only once. Speeches are repeated for emphasis, for the benefit of a new audience, for purposes of parody or sarcasm, or simply for the lack of anything new to say. Alleyne habitually repeats himself out of annoyance or rage: "You—know—nothing. Of course you know nothing"; "You impertinent ruffian! You impertinent ruffian!" (D, 91). In revenge, Farrington repeats his riposte, "I don't think that that's a fair question to put to me," numerous times in the course of the evening. His co-worker Higgins adds to the merriment by imitating Farrington and himself repeating the line (D, 94). The original cause of Alleyne's antipathy for his employee, as might be expected, was an incident when "Mr Alleyne had overheard him mimicking his North of Ireland accent to amuse Higgins and Miss Parker" (D, 92). Alleyne's revenge is to mimic Farrington's own words, in a parodic intonation:

> —But Mr Shelley said, sir—
> —*Mr Shelley said, sir.* . . . Kindly attend to what I say and not to what *Mr Shelley says, sir.* (D, 87)

> —I was waiting to see . . .
> —Very good, you needn't wait to see. (D, 88)

> —I know nothing about any other two letters, he said stupidly.
> —*You—know—nothing.* (D, 91)

Naturally enough, when Farrington takes his revenge on his son, he works up his own fury just as Alleyne had. "He began to mimic his son's flat accent, saying half to himself: *At the chapel. At the chapel, if you please!*" In his drunken anger he repeats both his accusation about letting the fire die out and his threat (D, 97–98).

Parodic repetition is clearly a fundamental category of dialogic interchange. Bakhtin discusses it under the general heading of parody: "Analogous to parodistic discourse is ironic, or any other double-voiced, use of someone else's words; in those instances too another's discourse is used for conveying aspirations that are hostile to it. In the ordinary speech of our everyday life such a use of another's words is extremely widespread, especially in dialogue, where one speaker very often literally repeats the statement of the other speaker, investing it with new value and accenting it in his own way—with expressions of doubt, indignation, irony, mockery, ridicule, and the like." Bakhtin then cites Spitzer's observation that reproducing a part of someone else's speech in one's own utterance *inevitably* adds an intonation of mockery (PDP, 194). Certainly in the interchanges of "Counterparts," where the mocking appropriation of the antagonist's words is generally carried out by men in the real or imagined presence of female onlookers, the element of aggression is highlighted. Conversation becomes less the exchange of information than a ritual of domination and submission. Thus Alleyne constantly adds to his statements such phatic interrogatives as "Do you hear me now?" and "Do you mind me now?" (D, 87) whose only purpose is to force a rhetorical, weak acknowledgment ("Yes, sir") from his subordinate. In "A Little Cloud" the reunion of friends is revealed as a disguised dialogical battleground, but in "Counterparts" the conversations are nearly devoid of any signification other than mutual hostility. As Foucault comments, "Discourse is not simply that which expresses struggles or systems of domination, but that for which, and by which, one struggles; it is the power which one is trying to seize."[3]

Repetition and difference are fundamental to the process of signification, but there is evidence that mimicry of language, gesture, and expression can occur outside the semiotic systems of human communication. Oliver Sacks notes that some variants of the neurological disorder known as Tourette's syndrome are manifested by an apparently spontaneous and uncontrollable compulsive mimicry of the speech, appearance, and actions of anyone within the sufferer's field of observation.[4] Sacks vividly conveys the nightmarish phenomenology of the disease, which presents itself as an assault on the very possibility of interpersonal communication. Joyce's story through its incessant repetitions has something of the same effect: the characters are caught in a compulsive, destructive round of mocking imitations and collapsing ironies. If we rapidly repeat a single word long enough, it loses its sense for us and takes on an aspect of *Verfremdung*, or sudden strangeness; once we notice the incessant repetitions of "Counterparts," the narrative begins to empty itself of meaning.

Indeed, the narration itself echoes the characters' compulsions. As Scholes notes, Joyce repeatedly strips Farrington of his identity.[5] He appears as "the man" throughout the office scene, briefly surfaces as "Farrington" in the bar, and at the story's end has become even further depersonalized, as "a man." The form of reference is numbing: "*The man* got up from his desk. Mr Alleyne began a tirade of abuse, saying that two letters were missing. *The man* answered that . . . he had made a faithful copy. The tirade continued: it was so bitter and violent that *the man* could hardly restrain his fist from descending upon the head of *the man*ikin before him" (*D*, 91, my emphasis). Similarly, the narrator tends to repeat epithets, such as Farrington's "heavy dirty eyes" (*D*, 94). Gradually we realize that the narrator has been implicated in the repetition-compulsion from the start, for the literal recording of repetitious dialogue is itself an unusual, "mannered" narrative gesture; classical narrative tacitly elides even ordinary conversational repetition. The effect is similar to that in "The Dead" when the party breaks up and each "Good-night" is scrupulously recorded, a process that spans half a page of text (D, 212). Such "empty" passages are highlighted, while the conventionally "meaningful" passages of the story are correspondingly deemphasized.

There is no defense against the assault of repetition except more repetition. The end of "Counterparts," horrifying enough as compulsively repeated brutality, is even more so when we realize that the boy, unable to escape his father's violence, is driven to offer repeatedly a repetition: "Don't beat me, pa! And I'll . . . I'll say a *Hail Mary* for you. . . . I'll say a *Hail Mary* for you, pa, if you don't beat me. . . . I'll say a *Hail Mary* . . ." (D, 98). There is no escape from the circle, for it is not only the circle of paralyzed Dublin life but the closure of fictional convention as well. "The engendering of replications" that Barthes equates to "the chain of signs" and "the regularity of the code"[6] has in fact a double face: when "naturalized" within ordinary discourse it is as soothing as a repeated lullaby to a child and forms our defense against the ruptures to which meaning is liable. But when, as in "Counterparts," repetition is subject to the estrangement consequent upon foregrounding, we are made painfully aware of the contingency of meaning in all speech.

"Clay": Repetition and Dialogism

The narration of "Clay" is somewhat paradoxical. It gives the overall impression of objective, naturalistic narration as in "Ivy Day" rather than narration through or centered upon a consciousness as in "The Sisters" or "Araby," and yet on examination virtually the whole of the narrative depends upon Maria's consciousness: it is a single extended character zone which asymptotically approaches *style indirect libre*. There is only one instance of directly reported individual dialogue in the entire story, the bakery clerk's "Two-and-four, please" (D, 102); the other instances are statements Maria remembers, like the Matron's "Maria, you are a veritable peace-maker!" (D, 99) or joint ejaculations like the children's "Thanks, Maria" (D, 103). Some dialogue, like Mrs. Donnelly's "*Do, please, Maria!*" (D, 105) is embedded in the narration, and the bulk of the conversation is indirectly reported without any mark of quotation, signalling far less of a rupture of the continuity of experience. The quality of Maria's experience is built into the very syntax of the narration, which is overwhelmingly coordinative. The sentences conjoin paratactically, with "and," "but," and "then," and their structure tends to be either simple or compound, and often repetitive. The effect is of a succession of unexamined experiences, none of which is subordinated to any other. By implication, Maria appears to be either simpleminded, childlike, or slightly drunk.

If "Counterparts" is a paradigm of linguistic aggression, "Clay" is the model of affirmative appeasement. Maria attempts to offer no resistance to the speech of others: "She talked a little through her nose, always soothingly: *Yes, my dear*, and *No, my dear*" (D, 99). Just as she allows Joe to succeed in forcing a drink upon her, she attempts to make no resistance to circumstance and eventually succeeds in affirming whatever is the case. She is not unaware of the uncomfortable situations in which she and others find themselves or of aggressive or embarassing statements directed toward her, but her characteristic movement is an immediate swerve toward something that can be affirmed—a better face to put upon the situation, another construction to be put upon a statement. The form in which her inner narrative expresses this tendency is characteristically "(negative) A *but* (positive) B":

> Often he had wanted her to go and live with them; but . . . she had become accustomed to the life of the laundry.

> She used to have such a bad opinion of Protestants but now she thought they were very nice people.

> There was one thing she didn't like and that was the tracts on the walls; but the matron was such a nice person to deal with, so genteel. (D, 100)

Occasionally the formulation must include an additional step, "(positive) A *but* (negative) B *but* (positive) C":

> She was sure they would [have a nice evening] but she could not help thinking what a pity it was Alphy and Joe were not speaking. . . . but such was life. (D, 102)

> Maria thought she would put in a good word for Alphy. But Joe cried that God might strike him stone dead if he ever spoke a word to his brother again. . . . But Joe said he would not lose his temper on account of the night . . . and soon everything was merry again. (D, 104)

As the last example indicates, these structures are not simply the characteristic form of Maria's inner narrative, but are underwritten by Joyce's dialogical collaboration with his character. Very seldom in the story does a locution occur that could not be attributed to Maria's consciousness. One such, however, is the description of Maria herself, "when she laughed her grey-green eyes sparkled with disappointed shyness and the tip of her nose nearly met the tip of her chin" (D, 101), the last clause of which is repeated twice in the course of the story (D, 101, 105). Another would be the observation that when she had omitted a verse of "I Dreamt that I Dwelt," "no one tried to show her her mistake" (D, 106). But aside from these, it is difficult to find an observation or sequence of events that does not appear to be filtered through Maria's presiding consciousness and thus structured by her mental strategies.

In an insightful article, Margot Norris argues that the narration "is split into testimonial and exposé, prattle and pantomime, empty language and expressive silence, and the reader is split into gullible narratee and cynical critic, flattered ear and penetrating gaze, consumer of realism and dupe of naturalism. This fractured discourse of 'Clay' is produced by the interplay between the two senses of *significance* working through the text: *significance* as an expression of psychological importance or ontological prestige, and *significance* as the linguistic or semiological meaning produced by nodes of signification."[7] Norris characterizes the narrative voice as for the most part describing Maria "as she would like to catch somebody speaking about her to somebody else," and further notes that the occasional instances of elevated language suggest that the narrator impersonates a social superior of Maria's who is nonetheless determined to present the old woman in the best possible light.[8] From a Bakhtinian perspective, the same effect is explicable as a result of Maria's and Joyce's dialogical "collaboration" in the narrative voice; Maria's voice is usually dominant, while Joyce supplies the sporadic literary elevation of tone and the more elegant periphrases for which the "Dublin by Lamplight" laundry's cognomen supplies the model.

Counterbalancing the Maria-centered discourse, Norris argues, is the semiological dimension of the text, which in turn she associates with the narrative gaps, lacunae, swerves, and silences that signal to the alert reader significances Maria would rather deny. The reader is forced to construct a text that does not mirror the numerous instances of narrative "repression," and that would answer questions such as "What is the *real* attitude of Maria's acquaintances toward her?" or even "What does Maria look like?" This is certainly an effect of reading "Clay," but it is less clear that it belongs exclusively to the sphere of "linguistic or semiological meaning." Indeed, such questions follow from our sensitivity to culturally coded *intonations* of Joyce's narrative, which in turn we must set against our reconstruction of Maria's historical milieu in order to detect those very gaps and silences. This operation is historical and dialogical rather than linguistic.

One aspect of the text that does belong to this purely rhetorical realm, however, is repetition. Like the characters in "Counterparts," Maria also employs repetition, but in a wholly different way: she repeats, privately and publicly, phrases that reassure her, such as the Matron's peacemaker comment, Ginger Mooney's comment regarding "what she wouldn't do to the dummy who had charge of the irons if it wasn't for Maria," or Joe's "Mamma is mamma but Maria is my proper mother" (*D*, 100). On taking out her purse, she reads again, probably for the thousandth time, the words "A Present from Belfast" (*D*, 100), which reassure her that she is loved and valued even though the present dates from a time when Joe and his brother were still friends. The consolation of these ritual verbal repetitions mirrors the pattern of her life, which is sustained by its regularity. She is joining Joe's family for Hallow Eve, as she no doubt does for most holiday celebrations. As she dresses herself she recalls dressing for Mass on Sunday mornings when she was a girl, and after she has arrived at Joe's the girls in their Sunday dresses suggest a continuity with this tradition. Of course the story is haunted by the past, increasingly toward the end, when Maria is asked to sing again "one of the old songs" (*D*, 105), and Joe observes that "there was no time like the long ago" (*D*, 106).

But this is obviously a story in which repetition, tradition, and habit ultimately fail to reassure. Joe introduces a sinister note in several ways. One is his "repeating for her a smart answer which he had made to the manager" (*D*, 104), which suddenly suggests the aggressive mode of dialogical repetition Joyce so thoroughly explored in the previous story. For an instant, Joe appears to drag Farrington and his sterile, vicious world into the pleasant family gathering. More obtrusively, Joe's quarrel with his brother underlines the realization that Maria most wants to avoid, that the past is irrevocably gone and no amount of ritual repetition will reestablish it. Significantly, the game in which Maria chooses the clay is a traditional one; but the folk tradition, with its possibility of brutal honesty, does not fit this bourgeois household in which everyone conspires to conceal from Maria what she has chosen in her life. Maria's turn is "no play" (D, 105), and so she must soothe herself and the family by taking another turn. But the climactic example of revelatory repetition is Maria's involuntary repetition of the first verse of "I Dreamt that I Dwelt," which critics generally read as a repression of the more sexual second verse with its ironic implications for the celibate Maria. The implication here is that repetition is set in opposition to progression, that Maria has frozen in a preadolescent stage of sexual development. Indeed, in this light all of Maria's habits are revealed as a compulsive attempt to stave off the realization of change—change encompassing both the general lapse from utopian childhood and the introduction of sexual relations among others that set her apart from them as an object of general pity. For Freud, the repetition compulsion is linked to the drive toward death, and death is of course the end toward which Maria's choice of the clay points.

The dialogical intervention of *The Bohemian Girl* here elaborates and expands upon some of these ironies. As the previous discussion of "Eveline" stipulates, the aria Maria performs is sung by the noble Arline to Thaddeus, the outsider; Arline recalls her luxurious youth only in dreams and perhaps senses that she must choose between her gypsy life with Thaddeus and that past. The irony produced by her unconsciousness of the situation gives the song much of its poignancy. Its sheer sentimental appeal is probably rooted in the fact, noted by Norris,[9] that the song articulates Freud's "family romance," the infantile fantasy that the child's mundane parents are imposters, while the real parents are aristocrats. This is precisely Arline's case: Thaddeus, whom she sees as a father, is a substitute for her real, noble father, and so she will be free to marry the false father while acquiring the status of her heritage. But in "Clay" the situation is reversed: it is the outsider Maria who sings the song to Joe, in the bosom of his own family. Maria acted as a surrogate mother to young Joe, as Thaddeus acted as surrogate father to the young Arline. And it is Maria who is now among "gypsies," the cultural outsiders in residence at the *Dublin by Lamplight* laundry. Her dream of marble halls is a dream of an impossible return to the natural place in the family that she never truly possessed. Arline's song represents the point of implicit change in Thaddeus's feelings toward her, from a pseudo-paternal attachment to active sexual involvement. Yet in Maria's rendition, the sexual element is ludicrous, and Maria's repression of it is only appropriate. What she asks is that Joe's feelings toward her remain those of child to mother: she dreams "that you loved me still the same" (*D*, 106).

This is poignant and impossible, but hardly laughable. Unexpectedly, Joe emerges as a very competent reader of the text she presents. He is so moved by her unwitting choice of the clay that "Maria had never seen Joe so nice to her as he was that night, so full of pleasant talk and reminiscences" (*D*, 105). He is even more moved by the song, "mistake" and all, and affirms the past and the old music, "whatever other people might say" (*D*, 106). The present is of little use to Maria; it is validated only by the past, and that is what Joe attempts to give her. The final irony of the story is what makes it, finally, unironic: Joe, drunken hunt for the corkscrew and all, is attempting to "mother" Maria; his maudlin sentimentality, at least in part, is assumed for her benefit in an attempt to affirm the thwarted repetitions upon which her consciousness depends.

Most readings of "Clay," including Norris's deconstructive reading and this one as well, assume at some points that the story is a spurious rendition of some more painful, repressed reality behind the self-deceptions in which Maria indulges. The narrative itself, superficially so committed to mimesis and yet everywhere undermining its own claims to objectivity, forces such readings. And yet, of course, there is no such unmediated reality that some other hypothetical narration might have presented, with all ideological veils torn aside. What "Clay" actually presents to the reader is a cacophony of ghost voices, inaudible in the narrative proper but eager to present their alternative perspectives on the reality of Maria. All the commentary others present on Maria the "veritable peace-maker" or Maria "my proper mother" is so obviously directed toward her, and so suspiciously univocal, that we are compelled to search for the missing statements other characters might make in her absence—and, beyond that, for the genuine, authoritative voice of Joyce, which would reveal Maria in her essence.

In this sense, there is no Joyce; his authorial voice sounds only dialogically in *Dubliners*, never wholly separable from the inner voices of the protagonists. There are other voices in "Clay," most notably Joe's ambiguous voice with his mingled scorn and sympathy for Maria, and the voice of Arline, so ideologically overdetermined and yet so revelatory when Maria assumes it. But what would be the voice of the children who arrange the embarrassing game and who "looked as if they did not like to eat cakes if they were to be accused of stealing" (D, 103), or of the gentlemanly drunkard in the tram, or of the "stylish young lady behind the counter, who was evidently a little annoyed by her" (D, 102)? The miniature mysteries of the narrative all point toward these voices for resolution, and yet they are present only in the weakest form of dialogism, as the "others" toward whom Maria's characteristic affirmative explanations are directed. Maria would like nothing more than to agree with everyone, as she agrees with the man on the tram that "youngsters should enjoy themselves while they were young" (D, 103) or even smiles to acknowledge what she takes to be a joke about wedding cakes by the impatient young lady behind the bakery counter. Yet even Maria cannot pretend that the world always offers a univocal and positive commentary. And so the text of the story, which might be regarded as a stylization of her inner narrative, is packed with explanation, excuse, periphrasis, and even denial, all in implicit response to the chorus of critical voices that surround her, just beyond her hearing.

"A Painful Case": The Rhetoric of Disembodiment

"A Painful Case" is unusual among the Dubliners stories in that the protagonist undeniably comes to a consciousness that his life has changed. The change, of course, is merely one of perspective: in the beginning he is a solitary and comfortable in that self-definition; at the end he "felt that he was alone," "outcast from life's feast" (D, 117). Nor is it surprising that he should react so strongly as to alter permanently his self-perception, for—in the context of the other stories—a truly dramatic event, the death of a friend, has occurred. Joyce was dissatisfied with the story, undoubtedly because it does contain the materials that might produce either tragedy or melodrama. The varying critical interpretations of the story register the attraction of these opposing generic poles. It is as if all the protective, distancing irony that Joyce so assiduously musters must struggle against Mr. Duffy's painful insistence that Mrs. Sinico's death has genuine and powerful resonance in his own life. The shock Duffy experiences and the depth of emotional indulgence into which he sinks suggest that no one is so sentimental as the lapsed ironist.

As with Maria, we grow to know Duffy as much through the narration in which he participates as through his explicit comments, thoughts, and actions. Indeed, Joyce foregrounds Duffy's dialogic participation in several places, suggesting that Duffy may be his own narrator. One such instance is the self-reflexive sentence, "He had an odd autobiographical habit which led him to compose in his mind from time to time a short sentence about himself containing a subject in the third person and a predicate in the past tense" (*D*, 108). Another is the curiously disembodied observation during one of his discussions with Mrs. Sinico, "he heard the strange impersonal voice which he recognized as his own, insisting on the soul's incurable loneliness" (*D*, 111). At least during the first half of the story, Duffy, like Conrad's Kurtz, remains little more than a voice. He is a man made of words, who confuses words with substance and nourishment. Inside his desk is the translation of *Michael Kramer* and the collection of his *sententiae* he has entitled *Bile Beans*, but when the desk lid is lifted one is likely to smell "an overripe apple which might have been left there and forgotten" (*D*, 108). He is in the habit of "read[ing] the evening paper for dessert" (*D*, 112). Words compose him. He eats them, pretends to artistic expression through them, and offers them to Mrs. Sinico in lieu of passion. Although their limbs never entangle, "little by little he entangled his thoughts with hers" (*D*, 110).

The patterns of Duffy's inner narration are those so often reflected in the story's narration: enumeration and inventory, classical balance and antithesis, analysis, neat causal connection, passive-voice construction. One of the sentences he inscribes in his book displays all these: "Love between man and man is impossible because there must not be sexual intercourse and friendship between man and woman is impossible because there must be sexual intercourse" (*D*, 112). In the story's narration, the elements are distributed, so as to avoid the extreme stylization of Duffy's writing. Enumeration is evident in the description of his room: "a black iron bedstead, an iron washstand, four cane chairs, a clothes-rack, a coal-scuttle, a fender and irons and a square table on which lay a double desk" (*D*, 107). Even his personal lacks are described in terms of a satisfying balance: "He had neither companions nor friends, church nor creed" (*D*, 109). Sometimes the urge to rhetorical balance obtains even when the items balanced differ so grossly that the effect is strikingly ironic. The observation, "His father died; the junior partner of the bank retired" (D, 112) recalls the threat that Pope's Belinda may "stain her honour or her new brocade." Analytic sentences are interjected even when the thing analyzed seems trivial or absurd, as when the narrator notes that the books in his library are "arranged from below upwards according to bulk" (D, 107). Similarly, sentences of causal analysis give the appearance of closing off a subject even when on inspection they raise as many questions as they answer: "Mr James Duffy lived in Chapelizod because he wished to live as far as possible from the city of which he was a citizen and because he found all the other suburbs of Dublin mean, modern and pretentious" (D, 107). But perhaps the most notable characteristic of the first paragraph, in which the majority of these sentences occur, is that their subject is curiously absent. "Writing materials were always on the desk. In the desk lay a manuscript translation of Hauptmann's *Michael Kramer*, the stage directions of which were written in purple ink, and a little sheaf of papers held together by a brass pin. In these sheets a sentence was inscribed from time to time and, in an ironical moment, the headline of an advertisement for *Bile Beans* had been pasted on to the first sheet. On lifting the lid of the desk a faint fragrance escaped" (D, 108). We cannot fail to notice that in the description of his most intimate activity Duffy is not present. He haunts the syntax of the sentences like a passive ghost, never appearing even as pronoun. Like a déclassé Deity, he is the absent cause of his own creation.

The theme of disembodiment, which has its syntactical reflection here, soon becomes explicit. Duffy, who "lived at a little distance from his body" (D, 108), has attempted to reduce his life to an intellectual and aesthetic dimension; attracted by Mrs. Sinico's "temperament of great sensibility" (D, 109), he "shared his intellectual life with her" (D, 110). It seems only appropriate that after her death she should return to haunt him as a spirit who is not even wholly disembodied: "As the light failed and his memory began to wander he thought her hand touched his. . . . She seemed to be near him in the darkness" (D, 116, 117). This evocation of the Jamesian ghost story adds much of the story's element of melodrama and is an interpretive crux as well. For we have the choice of seeing Duffy's ghostly encounter as a moment of genuine insight that is somehow underwritten by Joyce or as seeing it as another means of

egotistical self-aggrandizement for him, a ludicrous mock-epiphany for a
character who has inflated his own importance in Mrs. Sinico's life.
Michael West and William Hendricks have argued the latter view most
powerfully, claiming that Duffy is to be seen as a satirical butt, and that
his epiphany is "radically compromised by Duffy's intellectual, emotional, and stylistic limitations. His egotism remains ironically on display, undercutting his capacity to feel genuine grief, his ability to gain
genuine self-knowledge, and our desire to sympathize with him. . . .
With the quiet irony of the final word Joyce challenges us to realize that
Duffy, alone but no longer lonely, has returned gladly to the anesthetic
self-sufficiency that he enjoyed to begin with."[10] In defense of their view
West and Hendricks cite the pretentious "Dowsonesque image" of being
"outcast from life's feast" (D, 117), which Duffy repeats to himself, and
point mockingly to the train that seems to sound Mrs. Sinico's name
"for all the world like the Little Engine That Could."[11]

The case exactly parallels the notorious problem of distance in Portrait and, like our judgment of Stephen Dedalus, rests on our evaluation
of the rhetoric associated with the protagonist's mental processes. At
root, we are searching for the authoritative voice of Joyce, who unfortunately has emulated Duffy in effacing himself from his writing. And
unlike "Clay," in "A Painful Case" there is no host of other voices strain-
ing to be heard. Yet Duffy does not speak in a vacuum, as he imagines.
In a judgment with which Bakhtin would sympathize, J. Mark Heumann
has pointed out that Duffy is not genuinely a writer, because he shies
away from publication and thus from the implicit dialogue of all creative language.[12] But this is to overstate the case somewhat. Duffy engages in a sort of dialogue with Mrs. Sinico, however monologic he
attempts to make that intercourse. In a sense, his entire inner discourse
is what Bakhtin terms a "hidden internal polemic" (PDP, 195), a chaste,
objective, and scrupulous protest against the sloppy vulgarity of thought
and emotion that surrounds him. Just as he lives while "regarding his
own acts with doubtful side-glances" (D, 108), he speaks with continual
scornful side-glances at the anonymous others who are not kindred spirits. Still, within the story, these others do not speak; even Mrs. Sinico,
after her opening remark at the Rotunda about the poorhouse, has not a
single line of directly reported speech.

But there is a voice Duffy must confront, a voice that fittingly enough
represents precisely the public with whom Duffy refuses to engage in

dialogue. This is the newspaper. Two entire pages are filled with the account Duffy reads, which is cited verbatim—notable enough in a story where no other voice but Duffy's is allowed to sound. The technique is a version of that in the third chapter of *Portrait*, where the alien voice of the sermon suddenly intrudes into Stephen's nearly monologic reverie. Indeed, it has much the same effect on Duffy as does the sermon on Stephen. The brutal shock seems less the result of the signification of the passages than of the sheer weight of alien wordage. Duffy's immediate reaction is revulsion before the *style* of the excerpt: "The whole narrative of her death revolted him. . . . The threadbare phrases, . . . the cautious words of a reporter won over to conceal the details of a commonplace vulgar death attacked his stomach" (*D*, 115). Mrs. Sinico's death was banal, a cliché, he feels, and he is horrified to find his life entangled with such vulgarity.

Joyce thoroughly reworked the text of the newspaper "paragraph," giving it the sort of attention normally reserved for his own prose epiphanies. The finished version is a remarkable performance, in which the urges to sensational disclosure and to sympathetic or prudent reticence are carefully balanced, all within an enveloping verbal context of cool objectivity. The conservative *Mail* is naturally anxious to maintain its superior tone, yet for commercial reasons reluctant to ignore a melodramatic scandal. Matthew Arnold is said to have been appalled to read the report of a young woman accused of murdering her child under the heading, "Wragg is in custody." He lamented the "sex lost in the confusion of our unrivalled happiness, and the Christian name lopped off by the straightforward vigor of our Anglo-Saxon breed!"[13] The report of the "Painful Case" is nowhere near so brutal as this example of Victorian journalism, yet as Duffy recognizes, the careful periphrases such as "in view of certain other circumstances of the case" (*D*, 114) or "rather intemperate in her habits" (*D*, 115) serve as much to highlight the vulgar aspects of the event as to conceal them. Emily Sinico, a "Lady" in the heading, becomes "a woman" for the porter, "the deceased" for the surgeon (*D*, 114), and someone in the "habit of going out at night to buy spirits" (*D*, 115) in her daughter's testimony. Her identity, like her social station, becomes fluid and ambiguous.

Mr. Duffy is obviously shaken by reading the report; on returning to his house he reads it while "moving his lips as a priest does when he reads the prayers *Secreto*" (*D*, 113). He appears obsessed not so much by the item's significance as by the words themselves. Like Stephen collecting "words for his treasure-house" from "shops, on advertisements, in the mouths of the plodding public" and then "repeating them to himself till they lost all instantaneous meaning for him" (SH, 30), Duffy seems to be mesmerized. Perhaps some of this is the shock of recognition, for the newspaper report in some respects mimics his own narrative. It is narrated as if by no one, by a ghostly voice that subsumes the other voices it encounters in cool, logical paraphrase, and that has Duffy's odd insistence on concrete particularity; the "patent spring gates" mentioned by the railway's representative are a strange intrusion indeed into the tragic testimony. The Deputy Coroner's finding, "No blame attached to anyone" (D, 115), coming at the end of a general paraphrase, again appears to be an impersonal, cosmic judgment for which no individual is responsible. It has the putative impersonality of the popular ideas to which Yeats referred in his journal: "all these thoughts which were never really thought out in their current form in any individual mind, being the creation of impersonal mechanism—of schools, of textbooks, of newspapers, these above all."[14]

Duffy, of course, is horrified at having a part of his own experience reflected so banally in the public media. So absolute is his contempt for the public that he is probably incapable of realizing fully the links between this example of reportorial narration and his own inner narrative; he is doubtless unaware of this irony in his frantic effort to affirm the newspaper's conclusion. Yet his own characteristic rhetorical structures and those of the press are identical in aim: the denial of the subject through its subsumption in an unarticulated Authority. Like the press, Duffy attempts to envelop the conflicting voices that surround him, with all their aberrant patterns of signification, and to master them within his own cool, neat, closely bounded formulations. However dehumanizing the surgeon's observation that the "injuries were not sufficient to have caused death in a normal person" (D, 114), his own observation that evidently "she had been unfit to live" (D, 115) is more so. Just as the newspaper perforce arrays its formulations to appeal to the most hackneyed of public stereotypes, so Duffy immediately interprets Mrs. Sinico's action in terms of "the hobbling wretches whom he had seen carrying cans and bottles to be filled by the barman" (D, 115). For Duffy is at base a creature of cliché, much like Little Chandler but with a somewhat more sophisticated disguise of originality. After all, his vision of his relationship with Emily Sinico had been banally platonic; when he realized the relationship was more complex than that image, he preferred to abandon it rather than to reexamine his own motivations. Even when he himself is the narrative subject, his narration shares with the newspaper account the alternate motives of reticence and disclosure. His giant, romantic ego treasures every detail of his own daily existence, but takes care to present them through a defensive haze of cynicism and irony. He sees himself as heroic, a self expanded to the magnitude of impersonality, but takes care that his inner narrative should express that vision only indirectly.

The dialogical confrontation with the newspaper article shakes his very sense of self; the story's narrative alters substantially following it. Perhaps unsurprisingly, the magnitude of Duffy's shock is evidenced by frantic repetition. He reads the paragraph "over and over again" at the restaurant and again at home (D, 113), orders another punch (D, 116), twice feels her approach him, walks again through "the bleak alleys where they had walked four years before," hears the engine "reiterating the syllables of her name," and twice terms himself "outcast from life's feast" (D, 117). But this sudden, motivated repetition, while it signals a change in Duffy's construction of himself, also underlines what should have been clear from the beginning: that he has always depended upon repetition for the validation of his experience. This is an aspect of Duffy's curious habit of self-narration, and of his writing as well, for both processes are attempts at the reiteration of phenomenal experience. Indeed, Duffy's *sententiae* are attempts to generalize from repeated cases; his experience presents itself to him as a series of *exempla* whose validity depends upon their reduplication. Even his relationship with Mrs. Sinico, which he takes to be a unique event, is little more than his own attempt to replicate his own mind in another; when he "entangled his thoughts with hers" there is no doubt that his intent was the creation of a second Duffy.

Duffy experiences only so that he can reexperience, in memory. On first meeting Mrs. Sinico, even as they talk he attempts "to fix her permanently in his memory" (D, 109), and after reading the account of her death his initial revulsion first begins to alter when "the light failed and his memory began to wander" (D, 116). Duffy now has two "memories" of her, one idealized and one degraded, and only at this point does he begin to grow conscious of his own reliance upon memory: "As he sat there, living over his life with her and evoking alternately the two images in which he now conceived her, he realised that she was dead, that she had ceased to exist, that she had become a memory. He began to feel ill at ease" (D, 116). By the end of the story, with the train's reiteration of her name pounding in his ears, he "began to doubt the reality of what memory told him" (D, 117). But if memory fails, if his mental constructs may be inadequate to his experience, then what of his writing? Duffy is undergoing a revulsion against his entire mode of experience. That he has probably inflated the importance of his role in Mrs. Sinico's life and death, that his new self-perception is marked by sentimental self-pity, is beside the point. Like Stephen after confronting E. C. "point-blank in Grafton Street," Duffy now realizes that "all that I thought I thought and all that I felt I felt, all the rest before now, in fact . . . " (P, 252) was mistaken. Words and memory have failed him, have been inadequate to their referent; like Farrington, he is more repetition's victim than its master.

Stories of Public Life

The four stories of "public life," "Ivy Day in the Committee Room," "A Mother," "Grace," and "The Dead," explore varieties of public rhetoric. "The Dead" also makes a transition from the studied formality of Gabriel's address to the intimate dialogue he shares with his wife, thus making a connection to the familial dialogue of the early stories, but this story is unusual in many respects. In contrast, the other three stories form a neat triad, dealing respectively with politics, the arts, and religion, all in their more public aspects. The three rely heavily upon dialogue rather than action or introspection—"Ivy Day" and "Grace" do so almost exclusively—and even the narrative is more scrupulously neutral than in earlier stories. A greater number of supernumeraries are introduced in these stories, giving the effect of "crowd scenes" even when only four or five characters are actually present. Whereas many earlier stories such as "A Little Cloud" or "Counterparts" have a minor public dimension, with the dialogue taking place in a bar or in an office with onlookers present, in these last stories the subjects of discussion are themselves ideologically charged, already embedded in a dense network of assumptions and values. To speak about politics, religion, or the arts is to risk making an overt ideological commitment and thus to risk radically antagonizing one's interlocutor; the language appropriate for such discussion is thus highly formulaic, almost ritualized, and virtually every pronouncement is made "with a sideward glance." Politics and religion are notoriously dangerous topics for dinner-table discussion, and in turn-of-the-century Dublin the same might be said of the arts; each topic in turn comes up during the feast in "The Dead," and is responsible for increasing the sense of social unease which pervades that story.

All three stories turn upon a central irony produced by juxtaposing ideal values with mundane pragmatics. In "Ivy Day" the realm of the political is invoked first in its theological and mythical aspect by the evocation of Parnell as Savior and then in its quotidian aspect by the bickering about canvassing for a candidate about whom no one is enthusiastic. In "Grace" the religious sphere is invaded both by the tedious and inaccurate discussion of the minutiae of church history and by the question of its relevance to daily life. In "A Mother" the artistic and quasi-Nationalist production of the *Eire Abu* Society is threatened by Mrs. Kearney's insistence on the letter of her contract. All three, clearly, are instances of a kind of simony, but more significantly all three stories depend upon the confrontation of different languages embodying generally accepted but incompatible ideologies. In "A Mother" and "Grace" there is the remnant of an enveloping action—negotiation in the former, reconversion in the latter—but in "Ivy Day," in good Flaubertian style, there is almost nothing going on; the dialogue is supremely *undirected*, and as a consequence the forms and genres of speech are highlighted. Dialogical interaction in "Ivy Day" is all the purer for its lack of immediate motive.

"Ivy Day in the Committee Room": Consensus and Group Fantasy

The scene is the Nationalist party's ward headquarters, where canvassers for Richard Tierney—Henchy, O'Connor, Crofton, and Lyons—gather to take refuge from the inclement weather. Old Jack, the caretaker of the room, is present at the story's opening, and Hynes, a diehard Parnellite and sympathizer with the opposing leftist candidate, enters soon after. These two are the outsiders; Jack is accepted and ignored, because his inferior social station is fixed, but Hynes is an ambiguous figure, accused by Henchy of being a political spy yet also praised for his loyalty to Parnell and for his literary gifts. Like "Father" Keon, possibly a defrocked priest, Hynes's status is difficult to determine. Keon has no apparent means of support and is termed a "black sheep" by Henchy but on the other hand still wears a pseudo-clerical garb and manner, and has been observed to be "very thick" with Fanning, the sub-sheriff (D, 126). Henchy plays it safe and treats him with exaggerated deference. Hynes, on the other hand, is a socially powerless figure, tolerated for the sake of old acquaintance and the lingering, rather guilty memory the other men have of their former ideals. But if Hynes plays the role of their conscience, he also plays the role of entertainer, reciting a sentimental poem all present can appreciate because it asks no immediate action or commitment from them; as Henchy points out so brutally, "Parnell is dead" (D, 132).

Through the conversation the men are arrayed with respect to politics, with Hynes, who has socialist leanings, on the left, O'Connor somewhat sympathetic to him, Henchy in the amorphous center, Lyons somewhat right of center, and Crofton, a conservative Orangeman, on the far right. But, as Robert Boyle, S.J., notes, there is also a spectrum of commitment, ranging from the steadfast if ineffectual Hynes to the repellently unprincipled temporizer, Henchy.[15] Indeed, practical political considerations seem beside the point in this story, which features such a wide if vague span of ideologies. The men of the coalition are mainly concerned with their payment and their drink, only secondarily with the position of the candidate they represent. The only point of political action discussed is the upcoming welcome to Edward VII, and the men are unsure both of what Tierney's position will be and of what it *should* be in that purely symbolic matter. It is in any case Hynes who introduces this question, phrased in the political rhetoric to which his political commitment entitles him: "The working-man is not going to drag the honour of Dublin in the mud to please a German monarch" (D, 121). Soon after Henchy enters, Hynes leaves, with the parting irony, "It'll be all right when King Eddie comes" (D, 124), and the subject is dropped for seven pages until Hynes abruptly reintroduces it and Henchy offers his equally eloquent rejoinder, an encomium to Edward in a genre far removed from Hynes's oratory: "He's a jolly fine decent fellow, if you ask me, and no damn nonsense about him" (D, 132).

From a political standpoint, "Ivy Day" is clearly an anatomy of the

degraded state of Dublin politics in 1902, when a "Nationalist" candidate can devote a welcoming address to the British monarch and a representative group of Dubliners are willing to support him, if only for the
sake of the money and stout. The anniversary of Parnell's death and
Hynes's recitation both establish the immense ironic distance, thematically reinforced by the men's complaints about the decay of the younger
generation. But all this is made evident in the opening and closing pages
alone, whereas the bulk of the story is devoted to dialogue that seems to
evade the political issue. This dialogue is dominated by Henchy, who
shows himself a master of ostensibly nonpolitical rhetoric that is nonetheless ideologically charged. Henchy appeals to popular consensus and
to common sense, and as Gayatri Chakravorty Spivak observes, "What
is 'commonsense' if not ideology at its strongest?"[16] Of the two dialogical centers of power in the story, Hynes and Henchy, Henchy emerges
the stronger because he is himself a sort of living consensus. Where
Hynes asks the men to take a political stand based upon a coherent and
articulated ideology, that of radical Nationalism, Henchy allows them to
rest in the morass of conflicting and tacit ideologies that underlie social
inertia. Hynes's performance is the last in the story, but Henchy's performance subsumes it, undercuts it, and renders it even more nostalgic and
ineffectual than it would be were Henchy not present.

Henchy's speech demonstrates two ideological modalities, one negative, the other positive. He employs the former before the stout arrives,
the latter afterward, a fact which underlines the arbitrary nature of his
ideological commitment. Henchy's world view at any given moment
seems to depend primarily upon whether or not he has a drink in his
hand. Henchy's negative modality is essentially a form of massive de-
bunking; it expresses the proposition that nothing is what it seems, and
people with a worldly, cynical eye (like Henchy and his interlocutor) are
not taken in by appearances. In rapid succession Henchy asserts that
Hynes is a spy of Colgan's (D, 124), that "hillsiders and fenians" like
him are in the pay of Dublin Castle (D, 125), that Keon is a "black
sheep" (D, 126), and that Tierney and his associates owe money to the
City Fathers (D, 127). No one is safe from Henchy's denigration, but his
greatest vituperation is reserved for his own candidate, whom he terms a
"little shoeboy of hell" and a "mean little tinker," revealing that Tierney's father ran a "hand-me-down shop" and sold liquor illegally (D,
123).

The principles underlying Henchy's global critique are simple: first, anyone will betray anything for money, and second, those who pretend to an elevated social status are really from a lower, and thus despicable, social stratum. The principles are never stated as such, and so can never be examined critically by his listeners. Henchy's rhetoric depends upon innuendo and is buttressed either by an assertion of personal, privileged information ("O, but I know it for a fact" [D, 125]) or by appeal to the listener's presumed complicity ("Did you never hear that?" [D, 123]; "You know the patriot I'm alluding to" [D, 125]). His most frequently repeated conversational opener is an assertion of frankness, which draws the listener into a privileged dialogical space with himself: "I'll tell you my private and candid opinion" (D, 124, 125), "Between ourselves, you know ... " (D, 129). Henchy sometimes uses a qualifier to moderate the effect of his global negativity, one that imputes a degree of virtue to one person only in order to underline the degradation of another. Thus Hynes's "father was a decent respectable man," but Hynes doesn't have a "spark of manhood about him" (D, 124), and though Hynes may be "a stroke above" taking pay from the Castle, "there's a certain little nobleman" who is not (D, 125). In these speech structures Henchy's qualifiers function proleptically, as if to assure the listener that he is not simply deriding at random but is exercising reasoned judgment.

Henchy's observations have a surreal quality because he is so completely unaware of their application to himself. At every turn he demonstrates that he is presently being paid for supporting a candidate he scorns, and one who he claims is at least indirectly in the pay of political bosses. He joins old Jack in the sorrowful observation that the delivery boy has started on the road to alcoholism with a single bottle of stout— "the thin edge of the wedge" (D, 129)—even though he himself offered it to the boy seconds before. He piles abuse on the father of "Tricky Dicky" with his "tricky little black bottle up in a corner" (D, 123) and then himself proudly demonstrates a "little trick" with the bottles of stout (D, 130). He shifts his position on Hynes as soon as he sees that O'Connor is willing to defend him, and by the end of the story he is leading the acclamation for the man he had accused of spying. Similarly, when the sentiment of the party turns toward Parnell, whom he had impatiently dismissed minutes before, Henchy is bursting with admiration and ready to dramatize the great man's approach to the Irish delegation: "*Down, ye dogs! Lie down, ye curs!* That's the way he treated them" (D, 133). Henchy is the ultimate conversational opportunist, ready with a proverb or a vivid locution for any occasion, without the slightest regard for the consistency of his own position.

Henchy's praise is as dangerous as his vituperation. His main positive performance is his defense of Edward, and here he adopts a tone of bluff heartiness, a man-among-men style that loudly announces its own candid simplicity at every point: "Here's this chap come to the throne after his old mother keeping him out of it till the man was grey. He's a man of the world, and he means well by us. He's a jolly fine decent fellow, if you ask me, and no damn nonsense about him. . . . He's just an ordinary knockabout like you and me. He's fond of his glass of grog and he's a bit of a rake, perhaps, and he's a good sportsman. Damn it, can't we Irish play fair?" (D, 132). Since Henchy's praise depends on consensus to an even greater extent than his dispraise does, his language turns into an endless string of clichés without even the spurious vividness of his abuse. Toward the end of his peroration, his speech takes on a curiously British intonation, with the invocation of good sportsmanship and playing fair. But this is hardly surprising, since Henchy is a sort of ventriloquist, able to adopt whatever phrasing and vocabulary suits the occasion.

Indeed, he has a habit of throwing himself into the position of the person under discussion and speaking with that voice, as in his impersonation of Parnell quelling the Irish members or his version of Edward saying to himself, "The old one never went to see these wild Irish. By Christ, I'll go myself and see what they're like" (D, 132). The key to Henchy's success is not merely his ability to appeal to the unexamined prejudices of his listeners, but his dramatic flair. Several times during the story he presents such brief scenarios, involving his listeners dialogically much as Stephen Dedalus does when he dramatizes his Shakespeare hypothesis in the National Library. He is a master of the rhetorical power of the anecdote, whether implied or fully developed. Robert F. Boles has drawn attention to this process whereby a "group fantasy event" is elaborated in a small conversational group, each member of which may "chain out" the dramatic fantasy and thus help establish values and attitudes communally for the group.[17]

Henchy articulates such mini-dramas throughout "Ivy Day," most obviously when he imagines himself Lord Mayor, driving "out of the Mansion House . . . in all my vermin, with Jack here standing up behind me in a powdered wig," and O'Connor and Jack chime in with their own contributions (*D*, 127). The strength of this satiric vision is that it assumes just how far the company is from imagining an ordinary man like themselves in a position of political power. Hynes's question, "Hasn't the working-man as good a right to be in the Corporation as anyone else" (*D*, 121) is here answered with a resounding negative—not through an explicit statement of principles but through Henchy's dialogical manipulation of the group fantasy. The men here do not really know what they believe until they discover that they have unwittingly committed themselves to a position. "Motives do not exist to be expressed in communication but rather arise in the expression itself and come to be embedded in the drama of the fantasy themes that generated and serve to sustain them."[18] As "Ivy Day in the Committee Room" progresses, Henchy gains increasing power over the conversational group. Gradually the incoherent and self-contradictory social implications of his statements gather toward a paradoxical but nonetheless reactionary position: all Dublin politicians are corrupt and ordinary, and therefore deserve scorn and derision, but Edward VII, who is admittedly somewhat immoral, deserves praise and welcome *because* he is "an ordinary knockabout."

Henchy, like the popular press, is a great leveller. He claims to speak in Edward's voice and in Parnell's. He even imitates himself, as when he dramatizes his appeal to the conservative Ward on behalf of Tierney: Tierney is "respectable" and a "big rate-payer," "prominent and respected," and "doesn't belong to any party, good, bad, or indifferent" (*D*, 131). Surely this "commonsensical" approach to politics, the ideology that claims to avoid ideology, is the most insidious of all reactionary stances. Henchy's appeal is to common prejudice and to self-interest. "What we want in this country, as I said to old Ward, is capital. The King's coming here will mean an influx of money into this country" (*D*, 131). But of course it will mean no such thing, especially to the down-and-outers gathered in the Committee Room. Henchy is merely trying to associate himself with any apparent source of money and power, without any real regard for what that association will bring him; at best, like his canvassing for Tierney, it will bring him a couple of bottles of stout and the promise of token payment. Henchy is the blind leading the blind in this room, and he is the answer to Hynes's initial question, "What are you doing in the dark?" (*D*, 120). Nonetheless, his dialogical power outweighs that of Hynes, whose poem to Parnell is finally dismissed as "a very fine piece of writing" (*D*, 135). In the Committee Room, a fine piece of writing cannot compete against finely tuned speech. Hynes's monologic recitation appeals to popular mytho-political sentiment and demands approval on the basis of the nostalgic ideology the listeners all claim to share; but Henchy's dialogical conversation enmeshes his listeners through their own responses and finally holds their helpless allegiance.

"A Mother": Economic and Social Rhetoric

"A Mother" is by no means the subtlest of *Dubliners* stories, but in the dialogical relationship between narrator and protagonist it is one of the most interesting. In many respects the story parallels "The Boarding House," but on a slightly higher social plane: both mothers are concerned to advance their daughters's "careers," and both are sources of slippage in the social level of language within the stories. Both mothers are concerned with maintaining power in the face of opposition, a power they can claim only through association with a socially ratified ideology. In Mrs. Mooney's case this is moral, in Mrs. Kearney's, economic. Seen in this perspective, their situations are mirror images of one another. Mrs. Mooney gains the economic advantage of marrying off her daughter by invoking the rhetoric of bourgeois morality, while Mrs. Kearney attempts to invoke the rhetoric of contracts in order to maintain a social advantage for her daughter, that of association with a leading bourgeois "cultural" group. That Mrs. Mooney succeeds while Mrs. Kearney fails can be ascribed to the fact that Mrs. Mooney invokes a "higher" social rhetoric to disguise a "lower" motivation, while Mrs. Kearney is attempting the reverse. By reducing the concert to a matter of labor and remuneration, Mrs. Kearney embarrassingly demystifies this massively overdetermined cultural event.

Balance is a crucial metaphor in the story, most vividly evoked in Mr. O'Madden Burke's "magniloquent western name," the "moral umbrella upon which he balanced the fine problem of his finances" (*D*, 145). At the story's end, this "widely respected" interloper is still "poised upon his umbrella in approval" of Mrs. Kearney's discomfiture (*D*, 149), but the fine balance has been momentarily shaken by her outburst. The evening's difficult equipoise depends upon any number of crossing and conflicting cultural codes. It is meant to be both "entertainment" and "art," and thus embodies a conflict and compromise between the tastes of the Dublin audience, who would prefer music hall or pantomime, and the tastes of the organizers, who presumably would prefer grand opera and the recitation of poetry. As a manifestation of the Irish Revival the concert should be an expression of Irish culture, but the most authentic expression of that culture was folk forms that would not satisfy the organizers's bourgeois preference for socially elevated art. Similarly, the concert should draw exclusively upon Irish talent, but the need to feature recognized *artistes* leads the Committee to employ well-known (if incompetent) British performers like Madam Glynn.

Indeed, there is even a conflict between the desire to feature the most talented performers and the desire to feature socially acceptable *artistes*; Mr. Duggan has a wonderful voice but regrettably is the son of a hall porter and wipes his nose with his hand during performances (*D*, 142). But the most serious contradiction, the one underlined by Mrs. Kearney, is that between the concert as a profit-making endeavor, in which the labor of the performers should be rewarded by the appreciative audience, and the concert as a social ritual presenting art for art's sake, in which members of the privileged class mutually support and applaud one another's performances out of a disinterested appreciation of an aesthetic undertaking. The concert can be neither the one nor the other: the supporters are not wealthy or generous enough to sponsor such evenings gratis, while "elevated" musical presentations generally failed with Dublin audiences. The economic failure of the first evenings underlines a well-known cultural scandal of late-nineteenth-century Dublin, the inability of more than a couple of musical theaters to survive in this most "music-loving" of capital cities.[19]

As a result, both the performance and the organization are an explosive mix of amateurism and professionalism. Kathleen Kearney is the most dangerous example of this, a semiprofessional who is competent enough, but whose role can be adequately performed by Miss Healy at a moment's notice. The narrative makes it clear that she is chosen to perform on grounds at least as much social as musical. She is "talked up" by the Kearneys' musical and Nationalist friends, who recognize that she is "very clever at music and a very nice girl and, moreover, that she was a believer in the language movement" (*D*, 138). On the other hand, her one line of dialogue in the story makes it plain that she shares some of her mother's ignorance and vulgarity, when she asks about Madam

Glynn, "Where did they dig her up?" and asserts that she has never heard of her (D, 143). Kathleen is at best a medium-sized frog in a small, dark pool. But in her own story she is mostly silent, like Polly Mooney in hers; like Polly she is a counter in her mother's game of power rather than an independent participant. If she has any importance in the story's main conflict, it is because her mother *speaks for* her, but by the story's end she, like Mr. Kearney, must listen passively to her mother's vituperation.

An accompanist rather than a star turn, Kathleen is finally a super-numerary; this is her mother's story, not only in title but in the dialogical interaction of the narration. David Hayman has analyzed most percep-tively Joyce's device of "permitting the character's voice and reactions to usurp momentarily the narrator's prerogatives" in "A Mother."[20] As he points out, as early as the end of the first paragraph, with the observa-tion that "in the end it was Mrs Kearney who arranged everything" (D, 136) the woman's judgments and sensibilities have become unobtru-sively involved in the narration. Phrases like "she never weakened in her religion and was a good wife to him" (D, 137) bear the unmistakable mark of her consciousness.[21] Hayman also observes that by the end of the story the narrative has withdrawn from her, as if the narrator were, like the other performers, concerned to distance himself from such a troublesome character. But in fact Mrs. Kearney is not allowed simply to appropriate the narration from the beginning. The story's opening falsely suggests that Mr. Holohan will be the most significant character, until Mrs. Kearney gradually takes over center stage, along with Holo-han's functions. In a parallel manner, Joyce is careful to allow a distinc-tive narrative voice quite different from Mrs. Kearney's to establish it-self, before it is replaced by her characteristic attitudes and locutions.

This original narrative voice has much of the objectivity that charac-terizes it in all the other stories, but is rather more epigrammatic, even *précieux*, than is the norm in *Dubliners*. The narrator describes Mrs. Kearney as possessing "ivory manners" in her youth and refers to her sitting "amid the chilly circle of her accomplishments" (D, 136). The same voice is not averse to a polished comic turn, as when Mr. Kearney's "conversation, which was serious, took place at intervals in his great brown beard" (D, 137). Such language and such perceptions are cer-tainly far removed from Mrs. Kearney's rather bland, cliché-ridden locu-tions, which characterize her husband as a "model father" and herself as a "good wife to him" (D, 137). The effect of the dialogical interaction between authorial and protagonist's voices here is to destabilize Mrs. Kearney's social position, to suggest that her upper-middle-class manners disguise a lower-middle-class soul. Within the first several pages, Mrs. Kearney's voice has crowded out that of the original narrator and indeed has taken on a more vulgar intonation, as if in the heat of preparation she had forgotten her "ivory manners." Thus it is allowed that Kathleen's dress "cost a pretty penny" (D, 138), and when she seeks out Mr. Holohan following the first concert she "buttonholed him" (D, 140).

Throughout, "A Mother" revolves around the linguistic reflection of social position. Like Stephen in *Portrait*, Mrs. Kearney is inclined to judge others by their speech and accent rather than by their actions. When all goes well for her she is able to repress this tendency, but as soon as things begin to go wrong she is struck by the "flat" accent of the Society's secretary, Mr. Fitzpatrick, and rewards the "very flat final syllable" of his utterance with a "quick stare of contempt" (D, 139). Her immediate impulse when enraged is social mockery, the sort of cruel verbal mimicry that pervades "Counterparts" and helps establish that story's tone of universal aggression. When Fitzpatrick temporizes, "she had all she could do to keep from asking: —And who is the *Cometty*, pray?" (D, 141). This locution, with its icy formality and coded condescension, would itself be an artificial manner of speech for a woman who presses liquor on Mr. Holohan with the admonishment, "Don't be afraid! Don't be afraid of it!" (D, 138).

As if alerted by Mrs. Kearney's gesture toward pretentiousness, the narration now begins to distance itself again from the woman. When she speaks to her husband, their "conversation was evidently about Kathleen for they both glanced at her often" (D, 143), but the narrator has now assumed the position of a bystander who is not privy to Mrs. Kearney's experiences. After her confrontation with Holohan in the corridor, the narrative turns to follow the *Freeman* reporter, and the original narrative voice begins to reassert itself. The reporter is described as having "a plausible voice and careful manners" (D, 144), and during his conversation with Miss Healy it is observed that he "was old enough to suspect one reason for her politeness but young enough in spirit to turn the moment to account" (D, 145). The resurgence of genteel narrative phrasemaking climaxes at the epigram regarding O'Madden Burke's "magniloquent western name" (D, 145); still another narrative voice, as David Hayman argues convincingly, is "the oily blandness of a journalistic commentator, a voice we may perhaps identify as that of O'Madden Burke."[22] Both genteel and journalistic voices crowd out Mrs. Kearney's distinctive tones. Meanwhile, the narrator studiously turns his attention to the performers and managers waiting in the wings and backstage. In a parodic version of the performance onstage, these minor characters all have a line or two of characterization or of dialogue, as if they were taking their "turns" in dramatic, bathetic, or farcical performances. Like the narrator, the other performers by and large are doing their utmost to ignore the contretemps Mrs. Kearney has caused and to reassert the unified social front that her talk of contracts has jeopardized.

When the "star attraction" Mrs. Kearney returns, following the first part of the concert, her dialogue with Holohan signals the shifting of power. Where previously she has pursued him, now, emboldened by his sense that public opinion is on his side, Holohan confronts Mrs. Kearney. Significantly, her dialogue is parasitically dependent upon his statements; it is as if she has no language of her own in which to argue, but must attempt to turn Holohan's words against him. When Holohan says, "I never thought you would treat us this way," she replies, "And what way did you treat me?" (D, 148). He invokes "decency," she asks for a "civil answer" (D, 149). Her final blunder is to impersonate Holohan in a mockingly aggressive act of linguistic appropriation: "You must speak to the secretary. It's not my business. I'm a great fellow fol-the-diddle-I-do." It is after this interchange that "Mrs Kearney's conduct was condemned on all hands" (D, 149), and Holohan is able to accuse her of failing to be a lady. The crucial point is not that she has been proved wrong about the contract, or even that she has been shown another good of overriding value; it is that she has made a verbal slip which betrays her lower-middle-class origins. "I'm a great fellow fol-the-diddle-I-do" is more reminiscent of Simon Dedalus on a binge than of the woman who had aspired to demand, "What is the *Cometty*, pray?" The irreversible shift in power is again signalled verbally, when Holohan shows himself able to appropriate *her* words with impunity:

—I'm not done with you yet, she said.
—But I'm done with you, said Mr. Holohan. (D, 149)

Ironically, in a story whose situation cries out for adjudication, our judgment is necessarily suspended. Our sympathy is alternately with Mrs. Kearney, with Kathleen, with the other *artistes*, and even with Holohan. The point is not that Mrs. Kearney is right or wrong in insisting upon her daughter's contract, but that all the terms of the debate have been muddled beyond recognition. All the participants are engaged in an enterprise at once "artistic," economic, and social, and the rules applicable to one category are not applicable to the others. The failure of the concert series panics Mrs. Kearney and convinces her that the set of mutual assumptions upon which everyone has been operating may no longer hold. She attempts to maintain a sort of social superiority by invoking the economic perspective, but she is "trumped" when Holohan, in order to maintain economic advantage, invokes the principles of social interaction. No one is capable of the selflessness a purely artistic event would require, but everyone is constantly aware of the shifting social status of the participants.

Much of this confusion can be attributed to a sort of rampant nominalism exhibited by characters in "A Mother." Names are perpetually confused with things, or are thought to bear significantly upon their qualities, as with "Hoppy" Holohan and his game leg. The entire imbroglio begins when Mrs. Kearney, "determined to take advantage of her daughter's name" (*D*, 137), brings an Irish teacher to the house and generally encourages her to take an interest in things Irish.[23] O'Madden Burke supports himself greatly by virtue of his "magniloquent western name," which suggests a greater social standing than that to which he otherwise would be entitled; and having been designated by the official reporter as his unofficial stand-in, O'Madden Burke is perfectly willing to take upon himself the role of public arbiter and spokesman. Mrs. Kearney respects her husband "in the same way she respected the General Post Office" (*D*, 141), which is to say in his "abstract value" as husband and as male: he bears those important names and is therefore important. The fact that he fails to function in either of those traditional capacities is irrelevant to Mrs. Kearney, who is the story's premier literalist. Her insistence upon the letter of her daughter's contract is merely the climax of her nominalism, a desperate affirmation that things must *be* as they *say*. The language of the contract must be the guarantor of its reality. So it is curiously appropriate that she is defeated by a variant of the same sort of linguistic literalism. Mr. Holohan's telling point is that a lady *is* as she *speaks*; when Mrs. Kearney's language slips, she is no longer a lady. The nominalist fabric of linguistic social understandings is dense and interconnected: pull upon one strand too vigorously, and the whole may become unknotted. Woe to the one who, like Mrs. Kearney, insists too literally upon the strand she grasps.

"Grace": Periphrasis and the Unspeakable

In "Grace," which Joyce originally planned as the climax of his collection,[24] most of the themes of *Dubliners* converge. Simony is explicit here, as Joyce pointedly juxtaposes religion and the economic motive in Father Purdoin's sermon. Tom Kernan, unconscious on the lavatory floor, is the volume's premier paralytic. Like "Ivy Day," "Grace" features the interminable half-informed conversation of middle-class Dubliners, but the latter story highlights even more strongly its distinctive cadences and locutions.[25] Insofar as language, particularly speech and dialogical interaction, is the central preoccupation of Joyce in *Dubliners*, "Grace" could be an appropriate capstone. As Fritz Senn demonstrates in an insightful article, the story is greatly concerned with speech and rhetoric.[26] But the story also would give a certain degree of closure to the collection, in that it specifically reiterates many of the themes and concerns of "The Sisters." Here too we have a rather silent protagonist who does not share the language of the adults surrounding him. He feels himself the object of embarrassing and frightening attention from his pseudo-family, all of whom seem engaged in a vague plot and all of whom share knowledge withheld from him. A major concern of both stories is the protagonist's relationship to religion, especially as embodied in a charismatic priest who fails in his function. Both stories turn about silence, ellipsis, the unspoken, and the unspeakable; and in both, periphrasis, circumlocution, and verbal avoidance of a variety of sorts are highlighted.

The emphasis on silence and periphrasis is mirrored thematically in an entirely obvious way that nevertheless has gone relatively unremarked. "Grace" is a story about alcoholism and the attempted "rehabilitation" of an alcoholic, yet none of Kernan's friends and family ever broaches the subject. In the bourgeois culture Joyce examines—as, usually, in ours—alcohol is both pervasive and invisible. It seems never to occur to any of Kernan's friends that his problem is drinking and that the solution would be for him to drink less or to stop altogether; the retreat they plan is in place of such a direct approach, in the forlorn hope that, by a sort of sympathetic magic, spiritual involvement will lessen Kernan's need for spirits. Judging from Kernan's gin-drinking in *Ulysses* (*U*, 196–98/239–41), the plan is no more successful than might be supposed. Kernan's intemperance is given a kind of cosmic inevitability; it is, as Mrs. Kernan believes, "part of the climate" (*D*, 156). The consumption of alcohol is an inevitable concomitant to any social situation in the story, with effects that verge on farce. Kernan tries to thank his anonymous rescuer with a drink, and when Power brings him home Kernan's wife apologizes for being unable to offer one. The group of friends who gather to convince Kernan to "turn over a new leaf" (*D*, 155) are served drinks on their arrival, and when Mr. Fogarty joins them he brings whiskey, which is immediately opened and served. The group plans on meeting in a pub before the service. Even Kernan's memories of his previous experiences with religion are bound up with alcohol; he has only the vaguest memory of Father Tom Burke's sermon, but remembers vividly being "genuinely moved" by his discussion of religion with Crofton in Butler's afterward (*D*, 165). Certainly there is irony in the fact that the spiritual retreat to which Kernan is brought turns out to be so worldly and vulgar; but the greater irony is that anyone should think a general religious retreat of any sort would be the most effective approach to Kernan's problem.

If alcohol is an emblem of the unmentionable central subject, everywhere present and nowhere acknowledged, Kernan's injury also points to a disturbing *tacebimus*. At the story's beginning we are objective onlookers in the bar, without privileged information, and Kernan's identity is as much a mystery to us as to the constable and "curate." The constable's question, "Who is the man? What's his name and address?" (*D*, 151) is also ours, but is asked into a silence. Twice the constable asks him directly where he lives, without eliciting an answer; only when Mr. Power arrives is he identified as "Tom," and only when he takes leave of the young bicyclist does he identify himself as "Kernan." At first we take Kernan's barely understandable speech as a curiously exaggerated effect of his drunkenness, but finally Kernan explains to Power that he cannot give an account of his accident because "'y 'ongue is hurt" (*D*, 153).

The protagonist is distinguished first by being unable to speak, then by being unable to speak clearly; and as a man without speech, he is also a man without identity. In a sense, he does not exist until he is claimed by his friend; were it not for Power's intervention, he might well be imprisoned as a penalty for anonymity. Kernan's loss of speech highlights the "privilege of the *phonè*" that Derrida finds fundamental to the system of Western metaphysics: "The system of 'hearing (understanding)-oneself-speak' through the phonic substance—which *presents itself* as the nonexterior, nonmundane, therefore nonempirical or noncontingent signifier—has necessarily dominated the history of the world during an entire epoch."[27] The guarantee of presence, indeed of meaning itself, is found in the "logocentrism" or "phonocentrism" that assumes "absolute proximity of voice and being, of voice and the meaning of being, of voice and the ideality of meaning."[28] Kernan's silence, and even his distorted speech, are radically dangerous. The community must unite to expel or transform him. Walter Ong, S.J., argues that "Oral verbalization, unlike writing, is thus natural. The word comes to each of us first orally in our 'mother' tongue. Its association with mother and early nature and nurture is why speech is so closely involved with our personal identity and with cultural identity, and why manipulation of the word entails various kinds of alienation."[29] Kernan's injury in itself is suggestive: he has *bitten his tongue*, a common enough expression in Ireland as in America, which means that the biter is forcing himself to be silent because the words that occur spontaneously would be inappropriate or embarrassing. (Mrs. Kernan, for instance, might be said to "bite her tongue" rather than to tell Kernan's friends her opinion of the appropriateness of the accident—that "Mr Kernan's tongue would not suffer by being shortened" [*D*, 158].) Here again, Kernan's speech serves as metonym for his existence: Kernan the good husband and adequate businessman is also a hopeless drunkard, but his society cannot afford to admit that there may be a connection between these identities. What Kernan "says" cannot be allowed to be "spoken." Thus his friends will attempt to cover his silences and distortions with acceptable speech of their own, or better, with a publicly approved rhetoric like that of the church.

If Kernan can be "drawn in" to a conversation, can be taught to speak properly—that is, as everyone else does—then the threat he poses can be nullified. But this is more difficult than it seems. Even aside from his injury, Kernan is characteristically evasive and periphrastic; he turns aside inquiry, most notably with his reiterated "Sha, s'nothing," or finds himself verbally at a loss, leaving gaps to be filled by his friends:

> —. . .There's something keeps coming into my throat, phlegm or—
> —Mucus, said Mr M'Coy.
> —It keeps coming like from down in my throat; sickening thing.
> —Yes, yes, said Mr M'Coy, that's the thorax. (*D*, 158–59)

He cannot remember the name of the "little chap with sandy hair" with whom he was drinking and only under pressure admits to having been drinking with Harford, whose name he cannot pretend to have forgotten (*D*, 159). Kernan then immediately changes the subject, praising the "medical fellow," and asks ingenuously, "How did it happen at all?" (*D*, 160). Kernan is happier with his life a mystery strung together by anecdote. This time, however, Cunningham does speak the obvious, if euphemistically: "It happened that you were peloothered, Tom" (*D*, 160). Immediately afterward, Kernan deflects attention from the issue by working up a rage against the "country bumpkins" of the constabulary. He is silent during most of the religious discussion, but when he does join in calls the portion of the church in which he was seated the "pit" (*D*, 165), evoking theatrical and infernal connotations that his interlocutors would rather suppress. Even Kernan's anger is expressed through circumlocution, as when Mrs. Kernan pities the priest who will have to listen to his confession and he expostulates, "If he doesn't like it, . . . he can . . . do the other thing" (*D*, 171).

The goal of Power, Cunningham, M'Coy, and Fogarty is to establish a dialogue that Kernan cannot help but join, a unifying rhetoric turning about the Irish church. They wish to form a "speech community" that will include the speechless Kernan and thus transform him into a harmless dialogical participant in their ritual of recollection and praise. Yet this "Popish Plot" against the ex-Protestant is undermined both from within and from without by the inevitable dynamics of small-group dialogue and by Kernan's unconscious but effectively destructive misreading of the conversation. The general outline the group plans for its artificial conversation at Kernan's bedside is impeccable: "spontaneous" mention of the group's intent to attend a retreat, followed by a course of reminiscence of church history that establishes both the virtue of the church and the particular virtue of the Irish church, ending with a reaffirmation of the group's intention to attend the retreat. Along the way Kernan is to be reassured that nothing overly spiritual is intended, and indeed that religious belief is identified with common sense, with personal virility, and with Irish Nationalism—all *doxa* belonging properly to popular Irish Catholic ideology of the time. The tone is to be kept light, so that the group resolution will be, euphemistically, to "wash the pot" (*D*, 163), and any serious statement will be presented jokingly. Thus Power's statement that "we're going to make your man here a good holy pious and God-fearing Roman Catholic" (*D*, 170) is said "with abrupt joviality," and Fogarty's "Get behind me, Satan!" is said "laughing and looking at the others" (*D*, 171).

The first challenge to Power's planned confabulation is, appropriately enough, *power*: who will direct the conversation? Power's plan is to be a "weak" director who will keep the conversation on course, but otherwise allow considerable freedom to the discussants; but Cunningham soon seizes the reins of authority, proclaiming *ex cathedra* on matters of church history and doctrine, so that the rest of the group must eventually declare *credo*. For instance, when M'Coy threatens to derail the conversation by expanding vulgarly upon the Jesuits as "the boyos [who] have influence," Power rather primly regains the spiritual high ground by asserting that they are "a fine body of men"; but Cunningham immediately takes the initiative by asserting that the Jesuit Order is the only one never to have been reformed. Cunningham's near-anecdote easily effaces Power's generalization and elicits another of M'Coy's admiring queries, "Is that so?" Like nearly all of Cunningham's "facts" it is false, but this is irrelevant to the dialogical play of power in the group.[30]

Another of Cunningham's conversational advantages is precisely that exercised by Henchy in "Ivy Day," the ability to dramatize group fantasies. It is Cunningham who paints the picture of John MacHale's heroic defiance and heroic submission so dramatically that his "words had built up the vast image of the Church in the mind of his hearers" and "his deep raucous voice had thrilled them" (*D*, 170). No wonder that by the end of the conversation, Mr. Power "felt completely outgeneralled" (*D*, 171). But the problem with Cunningham's usurpation of dialogical authority is that it tends to undermine the dialogical unity of the group and to foreground its dynamics instead. Everyone must be fully aware of the tension between Cunningham and Power, just as everyone is aware that M'Coy is only reluctantly admitted to the group and is constantly being situated at the bottom of its conversational hierarchy. It is probably because of Cunningham's pontifical stance when he reminds the group that they must stand up with lighted candles to renew their baptismal vows that Kernan rebels; and because the lowly M'Coy has echoed Cunningham's reminder, he feels especially safe in doing so.

At this point Kernan has certainly realized that he has been cast as the "black sheep" being led back to the fold, and he has the opportunity to seize the romantic outsider's role of idiosyncratic opposition to authority: "I bar the candles, said Mr Kernan, conscious of having created an effect on his audience and continuing to shake his head to and fro" (D, 171). Kernan must be resentfully aware that Power and Cunningham have stooped in order to assist him. His decline throughout the story is presented in social terms: Power realizes the seriousness of Kernan's fall when he meets the younger children with their disturbing manners and accents. Kernan realizes he is in "low" company with Harford and feels he belongs there, so that he is reassured to find Harford and an assortment of business failures at the retreat. But of course his very realization of the fact that "the arc of [Power's] social rise intersected the arc of [Kernan's] decline" (D, 154) strengthens Kernan's resistance to the group's dialogical pressure. He knows he is the privileged focus of the conversation, but only because he has allowed himself to fall below the plane of ordinary social intercourse.

Kernan's dialogical resistance takes an especially pernicious form because it employs a popular fiction to which his interlocutors cannot help but assent. His technique, essentially an evasive tactic, is to neutralize general issues by personalizing each situation. Thus as soon as Cunningham confronts him with his drunkenness Kernan deflects attention to the "ignorant bostoon" of a policemen, which leads to Cunningham's "catch your cabbage" dramatization (D, 160–61). The four are easily seduced into indulging this bit of "compensatory group animosity" for Dubliners,[31] in part because it is an available group fantasy on which everyone may "chain out," in part because it allows them relief from the embarrassing prospect of confronting Kernan with his alcoholism. But throughout the conversation there is a tension between the desire— mostly on Power's part—to establish the virtue and importance of the church by means of general principles and the need—most pressing in Kernan—to reduce church history to character and anecdote. Kernan is inclined to believe Cunningham because of his "high opinion of Mr Cunningham as a judge of character and as a reader of faces," yet he distrusts the clergy because of "some of those secular priests, ignorant, bumptious . . . " (D, 164). His contribution to the discussion of papal infallibility is the suggestion, typically circumlocutory, that "some of the old Popes [were] not exactly . . . you know . . . up to the knocker" (D, 168). His only real interest in the conversation is ignited when he is led to talk of hearing "stars" such as Tom Burke or John MacHale; his enthusiasm for the former is based solely upon Burke's charismatic preaching rather than upon anything the priest may have said, while MacHale impressed him mainly by his "eye like a hawk" (D, 170). Theology, like most issues for Kernan, finally reduces to a matter of faces; when he arrives at the church it is only the "familiar faces" (D, 173) in the congregation that reassure him. Face is popular shorthand for character, and character as moral guide has the advantage that it is unchanging. Thus, once convinced that "I'm not such a bad fellow" (D, 171), Kernan can avoid examining or attempting to alter his pattern of actions.

Although Kernan's silence, circumlocution, and ideological evasions are central to the story, "Grace" makes it clear that everyone is to some extent implicated; evasiveness, like drink, is part of the climate. As Warren Beck points out, at the story's beginning the "commentators on Kernan's mishap" in the bar are "tactfully evasive," while at the conclusion "Father Purdon is heard in a professional job of glossing over."[32] Nor is the hapless Kernan the center of this verbal and ratiocinative infection; he is merely one of its more obvious victims. Cheryl Herr casts the institutionalized church as culprit, arguing that "the cult of personality which actor-preachers encouraged can be seen as of strategic importance to a church actively vying for a share of people's leisure time," and further that Father Purdon's glossing over the impossibility of serving both God and Mammon is a "function of hegemonic maneuvers" by a church anxious to increase its membership and social control.[33]

There can be no doubt that the vulgarizing rhetoric of figures such as Father Bernard Vaughan—and perhaps, as Herr insists, the institutionalized church itself—were primary objects of Joyce's satire.[34] But there is also little doubt that Joyce intended a blanket indictment of Dubliners in his presentation of popular speech. The discussion at Kernan's, especially the part dealing with ecclesiastical history, is clearly a Flaubertian *sottisier*, a compendium of popular blunders and misapprehensions. Further, the rhetoric of evasion centered on Kernan also permeates the story as a whole, making it difficult to ascribe to any single source. Distinctive narrative voices emerge in both the opening and closing sections of "Grace," so that the story is framed by voices in dialogical relationship with those of Kernan's comforters. The final voice, of course, is that of Father Purdon—who, at the story's conclusion, attempts to appropriate the voices of his listeners. The first voice, which narrates the story's opening, has been described as "ceremonious" and "mock-heroic,"[35] but in fact at times closely resembles the journalese that Joyce recreates in "A Painful Case." Thus the manager is said to "narrate what he knew" to the policeman, who "made ready to indite" (*D*, 151). After investigation, "they agreed that the gentleman must have missed his footing" (*D*, 152–53). Here too we have an element of court reportage presented in "the cautious words of a reporter won over to conceal the details of a commonplace vulgar" incident (*D*, 115).

But both the journalistic voice and the priestly voice are variants on the linguistic theme of euphemism, circumlocution, and evasion. The "curate," policeman, and priest are united in their wish to explain away the uncomfortable and to reassure their joint audience. A clear narrative signal of the continuity between the first and third parts in "Grace" is the reiterated term "gentlemen," whose ironic presence William York Tindall was probably the first to note.[36] But both narratives are also distanced, revealing little of the characters' internality. Like Father Purdon the narrator looks down upon these Dubliners only in order to excuse them, to bestow a peculiarly ineffective grace upon their lives. Yet paradoxically the narrative voice is a popular voice, in priest as in reporter an embodiment of the community's will. The community's will, confronted with sin or despair, is to ignore, to excuse, and to turn away—all features that find their rhetorical embodiment throughout the story.

These Dubliners are in no need of Father Purdon's benediction; they have been blessed by one of the *charisms*, the charismatic gifts not given to all men. As Senn points out, grace, which is "the 'gift' related to the Holy Ghost and 'the gift of tongues' [see Acts 2:4, 38, etc.], can be replaced by the gift of the gab, the ability to handle words."[37] But more specifically the grace to which Joyce alludes here is that of speaking in tongues and the interpretation of tongues, examples of *actual* grace as opposed to *habitual* grace, along with the specific roles of the apostles, the gift of healing and prophecy, and so forth.[38] Kernan's garbled mutterings at the beginning of the story are interpreted easily enough by Power; indeed all these Dubliners speak in tongues, evasive and circumlocutory dialects incomprehensible to the uninitiated but—with the help of the proper spirits—clear enough to the Elect. This linguistic grace is also their damnation, as they are condemned to an inferno of perpetual conversational circling around an unspeakable center, like the horse Johnny in Gabriel Conroy's story mindlessly circling King Billy's statue (D, 208). In "Grace" the tongue is the tongue of Kernan, but the voice is the voice of Dublin.

"The Dead": Women's Speech and Tableau

Most critics have noted that "The Dead" is something of an anomaly among the stories of *Dubliners*. A late addition to the collection, it is often seen as anticipating some of the techniques and concerns of *Ulysses*. The majority of commentators have argued that the story is a belated attempt to redress the imbalance in tone of the collection: unlike the other stories, which seem increasingly to stress the sterile frustration and paralysis of Dublin life, "The Dead" is often read as offering positive hope for Gabriel's regeneration through self-knowledge. From a dialogical perspective as well, "The Dead" marks an abrupt break in the progression of the stories. Where the stories of public life generally rely far more heavily on dialogue than did the earlier ones, "The Dead" incorporates both large stretches of seemingly undirected dialogue, like "Grace" or "Ivy Day," and long passages of introspection by the protagonist as well as blocks of scenic description, like "Araby" or "An Encounter." Technically, the story seems a hybrid of the earlier and later stories. This is also true with respect to the position of the protagonist. Gabriel Conroy is as intelligent an observer as any protagonist in the collection, possibly excepting Mr. Duffy, but unlike Duffy, his character is not obviously pathological. Yet he is clearly limited, at once an ironist and an object of irony. Thus his dialogical intervention in the story is both crucial and ambiguous. His "reading" of himself is at different times both more generous and more critical than any reading we are likely to give him.

One clear reason for the story's hybrid technique is thematic: "The

Dead" is the only story of "public life" that deals equally with a character's intimate, personal life. Gabriel's confrontation with Gretta reflects upon and in turn is problematized by his experience of the party. Further, there is an apparent split in Gabriel's consciousness throughout the story that is embodied in the two distinct kinds of language in which his inner monologue is represented, just as there is a split between his immediate concerns during the evening—worry about his speech, annoyance at Miss Ivors, and so forth—and some unspoken, unrealized source of tension. It is tempting to suppose that his public concerns are conscious, his private ones less conscious, but the dialogical interplay between the two categories negates any such simple solution. There are many indications that Gabriel is under unusual tension in the course of the evening: he laughs nervously (D, 180), has sudden fits of unexplained anger (D, 181), irritation (D, 186), and despair (D, 179), each time without any obviously sufficent motivation. Twice the narration focuses on Gabriel's trembling fingers; both times this is followed immediately by an impulsive and unusual movement of his mind outward to the snowy landscape, as if in the frantic desire for escape:

> Gabriel's warm trembling fingers tapped the cold pane of the window. How cool it must be outside! How pleasant it would be to walk out alone, first along by the river and then through the park! The snow would be lying on the branches of the trees and forming a bright cap on the top of the Wellington Monument. (D, 192)

> Gabriel leaned his ten trembling fingers on the tablecloth and smiled nervously at the company. Meeting a row of upturned faces he raised his eyes to the chandelier. . . . People, perhaps, were standing in the snow on the quay outside, gazing up at the lighted windows. . . . The air was pure there. In the distance lay the park where the trees were weighted with snow. The Wellington Monument wore a gleaming cap of snow that flashed westward over the white field of Fifteen Acres. (D, 202)

Both passages are distinct in tone, syntax, vocabulary, and imagery from the ordinary course of his ruminations during the evening, and both of course anticipate his final, even more lyrical meditation upon the snow, brought on by "a few light taps upon the pane" (D, 223).[39]

"The Dead" progresses by means of a dual movement. On the one hand Gabriel's experience is shaped by the series of outwardly manifest dialogical encounters with others, culminating in his dialogue with his wife; on the other, his perceptions are increasingly dominated by an internal dialogue between his everyday inner monologue and the disturbing, unwonted inner voice that calls him lyrically to the outdoors, to the snow, to the west, and to the dead. The implied metaphor for his experience of this second inner voice is *possession*, with all of the Jamesian ghostly associations that implies: "Other forms were near. His soul had approached that region where dwell the vast hosts of the dead. He was conscious of, but could not apprehend, their wayward and flickering existence. His own identity was fading out into a grey impalpable world: the solid world itself which these dead had one time reared and lived in was dissolving and dwindling" (*D*, 223). This rather sinister "inner dialogism" certainly corresponds to his conscious experience in some respects—after all, it is Gretta's story about Michael Furey that provokes this last meditation—but in other respects it is spookily unmotivated. Gabriel is preoccupied with the cap of snow flashing westward long before he has heard of the dead young man. He wishes to escape the party long before anything unpleasant has occurred. The fatidic tone established by these apparently unmotivated impulses culminates in the mythic expansion of Gabriel's consciousness at the story's end, as he muses, "The time had come for him to set out on his journey westward," and "Yes, the newspapers were right: snow was general all over Ireland" (*D*, 223). The first statement suggests that a journey, ritual or final, has been assigned him, and he has just gained knowledge of that fact; the second implies that his vision has so broadened that he is able to verify the newspapers' account of an extremely unusual meteorological event through some absolute visionary awareness.

The inner dialogue between Gabriel and the ghosts is curiously balanced by the outer dialogues that make up much of the story's substance and establish its "psychological" themes. Surprisingly, few critics have noted that Gabriel's significant encounters in the story are all with women, especially the three encounters with Lily, Molly Ivors, and Gretta. Edward Brandabur does note this fact, but only in order to characterize the women as "distracted," with "corrosive sensitivities" that lay bare Gabriel's essentially sadomasochistic sexual orientation.[40] The encounters with the women are crucial, not because Lily, Molly, and Gretta are abrasive or aggressive toward Gabriel but because all three refuse the conversational role he wishes to thrust upon them. Their refusals, however, are remarkably gentle, considering the provocation in each case. Lily's famous retort to Gabriel's jocular and patronizing question about marriage is, "The men that is now is all palaver and what they can get out of you" (D, 178). Although Gabriel seems to take it as a direct insult, this reply in fact carefully excludes men of his generation from her cynical evaluation. Miss Ivors is flirtatiously gentle in pointing out what would be obvious to any politically engaged person of the time, that writing for an antinationalist newspaper has political implications. Even Gabriel realizes that he cannot get away with saying that literature is above politics, because she is his intellectual equal and will not be taken in by "a grandiose phrase." When Gabriel remains "perplexed"—by what is not clear—she reassures him, "Of course, I was only joking" (D, 188). She has merely called attention to an embarrassing professional oversight of Gabriel's, the way Mr. Brown discreetly calls attention to Freddy Malins's unbuttoned fly.

Similarly, Gretta's response to his advances is, considering her own state of stress and romantic nostalgia, a model of tact. When, typically evading the subject he wishes to broach, he tells her of his loan to Malins, she wrenches herself from self-preoccupation, kisses him, and tells him he is a "generous person" (D, 217). Unable to escape from his own self-preoccupation in turn, Gabriel assumes that her kindness is erotic—that, in his embarrassing phrase, "she had fallen to him." He begins a sort of stilted verbal foreplay by asking what she is thinking about, and insisting, "Tell me what it is, Gretta. I think I know what is the matter. Do I know?" (D, 218). Gretta meets this puerile erotic gambit by telling him what she is thinking about—a gesture of genuine intimacy to which he reacts with astonishment and then anger. The remainder of his questions are asked with a defensive irony intended to point out the silliness or sordidness of Gretta's youthful experience, a ploy which Gretta defeats by means of her simple, literal answers, until her husband is "humiliated by the failure of his irony" (D, 219). The two are speaking different languages, and Gretta's is the more powerful.

One source of that power, of course, is her direct, literal answers that fail to recognize or respond to Gabriel's sophisticated irony, much as Bloom defangs Stephen's epigrams in "Eumaeus" by failing to understand them. Another source of power in Gretta's speech is its rootedness in the folk speech of Galway, the language of her girlhood, which she has not spoken previously during the evening. Donald Torchiana has sensitively analyzed Gretta's use of the "local but formal and general language and gestures of Galway," pointing out the poetic force of locutions like "I used to go out walking with him" and "I was great with him at that time."[41] Gretta here speaks like a character out of Synge, but without the rather self-conscious stylization Synge often imposed; when her language is compared to Gabriel's coarse irony—or his flatulently platitudinous postprandial speech, for that matter—it is apparent that artist and philistine have exchanged roles. But in this dialogical interchange Gabriel is only halfheartedly his wife's conversational antagonist. Another voice continually mitigates the effect he intends, as when a "kinder note than he had intended went into his voice" (D, 218) or he "tried to keep up his tone of cold interrogation but his voice when he spoke was humble and indifferent" (D, 220) or even when a "strange friendly pity for her entered his soul" (D, 222). The second inner voice, the one associated with Furey and the ghosts, has begun to creep into his thought and his speech, causing him to pull his conversational punches. That that voice should be more "kind" and "humble" than his own is an irony far greater than any Gabriel can muster.

Gabriel's dialogical tactic with his wife is *interrogation*, a ploy which in theory should put the inquisitor in charge of the conversation; this fails because the language of her response is so much more powerful than the language of his questions, and because his own desires are conflicted. But he elects to interrogate Gretta in the first place because he still smarts from the confrontation with Miss Ivors, who, much to his surprise, interrogates *him*. Molly Ivors's dialogical authority, for which Gabriel is unprepared, is rooted in her ideological commitment—like that of Hynes in "Ivy Day"—and in the frank simplicity of her questions, which demand specific and coherent answers Gabriel is unwilling or unable to give:

—The fact is, said Gabriel, I have already arranged to go—
—Go where? asked Miss Ivors.
—Well, you know, every year I go for a cycling tour with some fellows and so—
—But where? asked Miss Ivors.
—Well, we usually go to France or Belgium or perhaps Germany, said Gabriel awkwardly.
—And why do you go to France and Belgium, said Miss Ivors, instead of visiting your own land? (D, 189)

Miss Ivors's language is overt polemic, whereas Gabriel is unable to reply, reluctant as he is to give voice to his vague and self-serving dissatisfactions.[42] As soon as he is able, he retreats to the company of Mrs. Malins, who will reward him with sufficiently inconsequential conversation.

Miss Ivors's speech is doubly disconcerting to Gabriel not merely because of its content but because of the dance of gesture that accompanies it. If he were confronted with a similar political discussion from someone like Hynes, but of his own social class, he would be far less distressed. But Miss Ivors is engaged in the ritualized courtship of the dance and uses a series of gestures like pressing his hand warmly and whispering into his ear (D, 190) at the same time that she advances her criticism. Gabriel, unable to reconcile her admiration for his review, her detestation for the political gesture of publishing it in *The Daily Express*, and her personal fondness for him, is left unable simply to reject her and her arguments—as he might well do were he approached coldly —or to enjoy her unalloyed admiration. His confusion is deepened when she leaves the party before dinner, but not because she is angry or distressed. The notion that she has an active and independent life of her own, and perhaps other conflicting social commitments as well, never crosses his mind. She departs the story, as Bonnie Kime Scott observes, unaccompanied, confident, and attractive.[43] "I'm quite well able to take care of myself," she says gaily (D, 195). Even Gabriel's erotic being is frustrated by this stance because his potency is a function of his partner's helplessness: when he feels attracted to his wife, "he longed to defend her against something and then to be alone with her" (D, 213). For him, Molly Ivors's advances are immediately cancelled by her competence.

The underlying fact of Gabriel's dialogical interchanges with Lily, Molly Ivors, and Gretta is that they speak *as women*, and here Bakhtin is unable to help; as Wayne Booth suggests, Bakhtin's failure to recognize a woman's voice produces an unexpected blind spot in his criticism.[44] Perhaps one barrier to the dialogical analysis of women's speech is that an understanding of it rests upon an analysis of women's *position* rather than upon verbal texture or rhetorical characteristics.[45] In "The Dead" virtually all of Gabriel's speech is addressed to women and is formed and delimited by that situation, by the ideological positioning of male versus female in turn-of-the-century Dublin's bourgeois circles. Such interchanges are highly ritualized, and in fact it is the departure of

Lily, Molly Ivors, and even Gretta from the conversational format Gabriel expects in each case that so disturbs him. And when we attempt to characterize Gabriel's expectation of the dialogical position of women, an unsurprising answer emerges: the woman should be silent or at least provide perfect counterpoint to his own inner monologue. Lily should blush and giggle at his comment about matrimony; Miss Ivors should praise his review without having guessed that he is its author; and as for Gretta, he elaborates an entire scenario:

> When the others had gone away, when he and she were in their
> room in the hotel, then they would be alone together. He would
> call her softly:
> —Gretta!
> Perhaps she would not hear at once: she would be undressing.
> Then something in his voice would strike her. She would turn and
> look at him. . . . (D, 214)

The rest, in Gabriel's scenario, is silence. Once they have arrived at the hotel he goes to considerable trouble to arrange the proper lighting for his seduction of Gretta. Like a stage-manager he has the porter remove the candle and then stands in a position of dramatic dominance with his back to the light from the street, watching her for a beat as she undresses, and then calling her name (D, 216).

Gabriel's imagination is highly theatrical, and despite his claims to literary sophistication, it is theatricality of a low order. His desire revolves about the *tableau*, that staple of nineteenth-century popular entertainment.[46] In this he is a typical product of his age, whose tastes ran to the emblematic illustration, laden with melodramatic and moral implication; the pictures in his aunts' house of the balcony scene from *Romeo and Juliet* and of the two murdered princes in the tower are obvious examples of this, as—in a different mode—is the photograph of Gabriel's mother with an open book, pointing out something to Constantine, who lies at her feet (D, 186).[47] But the most prominent tableau in the story, the one which stirs his desire, is his sight of Gretta listening to "The Lass of Aughrim." "A woman was standing near the top of the first flight, in the shadow also. He could not see her face. . . . It was his wife. She was leaning on the bannisters, listening to something. . . . He asked himself what is a woman standing on the stairs in the shadow, listening to distant music, a symbol of. If he were a painter he would paint her in that attitude. . . . *Distant Music* he would call the picture if he were a painter" (D, 209–10). Gabriel's inner monologue, with the awkward "a symbol of" and the childish repetition of "if he were a painter," has a comic dimension of which he is unaware. If he were a painter, Gabriel would paint the way a third-rate Tennyson imitator would write. This is, in fact, the way he wrote in a loveletter to Gretta: "Why is it that words like these seem to me so dull and cold? Is it because there is no word tender enough to be your name?" It would be unfair to judge Gabriel's aesthetic abilities from an early love letter, were it not for the fact that it is precisely "like distant music" that these words of his "were borne towards him from the past" (D, 214). Gabriel's erotic inspiration this evening is an amalgam of his own self-consciously literary words of seduction and the image of his wife, objectified, aestheticized, and entitled by him in a *tableau vivant*. Gabriel's language here displaces Gretta in her own complexity, just as his title for the painting into which he makes her points toward the painting's significance in a gesture of total hegemony.

At least since de Beauvoir, feminist criticism has emphasized the objectification of women as Woman, and in recent years has added a stress on the repression of women through the language of the patriarchy. Derrida's association between "phallocentrism" and "logocentrism" has obvious relevance to the role Gabriel attempts to play in "The Dead." But perhaps the most suggestive recent formulation of woman's position is that of Lacan, who argues that "The Woman" does not exist, in that "phallic sexuality assigns her a position of fantasy."[48] Woman is sought by men to fill the lack or absence that they experience as a concomitant of consciousness. Further, Lacan teasingly argues that the "jouissance that goes beyond," the "jouissance of the body" that is associated with the place of women, is the domain sensed by mystics—the realm of the *supplementary*, which has often been interpreted theologically.[49] Lacan takes courtly love to be symptomatic of this set of relationships, a way in which man as speaking being attempts to take responsibility for the impossibility of erotic love. Given the theological resonance of "The Dead" to which so many commentators have attested, Lacan's formulation seems particularly relevant.[50]

Throughout the story Gabriel has been in a universe of women. The party is presided over by three women whom he attempts to characterize as the "Three Graces," so that he can play the role of Paris, judging (or refusing to judge) among them, but who equally suggest the three Fates or even a more famous Trinity—Julia as the Patriarch (Matriarch), Kate as the Spirit (the spirited woman who keeps the party going), and Mary Jane as Son (Daughter), sent to play for the company, lifting her hands like "a priestess in momentary imprecation" (D, 186). Music, of course, alternates with religion as an explicit topic of discussion, and within the party's cultural codes signifies "higher things," the realm of the spiritual. Gretta's tableau, a nineteenth-century topos, embodies that century's assumption that the woman's place is to heed the call of the spirit, often inaudible to man, and to lead him toward it; it is a degenerate version of woman's role as spiritual mediator in Neoplatonism or in the ideology of courtly love. In Lily, Molly Ivors, and Gretta, Gabriel encounters a second trinity, this one coded by the conventional typology of women as Virgin, Temptress, and Wife. Yet each escapes that categorization: Lily's comment suggests she may no longer be virginal, Miss Ivors's temptation is undercut by her political critique, and Gretta's story implies that in a romantic sense she belongs to another man.

From the beginning of the story, Gabriel has found himself more and more firmly situated in the woman's position. He is established as "old-womanish" in his fussy preoccupations with galoshes, green eyeshades for his son, and proper nourishment for his daughter (D, 180). He is at his aunts' beck and call, and—however ineffectually—acts for them, as their substitute and emissary. Each of his dialogical confrontations with women places him in the woman's position of passivity, inarticulateness, or dialogical defeat, and in the conversation with Gretta he becomes a spiritual cuckold as well, a castrato of the imagination. It is made clear to him that he has never really lived, never been a part of the male domain of passion and action in the world. Instead, Gretta has. It is she who has had the passionate, death-bound romance that to Gabriel's romantic sensibilities signifies true, transcendent love: he "had never felt like that himself towards any woman but he knew that such a feeling must be love" (D, 223). Meanwhile he has been "a pennyboy for his aunts, a nervous well-meaning sentimentalist, orating to vulgarians and idealising his own clownish lusts" (D, 220). Similarly, Miss Ivors is a part of the outside world of politics and adventure into which she vanishes, and even Lily has obviously had some bitter erotic involvement. And as the women in "The Dead" have played roles culturally coded as masculine, from the trinity of women overseeing everything to the young country girl with her painful worldly wisdom, Gabriel, in a kind of compensatory movement, moves farther toward the position of the woman.

The paradox of "The Dead"—that within a society in which women are disempowered there should arise an opposing imaginative scenario in which women are omnipotent—is wholly parallel to the original paradox of courtly love to which Lacan points in an analysis of the phenomen's historical rise: "Here, it is a matter of things which are all the more surprising to see arise, given that they arise in an era whose historical coordinates show us that contrary to expectation, nothing seemed—indeed, far from it—to respond to what one might call an advancement, much less a liberation of women. . . . Nonetheless, these ideals, in the foreground of which stands the ideal of the Lady as such . . . are those which turn up again in subsequent eras, even in our own, and witness their impact borne out concretely in the way in which contemporary man lends organization to feeling."[51] There is of course an element of what conventional psychology would term masochism in the courtly love scenario, especially in the version presented in Michael and Gretta. Gabriel, whose erotic consummation with his wife is withheld by her reminiscences and by his new vision of her as a different sort of being, joins Michael in his distant, courtly worship and moves toward death in emulation of the young man. But Michael is, after all, Gretta's creation, and in doing this Gabriel places himself within the domain of her imagination, becomes her creature.

Gabriel's final "epiphany" is in fact an act of self-abasement, an extremity of *Schadenfreude* that enables him to identify with his wife, to take her position, and simultaneously to join the hosts of the dead. Vincent P. Pecora has argued convincingly that Gabriel's transcendent "realization" at the story's ending is in fact no escape from the stultifying cultural codes that surround him: "Gabriel in no way overcomes or transcends the conditions of his existence. Rather, he merely recapitulates them unconsciously in this self-pitying fantasy."[52] Certainly, as Pecora asserts, Gretta mythifies her relationship with Michel Furey and Gabriel assents willingly, even contributes to this mythification, but we can go further. What Gretta and Gabriel interpret as the *Liebestod* of Michael Furey is a quintessence of the courtly love relationship, a relationship Lacan assigns to the side of the Woman and associates with the theological domain. In appropriating Gretta's story, wrapping his inner monologue around it, Gabriel attempts to become woman. There is, of course, nothing essential about the woman's position to which he aspires: it is the product of dense, pathological cultural codes that prescribe for her immobility and passivity and in consolation yield her the transcendent domains of the spirit. But Gabriel's movement in "The Dead" is toward silence, passivity, death, and the position of the emblem or tableau. He embraces the ghosts and their insistent voices, which we may now read as the female voice within him that he has unsuccessfully repressed throughout the story. His embrace is entirely passive—"his soul swooned slowly" (D, 224)—as he drifts to sleep in a universe filled with the gentlest of deaths.

In the light of the foregoing discussion, it should not be surprising that the major intertextual interventions in "The Dead" point variously to male-female confusions, disguised and mistaken identities, and sexual ambivalences and frustrations. Bret Harte's *Gabriel Conroy* (1871), for instance, features a man who is all but completely passive during his own story. Huge and strong but shy, unlettered, and inarticulate, Gabriel Conroy first appears as one of a group of settlers trapped in the mountains by the snow of the opening paragraphs. His outstanding qualities are all conventionally coded as feminine:

> Added to his natural hopefulness, he had a sympathetic instinct with the pains and penalties of childhood, not so much a quality of his intellect as of his nature. He had all the physical adaptabilities of a nurse—a large, tender touch, a low persuasive voice, pliant yet unhesitating limbs, and broad, well-cushioned surfaces. During the weary journey women had unhesitatingly intrusted babies to his charge; most of the dead had died in his arms; all forms and conditions of helplessness had availed themselves of his easy capacity. No one thought of thanking him. I do not think he ever expected it; he always appeared morally irresponsible and quite unconscious of his own importance, and, as is frequent in such cases, there was a tendency to accept his services at his own valuation.[53]

In short, Gabriel is a wife, a man who is "gentle as a lamb" and "blushes like a girl."[54] Certainly he is an antiheroic figure in an adventure novel; the role of the conventional rogue-hero is played by the lover of his sister, and that man and a succession of villains and dubious women, most of whom plot against Gabriel, supply the novel's motive force. The elaborate plot is of little relevance here, except to note that

Gabriel is inevitably seen as either villainous or devious by both his enemies and uninformed observers when in fact he is simple and trusting, nearly saintly. His main goal is to trace and then care for his sister Grace, who escapes from the snowbound group with her lover and then, abandoned by him, assumes a false identity; he spends much of the book married to a woman who has falsely identified herself and who marries him for money she mistakenly believes he possesses. Near the book's end, she has been captivated by his goodness and loves him despite the fact that he has penetrated her disguise and now despises her. He and she at last are reconciled, and at the conclusion Gabriel, she, their baby, and Gabriel's second sister are living hapily together. At no point has Gabriel appeared as a sexual being, despite his size and strength; instead, he is a nurturer, far more concerned with his sisters Grace (Gretta?) and Olympia than with a mate. Grace, meanwhile, has spent most of the book as the beautiful, wealthy, and mysterious Dona Dolores, a masterful figure who toys with her lover with Spanish passion, secure in the knowledge that he cannot recognize the Grace Conroy he once betrayed.

If Harte's novel provides a suggestive intertext for Joyce's story, so do the three operas invoked by Mary Jane and Mr. Browne during dinner, *Mignon*, *Dinorah*, and *Lucrezia Borgia*. *Mignon*, by Ambroise Thomas, is based on Goethe's *Wilhelm Meister*, *Dinorah* is by Meyerbeer, and Donizetti's *Lucrezia Borgia* is based on Hugo's novel. Like *Gabriel Conroy*, *Mignon* features a couple in which the woman is disguised and the man to whom she is passionately attached fails to reciprocate or even recognize her feelings. In the opera, Mignon has been stolen by gypsies from a noble home and is rescued by Guglielmo from mistreatment at their hands. Meanwhile, her father Lotario is madly wandering as a minstrel in search of his daughter; without recognizing her, he saves Mignon as she is about to commit suicide because of her unrequited love for her protector. *Dinorah* has certain similarities to *Mignon*, in that the female lead spends much of her time in a state near madness, unrecognized by her lover; she is taken for the mad girl of the mountains, and only when she appears to be dead does Hoël recognize his fiancée. In *Lucrezia Borgia* the unrecognition and unrequited passion are compounded and made ambiguous; there, Lucrezia Borgia is irresistibly compelled to follow a young man whom she believes to be her son by a previous husband, abandoned as a child. Her passionate avowals and distracted air convince her husband and the boy's friends—and might well convince the audience, considering her rhetoric—that her feelings are amorous rather than maternal. Because of the young man's failure to recognize his mother and the scorn he wants to show for her notorious family, he is poisoned inadvertently by Lucrezia, who also dies.

All three intertexts turn upon the figure of the passionate, unrecognized woman whose love is not reciprocated; in all three death threatens as a result of the young man's failure to recognize the woman and her passion. Madness wanders through all of the texts, and there is a certain confusion or conflation between fathers and lovers, lovers and sons: they play parallel or complementary roles or—like Borgia's son—play both. Naturally, there is also an abundance of passionate triangles: in *Lucrezia Borgia* Gennaro scorns his mother and pays court to the Princess Negroni, while in *Mignon* Guglielmo is captivated by the young actress Filina while Mignon pines after him. The underlying romantic ideologies affirm either fatal love, allied to madness and to death, or fatal love that at the last moment is transformed into something less lethal in a bourgeois gesture of social affirmation.

Set against "The Dead," the parallels and ironies of these operas proliferate. Gretta cannot reciprocate Michael's fatal passion, except after his death, at which point it keeps her from responding passionately to Gabriel: this reverses the operas' characteristic structure of desire. But when Gabriel is seen in his female role, the structure is affirmed. The ambiguities surrounding fathers, mother, and lovers are echoed faintly in Joyce's story by the suggestions that Michael is a sort of son to Gretta, just as Gabriel is a sort of father. Michael, committing slow suicide in the rain, is the marker of madness in "The Dead," and so holds a position of privilege that all the operas associate with recognition scenes, fulfillment, or death. But while these implications all deepen Joyce's text, the main force of the operatic intertexts, like that of Harte's novel, is to suggest that there is a fundamental sexual reversal in "The Dead"; once Gabriel learns to speak as Woman, the intertextual tensions are resolved, though perhaps at the price of "the descent of their last end, upon all the living and the dead" (*D*, 224).

A DIALOGICAL PORTRAIT

Dialogical Variations

To move from *Dubliners* to *A Portrait of the Artist as a Young Man* is to move from narration in which at most two or three narrative voices interact dialogically with protagonists' voices to a narration that is radically destabilized, both dependent upon the protagonist's voice and unable to be identified with it. Where in *Dubliners* the narration responded preeminently to the protagonist's voice, only infrequently allowing subsidiary characters to affect its tonality, in *Portrait* many subsidiary characters from Uncle Charles to Cranly enter into dialogical relationship with the narrative; each has a discrete zone of dialogical influence. In addition, larger group-languages exert a tidal influence upon the narration of *Portrait*: the language of Clongowes schoolboys in chapter 1 is a minor example, the language of the Irish Catholic church in chapter 3 a major one. Whereas in *Dubliners* the usual relationship of a young protagonist to the dominant discourses of his culture is antagonistic, Stephen Dedalus moves from an attempt to assimilate and adapt to surrounding languages in the opening chapters to a programmatic opposition to them in the final one—an opposition that itself is culturally coded, descending from the conscious opposition of virtually every major artist in nineteenth-century France to bourgeois or Philistine culture.[1]

But in a sense all of these linguistic interactions belong to the realm of speech genres; they are dependent on living conventions of speech, not upon texts. In *Portrait* we also see in Stephen's inner monologue a depth and complexity of intertextual dialogism that exceeds anything to be found in *Dubliners*. Like the boys of the first three stories, like Mr.

Duffy and Gabriel Conroy, and, to a lesser extent, like Chandler, Stephen is a reader; but it is arguable that his reading permeates his consciousness more deeply than is the case with any of those. Language is thematized to such an extent in *Portrait* that any text with which Stephen comes in contact, whether or not it is specified in the narrative, leaves a narrative mark. The classic "school stories" like *Tom Brown's School-Days* and *Eric, or Little by Little* are ghost narratives framing, shaping, and counterpointing the opening chapters of *Portrait*, while the school play *Vice-Versa* and the classic romance *The Count of Monte Cristo* lend their fantastic coherence to the pattern of Stephen's experience. Indeed, nineteenth-century bourgeois romance in its infinite avatars, from the adolescent fantasy of *A Modern Daedalus* to the slick dramas *Ingomar the Barbarian* and *The Lady of Lyons*, furnishes an ambiguous countertext to the novel as a whole; Stephen both realizes the degree to which its basic movements and patterns are elements of the philistine culture around him and at the same time depends upon them for psychological sustenance. After all, the very stance of opposition to which he inevitably comes as an intellectual and an aspiring artist in the late nineteenth century is so heavily coded by the texts of bourgeois romance that it would be all but impossible to imagine a site of opposition that did not participate in that ideology. In the same way, it is impossible for him to imagine that from the privileged position of exile to which he aspires—a position "outside" his culture—he should not then be enabled to reinsert himself into that culture with all the omnipotent energy of the Count of Monte Cristo in order to forge "the uncreated conscience of my race" (*P*, 253).

The texts of Stephen's youth are unusually powerful presences in his consciousness and persist in their dialogical effects long after his initial encounters with them. But by the time he has entered Belvedere College and University College Dublin, Stephen is more concerned with the "subversive" serious authors he has discovered. Shelley, Ibsen, Yeats, d'Annunzio, and the like are of course powerful dialogical influences, and the intervention of their texts in his thought is not difficult to trace. Similarly, the effects of the boy's prescribed curriculum are pervasive in his speech and thought; after all, Stephen is a consciously allusive speaker whose basic intellectual tactic is to harness the words of authorities like Aquinas or Aristotle to his own radical formulations. But for Stephen explicitly to cite a writer he must belong to one of three classes: those who are recognized classical authorities; those who are evocatively obscure, and thus can be presented as Stephen's own intellectual property (such as Galvani, Bruno, or Mangan); and those who are important embattled contemporaries, preferably ones who have not yet been discovered by Stephen's fellow students. Yet when Stephen's discussion of socio-literary questions is set in the context of its time, it becomes evident that his voice echoes and responds to specific voices in the popular intellectual debate whom he does not specifically acknowledge. Perhaps the most important of these voices is Havelock Ellis's in *The New Spirit*, a book in Joyce's library that echoes many of the concerns and much of the language of Stephen in both *Portrait* and *Stephen Hero*. Ellis's book also has clear relevance to Joyce's nonfictional writing of the time, especially his discussions of Ibsen.

Of course, dialogical interaction with other texts is not the prerogative only of protagonists, but is inescapable for the authorial voice as well. Indeed, with a writer as autobiographical as Joyce, such a distinction is often difficult to draw. And even ignoring the autobiographical element, in a book as dependent upon the protagonist's consciousness as is *Portrait* we find it difficult to ascribe the "shape" of a chapter or an episode either to the impress of Stephen's consciousness in the organization that he imparts to his experience, on the one hand, or to the aesthetic intention of Joyce, on the other. The adolescent Stephen is roughly as well-read as the Joyce who creates him, and the general argument of the present chapter is that *Portrait* should be read as a rather literal record of Stephen's inner speech. Nonetheless, there are areas, such as those involving the structure of the entire book, in which it is not practical to ascribe a primary role to the protagonist, whose mind, language, and sense of structure are in continual change. *Portrait* participates in a multiplicity of genres—*Bildungsroman*, *Künstlerroman*, heroic romance, Victorian novel incorporating classical mythic parallels, Victorian/Edwardian novel of the rebellion of Youth, Irish novel of departure, Catholic novel of apostasy, naturalistic novel of urban poverty, to name several—and each generic identification carries with it a multitude of intertexts of greater or lesser resonance.

In the present chapter, two novels by the American author James Lane Allen and one by Edouard Dujardin are discussed, all three of which treat the development of a "sensitive" youth with particular attention to sexuality and religion, and all three of which Joyce read with some attention. Two of the novels discussed in the following chapter, Filson Young's *The Sands of Pleasure* and Marcelle Tinayre's *The House of Sin*, might also usefully be studied in the same context. This is not to imply that any of these books is a more significant influence upon *Portrait* than, say, *A Sentimental Education* or *The Way of All Flesh*.[2] Rather it is to show, as William Veeder has in the case of Henry James, that even as ground-breaking a work as *Portrait* is indebted to a greater extent than has been recognized to the normative conventions of popular literature even in its style, imagery, and structure.[3] The books by Allen and Dujardin may be taken as metonyms for entire subgenres of novels turning about many of the basic concerns of *Portrait*, concerns that are rooted in the imaginative discourse of that period and cannot be separated from their historical moment without penalty.

Dialogism and Incremental Repetition

Bakhtin has remarked that "language, for the individual consciousness, lies on the border between oneself and the other. The word . . . becomes 'one's own' only when the speaker populates it with his own intention, his own accent, when he appropriates the word, adapting it to his own semantic and expressive intention" (*DI*, xxix). Much of *Portrait* reflects—or embodies—Stephen's possession by the languages that surround him, and his attempts to appropriate them in turn. First, in remarkably explicit terms, each of the phases of Stephen's life appears—to him and to the reader—as a language. Near the end of his stay at Belvedere, he feels "regret and pity as though he were slowly passing out of an accustomed world and were hearing its language for the last time" (*P*, 156). His harrowing experience at the Christmas dinner is at root a battle between two highly developed rhetorics, the nationalist and the Irish Roman Catholic, in each of which he has some investment. Dante proclaims that he will remember when he grows up "the language he heard against God and religion and priests in his own home," while Mr. Casey cries, "Let him remember . . . the language with which the priests and the priests' pawns broke Parnell's heart" (*P*, 33–34). Stephen, like the modern novel itself, is a product of heteroglossia. There is no language in which he is "at home." English, the language of the dean of studies and of Stephen himself, is alien; Stephen thinks, "His language, so familiar and so foreign, will always be for me an acquired speech. I have not made or accepted its words" (*P*, 189).

Yet the novel is permeated with the nostalgic sense of a lost linguistic innocence, a time when language was natural, without its burden of alterity. The opening of *Portrait*, the voice of the Father, is also the opening of narrative possibility: "Once upon a time and a very good time it was" (*P*, 7). The time is what Bakhtin terms the "absolute past" (*DI*, 34), the infinitely distant time of earliest narrative. There is no separation between this narrative event and Stephen himself: "He was baby tuckoo." Yet, as soon as this relationship is posited, it collapses; the "wild rose blossoms" song is deformed through lisping and transposition in Stephen's mouth to emerge as a "new song" that is "his song." From this point on there can be no unmediated, purely received language for the boy; indeed, the narrative patterns that had been so easily committed to memory in the child's infancy—his perfect past—take on a life of their own. The "Pull out his eyes, / Apologise" rhyme, which, eerily, seems to be narrated by no one at all, serves as metonym for alien language. Hiding under the table is no protection; as Kenner has pointed out, the chiasmic structure of the rhyme will be echoed throughout the remainder of the book, and becomes one of the most easily identifiable patterns of Stephen's thought.[4]

At each significant stage in the development of Stephen's consciousness, he undergoes a period of painful sensitivity to "raw" language, language that seems in some respects to lack denotation. In structuralist terms, he is confronted by the signifier in the absence of the signified. In the first chapter, he dwells upon his own name and God's name (which seem to "mean" nothing) (*P*, 16), the self-describing word "suck" (*P*, 11), the ambiguous word "belt" (*P*, 9), the deceptive word "heartburn" (*P*, 11), and even the sounds that are almost-words, like the "little song of the gas" (*P*, 14). On the trip to Cork, the word "Foetus" triggers a series of vague realizations that seem to have no rational connection with the word's reference, and he is driven to mindless narration: "I am Stephen Dedalus. I am walking beside my father whose name is Simon Dedalus. We are in Cork, in Ireland. Cork is a city. Our room is in the Victoria Hotel. Victoria and Stephen and Simon. Simon and Stephen and Victoria. Names" (*P*, 92).

Throughout, names, with their purely ostensive quality, rush in to fill the empty spaces in his thought. When he attempts to write a poem for

Parnell, the names of his Clongowes classmates appear beneath his pen (*P*, 70). During the retreat, Stephen begins to fear that he is a mere beast, and "a faint glimmer of fear began to pierce the fog of his mind. . . . The letters of the name of Dublin lay heavily upon his mind, pushing one another surlily hither and thither with slow boorish insistence" (*P*, 111). Yet there is a reassurance in the very alienness of these words over which he has no power, a reassurance like that offered by the embrace of patriarchal language, which is simply there, given and unmediated. After his performance in the Whitsuntide play, in a state of agitation and unable to face his family, he can only calm his heart by staring at "the word *Lotts* on the wall of the lane (*P*, 86). And words that are not names can be made to relinquish their denotations, to become "empty," and thus no longer a threat. Stephen awakens from sleep on the train to Cork filled with vague fear: "His prayer . . . ended in a trail of foolish words which he made to fit the insistent rhythm of the train; and silently . . . the telegraphpoles held the galloping notes of the music between punctual bars. This furious music allayed his dread and, leaning against the windowledge, he let his eyelids close again" (*P*, 87).

During his self-consciously aesthetic phase, Stephen begins to learn to allow a dialogue between the alien language that surrounds him and his own generative power, so that the menacing quality of words is first converted to a reassuring empty neutrality, and then to "creative" possibility in the form of a literal heteroglossia and an abandonment to language: "He found himself glancing from one casual word to another on his right or left in stolid wonder that they had been so silently emptied of instantaneous sense until every mean shop legend bound his mind like the words of a spell . . . as he walked on in a lane among heaps of dead language. His own consciousness of language was ebbing from his brain and trickling into the very words themselves which set to band and disband themselves in wayward rhythms. . . . The word now shone in his brain, clearer and brighter than any ivory sawn from the mottled tusks of elephants. *Ivory, ivoire, avorio, ebur*" (*P*, 178–79).

Stephen is at least partially aware of his relationship with *disembodied* forms of language, language without context, *parole* magically divorced from *langue*. He is much less conscious of his assimilation of embodied forms, languages that approach the sequentiality of narrative. Yet these are clearly signalled in the text of the novel, first by the multitude of sentences and phrases that we must enclose in Bakhtin's "intonational quotation marks" (*DI*, 76) and then by Joyce's striking use of incremental repetition in the narration of *Portrait*. Both of these effects are most prevalent in the first chapter, during the critical period when Stephen is exposed to the varieties of public language of his schoolfellows and masters, and both are embedded in the *style indirect libre* through which we experience much of Stephen's life.[5]

The intonational quotation marks make their appearance almost immediately in the second section of the first chapter. Stephen is brooding over new and strange expressions—those that are not "nice," those that have the odd authority of schoolboy jargon, those that have the ring of the adult language-world of moral imperatives, or those that unmistakably smack of mysterious taboos:

> Rody Kickham was not like that: *he would be captain of the third line* all the fellows said.
>
> Rody Kickham was *a decent fellow* but Nasty Roche was *a stink*.
>
> And his father had told him if he wanted anything to write home to him and, whatever he did, *never to peach on a fellow*. (*P*, 8–9)
>
> Was it true about the black dog that walked there at night *with eyes as big as carriagelamps*? (*P*, 19)
>
> What did that mean about *the smugging in the square*? (*P*, 42)

The boy tries the strange phrases in his mind, repeating them over and over, placing them within changing contexts, conjugating them as he would his Latin verbs: "Was that a sin for Father Arnall *to be in a wax* or was he allowed *to get into a wax* when the boys were idle because that made them study better or was he only letting on *to be in a wax*?" (*P*, 48).

For long stretches, during this phase of his development, Stephen's thoughts simply are not his own. His mind buzzes with borrowed expressions, languages that he tries on like suits of clothing; but unlike his gray-belted suit he cannot discard them at will. Just as with the words emptied of meaning, there is a certain reassurance in repeating word sequences he has learned; ironically, in his illness he enjoys repeating "Canker is a disease of plants / Cancer one of animals" (*P*, 21). But even when the words are ostensibly his own, Stephen characteristically *recites* them, rehearsing these miniature narratives in a form that he later repeats, with minor variations. While pretending to play football, he thinks,

> That was mean of Wells to shoulder him into the square ditch because he would not swop his little snuffbox for Wells's seasoned hacking chestnut, the conquerer of forty. How cold and slimy the water had been! A fellow had once seen a big rat jump into the scum. (*P*, 10)

Soon after, in the playroom, he is taunted by Wells, and thinks:

> It was Wells who had shouldered him into the square ditch the day before because he would not swop his little snuffbox for Wells's seasoned hacking chestnut, the conquerer of forty. It was a mean thing to do; all the fellows said it was. And how cold and slimy the water had been! And a fellow had once seen a big rat jump plop into the scum. (*P*, 14)

Here not only can we hear the echo of the schoolboy phrases describing the items to be exchanged—almost kennings in their ritual, formulaic quality—but we can also witness the development of a narrative Stephen prepares *as if* to tell his classmates. The second, somewhat more sophisticated version, has the advantages of an appeal to consensus and a "literary" touch ("plop").

Caryl Emerson has pointed out that in Bakhtin's model the individual "forms lateral ('horizontal') relationships with other individuals in specific speech acts, and he simultaneously forms internal ('vertical') relationships between the outer world and his own psyche. These double activities are constant, and their interactions in fact *constitute* the psyche."[6] As Joyce's narrative presents the processs of Stephen's consciousness, the formation of "vertical" relationships is suggested by the boy's mulling upon the universe of "given" words and phrases. The formation of "horizontal" or interpersonal relationships is mirrored not simply in the passages of dialogue—where, in fact, Stephen does his best to perform uninterrupted monologues—but in repeated meditations such as the passage on Wells. The potentially public context of this narrative fragment should not mislead us; Stephen's mind works in much the same way when he has no intention of presenting his thoughts to an audience.

For instance, his Christmas Dinner meditation on Eileen recurs, hardly altered, on his return to Clongowes, triggered by the thought of Tusker Boyle's fingernails.

> Eileen had long white hands. One evening when playing tig she had put her hands over his eyes: long and white and thin and cold and soft. That was ivory: a cold white thing. That was the meaning of *Tower of Ivory*. (P, 36)

> Eileen had long thin cool white hands too because she was a girl. They were like ivory; only soft. That was the meaning of *Tower of Ivory* but protestants could not understand it and made fun of it. (P, 42)

Repetition lulls Stephen, like any child; he identifies the smell of the peasants in the back of the chapel as "air and rain and turf and corduroy," and then immediately afterwards imagines himself in their cottage breathing "the smell of peasants, air and rain and turf and corduroy" (P, 18). Sometimes, indeed, the thought of repetition itself evinces a formal repetition. In the refectory,

> He leaned his elbows on the table and shut and opened the flaps of his ears. Then he heard the noise of the refectory every time he opened the flaps of his ears. It made a roar like a train at night. And when he closed the flaps the roar was shut off like a train going into a tunnel. . . . He closed his ears and the train went on, roaring and then stopping; roaring again, stopping. (P, 13)

Shortly afterward, in the study hall, he thinks of the alternation of term and vacation:

> It was like a train going in and out of tunnels and that was like the noise of the boys eating in the refectory when you opened and closed the flaps of the ears. Term, vacation; tunnel, out; noise, stop. (P, 17)

Several things are going on simultaneously in such passages. Certainly we are being shown the young verbal artist, forming and treasuring his phrases before he is aware he is doing so, just as later, in a moment of stress or exaltation, he will draw forth "a phrase from his treasure" (P, 166). We are also being played upon by Joyce's most characteristic rhetorical turn, lyrical repetition.[7] But most importantly we are being shown a mind whose mode of conscious perception is in a radical sense *narrative*. Stephen not only thinks, but perceives in phrases and sentences. His consciousness, we might say, is "narratized."[8]

But the most arresting examples of incremental repetition are not, strictly speaking, repetitions for which Stephen is directly responsible at all, in that they are embedded in sections of the narrative that only obliquely represent his train of thought. The relationship between narrator and protagonist has been a crux of Joyce criticism for years; for the present argument it is probably most important to realize that although the narration eschews overt retrospection, moving through time with Stephen and altering its language as his consciousness grows more sophisticated—most obviously in the movement from paratactic to hypotactic structures between the first and second chapters—nonetheless, at least until the final section of the book, where Stephen himself "narrates" through his diary, the narration is always in advance of Stephen.[9] Perhaps this enveloping narration can best be imagined as a more articulate, more sophisticated version of the narrative he is constantly creating about himself. Yet despite its relative sophistication, it is more closely linked with the verbal structures of Stephen's mind than is the case in any earlier *Bildungsroman*. For Joyce as for Bakhtin, consciousness itself is all but identified with language, and both consciousness and language develop through interactive processes. "Consciousness becomes consciousness only once it has been filled with ideological (semiotic) content, consequently, only in the process of social interaction," and language is "the semiotic material of inner life—of consciousness (inner speech)" (*MPL*, 11, 14).

Yet it is the very literal way in which Joyce's text shows language to be the material of Stephen's inner life that is responsible for the difficulty in ascertaining the epistemological status of the book's narration. This problem is most acute in the early sections of the novel. The opening paragraph of the Clongowes section, which moves from a description of the playground to Stephen's thoughts about himself and Rody Kickham, is a case in point: the sentences become smoothly and increasingly "internal." Midway through the paragraph, we read, "after every charge and thud of the footballers the greasy leather orb flew like a heavy bird through the grey light" (*P*, 8). Later, ill in bed, Stephen remembers himself "a long time ago then out on the playgrounds in the evening light, creeping from point to point on the fringe of his line, a heavy bird flying low through the grey light" (P, 22). Clearly, the language that had been ambiguously attached to the narration has by now become more intimately associated with Stephen, as in the second passage we are being given something close to a hallucinatory stream-of-consciousness. But is the bird image Stephen's? And if so, are we to assume he is conscious of this? It has undergone a transformation during the intervening time, so that now it seems to refer to the boy himself, the fledgling poet-albatross, rather than simply to the football.

This effect is still more evident in another repeated passage describing the sound of the cricket bats "through the soft grey air. They said: pick, pack, pock, puck: like drops of water in a fountain slowly falling in the brimming bowl" (P, 41). At the chapter's close, Stephen listens in the "soft grey silence," and hears "through the quiet air the sound of the cricket bats: pick, pack, pock, puck: like drops of water in a fountain falling softly in the brimming bowl" (P, 59). Again, where the first version of the passage might be taken as external narrative comment, in the second we are clearly signalled ("*he could hear* the bump of the balls . . . and . . . the sound of the cricket bats") that the words of the description are Stephen's. Unlike the passages of "schoolboy" language, we are given no implied source for the words; they simply "come to" Stephen, as if they had been "given" by the narrator. Yet what can this mean? The passage, in both versions, is a sort of "Edwardian novelese" (to use Kenner's term)[10] with echoes of Pater, Meredith, and, particularly, Swinburne; on the level of symbolism, the referents are only slightly more mysterious than those of the "heavy bird" passage. The drops of water suggest the passing seconds of experience, the bowl perhaps life itself; and the bowl is of course connected to the ciborium at the close of the third chapter and to the other containers and chalices throughout the book. At least since Joseph Frank's "Spatial Form in Modern Literature" we have learned to accept such language and imagery as part of the mosaic pattern of the book, as formal markers of Joyce's presiding aesthetic consciousness.[11] Yet to read the passages thus is a betrayal of the very language before us and of the phenomenological acuity of the novel. The words are Stephen's, only slightly less so than if he had spoken them aloud. If we must specify a source, it is the language of his own future consciousness, which is to be formed in part by the "subversive authors" (P, 78) from whom his verbal style will derive.

The text of *Portrait*, with all its stylized incremental repetition and all its virtuoso verbal effects, is nonetheless fundamentally bound to the narrative of Stephen's consciousness; it is to be read more mimetically than we are accustomed to reading it. The boy is learning a language, and the incremental repetition witnesses to that process. Within the context of the chapter, perhaps, we are tempted to regard it as Stephen's own language; but in the context of the book as a whole we may well doubt that such a characterization has much meaning. Neither Stephen nor Joyce (as "implied author") possesses a language purely his own here; as Bakhtin has noted with respect to *Eugene Onegin*, there is a mutual interpenetration of author's and protagonist's speech. "The hero is located in a zone of potential conversation with the author, in a zone of *dialogical contact*"; the author "dialogizes [the protagonist's language] from without" (*DI*, 45, 46).

Stephen is a product of his listening and reading, an irrational sum of the texts, written and spoken, to which he has been exposed. He is aware that his reading emerges, in distorted and syncretic form, in his writings, as when he admits that "all the leisure which his school life left him was passed in the company of subversive writers whose gibes and violence of speech set up a ferment in his brain before they passed out of it into his crude writings" (*P*, 78). He is much less aware that the very structure of his consciousness is dependent upon these texts, but it is significant that when he inadvertently alters a text he reacts with inordinate self-disgust. Misquoting a line of Nashe's can convince him that "his mind bred vermin" and his "thoughts were lice born of the sweat of sloth" (*P*, 234).

To a surprising extent, his relationship with the church is a linguistic affair; during the retreat sermon, the distinctions among the text of the sermon proper, Stephen's retrospective paraphrase of it, and his inner reflections become hopelessly blurred. His religious crisis thus appears a clear case of possession by liturgical language, which will require exorcism by the prostitutes. Even his temptation to join the priesthood seems, almost ludicrously, largely a matter of curiosity about definitions: "He would know then what was the sin of Simon Magus and what the sin against the Holy Ghost" (*P*, 159). We are reminded of the young boy's painful curiosity about the words around him, and his attempts to assume the languages he hears, just as "he had assumed the voices and gestures which he had noted with various priests" (*P*, 158). In a similar manner, but silently, he had narrated his imaginary reconciliation with

Emma in the voice of the Blessed Virgin, a voice drawn from the religious texts of his childhood: "Take hands, Stephen and Emma. It is a beautiful evening now in heaven. You have erred but you are always my children" (*P*, 116). At the opposite extreme of experience, Stephen is appalled to discover that his most heartfelt cry of bestial anguish is "but the echo of an obscene scrawl which he had read on the oozing wall of a urinal" (*P*, 100).

For Stephen, the distinction between text and voice is minimal, not only because he is hypersensitive to intonation and style in written language but also because public discourse in Ireland was then, as it is now, a highly "written" phenomenon; *phonè* and *graphie* interpenetrate. The speech he hears is unusually literary, not as regards context and content, but in its discrete stylization, its consciously idiosyncratic formulation, and its rich and precise allusiveness. Dismissing the Irish public leaders of today, in contrast to the great men of the past, Simon Dedalus says, "No, Stephen, old chap, I'm sorry to say that they are only as I roved out one fine May morning in the merry month of sweet July" (*P*, 97). Simon's use of language itself as metonym here is a characteristically sophisticated colloquial turn.

Throughout the book Stephen studies accents, vocabularies, intonation, and delivery much like an actor unsure which of an infinity of possible parts he will be called upon to play. Having heard his father imitate the "mincing nasal tone of the provincial" Father Conmee (*P*, 72), Stephen establishes a schoolboy reputation as mimic, assuming "the rector's pedantic bass. . . . *He that will not hear the churcha let him be to theea as the heathena and the publicana*" (*P*, 75–76). He imagines the "sleek lives of the patricians of Ireland" in Maple's Hotel who "gave orders to jarvies in highpitched provincial voices which pierced through their skintight accents" (*P*, 238). The "genteel accent, low and moist, marred by errors" of the old captain in the National Library suggests to him a noble lineage which has been diluted by incest (*P*, 228). He notes the "sharp Ulster voice" of MacAlister (*P*, 193) and the "hard jingling tone" of the dean of studies (*P*, 187); while his attitude toward his friends seems disturbingly determined by their speech habits. He is "won over to sympathy" by Davin's "simple accent" (*P*, 181). Lynch is favored for his habit of swearing in "yellow" and his detection of Cranly's pretentious solecism "let us eke go" (*P*, 204), while Cranly's usage of "sugar" as a vulgarism to denote dead friendships strikes Stephen as a "heavy lumpish phrase" and brings on a gloomy meditation on his companion's speech: "Cranly's speech, unlike that of Davin, had neither rare phrases of Elizabethan English nor quaintly turned versions of Irish idioms. Its drawl was an echo of the quays of Dublin given back by a decaying seaport, its energy an echo of the sacred eloquence of Dublin given back by a Wicklow pulpit" (P, 195). Stephen finds a certain derivative shoddiness in Cranly's voice before he becomes aware of his friend's limitations; he anticipates betrayal in Cranly's language before he detects a hint of it in his friend's actions and manner.

In an essay stressing the social dimension of Stephen's language-consciousness, James Naremore has pointed out that "Stephen's own rather prissy, formal way of speaking is, as he himself tells us, a carefully acquired habit, an attempt to disentangle himself from his environment and the 'nets' which have been flung at him."[12] But of course this attempt is foredoomed; Stephen has no choice but to select among the languages surrounding him, which speak through and within him regardless of his wishes. For all of his "objectifying" analysis of the social and literary languages surrounding him, all of his attempts to eschew "the language of the marketplace," Stephen eventually must become aware that his own language is a hybrid, that he is "spoken through" even in his private thoughts, in a sort of mental ventriloquy. He could hardly ignore this, since his entire formal education has been based upon the inculcation of "key passages" from a variety of sources; his accomplishment has been evaluated with an eye to his ready and graceful appropriation of such tags and passages in his own essays. As Don Gifford has noted, "Stephen's knowledge is based on a study of selected passages, key points or moments, presented in textbooks which advertised themselves as *Synopsis of the Philosophy of.* . . . As Stephen puts it to himself, he has 'only a garner of slender sentences.' The educational practice of focusing study on memorable key quotations provided the student with a package of quotable phrases and tended to suggest that thought was aphorism."[13]

That Stephen has a reputation for originality is not a reflection of any putative originality of discourse; rather, it is due to his ability to harness traditional authority to unusual contexts—as when he quotes Aquinas and the physiologist Luigi Galvani in support of a Pateresque aesthetic— and to call upon unusual or obscure sources such as Giordano Bruno. And this is true not only of Stephen's "public" performances within the book, but of the current of his thoughts as well. There it also becomes clear that Stephen's internal discourse is composed of a spectrum of popular languages as well as literary ones. In the two concluding chapters Stephen assumes a variety of voices and is sometimes disturbed to discover himself doing so. Annoyed by a fellow student's dully pragmatic question at a lecture, Stephen thinks that "the student's father would have done better had he sent his son to Belfast to study and have saved something on the train fare by so doing"; and then immediately he corrects himself. "That thought is not mine, he said to himself quickly. It came from the comic Irishman in the bench behind" (*P*, 193). As we immediately recognize, it came from Simon Dedalus, the comic Irishman whose language Stephen so reluctantly shares.

A complete acknowledgment of the extent to which his mind is an amalgam of preexisting texts would be difficult and painful for the young artist. He has a personal investment in the Romantic concept of self, an authentic and vital soul which, like God, creates *ex nihilo*. In his aesthetic, the artist's personality, purely expressed in the lyric, is passed into the narration itself in the epic, and finally refined out of existence in the dramatic form. But in *Portrait* the reverse is more nearly the case: an originally undifferentiated ego slowly takes on form and "selfhood," expressed as inner narrative, by way of a continuous series of dialogic encounters with and among the languages surrounding it, from which the solitary artist has always already vanished.

Stephen's Schooldays

In an early essay on Bakhtin, Julia Kristeva stresses that his thought leads inevitably to a concern with *intertextuality*:

> Writer as well as "scholar," Bakhtin was one of the first to replace the static hewing out of texts with a model where literary structure does not simply *exist* but is generated in relation to *another* structure. What allows a dynamic dimension to structuralism is his conception of the "literary word" as an *intersection of textual surfaces* rather than a *point* (a fixed meaning), as a dialogue among several writings: that of the writer, the addressee (or the character), and the contemporary or earlier cultural context. . . . By introducing the *status of the word* as a minimal structural unit, Bakhtin situates the text within history and society, which are then seen as

texts read by the writer, and into which he inserts himself by rewriting them. . . . The word's status is thus defined *horizontally*
(the word in the text belongs to both writing subject and addressee) as well as *vertically* (the word in the text is oriented toward an anterior or synchronic literary corpus.[14]

For Kristeva character, "addressee," and culture all are—or become accessible as—text, and all are involved in the continuing dialogue of the
novel. She attributes to Bakhtin the insight that "any text is constructed
as a mosaic of quotations; any text is the absorption and transformation
of another." Thus "the notion of *intertextuality* replaces that of inter-
subjectivity."[15] While this attempt to insert Bakhtin into a structural-
ist/poststructuralist context may do some violence to his model of dialogism, there is no doubt that his idea of the novel depends upon a
dynamic relationship among a multiplicity of voices, both written and
spoken, voices both "internal" and "external" to the text.

The preceding section explored dialogism in *Portrait* primarily in its
intratextual dimension; the following sections will be devoted to *intertextual* dialogism in the novel. It has been an assumption of modern
criticism at least since Eliot's "Tradition and the Individual Talent" that
literary texts necessarily enter into relationships with significant preceding texts, in the course of which both are altered; thus the relationship
of *Portrait* to important exemplars of the *Bildungsroman*, for example,
has been explored at length. Far less attention has been paid to the
immediate, popular context of *Portrait*, i.e., to the pseudo-literary and
subliterary works to which the novel alludes either explicitly or implic-
itly. Yet *Portrait* evokes a constellation of popular texts: schoolboy stories, to which Joyce's novel alludes formally; adolescent Irish heroic romances, which would be among the staples of Stephen's schoolmates'
reading; hugely influential romances like *The Count of Monte Cristo*,
which play an important role in the formation of Stephen's image; nineteenth-century bourgeois-romantic dramas, which Stephen attends; and
a group of novels in Joyce's library, each of which addresses the development of a sensitive young man in the context of a strong religious environment. None of these is of great significance in canonical literary history; but if there is a major thesis to Bakhtin's rewriting of the generic
canon, it is that the novel develops through unfastidious cross-fertiliza-
tion from obscure and popular genres.

Several critics have observed that the final section of the first chapter of *Portrait*, which recounts Stephen's unjust pandying and his protest and vindication, is told in the style of a schoolboy story.[16] Here, it is as if Stephen's tendency to "narrate himself" has taken on recognizable form by assuming the shape of a popular genre. The distinctive shape and intonation of the final section can be seen in clearer relief by comparing it to the earlier sections of the chapter. The short, enigmatic, and apparently disorganized first section functions as a thematic prelude, much like the beginning of the "Aeolus" episode in *Ulysses*; it is succeeded by the first Clongowes section, a somewhat chaotic and elliptical narrative spanning two days soon after Stephen's arrival at school; the Christmas dinner scene follows, a continuous narrative made up almost entirely of dialogue overheard by Stephen; and this gives way to the final Clongowes section, which is not only continuous but plot-centered in a way none of the preceding sections has been.

While the Christmas dinner scene is in one sense more "sophisticated" than the pandying sequence—on the surface it resembles a *Dubliners* story—nevertheless, with regard to the narrative portrayal of Stephen's developing consciousness it is more primitive. Stephen is a helpless nonparticipant in the harrowing dinner scene, whose organizing and structuring principles are, we must feel, tacit: we, not Stephen, are aware of the thematic resonance of the church-country split, the "dead king" motif, and the "blinded and drownded" harridan on whom Mr. Casey has spat. The considerable richness, the "density" of this section is in a sense *external*; there is relatively little dialogic interchange between author and protagonist. In the last Clongowes section, on the other hand, Stephen clearly participates in the narration; he is aware of his central role and correspondingly aware of the audience of his schoolfellows. He is also aware, it would seem, that his is a drama of injustice; he becomes responsible for the narration in a way he had not been previously. Virtually nothing that does not relate to the problem of transgression, punishment, and vindication is included in the section, either in overheard dialogue, in reported action, or in the stream of Stephen's consciousness. To a great extent, it is this radical thematic simplification that suggests to readers the conventional schoolboy story. Action, speech, thought, and observed detail are unified here through a narration that begins to resemble a performance of the boy's consciousness; this is *his* story in a way none of the preceding sections had been, and its naiveté is directly attributable to Stephen. The climax of the section and of the chapter, with the admiring schoolboys' praise for Stephen and cheers for Conmee, conventionalizes the episode even more clearly. Here, as in all good boys' stories of the nineteenth century, we have Virtue (or at least Innocence) Rewarded. Only the final paragraph, with its reiteration of the "brimming bowl" motif, sounds an unfamiliar note.

The school story was a relatively late arrival on the popular cultural scene, if only because children were not viewed as a potential market for writing until the nineteenth century was well advanced. The ambiguous moral status of the novel itself naturally appeared to be an even more urgent concern with respect to children than it had been with respect to women. The first impulse of writers addressing a young audience was to present irreproachable moral tracts thinly disguised as narratives of adventure or domestic romance, the staples of the adult market. These stories were ideological in the most restricted sense and were on the whole scrupulously self-censored. Only after Captain Marryat's *Mr Midshipman Easy* (1836), intended for an adult audience, had been adopted by schoolboys did he venture into the field of fiction for children, and then *Masterman Ready* (1841) dared none of the easy morality, racy humor, and picaresque naturalism that had made the earlier book so popular.[17] Still, moral irreproachability and a thick interlarding of pious sermons were not necessarily a sufficient excuse for a literature aimed at such impressionable minds. Charlotte Yonge, herself a prolific writer of books for children, observed more in sorrow than in anger that boys simply will not read the "mild tales" that content girls, so that to make up a list of recommended reading for boys is at best a compromise with the regrettable: "The solid, therefore, is not attempted in the present list. What it aims at giving is such a choice of books as boys will listen to with interest, or if they read in quieter moments, or in illness, may find so amusing as not to be tempted to think that nothing diverting or stimulating is to be found beyond the Penny Dreadful. If their taste can be kept unsullied during the time of growth, there is more hope for it afterwards."[18]

Tom Brown's School-Days

Within this dubious context, the first major school story, Thomas Hughes's *Tom Brown's School Days* (1857), appeared as exceptional in several regards. Like his friend Charles Kingsley, Hughes was a Christian Socialist, and unlike him admired Dr. Thomas Arnold, the former headmaster at Rugby, to the point of adulation.[19] *Tom Brown*, published fifteen years after Arnold's death, is in part a tribute to "The Doctor," in part a surprisingly realistic story set in a real school, and in part an embryonic *Bildungsroman* featuring "the English schoolboy as he is popularly supposed to be, tough, gregarious, reckless, a creature of outdoor tastes, intensely loyal to the community to which he belongs."[20] He also appears as a creature of suppressed but profound religious and moral instinct who is nonetheless easily led astray, and whose salvation during these formative years is a chancy matter.

Traditionally enough, Hughes establishes Tom's rural childhood home in the Vale of White Horse as a place of rather combative innocence, full of mischief-making but without the potential for real moral damage; ironically, Hughes observes that the son of Squire Brown "got more harm from his equals in his first fortnight at a private school . . . than he had from his village friends from the day he left Charity's apronstrings."[21] Although Hughes is at pains to present Rugby as a greatly superior alternative to the dubious "private schools" of the time, much the same could in fact be said of that institution. As the boy is leaving home, Tom's father warns him, "You'll see a great many cruel blackguard things done,"[22] an opinion that understates the case. At least by modern standards, and sometimes even by the standards of Britain in 1857, the reader must be taken aback by the organized and random bullying, the wholesale exploitation of the smaller by the larger boys, the organized cheating on examinations, and the recreational destruction of property and livestock belonging to neighboring farmers.

Although he offers occasional apologies for these events, and even assures the reader that some of the abuses have since been corrected, Hughes clearly regards this schoolboy world as natural, even bracing in its moral climate. As soon becomes clear, Rugby is a spiritually Darwinist world where the innocent are exposed to temptation and vice in order that they may overcome them, and where they are unjustly attacked in order that they may learn to demonstrate their manhood. In this system education itself is curiously irrelevant: "the object of all schools," Hughes comments, "is not to ram Latin and Greek into boys, but to make them good English boys, good future citizens; and by far the most important part of that work must be done or not done, out of school hours."[23] The true testing ground of boys is sports, particularly football, in this seed-bed of Muscular Christianity, and to a lesser extent social interaction within the community of boys. The boys' personal relationships to the masters, like their academic accomplishments, are also curiously irrelevant; one of the boys observes that masters are the "natural enemies" of the students, and just as it is the job of the former to attempt to enforce study it is the job of the latter to attempt to evade it.[24] The one possible exception to this paradigm is the headmaster, Dr. Arnold, who presides over the fortunes of each boy like a benevolent but infinitely distant deity, and who intervenes in the life of the school only as a "hidden hand." Toward the end of Tom's stay at Rugby, it is revealed to him that Arnold was responsible for putting him in charge of George Arthur, a physically weak but spiritually evangelical boy, in order to save Tom from directionless dissipation by thrusting responsibility on him. When Tom shows surprise that so lofty a personage would bother with him, a friendly teacher explains: " 'The Doctor sees the good in everyone, and appreciates it,' said the master, dogmatically."[25]

Like most schoolboy stories, *Portrait* can be viewed as a commentary upon *Tom Brown*; Stephen's experience, for early twentieth-century readers, would consciously or unconsciously be compared and contrasted to Tom's, the original model. Certainly the basic plot and thematic elements are similar, not only in the Clongowes sections, but throughout Joyce's book. The stress on a spiritual element in the lives of the boys at Rugby, which is somehow related to both personal and civic responsibility, means that there is less difference from Jesuit Clongowes than might be supposed. Both schools are self-consciously elitist, and in both a boy's status—at least among the boys—is greatly determined by his prowess in sports. Tom's introduction to Rugby's ethic comes through a valedictory speech by "old Brooke," the house captain, who announces, "I'd sooner win two school-house matches running than get the Balliol scholarship any day," and is roundly cheered.[26] Stephen immediately understands that Clongowes's "model" boys are athletic stars; he knows he is justified in resenting Nasty Roche because he is not a "decent fellow" like Rody Kickham, who is destined to become captain of the third line (*P*, 8).

The year at Clongowes—and the Clongowes section of *Portrait*—begins with football and ends with cricket,[27] just as does the year at Rugby and the book *Tom Brown*. But of course where Tom is immediately in the thick of things, Stephen reluctantly keeps on the fringes of his line, pretending to run from time to time to avoid the displeasure of the prefect. Tom's enthusiasm in "playing up" as soon as he arrives is all the more impressive when we realize that he is playing against students as old as seventeen, while the younger players may be no more than seven. Before the game, his friend East explains to Tom, "It's no joke playing-up in a match. . . . Why, there's been two collar-bones broken this half, and a dozen fellows lamed. And last year a fellow had his leg broken."[28] Undaunted, Tom plays up, and is carried off the field unconscious, but he has won the approbation of the student leaders. That night, to save a younger and weaker boy from harassment, he volunteers to be tossed against the ceiling in a blanket by the older boys; apparently, an element of masochism was most useful in winning social success in the world of Rugby. Stephen of course has some excuse for his reluctance to play up, as at "half-past six" he is easily the youngest (and smallest) boy at Clongowes; but then, the variety of "gravel football" played there did not pit so much older against so much younger boys.[29]

The basic justification for the brutality of the Rugby world, in Hughes's eyes, is simply that it is preparation for the essential activity of life. "After all, what would life be without fighting, I should like to know? From the cradle to the grave, fighting rightly understood is the business, the real highest, honestest business of every son of man."[30] Tom's initial struggles are physical: against his football antagonists, against the "brute" Flaxman, against a group of higher-form bullies who abuse the "fagging" system. Tom and his lower-form friends instinctively understand that they must not appeal to the authorities about the bullying, because "blabbing won't do."[31] In his final advice before Tom's departure, his father had told him to "tell the truth, keep a brave and kind heart, and never listen to or say anything you wouldn't have your mother and sister hear,"[32] but only because Simon's advice to Stephen "never to peach on a fellow" (P, 21) would have been insultingly superfluous. In Tom's family, this part of the code needs no articulation; in Stephen's it does, either because Simon is less secure in his status than Mr. Brown or because he already suspects that his son has no inborn appreciation for the Rugby ideology.

Despite their enormous differences in personality, Tom and Stephen experience many of the same things in school. Soon after his arrival, Tom is quizzed by the older boys: "You fellow, what's your name?

Where do you come from? How old are you?"[33] Unlike Stephen, Tom is not asked what his father does. In fact, Tom's father is a magistrate, but his schoolfellows' silence here probably indicates that they are easier in their role as young gentlemen than are Stephen's cohorts. But when he arrives at his first school Tom misses his mother as strongly as Stephen, at least at first, and when his letter to her is delayed he cannot help bursting into tears, at which he is taunted by another student who calls him "young mammy-sick."[34] At Rugby Tom soon makes a friend (East) and, through no fault of his own, an enemy (Flaxman), just as Stephen is befriended by Fleming and arbitrarily persecuted by Wells. Both boys gain fame and the admiration of their fellows by standing up against unjust punishment, Tom by organizing the lower-form boys in a kind of passive-resistance movement against higher-form bullies, Stephen by appealing Father Dolan's punishment to the rector. Like Stephen, Tom has been caned in the hand, but for Tom this is an unimportant event: three-quarters of his form has been caned, and though he may have been unjustly punished on some occasions, he knows he has escaped numerous times. Tom's stirring sexual and romantic urges are centered on George Arthur's beautiful mother, who becomes his personal representation of Christian purity, a kind of secular saint who evokes from him much the same feelings and associations that Stephen in his early youth feels for Mercedes, Eileen, and the Virgin. Both boys gain the sympathy of their classmates through illness, and both hear of the death of a fellow student.

Illness—the first confrontation with the idea of death most children undergo—provides a striking parallel between the books. When Tom is sent to bed in the housekeeper's room after he has been burned by bullies, he is comforted by his friend East and then goes to sleep murmuring a verse from a hymn he learned in childhood: "Where the wicked cease from troubling / And the weary are at rest." Stephen, who is comforted both by Fleming and (somewhat ambiguously) by Athy, is slightly more secular in his choice, reciting the "Bury me in the old churchyard" verses to himself. Although Tom has no dream-vision like Stephen's when he is ill, his friend George Arthur does, and recounts it to Tom, on whom it has a great spiritual effect. Like Stephen, George, who has been near death, dreams of a river; but where Stephen's dream of Parnell's ship, Dante, and Brother Michael is mysteriously symbolic, George's is flatly allegorical. He knows the river is death, sees the happy people on the other side, and longs to join them; but a voice stops him and directs his attention to the toilers on the near side. George then sees himself, "and I was toiling and doing ever so little a piece of the great work."[35] Tom naturally is embarrassed by the heavy spirituality and emotionalism of all this, and—along with the reader—is somewhat nonplussed when George Arthur's deathbed request turns out to be that Tom should forego the use of "cribs." But Tom does so and even manages to make it look manly, just as earlier he had defended with his fists George's practice of praying before bed.

George Arthur's brush with death and Tom's ameliorating experience is the spiritual climax of the book, but a secondary climax involves his relationship with East. Throughout the book, East has represented the "natural" boy, with decent instincts but without the moral and spiritual convictions of George; George stands for the model Anglo-Catholic youth. Both, clearly, are aspects of Tom himself, and together they form the extreme potentials of his psyche. But after his "conversion" by his less robust friend, Tom attempts to save East as well. East is receptive, but reluctantly confesses his "secret" to Tom, the fact that he has never been confirmed. Hughes's persona, narrating this episode, sounds almost as reluctant as East to speak about intense emotional experiences, but insists that Tom's discussion with East is not only necessary, but universal, even archetypal: "What a bother explaining all this is! I wish we could get on without it. But we can't. However, you'll all find if you haven't found it out already, that a time comes in every human friendship, when you must go down into the depths of yourself, and lay bare what is there to your friend, and wait in fear for his answer. A few moments may do it; and it may be (most likely will be, as you are English boys) that you never do it but once. But done it must be, if the friendship is to be worth the name."[36] The parallel here is to Stephen's discussion with Cranly, and it is, of course, ironic. Where Tom painfully confesses his faith and East confesses his wish for confirmation, Stephen confesses his religious unfaith and his devotion to a romantic, personal aesthetic creed. But there is still a correspondence to Tom's interchange as a climax to the school experience. And while Stephen comes more naturally by this sort of intense discussion, this is almost the only time we see him speaking to a friend without his habitual layers of protective irony and without assuming defensive poses.

The differences between *Tom Brown's School-Days* and *Portrait of the*

Artist are plain, but some of these also are significant when *Portrait* is read as a dialogical response to the earlier book. At least in this final version of *Portrait*, Stephen is foregrounded at the expense of the other "balancing" characters who, in the convention established by *Tom Brown*, might represent alternatives to the hero's development. Perhaps Cranly and Davin remain to suggest Stephen's orthodox intellectualism on the one hand and his native roots on the other, but both are shadowy figures, subsumed by stronger representations of church and nation. In personality, Stephen is almost as unlike Tom Brown as possible; but it is interesting to note that some of the differences between the protagonists suggest that Stephen has been constructed as Tom's antitype, rather than merely reflecting an autobiographical image of his creator. According to Bruce Bradley, Joyce was in general as happy at Clongowes as Tom was at Rugby,[37] while Stephen often appears miserably out of place. Like Tom, Joyce was rather good at sports; like Tom he also raided the school orchards with his closest friend, a boy named Furlong, and was probably pandied on several occasions for vulgar language.[38] Undoubtedly such conventionally boyish details were deleted or changed in order to show in higher relief the figure of the young artist in opposition to his community. But they also serve to establish Stephen as the dialogical inverse of Tom Brown, the most famous example of the British bourgeois as schoolboy.

If the contrast in character between the two protagonists is apparent, the contrast in the worlds of the two books is no less so. *Portrait* is radically developmental while *Tom Brown* is essentially static; *Portrait* is internal where *Tom Brown* is external; and of course *Portrait* has the resonance and complexity of great literature in the modernist mode while *Tom Brown* has the naive archetypal solidity of a major example of popular art. The final section of the first chapter of *Portrait* is closest to *Tom Brown* in texture, although the absence of Hughes's interpretive and moralizing narrator gives it more immediacy and a greater surface simplicity. Stephen's punishment, his bravery in appealing it, and the deus ex machina role of Conmee all suggest the Christian Darwinism of the earlier book, but this exemplary drama is so thoroughly undercut by succeeding chapters that its function within the book as a whole is almost purely ironic. Certainly Joyce's book remains a novel of trial and testing, but for Stephen the tests gradually become framed in what he believes to be his own terms rather than the public terms in which Tom is tried—and which neither he nor Hughes's narrator ever questions.

Tom Brown closes with the mature Tom standing at the altar of the chapel where the Doctor is buried, feeling a unity with the students who had gone before him and reverent gratitude for Arnold. Arnold's secret intervention in Tom's life, we realize, is precisely parallel to the operation of divine grace in a world otherwise characterized by struggle and temptation. The world of his schoolboy experience perfectly mimics the greater world beyond; the epistemology is that of the microcosm. And Tom's revelation is simply a realization of the moral and divine order of the world. Nothing is asked of him but to accept it. For Stephen, in a school run by Catholic priests, the purported parallel is all the more obvious, though he reacts differently from Tom to the school's theocracy—instead of passively waiting for Conmee's grace to intervene he actively seeks it out. And the model of active heroism this implies is sustained through the book long after Stephen has rejected the superstructure of religious authority. Surprisingly enough, the initial contrast between Tom's active, aggressive character and Stephen's weak passivity has been reversed by the end of the books. Tom has assimilated an ethic of acceptance, has completely internalized the voice of authority, while Stephen has moved toward what he sees as an ultimate rebellion. While still an adolescent, Stephen is perfectly capable of objectifying the schoolboy ideology that descends from *Tom Brown* and seeing it as an arbitrary structure of demands parallel to those of Irish Nationalism or of the bourgeois family: "When the gymnasium had been opened he had heard another voice urging him to be strong and manly and healthy and when the movement towards national revival had begun to be felt in the college yet another voice had bidden him be true to his country and help to raise up her fallen language and tradition. In the profane world, as he foresaw, a worldly voice would bid him raise up his father's fallen state by his labours and, meanwhile, the voice of his school comrades urged him to be a decent fellow, to shield others from blame or to beg them off and to do his best to get free days for the school" (P, 83–84). Already these imperative voices, all claiming to speak with monological authority, are "hollowsounding in his ears" (P, 83).

Eric, or Little by Little *and* The Harrovians

The second major schoolboy novel of the Victorian age, and one which rivaled *Tom Brown* in popularity at the time of their writing, was *Eric, or Little by Little: A Tale of Roslyn School* (1858) by Frederick Farrar, a Fellow of Trinity College and a Doctor of Divinity. If the tone of *Tom Brown* is frank and manly, *Eric* represents the emotionally enthusiastic side of the Victorian character with its eighteenth-century inheritance of sensibility. Eric begins as a far nobler and more devout character than Tom, although he strikes the twentieth-century reader as something of an egotistical prig. The book is more episodic and less coherent than Hughes's novel and is packed with sentimentality, deathbed scenes, tears, beating of breasts, and intimate, passionate interchanges between pupils and masters. Although Farrar's book went fairly quickly out of fashion, so that by the 1890s the popular heroes of Kipling's *Stalkey and Company* found Eric a figure for derision, it probably represented an aspect of school life in Arnold's time fairly accurately. David Newsome observes, "The doctrine of the stiff-upper-lip was no part of the public-school code of the Arnoldian period. This gradually came in with the manliness cult of the 1870s and 80s. . . . But tears were usual, the expected consequences of reproof. . . . Headmaster and assistant masters occasionally wept together in the course of a difference of opinion. And the word 'love' was more frequently on their lips, used with real sincerity. The association between master and pupil seems to have often been very intimate, admitting of expressions of emotion on both sides."[39]

In at least one regard, *Portrait* is closer to *Eric* than to *Tom Brown*, and this is in its representation of adolescent passions and emotions; although Stephen quickly learns to fight the tears that spring to his eyes on numerous occasions, and even to surpass Tom in imperturbability of demeanor, his inner life is as tumultuous as Eric's. Stephen is also closer to Eric in his character and interests, at least initially. Farrar's narrator says of Eric at twelve, "His mind seemed cast in such a mold of stainless honor that he avoided most of the faults to which children are prone. But he was far from blameless. He was proud to a fault; he well knew that few of his fellows had gifts like his, either of mind or of person, and his fair face often showed a clear impression of his own superiority. His passion, too was imperious."[40] Undoubtedly it is these initial faults of character, as well as the old Adam within him, that are responsible for the manifold sufferings of Eric in the course of the book. Like Stephen and Tom he is unjustly caned on the hand, although the vividness of the episode recalls Joyce's book more than Hughes's: "for some weeks after there were dark weals visible across Eric's palm, which rendered the use of his hands painful."[41] Eric is punished for innocently passing a "crib" from one boy to another, and when he refuses to betray the responsible boys he becomes a hero with his form. Like Stephen, who refuses to "peach" on Wells for pushing him into the square ditch, Eric has his cap thrown into a puddle by a bully and refuses to turn him in. Also like Stephen, Eric is an enthusiastic and competent scholar, and within Farrar's world academic performance is taken more seriously than in Hughes's Rugby.

But scholarship cannot save him from a most grievous fault, which is hearing "foul language" without protest—a particularly pernicious example cited by Dean Farrar is one boy's referring to another as a "surly devil." The narrator makes it clear that assenting to one sin is equivalent to committing the lot: "Ah, Eric, Eric! how little we know the moments which decide the destinies of life! . . . Ah Eric! moodiness and petulance cannot save you, but prayerfulness would; one word, Eric, at the throne of grace—one prayer before you go down among the boys, that God in his mercy would wash away, in the blood of his dear Son, your crimson stains."[42] The emotional intensity and overt religiosity of *Eric* make it a closer parallel to the third chapter of *Portrait* than to the first, despite the overlap of some episodes; and indeed that is the point at which the protagonists' ages coincide. Farrar's book at times suggests the sort of text that might be produced by a less intelligent Father Arnall attempting to narrate Stephen's spiritual history.

But even if *Eric* is not a direct model for *Portrait* it represents a major tendency of the nineteenth-century schoolboy story that is less clearly represented in the heartier tradition of *Tom Brown*. While modern readers often ascribe the violence of Stephen's moral and religious guilt to his Irish Catholic environment, the paradigm of sin, punishment, and repentance was already firmly established in the schoolboy genre by the time Joyce wrote. Indeed, the physical masochism that often surfaces in *Tom Brown* is easily surpassed by the "spiritual" masochism of Farrar's influential book. Despite the kindly words of a master, Mr. Rose, Eric plunges into iniquity after iniquity, and after three or four years of exposure to blasphemy, dishonesty, drunkenness, and homosexuality his only salvation lies in death. Yet Farrar no more questions the benefits of such an education than does Hughes: "The true preparation for life, the true basis of a manly character, is not to have been ignorant of evil, but to have known it and avoided it." Farrar's world seems less a ground for fair testing than a minefield of inevitable error, and the modern reader is at times led to question whether we are intended to take warning from Eric's tribulations or simply to revel in his sufferings.

By the turn of the century, of course, the bourgeois ethic had shifted; not only did Eric's *askesis* appear to the reading public overly emotional and self-consciously didactic, but even Tom's bluff and hearty moral tale was seen with an increasingly cynical eye. The schoolboy story, besides, was capable of relatively few permutations before the genre was exhausted; unjust accusations and punishments, betrayals, and athletic triumphs with a seasoning of lighthearted pranks or deathbed scenes yielded a recipe for extreme conventionalization. Arnold Lunn's *The Harrovians* (1913) plays on those conventions by making its protagonist, Peter O'Neil, an avid reader who has no distance on his reading: "His poses were delivered weekly from Mudie's, for his pet roles varied with current literature."[43] Peter is a sort of Mme Bovary of the public school, forever betrayed by reality: "As he strolled up the Trollope House drive, he knew exactly what to expect. . . . 'What's your father,' some ill-natured lout would ask, to which he would reply with some variation of the traditional reply, 'My father was a gentleman; what was yours?' This retort would provoke a murmur of amused applause."[44]

Obviously by the time of Joyce's novel, both the question and the proper response were stock, although Stephen is too young and too unread to realize this. Peter, who is well prepared for life in a schoolboy novel, unfortunately finds that Harrow has little to do with his expectations. No one will ask him what his father does. He realizes that the way to become popular is to win a fight and so picks a fight with a Spanish boy on the grounds that any Englishman can beat any three foreigners. The Spaniard fails to realize this and beats him handily, upon which the other boys throw him in the "new Boys' Bush." Here—although the source is not specified in the book—Peter is basing his expectations on the "Jack Harkaway" series, the creation of one Bracebridge Hemyng, which flourished in magazines like *Boys of England* and in "penny parts" from 1871 well into the twentieth century. Harkaway's adventures were not confined to school, but successive avatars returned there periodically, so that in *Jack Harkaway's Journal for Boys* (1893) Jack Harkaway III arrives at Plato House. There he accuses a fellow pupil of foreign appearance of having "touch of the tarbrush" about him and of being a "half-bred Spanish cur." Jack beats the boy in a fair fight, but afterward the un-English coward sneaks up behind the hero and brains him with a cricket bat, upon which "all were inclined to cry, 'Out upon the dastard!' "[45] Unfortunately for Peter, either Harrovian schoolboys of the period were far less sympathetic to brutal chauvinism than were "Platonians," or else the resident Spaniards were tougher. As Bruce Bradley has noted,[46] there are a few other correspondences between *The Harrovians* and *Portrait*, including a scene where several boys discuss a caning on the hand: "Thompson says he raised his hand above his shoulder, which is against the law."[47] Later, after Peter's wit has earned him some acceptance, the schoolboys depend on him to postpone their German lesson indefinitely by asking the professor delaying questions, a technique Stephen also employs. Considering their respective dates of publication, it is unlikely that either Joyce's or Lunn's novel borrowed such details from the other; what the correspondences do suggest is that both schoolboy experience and its literary reflections had become highly conventionalized.

Lunn's book thus shows a new self-consciousness within the school-story genre and employs a new sort of irony in its portrayal of childhood. The popularity of books such as this around the turn of the century was due to two related aspects of the shift in bourgeois taste: first, the waning of the demand for explicit moralism in literature, illustrated by the paradoxical rise of both naturalism and aestheticism; and second, the major post-Romantic change in the popular view of childhood. Where for the Victorians childhood had been seen as primarily a period of testing and preparation for adulthood, a clearly imperfect stage during which the formation of the citizen's character takes place, for the Edwardians childhood began to be seen as an end in itself, a golden age of innocence and intuitive virtue that was contrasted to the fallen state of hypocritical adulthood. To a degree, this was simply a translation into popular terms of the original Wordsworthian vision of childhood, allowing for the necessary delay before a radical literary movement could be assimilated by mainstream culture—it was, after all, late in the Victorian period before Byron became a "bestseller." To a degree, also, the transformation in the image of childhood was made possible by the Victorian reform movements addressing the situation of the child. Perhaps the best exemplars of the new sensibility are Kenneth Grahame in *The Golden Age* (1895), *Dream Days* (1898), and *The Wind in the Willows* (1908) and James Barrie in *The Little Minister* (1891) and, preeminently, *Peter Pan* (1904). But virtually all the school stories published around the turn of the century also reflected the new vision of childhood.

Where Barrie and Grahame stress the lyrical note in their portrayals of childhood, Kipling obviously sounds a more sardonic tone; the other side of the coin of childhood innocence is childhood experience, but (as Blake suggested) the two are interrelated. If childhood is no longer merely preparatory but a valid and significant realm of experience in itself, then the events in which the child participates may have weight of their own, and not simply as an allegory of adult experience. In Kipling's *Stalkey and Company* the terms of reader identification are changed: the masters generally represent a hypocritical and hidebound conformity, while the three boy-heroes are allowed to triumph over them through cunning and a rather shifty but fundamentally decent morality. By comparison with *Eric*, or even *Tom Brown*, the world of the book is far closer to the world of "adult" novels; there is a mundane seriousness about the events—even when they are trivial or humorous— which strangely parallels the imaginative seriousness of the fantasies of Grahame and Barrie. Certainly it is the transformation in the image of childhood that these writers in their different ways epitomize that allows Joyce to imbue the early chapters of *Portrait* with such striking immediacy and emotional sincerity.

Vice-Versa

A somewhat earlier work that, like Kipling's, reverses the moral status of boys and masters is F. Anstey's *Vice-Versa*, the Whitsuntide play in which Joyce performed, which we may assume is also the "play within a play" of *Portrait*. Thomas Anstey Guthrie first published *Vice-Versa, or a Lesson to Fathers* in 1882. The novel was unexpectedly successful; it was reprinted nineteen times in its year of publication and frequently for forty years thereafter. The book's success led to a dramatic version attributed to Edward Rose in 1883, which is the play in which Joyce performed at Belvedere, probably in 1898. Later, Guthrie published an expanded dramatic version of his own under the title *Vice Versa: A*

Farcical Fantastic Play (London, 1910).[48] As several critics have noted,[49] Anstey's play, a comic father-son reversal, treats farcically the father-son relationship that is a central theme in *Portrait*, *Ulysses*, and the *Wake*.

The main characters of the play (and novel) are Paul Bultitude, an extremely pompous and rather hypocritical Colonial Produce Broker whose wife has died; his son Dick, a fifteen-year-old virtually indistinguishable from Tom Brown; and Dr. Grimstone, the Principal of Crichton House School, who is pedantic, overbearing, and egotistical. In a clear Arnoldian allusion he is referred to as "The Doctor," although his school is a cut-rate private imitation of Rugby. Joyce, with his height and elocution, was cast as Dr. Grimstone; according to Eugene Sheehy, he "ignored the role allotted to him and impersonated Father Henry (the rector of Belvedere College). He carried on, often for five minutes at a time, with the pet sayings of the Rector, imitating his gestures and mannerisms. The other members of the cast collapsed with laughter on the stage—completely missing their cues and forgetting their parts—and the schoolboy audience received the performance with hysterical glee."[50] There is no direct evidence that Stephen has done this in *his* play, although he too is known for his "impressions" of the school authorities (*P*, 75–76). But Anstey's farce undoubtedly contributed elements to Joyce's notion of the schoolboy story, and considering the importance of the father-son theme in Joyce's early life as well as in his work—and the vague border between the two—the play has undeniable relevance to *Portrait*.[51]

The success of the work is due to its simplicity of conception. Bultitude's bounder of a brother-in-law, Marmaduke Paradine, has given Bultitude a "wishing stone" he was given by the fakir Ram Dass, but without realizing it is the genuine article; as Bultitude is sending his reluctant son off to school again, he expresses the hypocritical wish that the two of them could exchange places. Childhood, he feels, is a joyous, carefree time and Grimstone's school above reproach. Naturally Bultitude gets his wish and finds himself in his son Dick's body. Once he understands about the stone, he attempts to bluster and bully his way out of the situation, so Dick feels forced to send his father off to school. There Bultitude encounters the familiar list of abuses we know from *Eric* and *Tom Brown*—bullying, tale-bearing, the keeping of "tuck" (or forbidden possessions, such as sweets), vandalism, and of course the danger to life and limb occasioned by "playing up" in football matches. Bultitude of course attempts to stand on his dignity and refuses to participate in any of this; much of the play's humor comes from his retaining the language and behavior of a stuffy middle-aged man while trapped in an adolescent body, unable to convince anyone of his situation.

Gradually Bultitude loses the considerable popularity Dick had enjoyed, without really gaining any popularity among the masters, by siding with those whom Tom Brown's friend called the boys' "natural enemies." Soon after arriving at school, he remarks to Grimstone, "I may be old-fashioned . . . but I decidedly disapprove of taking children to dramatic exhibitions of *any* kind. It only *unsettles* them." Also morally unhealthful, he feels, are sucking peppermints, eating sweets, and long vacations.[52] But of course he has no appreciation for the schoolboy "code," and soon becomes known as a "regular rotter" because he betrays the boys to the masters, attempts to deny his (actually Dick's) debts, and refuses to fight either to avenge an insult or to protect his girlfriend from a rival. He is bullied and ostracized, and his misery is only increased when his son comes to visit, awkwardly playing the part of a conservative paterfamilias, and rescues him from a whipping.

At first glance, it would seem that the comic tension here is produced by the confusion of two worlds, the adult and the schoolboy, with their attendant values. But in fact, the "adult" world has no real, unironic representatives; Bultitude's egotistical stuffiness disqualifies him, and Grimstone is a farcical pedant who skimps on meals for the students, hires unqualified masters, and in emotional matters is totally out of touch with reality. "I'll establish a tone of unmurmuring happiness and trustful content in this school," he announces to the boys, "if I have to flog every boy as long as I can stand over him."[53] Above his desk is the motto, "The Child is Father to the Man," an unexceptionable text rendered ludicrous by the situation. Indeed, one of Grimstone's sins is that his condescending, opinionated paternalism, the image of Bultitude's own relationship with his son, allows the boys no dignity.

But the plainest indictment of Grimstone's values comes at the end of Bultitude's stay, when he is caught receiving a note from a girl at a neighboring house, and another student shows Grimstone a note from Dick to the girl written the previous term. The Doctor assembles the students to witness his pupil's punishment, and thunders, "Look upon him, as he cowers before you in all the hideousness of his moral depravity. . . . [He] has not scrupled to conduct a secret correspondence with—with a young person of the opposite sex."[54] When Grimstone attacks an innocent youthful flirtation with such comic fervor, it becomes obvious that he is unable to distinguish among different degrees of transgression. Even Bultitude has had enough of his own medicine by then, and when a master observes to him that "No time is . . . so thoroughly happy, as the days we spend at school," he replies, "Bosh, sir, bosh! I'll be dashed if I stand that infernal cant and humbug from you or anybody else!"[55]

The play ends happily when Bultitude escapes from school and finds his way home. Dick has begun to find adult life palling on him and reluctantly cooperates in exchanging places once again. In Ulyssean fashion, Bultitude ousts the parasite Parradine and takes charge of his household once again. But he has reformed, will be more generous and lenient in the future, and seems to feel some real affection for the boy at last. This classical denouement, however satisfying in abstract dramatic terms, does not settle the genuine questions the farce has managed to raise. Aside from his position of power, what gives Bultitude authority over Dick, who seems much the more reasonable person? Why will Dick be returning to a school that has been shown up as a mockery of education, not to mention socialization? Just what are the "adult" values to which the schoolboy values must give place? Joyce's instincts were sound in turning his part in *Vice-Versa* into an extended mockery of his own Rector, because in essence the play is little more than a demolition of the world of the masters through parody.

The central device, the exchange of roles between parent and child, is a minor theme in *Portrait* as well. Simon Dedalus is full of high sentence, but more than a little obtuse when it comes to the welfare of his family. After the first chapter, Simon is more concerned with his own pride and pleasures than with his children's needs. Stephen confronts this fact about his father most directly during the painful trip to Cork, when Simon shocks even his barroom cronies by belittling his son: "There's that son of mine there not half my age and I'm a better man than he is any day of the week. . . . I'll sing a tenor song against him or I'll vault a fivebarred gate against him or I'll run with him after the hounds across the country . . . and the best man for it" (*P*, 95). In virtually every action, Simon claims the license of a child, while refusing to abandon the authority of a father. Even his likeable qualitites spring from a childlike naiveté and enthusiasm and his comic inability to gain any perspective on himself. Perhaps unconsciously realizing that he cannot fill the traditional role of the father, he attempts to play the pal: "I'm talking to you as a friend, Stephen. I don't believe in playing the stern father. I don't believe a son should be afraid of his father. No, I treat you as your grandfather treated me when I was a young chap. We were more like brothers than father and son" (*P*, 91). Stephen, of course, is unable to respond to this overture, knowing that half of Simon's emotional outbursts are only drunken sentiment to be forgotten in the morning and realizing that his father will resume the authoritative and authoritarian mantle whenever it suits him. Immediately following the Cork trip, Stephen with his Prize money—a substantial proportion of the family budget—assumes the paternal role, taking his subdued father out to dinner and tabulating money lent to the rest of the family in an effort to build a breakwater against the "disorder, the misrule and confusion of his father's house" (*P*, 162). Stephen is early aware of his intellectual superiority over his parents and at first probably feels as much pain as pride in that fact.

Later, in *Ulysses*, he will be searching for a spiritual father to replace the merely "consubstantial" Simon Dedalus; without ever quite articulating it, he seems to share the common adolescent fantasy that he is not genuinely the son of his parents—a conviction so common that Freud dubbed it the "family romance." Indeed, without that presumption, his relationship with Bloom would lose most of its point and potential. By the time he is living with Mulligan in the tower, Stephen is also seeking to become his own father, as the artist fathers his own image; Shakespeare is not Hamlet the son, but the ghost of the dead king. Mulligan parodically explains this to Haines: "He proves by algebra that Hamlet's grandson is Shakespeare's grandfather and that he himself is the ghost of his own father" (*U*, 15/18). In *Vice-Versa*, the mocker Parradine is similarly skeptical when Bultitude explains that he is not really Dick: "Not your own son, but your own father, eh?"[56]

Like the literal father-son relationship, the school's status in loco parentis is ridiculed in *Portrait* much as it is in *Vice-Versa*, although Joyce's tone is at times closer to tragedy or even melodrama than to farce. From Father Dolan's sadistic and unjustified punishment through the Dean of Studies's unfortunate solecism over tundishes, the ethical and intellectual pretensions of Clongowes, Belvedere, and University College are exploded by the precocious Stephen. Although none of his mentors resembles Grimstone in character, he himself at times sounds like a more sophisticated Bultitude, turning out orotund, Johnsonian periods at every opportunity.[57] Stephen's role in the novel imperceptibly modulates from the "chiel amang ye takin' notes" to the unsuspected adult in a schoolboy world. At roughly the age of ten, "the noise of children at play annoyed him and their silly voices made him feel, even more keenly than he had felt at Clongowes, that he was different from others. He did not want to play. He wanted to meet in the real world the unsubstantial image which his soul so constantly beheld" (P, 64–65). By the age of fourteen, observing Simon and his cronies in Cork, he reflects morosely, "His mind seemed older than theirs. . . . No life or youth stirred in him as it had stirred in them. . . . His childhood was dead or lost" (P, 95–96). Like Bultitude, he feels himself a mature, suffering soul in a child's body, incomprehensibly at the mercy of the childish adults around him.

Romantic Image

In the "Scylla and Charybdis" episode of *Ulysses*, Stephen's audience grows restive as soon as they realize the thrust of his argument. "I may as well warn you that if you want to shake my belief that Shakespeare is Hamlet you have a stern task before you," comments John Eglinton. Stephen counters with an attack on the notion of physical and spiritual identity that has unexpected implications for the idea of the artist:

> As we, or mother Dana, weave and unweave our bodies, Stephen said, from day to day, their molecules shuttled to and fro, so does the artist weave and unweave his image. And as the mole on my right breast is where it is when I was born, though all my body has been woven of new stuff time after time, so through the ghost of the unquiet father the image of the unliving son looks forth. In the intense instant of imagination, when the mind, Shelley says, is a fading coal, that which I was is that which I am and that which in possibility I may come to be. So in the future, the sister of the past, I may see myself as I sit here now but by reflection from that which then I shall be (U, 159–60/194).

In this celebrated and confusing passage metaphor is piled on metaphor until God, the artist, the self, the work, the father, the son, the past, and the future all are conflated in a Heraclitean flux of imagery. If Socrates learned dialectic from Xanthippe, as Stephen suggests (*U*, 156/190), he himself has learned to abuse it, perhaps with the aid of Bruno, Shelley, and Drummond of Hawthornden.

Yet one implication seems undeniable: that the artist's "image" is *himself*, however construed or bodied forth. Of course, Stephen is engaged in an exercise in biographical criticism, arguing that Shakespeare "is" the dead king in *Hamlet*, so that the Romantic premise that the artist's self and work are interchangeable is apposite here, at least metaphorically. Stephen extends the idea in several directions. In the "intense instant of imagination," the Pateresque moment of creation or aesthetic perception, the artist's identity becomes unified in time; his past and his potential contribute to his identity along with the mundane present self, Yeats's "bundle of accident and incoherence that sits down to breakfast."[58] It is as if, in those charged moments, the artist became a supertemporal *Ubermensch*, a giant and essential figure standing like an archetype above the flux of daily existence. "His own image to a man with that queer thing genius is the standard of all experience," Stephen continues. "The images of other males of his blood will repel him. He will see in them grotesque attempts of nature to foretell or to repeat himself" (*U*, 161/195–96). Here again "image" means "self" or "life," with the additional implication that this image is inextricably bound to the artist's personality, his desires and fears, and not merely to the ideal self of the artist qua artist. If, in Freudian fashion, the artist finds the image of other males of his blood—his father or son—repellent, then the interaction among images reduces to the interaction among persons.

This is not in itself a surprising assertion, if we are content to see Stephen as an Irish d'Annunzio, a Wildean aesthete paradoxically claiming more for the artist than even Shelley had (for example, "A man of genius makes no mistakes. His errors are volitional and are the portals of discovery" [*U*, 156/190]). And it must be remembered that, in dialogical fashion, he is overstating his case before an audience all of whom will condescend to be entertained but are inclined to disagree. Stephen is *performing* the role of the artist in this play within a play: in a contemporary sense of the word, he is developing an "image." Like Wilde, Stephen is conscious of the element of falsification in such a performance. He is seducing his listeners, using artifice to involve them dialogically in the necessary falsehood of art: "Local colour. Work in all you know. Make them accomplices" (*U*, 154/188). Again like Wilde,

Stephen is aware of a somewhat sinister element in this process: "They list. And in the porches of their ears I pour" (*U*, 161/196).[59]

The problem here is the difficulty in reconciling such an aesthetic with the more impersonal notion of the epiphany, as developed in *Stephen Hero* and in *Portrait*, or with the use of the term "image" there. In his famous disquisition to Lynch, Stephen distinguishes among "the lyrical form, the form wherein the artist presents his image in immediate relation to himself; the epical form, the form wherein he presents his image in mediate relation to himself and to others; the dramatic form, the form wherein he presents his image in immediate relation to others" (*P*, 214). Further, in the "highest" form of literature, the dramatic, "the personality of the artist . . . finally refines itself out of existence, impersonalizes itself, so to speak" (*P*, 215).[60] Undoubtedly the implications of this metaphor are quite different from the implications of those Stephen employs in the National Library; so much so that they have allowed the "Classic versus Romantic" controversy to dominate an area of Joycean criticism to the present day.[61] But Stephen's stress on impersonality in this passage should not mislead us; in both arguments he relies on a radically generative theory of art that takes as its point of departure the moment when "the artist prolongs and broods upon himself" (*P*, 214), not the moment when he confronts the world. If Stephen's performance for Lynch is to be reconciled with Stephen's performance for the Library group we must understand that the "refining" of the artist's personality in his work involves an infinite expansion of that personality rather than a diminishment. His daily self is subsumed by his Self as Artist so that "like the God of the creation" the artist is "within or behind" his handiwork, nowhere distinguishable but everywhere pervasive in it (*P*, 215).

If the two aesthetic discussions still seem to point in two different directions, we must recall that they are different performances before different audiences; as dramatic and dialogical utterances, Stephen's words are in "immediate relationship" to others. Addressing Lynch, Stephen chooses them to draw forth his fellow student's highest accolade, that they have "the true scholastic stink" (*P*, 214). For the more idealist audience in the Library, all in varying degrees influenced by A. E.'s mystical folk Platonism, Stephen realizes that he must not merely pontificate but "make them accomplices." Any assent that Best, Eglinton, and Lyster will give must be emotional or "spiritual." The *Portrait* speech turns upon abstract "scholastic" distinctions, as if to win a school prize;

the *Ulysses* speech turns upon hypostatic poetic assertions embellished with vivid details, as if to win insertion into a Michael Robartes narrative. Both show the critic as artist and the artist as performer.

From the beginning Stephen has been conscious of himself as performer, choosing—or being chosen by—a language, striking a stance, adopting a posture toward whatever audience he confronts. As he matures he grows capable of observing and evaluating his own verbal and physical gestures with an eye to their effect upon those around him. His parting from E. C. at the end of *Portrait* would be a nightmare of self-consciousness, were it not for the unprecedented sympathy he has started to feel for the girl and the ironic distance from himself that he has begun to cultivate: "Asked me, was I writing poems? About whom? I asked her. This confused her more and I felt sorry and mean. Turned off that valve at once and opened the spiritual-heroic refrigerating apparatus, invented and patented in all countries by Dante Alighieri. Talked rapidly of myself and my plans. In the midst of it I made a sudden gesture of a revolutionary nature. I must have looked like a fellow throwing a handful of peas into the air. People began to look at us" (*P*, 252). Although his metaphors here are comically mechanistic, what Stephen is portraying is his awareness of a language made of words, movements, and stances; he is anticipating the discussion at the beginning of "Circe" that Lynch characterizes as "Metaphysics in Mecklenburg Street," where he posits a "universal language" of gesture (*U*, 353/432).[62]

We have already explored the dialogical formation of Stephen's language through *Portrait* and the intimate and implicit connection of that language with his consciousness. As Bakhtin recognizes, a person speaking in a novel is inevitably an ideologue and his words, already stratified by social tradition or literary genre, may be called "ideologemes" (*DI*, 333). But Althusser takes the relationship between character and ideology one step further. In a discussion of Freud and Lacan he suggests that the bourgeois notions of the self and of consciousness may be revised so as to show their contingency on ideology: "Freud has discovered for us that the real subject, the individual in his unique essence, has not the form of an ego, centered on the 'ego,' on 'consciousness' or on 'existence'—whether this is the existence of the for-itself, of the body-proper, or of 'behavior'—that the human subject is decentered, constituted by a structure which has no 'centre' either, except in the ideological formations in which it recognizes itself."[63]

In this Marxist/postmodernist characterization of the self, the individual mind is structured by an open system that Lacan would call linguistic, Althusser ideological, but which would in any case embrace the semiological formations of the surrounding society. Elsewhere, Althusser stresses the psychic depth at which ideological formations function: "Ideology has very little to do with 'consciousness.' . . . It is profoundly *unconscious*, even when it presents itself in a reflected form. . . . Ideology is indeed a system of representations, but in the majority of cases these representations have nothing to do with 'consciousness': they are usually images and occasionally concepts, but it is above all as *structures* that they impose on the vast majority of men, not via their 'consciousness' "[64] Although Althusser's use of "structures" here remains somewhat vague, his thrust is clear: ideologies permeate the individual psyche below the level of consciousness, in part through the societal repertoire of images—no doubt including those structured sets of images Barthes terms "mythologies"—and in part through the underlying linguistic structures that society does not even recognize consciously as communications, much less as constituents of ideology.

For Althusser popular culture is a major agent and witness of this process; variants of the dominant ideology, inevitably and deeply embedded in popular cultural forms, perform their structuring function upon the minds of the populace. Yet we must recognize that if Althusser's characterization is at all accurate, it would be ludicrous to except from this process the intelligentsia; as the testimony of Joyce and many other twentieth-century writers makes clear, their lives are surrounded and informed by popular culture to the same degree as the rest of the bourgeoisie or the proletariat. Stephen's formulation of the myth of the transcendent artist certainly has its roots in the intellectual tradition stretching from Plato through Sidney, Shelley, Nietzsche, d'Annunzio, Ibsen, Yeats, and Wilde, and in the light of Derrida's work can also be seen as a hypertrophy of the myth of presence. But the particular intonation Stephen gives to the artist's *image*, both in his aesthetic discussions and in his performances throughout *Portrait* and *Ulysses*, owes just as much to the ideology of a major genre of the nineteenth-century popular novel, the mundane-heroic romance. Stephen's idea of selfhood is shaped by his reading, and to a far greater extent than he recognizes by his *early* reading; like the protagonist of *The Harrovians*—or, to elevate the company, like *Le Berger extravagant*, Quixote, Julien Sorel, Emma Bovary, Raskolnikov, and Lafcadio—he is a victim of the ideology of romance. The form of this imposition upon his psyche is in great part linguistic; indeed, with Lacan, we could assert that because it is structural, it is by definition linguistic. But at least in mediated form Stephen's internalization of the ideology of popular romance is also imagistic; he acts and speaks from within a grammar of images—images of whose popular and derivative nature he remains profoundly unconscious.

A Modern Daedalus

The mundane-heroic romance that flourished in the mid- to late nineteenth century is one of the clearest examples of Bakhtin's "novelization" process, and one of the more interesting examples of the way in which the character of a genre is altered by its novelization. Its immediate progenitor is the heroic romance of Byron, notably *Manfred*, but as that form is novelized a mundane or "realistic" quality is superimposed upon what in the poetic narrative had been symbolic heroic action. Thus an inevitable ironic note is introduced, a disparity between action and context. At the same time, wildly exotic or supernatural elements, which are simply asserted in the poetic narrative, must be "naturalized" within a genre whose essential tendency is toward bourgeois realism. Within the more popular exemplars of this genre, the resulting tension produces novels filled with absurd coincidence, superhuman feats, a dense, poetic, mystifying narrative voice, and a plot that culminates periodically in symbolic *tableaux*. Gesture is paramount, not coherent plot-oriented action. Even dialogue becomes a variety of gesture, of "pure" expression, oriented toward the reader, rather than communication, oriented toward another character. The most important and influential example of the genre, and the one with most importance for Stephen, is probably Dumas's *The Count of Monte Cristo*.

But before considering this novel let us turn to a more obscure example of the genre, a book which enjoyed considerable popularity in Ireland in the late 1880s. This is Tom Greer's *A Modern Daedalus* (1885), a politically revolutionary fable that may in fact have inspired Joyce in choosing his early pseudonym, but which, whether or not it was known to Joyce, has immense relevance to the image of his protagonist. In his preface, Greer asserts that although his story is imaginary, "the ideas and forces with which it deals are real, and may at any moment be brought into active play by the inevitable development of 'the resources of civilisation.'" Although the change in Ireland's fortunes may not come in this form, "come it will in some form as little expected, as impossible to control." This sincere and rather apocalyptic warning is then paralleled by an "introduction" by the protagonist of the book, John O'Halloran, who speaks as if after the events of the novel have transpired, in defense of his actions: "All I desired was liberty to pursue my work in peace and quiet," but "the State, so far from protecting or assisting, became my chief persecutor and the main obstacle in my path."[65]

The protagonist was born to a large family in a wild and secluded area of Donegal. He soon distinguished himself intellectually, winning prizes and exhibitions, but was shy and unsociable. Although he worked briefly at a local foundry, he was disliked by his fellow workers, "who soon discovered I was not one of themselves."[66] After the death of his mother, the boy's father and brothers, all active, strong, unintellectual types, become revolutionaries in response to the worsening political situation. The boy regards the revolutionary cause as hopeless, though, and devotes himself to his experiments. These soon succeed, and he invents a winged device that enables him to fly. Despite the mechanism he employs, flight appears to be greatly a spiritual activity for him. Almost mystically, it is bound up with his ideas of the growth of the human soul and the advancement of the race. In a paean to flight, he describes feeling "as if I floated there / By the sole act of my unburdened will / Which buoyed me proudly up."[67]

His family, busy with revolutionary activities in which he refuses to participate, regard him with scorn: "my position in the family had been rather that of a tolerated intruder, than that of a son and brother."[68] Just so, Stephen feels "his own futile isolation" within his family and is unable to bridge "the restlesss shame and rancour that divided him from mother and brother and sister" (P, 98). Naturally, O'Halloran's family also refuse to believe he has discovered the secret of flight until he demonstrates it for them and gives one of his brothers some training. The symbolic nature of flight is underlined as he warns that the knack of flying is not for everyone; "many might be constitutionally unable ever to acquire it."[69] His family argue that flight should be used for the Irish cause, but the boy is reluctant. He feels that their vision of the British Empire as the embodiment of evil is simplistic jingoism: "I don't believe that men are parcelled out into tribes and nations, one all good and the other all bad."[70] Like Stephen refusing Davin's nationalistic advances, O'Halloran tries to take a larger view. After some argument, the boy is banished. His family agrees to keep his secret, but also keep the wings he has devised. The boy goes to stay with friends elsewhere in Ireland, to meditate on the implications of his work. Meanwhile, the guerrilla activities of his family are being compared to the work of the "Invincibles," and the leader of the Irish party (obviously Parnell) is challenged to disavow any sympathy with "the advanced wing of the Nationalists." The leader, it is reported, "coldly declined to answer questions which were insults," a response that earns the boy's admiration.[71]

O'Halloran decides to fly to London and, with a new pair of wings that enable him to fly at 100 miles per hour, crosses the Channel, landing on Nelson's Monument in Trafalgar Square and drawing a huge crowd. The newspapers feed the crowd's fear that such a strange apparition must be connected with some nihilistic "dynamite conspiracy," but the boy contacts an editor and writes a column himself for the *Echo*. He is brought to the House, where a Swiftian debate ensues about what he represents. The Irish members are irrationally convinced that a flying man must be connected to Irish Nationalism, because "they felt as if by instinct that anything which had the effect of elevating and educating men must work to their advantage."[72] Again the Irish leader distinguishes himself from the squabbling British statesmen in his appreciation of the boy's feat: "how unutterably paltry and contemptible the little tricks and dodges ... in which the lives of parliamentary leaders were passed appeared when compared with the lofty themes which engaged this man of science in his unselfish, beneficent labours for mankind!"[73]

The boy is brought to meet the Home Secretary and, flattered by the attention of all these notables, agrees to give a demonstration of flight the next day. That night, however, he overhears a discussion between two of his hosts. The Tory asserts that "no government could afford to let such a thing go on without control," while the Liberal is captivated by the possible benefits to private enterprise. The boy is disillusioned with the strictly monetary aspect of the conversation, a dimension of his discovery which had not even occurred to him. "My dreams had been of knowledge," he says, "of human brotherhood, of universal peace."[74] Although a detective discovers and seizes him, he escapes and takes flight, looking in disgust at the "crawling wingless insects below." "Why should I hold myself at their beck and call? . . . I laugh at their puny authority," he exults.[75] He considers flying to the "land of freedom beyond the Atlantic," and resolves that his invention must be given to the whole world, as individual governments are too short-sighted and corrupt to be entrusted with the responsibility.

Meanwhile, armed revolt has broken out in Donegal and a wave of fear begins to sweep Britain. The boy is injured in a crowd and is recaptured by the Home Secretary, who puts him under medical restraint. The Rising sweeps through Ireland and a Provisional Government is set up in Dublin. In the grip of jingoism, the British government prepares an expedition to crush the rebellion. O'Halloran is offered a million pounds by his captors for the secret of flight, but refuses. He had come to the seat of British government to offer his invention for the betterment of mankind, but by their attitudes and treatment of him the British have turned him into a rebel. He is rescued from incarceration by his brother, who still has the boy's original pair of wings, and is flown back to Dublin.

In the climax of the book, O'Halloran offers his services to the Irish revolutionary leader and is set to making wings for a squadron of fighters. He leads aerial attacks on the Castle and upon a blockading ship, both of which are horribly effective thanks to his use of incendiary devices. The revolution is a success, and the boy is embarrassed by the exuberant admiration and gratitude of his countrymen. Although he is appalled by the destruction he has wrought, O'Halloran has no qualms about the political use to which his invention has been put. He feels he had no choice, and in any case he still sees it in transcendent terms. In a concluding Whitmanesque peroration, he expands upon the ability flight can give him to see the whole of life: "I see everything, I sympathise with everything." "It will never be given to the sons of man to know and feel so much, to aid so signally in the forward march and progress of the race," he predicts. Mankind itself will be transformed by flight—"it will not be fulfilled in me; but in my successors, it may." As the book closes, O'Halloran is basking in the adulation of his countrymen, but looking ahead to still greater freedom: "So, one day, I will go forth free and unknown, to realize my old dream, and for a time my place will know me no more."[76]

Although by literary standards Greer's book is little more than a curiosity of the early Irish renaissance period, it does forcefully and schematically portray the situation of the Irish intellectual caught between his own spiritual, mystical, or even scientific aspirations and the call of nationalism. Flight in *A Modern Daedalus* serves as symbol for the awakening spirit—the sense of intellectual adventure which we find toward the end of the Victorian period expressed in writers as diverse as Nietzsche, Wells, d'Annunzio, and Havelock Ellis. Similarly, "science" is a heavily coded term implying spiritual aspiration, social progressiveness, and a putatively disinterested openness to revolutionary ideas. As it had been in its original romantic articulation, the freedom of flight is usually linked to a new political order as well. Like Stephen, Greer's protagonist is a solitary, intellectual boy, alienated from those around him and their values, but stirred by the example of dignity and high-mindedness of Parnell. O'Halloran's confrontation with his father and brothers is most closely paralleled by Stephen's argument with Davin. For both, the real issue is the freedom of the soul, and in Stephen's famous formulation, "When the soul of a man is born in this country there are nets flung at it to hold it back from flight. You talk to me of nationality, language, religion. I shall try to fly by those nets" (*P*, 203). Davin's response is, "Too deep for me Stevie," while O'Halloran's father responds to his vague internationalism by insisting, "We will soon teach you to sing a more manly tune."[77] Of course, one major difference in the two books is that Stephen moves from his early identification with Parnell to a disillusionment with Irish nationalism, while O'Halloran comes to embrace it, having passed through Stephen's attitude of proud aloofness and his scorn of the "rabblement" below him as well.

Greer's book does not face squarely the issues it raises; instead, it embraces Irish revolutionary ideology, wherein the liberation of the country more or less automatically resolves all other conflicts. The vision is that of the Young Ireland movement, where spiritual exaltation and politics are naturally conjoined, whereas in *Portrait* the two are seen as antagonistic and mutually exclusive forces. But the closing perorations of the two books are quite similar in feeling, with Stephen setting out on the wings of his "terrible and exultant youth" to express himself freely, and O'Halloran foreseeing the time when he will fly off "free and

unknown, to realize my old dream." Both have moved from early ignominy, in a subculture that values only physical action, toward a heroism
earned by the mind; but in Stephen's case the heroism is only potential
in his pure opposition, while in O'Halloran's it is fully achieved because
the world itself has been remade. A *Modern Daedalus* is a child's fantasy
of heroism, in which no choice among values must be made: the boy
becomes a military hero as well as a free intellect, transforms the world
so that it must recognize his superiority in his idealistic terms as well as
its own pragmatic, materialistic ones. Perhaps because it is so deeply
embedded in the romantic vision, the aspiration of both protagonists is
finally a renunciation, because perfect freedom can be imagined in no
other terms: Stephen proudly turning away from Mercedes or taking
flight from his family and country, O'Halloran refusing a million pounds
or leaving the scene of his perfect triumph.

Despite Greer's affirmation of Irish nationalism, it should be noted
that Ireland itself has relatively little role in the book's resolution. The
Irish people function as a chorus, expressing scorn for the boy at the
book's beginning and adulation at the end. But the book is not so much
an affirmation of an Irish political revolution as it is an affirmation of
the total expression of the self through individual heroism. O'Halloran's
early internationalism may be proved naive, but at the book's end he is
no less dedicated to spreading the secret of flight to all mankind, the
British (presumably) included; and he is no less alone than in his early
ignominy. Ironically, by delivering his country he has risen above countries, and from his unprecedented height he can view the unity of mankind.

The Count of Monte Cristo

The figure of the artist/scientist as transnational savior is in fact a staple
of the late nineteenth-century popular imagination, but there is an essential ambivalence at the core of the image: although he may express
his will by uniting mankind, righting political or personal wrongs, or
serving as the hand of God, he remains solitary and aloof. His freedom
from personal and national ties allows him extraordinary power to
benefit others, but by the same token he may become a dangerous and
sinister figure because he is free of the ordinary restraints upon men.
Edmond Dantes, Alexandre Dumas *père*'s Count of Monte Cristo, is

surely the most vivid and influential avatar of this image. The Count, whose mainspring is revenge, became the ideal fantasy self of an alienated bourgeoisie during the mid-nineteenth century. Betrayed by his coworkers, he makes an immense fortune abroad in the East—where everything is conventionally transformed into luxury—and returns, ennobled and transfigured by wealth, to wreak his vengeance.

Even Leopold Bloom, for all his self-abnegation, is sufficiently wounded by Molly's adultery to consider self-exile and return as a fantasy solution. He imagines himself a wandering comet: "Whence, disappearing from the constellation of the Northern Crown he would somehow reappear reborn above delta in the constellation of Cassiopeia and after incalculable eons of peregrination return an estranged avenger, a wreaker of justice on malefactors, a dark crusader, a sleeper awakened, with financial resources (by supposition) surpassing those of Rothschild or the silver king" (*U*, 598/728). As Bloom's fantasy suggests, the source of the Count's empowerment, paradoxically, is his exile, his essential solitude. On his return from exile, in a chapter entitled "Ideology," the Count of Monte Cristo explains to a naive and horrified listener (who ironically will be a principal target for his revenge) why he is among "those men whom God has placed above kings and ministers": "My kingdom is bounded only by the world, for I am neither an Italian nor a Frenchman, nor a Hindu nor an American nor a Spaniard. I am a cosmopolite . . . I adopt all customs, speak all languages. . . . You may, therefore, comprehend, that being of no country, asking no protection from any government, acknowledging no man as my brother, not one of the scruples that arrest the powerful or the obstacles which paralyze the weak paralyze or arrest me. Unless I die, I shall always be what I am, and therefore it is that I utter the things you have never heard, even from the mouths of kings."[78] Undoubtedly the figure of this "dark avenger" came to haunt the young Joyce as it did the young Stephen, for whom it "stood forth in his mind for whatever he had heard or divined in childhood of the strange and terrible" (*P*, 62). The "Man Without a Country," in Edward Everett Hale's memorable phrase, was a permanent exile, without the protection of the social contract; yet as a man without allegiances or hostages to fortune he was uniquely master of himself. He was, in a dangerous sense, *privileged*, able to speak the unspeakable in the language of the outlaw.

The image became increasingly seductive to Joyce as he identified with a series of pariahs and exiles, beginning with Parnell and culminating in Ibsen. Their personal aloofness, their dazzling coolness and total dedication to their chosen missions, their ability to use social formality as an aggressive weapon—all these were qualities he emulated as an adolescent. But equally important was the refusal to accept a national context: Joyce's notorious denial of his place in the Irish Literary Renaissance was only partly due to his aesthetic distance from the Celtic Twilight or his bitterness over what he saw as early neglect. In great part he saw himself as European, not so much because of his affinities for Ibsen or Flaubert as because Europe was *other* to Ireland's Rabblement. "Before Ibsen's letter (to him) Joyce was an Irishman," asserts Ellmann; "after it he was a European."[79] But Europe to Joyce meant an escape from provinciality; if he argued in "The Day of the Rabblement" that "a nation which has never advanced so far as a miracle-play affords no literary model to the artist, and he must look abroad" (CW, 78), nonetheless Joyce was less interested in finding a European tradition than in shocking the country he called "the eternal caricature of the serious world" (CW, 176). This point was not lost upon his contemporaries, who easily perceived that Joyce was using arcane references to "the Nolan" as a stick with which to beat Kathleen Ni Houlihan. Arthur Clery, reviewing Joyce's essay in *St. Stephen's* magazine, commented archly that Joyce had been "corrupted, as we do verily believe, by the learning of Italie or othere foreigne parts."[80]

For Stephen, Europe is a promise, at least a promise of difference. Certainly the notion that he had spiritual kindred in Europe was a seductive one. In his famous walk to the Bull, Stephen watches the dappled clouds drifting over Ireland: "The Europe they had come from lay out there beyond the Irish sea, Europe of strange tongues and valleyed and woodbegirt and citadelled and of entrenched and marshalled races. He heard a confused music within him as of memories and names which he was almost conscious of but could not capture even for an instant. . . . A voice from beyond the world was calling" (P, 167). "Confused music" indeed: the Europe evoked here belongs more to Tolkien than to Flaubert. It is a promise of "strange tongues" that he may one day speak and "marshalled races" among which he can lose his national identity, to be born again without the stifling daily contingency of his Irishness.

Indeed, the suggestion is that whatever he shares with the races "beyond" is already within him, so deeply buried that only the dimmest memory stirs at its call. The tone and imagery is continuous with that of Stephen's final vision of "the spell of arms and voices"—the arms of roads and ships that are held out to him, the voices that "say with them: We are your kinsmen. Come." The disembodied, foreign voices call Stephen, "making ready to go, shaking the wings of their terrible and exultant youth" (P, 252). Just as later Stephen searches for a "spiritual father" to replace the egregious Si Dedalus, here he claims a spiritual family "from beyond the world" to replace the rabblement of Firbolgs skinnydipping below him. The logic of the image is associative, but clear: to be European is to be superhuman, winged, and newborn; to be Irish is to be human or subhuman, trapped, and mundane.[81] The attraction of the European pose is that to be European, for Stephen, is to approach the rootlessness of Dantes. For the Irish boy the distance of Europe lends it its total lack of definition; its lack of definition means that it cannot define him, as Ireland has attempted to do.

Ironically, although Stephen cannot realize this, his seduction by the romantic and heroic image of the Count of Monte Cristo will define him more thoroughly than any national allegiance could hope to do. For Dantes's homelessness is only one of a set of defining characteristics of this powerful and overdetermined image. Stephen's first confrontation with the image is enlightening in several respects. After pouring over his "ragged translation," Stephen builds on the parlour table "an image of the wonderful island cave" out of the materials he has at hand and meditates on the picture of sunny Marseilles where the story opens and closes. He identifies a whitewashed cottage outside Blackrock with Mercedes's house,

> and in his imagination he lived through a long train of adventures,
> marvellous as those in the book itself, towards the close of which
> there appeared an image of himself, grown older and sadder,
> standing in a moonlit garden with Mercedes who had so many
> years before slighted his love, and with a sadly proud gesture of re-
> fusal, saying:
> —Madam, I never eat Muscatel grapes. (P, 63)

Following this reverie, Stephen is repelled by the filthy cowyard at Stradbrook, which shatters his childish image of pastoral beauty, and he becomes increasingly conscious of the decline in his father's fortunes, with a "foreknowledge" that "dissipated any vision of the future" (*P*, 64). As this "dusk" closes in on his mind, he again broods on the image of Mercedes, and this time his reverie is not one of proud rejection but of salvation: "He did not know where to seek it or how: but a premonition which led him on told him that this image would, without any overt act of his, encounter him. They would meet quietly as if they had known each other and had made their tryst. . . . They would be alone, surrounded by darkness and silence: and in that moment of supreme tenderness he would be transfigured. He would fade into something impalpable under her eyes and then, in a moment, he would be transfigured. Weakness and timidity and inexperience would fall from him in that magic moment" (*P*, 65). Stephen does not seem to be conscious of the disparity between the two images he evokes for himself, the woman as scorned betrayer and the woman as transfiguring savior. And in a sense this is true to the ideology of the romantic image; even in its medieval chivalric formulations the woman must be both present and absent, both the object of the hero's love and unable to reciprocate his passion. But the radical ambivalence of the image is also rooted in the particular ideology of the nineteenth-century romantic novel.

At the opening of Dumas's novel, Edmond Dantes approximates the pastoral hero, insofar as that is not a contradiction in terms. He is handsome, brave, reverent, popular, and betrothed to the beautiful Mercedes, a somewhat exotic girl from a village which is half Moorish, half Spanish. Although he is neither aristocratic nor wealthy, he is about to accede to the captaincy of a vessel owned by a generous and kind merchant. Indeed, he is made uneasy by the extent of his own happiness, because "man does not appear to me to be intended to enjoy felicity so unmixed."[82] As if to fulfill his premonition, guards interrupt his wedding to arrest him for carrying a secret Bonapartist message from the former captain of his ship. Dantes, who had no idea of the content of the message, has been betrayed by a spurned suitor of Mercedes and a false friend who envies his success. Compounding the injustice, the deputy public prosecutor in charge of his case and his appeal, Villefort, realizes that his own father would be implicated by the message and so "buries" Dantes in the infamous Château d'If.

The remainder of the novel is quite simple in outline, which has led to the multitude of abridgments in the book's popular history; its enormous length in its original form is due to the numerous subplots, complications, and unrelated episodes interpolated by Dumas and his collaborator Macquet. In prison, having gone nearly mad with solitude, Dantes finally makes contact with a fellow prisoner, the Abbé Faria. The old monk has become a master of the arts and sciences by dint of superhuman study and teaches Dantes all that he knows. He also tells Dantes the location of the immense treasure of the Borgias. After the Abbé's death Dantes escapes by substituting himself for the body, which is thrown from the dungeon into the sea, and by joining a group of pirates he makes his way to the island of Monte Cristo. After finding the treasure he purchases the island and a noble title to it. For a time he resides in a luxuriously appointed cave on the island, accompanied by an Arabic servant and by an Eastern princess whom he introduces as his slave. He becomes known as "Sinbad the Sailor" (with whom Bloom, falling asleep at the end of "Ithaca," has travelled). Under this and a variety of other disguises—his incarceration has made him physically almost unrecognizable—he returns to Paris to reward his faithful friends and to wreak vengeance on his enemies, all of whom have now attained positions of wealth and prominence. At least in the original version of the book his vengeance is incredibly prolonged and indirect, and by the time it has started to destroy the blameless members of his victims' families, he begins to wonder whether he has—as he had previously assumed— genuinely been the hand of Providence.

At the start of the story is his transcendent love for Mercedes, who vows to remain faithful to him during his imprisonment; as the boat transports him to the Château d'If he sees the single light from her chamber, which gives him his only hope (an image echoed by the light from Molly's window in "Ithaca"). But when his appeals fail and he is believed to be dead, Mercedes betrays him by marrying one of his betrayers. It is this, more than any of his other injustices, which motivates Dantes's revenge and triggers his transformation into the superhuman Count. Dumas underlines the theme of the woman's betrayal by interpolating the story of a young Italian boy who is transformed into the outlaw Luigi Vampa when his innocent love is betrayed by Teresa, whom the narrator ironically terms a "worthy daughter of Eve."[83] Later, in the scene that so haunts Stephen, the mysterious Count is the toast of Paris and is being entertained by his betrayer; although Mercedes half-recognizes Dantes and begs him to take some refreshment, he refuses coldly and politely. It is understandable that Stephen should dwell on this scene, as it is one of the *tableaux* that punctuate the novel, and toward which the action tends. The Count has several other powerful scenes with Mercedes: in one she begs him to spare the life of her son, who has challenged the Count to a duel, and Dantes bitterly resolves that he will forfeit his own life, as a final gesture for the woman he still loves but must forsake. Still later, at the end of the book, he establishes her in his father's house in Marseilles and preserves her from ruin; once again she offers herself and once again he refuses, content to remain her savior. The *tableaux* are of course repetitive; like pornography, this variety of romantic novel, having moved toward a culminating scene, can then only reenact that scene.

The motive force in the transfiguration of Edmond Dantes is his betrayal by his friends, by the representative of the State, and ultimately by his fiancée. Once in the Château d'If, he officially ceases to exist, and this official death is mirrored by a series of death-images, as he impersonates the Abbé's corpse and is thrown from the battlements. Even when his trick is discovered, he is assumed to have died, since his jailors do not realize that he has hidden upon him a knife with which he cuts the bonds around his shroud. Having died, he is then reborn from the sea with a new identity and a new personality. Christian imagery naturally surrounds this process. He escapes from the Château fourteen years to the day from his imprisonment, at the age of thirty-three. And in order to discover the hidden treasure on the island—the treasure that enables him to be born again with the name Monte Cristo—he must roll away the stone from a tomb. Afterward, in rewarding those who remained faithful to him, he sees himself as "heaven's substitute"[84] and in punishing the wicked as the agent of Providence.[85] In case Mercedes has missed any of the symbolism, in his final farewell to her he explains that he is a "Divine instrument" who "would have sacrificed my life to you."[86]

But the perverse power of Monte Cristo's image does not come simply from his reenactment of Christ's agony on Gethsemane and his miraculous return to judge the living and the dead; it comes from the substantial diabolic imagery and language that surrounds him as well. To become superhuman, Dantes must also become inhuman, and those he encounters sense this uncanny transformation with a mixture of attraction and repulsion. Early in his incarceration, Dantes's original asceticism gives way to a rage which never leaves him, which possesses him.[87]

On his escape he finds that he has been made superior by his suffering and indeed has learned to take an inhuman pleasure in his own pain and that of others; "Pain, thou art not an evil," he exclaims.[88] The sight of a dead man "had made but slight impression upon him," as his "heart was in a fair way of petrifying in his bosom."[89] As he begins his course of vengeance, he further hardens his heart, exclaiming, "Farewell kindness, humanity, and gratitude."[90] He has become the complete misanthrope, whose only companions are pirates and outlaws. Indeed, there is a clear element of sadism in his prolonged and elaborate courses of revenge; instead of simply challenging each of his enemies, he acts from behind the scenes, pretending to befriend them while subtly setting in motion the mechanism of their ruin.

Throughout, the Count acts as a lethal and enigmatic artist, specifically a dramatist, who works with the materials of life itself. With the aid of the knowledge he has gained of his enemies' shameful secrets, he stages scenes to harrow their souls and looks on with ironic enjoyment. In arranging a particularly elaborate revenge, where the daughter of one of his enemies will be led to marry a young criminal, he hires two plausible rogues to enact a mock-reunion of father and son, thus parodying one of the topoi of sentimental literature.[91] And like the Flaubertian artist, he takes care always to remain in the background of his own plots. When his victims accuse him of having recommended a man who turns out to be a villain and the agent of their ruin, he can reply with honesty and perfect detachment that he has done no such thing: he merely allowed them to infer that the man had his recommendation. The Count will lie only by misdirection and omission, never in direct speech. An artist in the theater of cruelty, he is in equal parts godlike and diabolic, and indeed he is fully conscious of this creative ambiguity. In perhaps the book's most remarkable scene, a clear anticipation of the "Grand Inquisitor" passage in The Brothers Karamazov, the Count tells a parable to his chief enemy, Villefort:

> "I, too, as happens to every man once in his life, have been taken
> by Satan into the highest mountain in the earth, and when there he
> showed me all the kingdoms of the earth, and as he said before, so
> said he to me, 'Child of earth, what wouldst thou have to make
> thee adore me?' I reflected long, for a gnawing ambition had long
> preyed upon me, and then I replied, 'Listen, I have always heard
> tell of Providence, and yet I have never seen Him, nor anything

that resembles Him or which can make me believe that He exists. I wish to be Providence myself, for I feel that the most beautiful, noblest, most sublime thing in the world is to recompense and punish.' Satan bowed his head and groaned. 'You mistake,' he said; 'Providence does exist, only you have never seen Him, because the child of God is as invisible as the parent. You have seen nothing that resembles Him, because he works by secret springs and moves by hidden ways. All I can do for you is to make you one of the agents of that Providence.' The bargain was concluded. I may sacrifice my soul, but what matters it?" added Monte Cristo. "If the thing were to do again, I would again do it."[92]

So far, the parallels to Stephen's developing image as artist are too clear to belabor. In *Portrait* both Christian and Satanic imagery and allusions cluster around him; with Cranly the Baptist looking on, he is crucified by Ireland while simultaneously falling from an angelic state, announcing that he will not serve (*P*, 239). If he is not actually betrayed by E. C. with one of his false friends, at least he needs to convince himself that he has been, and that betrayal is the spur to his art. In *Ulysses* the betrayal by false friends, Mulligan in particular, is paramount, and Stephen's revenge through art is introduced. He is writing a book, and all his "friends" are in it; even Mulligan "fears the lancet of my art," Stephen thinks (*U*, 6/7). At the book's beginning Mulligan finds Stephen's refusal to pray for his dying mother inhuman, and remarks, "There is something sinister in you" (*U*, 5/5). Rather than discourage this reading of his image, Stephen seems to cherish it. In "Circe" he has become fully diabolic, attending the black mass and leading the dance of death, then finally destroying the universe with his cry, "*Non serviam!*" (*U*, 475/582).

But solitude and exile, betrayal, revenge, and Christian/Satanic symbolism are only the initial themes linking Stephen and the Count. Disappointed young idealists, both become powerfully misanthropic egotists. In his talk with Villefort, Dantes preaches the politics of egotism, not socialism: "I never seek to protect society, who does not protect me."[93] Stephen, outraging his own bourgeois, responds to Bloom's advocacy of socialism in Ireland by retorting, "You suspect . . . that I may be important because I belong to the *faubourg Saint Patrice* called Ireland for short. . . . But I suspect . . . that Ireland must be important because it belongs to me" (*U*, 527/645). Yet the egotism of both men is licensed, even depersonalized, by their extreme dedication to a mission. Dantes, in his role as Monte Cristo, taunts Villefort by asserting that as one of those "whom God has placed above kings and ministers by giving them a mission to fulfill," he is above the prosecutor's justice: "the procureur de roi, be he who he may, with whom I should have to deal would assuredly be more embarrassed than I should."[94]

Elsewhere, it is suggested that the Count is like Manfred, Lara, and Werner, Byronic heroes "whom Misery has marked with a fatal brand— some Manfred, some Lara, some Werner, one of those wrecks, as it were, of some ancient family, who, disinherited of their patrimony, have achieved one by the force of their adventurous genius, which has placed them above the laws of society."[95] This secular, romantic license is of course closer to Stephen's artistic one than is the Count's mission on God's behalf; because Stephen's task is to "forge in the smithy of my soul the uncreated conscience of my race" (P, 253), he refuses to serve "that in which I no longer believe whether it call itself my home, my fatherland or my church" (P, 246–47). His weapons—silence, exile, and cunning—are precisely those employed by the Count of Monte Cristo in that artist's long revenge. Dantes's exile is literal, and his cunning diabolical. His silence, like Stephen's, is less a matter of withholding speech than of disguising his intent and his emotional investment in his actions. As the Count tells Villefort, his superiority lies not in having never sinned, but in being "impenetrable" and in maintaining his pride.[96]

The key to the Count's powerful impression on others is his *affect*, the set of gestures, expressions, stances, and languages he employs in his centerless impersonation. His appearance contributes to this, as he is tall, strikingly pale, powerful. He habitually dresses in black and bears the marks of suffering on his face. His speech is formal and precise, and although he may talk about himself in grandiose terms, as he does with Villefort, he is more inclined to hold his silence; naturally, he admits nothing of his true background and identity. A "keen and cutting politeness"[97] is his invariable social armament. His mind is his most dangerous weapon, though; he has absorbed the Abbé Faria's almost supernatural scholarship and faultless logical methodology and has trained his memory to perfection.[98] In a scene echoed toward the end of *Portrait*, immediately before his escape Dantes stands watching a bank of clouds sweep by and muses that, whatever the extent of the hidden treasure of which the Abbé has told him, his real treasure is his learning. During his

Paris career, this is yet another weapon. He is a demon debater who uses epigram, aphorism, and paradox to manipulate or demolish any who question him. Yet he remains a fatally attractive figure because he is unique. A Parisian socialite asks another who has seen the Count at the Opera, "Did the eccentric person commit any new originality?" and she replies, "Can he be seen without doing so?"[99]

Just as the Count is a symbolic oxymoron, simultaneously Christ and Antichrist, so his social image combines the extremes of cold, polite, formal behavior with a constant suggestion of decadent sensuality and total outlawry. Like the figure of the dandy he presents a facade of extreme social conformity that, stripped of any of the coloration of a natural, spontaneous ego, turns to parody.[100] The mask is so perfect that there can be nothing behind it, and so the sentimental illusions that support the rituals of courtesy must collapse. The Count's politeness is dangerous. The result of superhuman self-discipline, his self-possession is perfect. At the same time, without ever quite violating society's explicit taboos, he manages to outrage its tacit assumptions. At the Opera, his "originality" is to appear accompanied by a slave girl in harem outfit—an indulgence that by implication effectively strips the social facade from other gentlemen sitting with their expensive wives and mistresses. On his island, as Sinbad the Sailor, a reputed pirate king, the Count entertains a young Parisian with hashish and the finest foods, wines, and perfumes: his Aladdin's Cave is the perfect image of the nineteenth-century bourgeois dream of *luxe et volupté*. And yet this paragon of forbidden indulgence seldom eats or drinks in public, much less commits any of the minor improprieties.

Because Stephen is seldom described in *Portrait* or *Ulysses* it may not be obvious how closely he is modeled on this figure. Yet it is clear that from his original conception this ultimate aesthetic rebel was envisaged as cool, formal, suave, aggressively articulate, but always at an ironic distance from his interlocutors. In the 1904 essay "A Portrait of the Artist," Joyce describes his artist after having undergone a period of violent religious zeal alternating with disillusionment: "About this period the enigma of a manner was put up at all corners to protect the crisis. He was quick enough now to see that he must disentangle his affairs in secrecy and reserve had ever been a light penance. His reluctance to debate scandal and to seem curious, of others aided him in his real indictment and was not without a satisfactory flavour of the heroic.

It was part of that ineradicable egoism which he was afterward to call redeemer that he imagined converging to him the deeds and thoughts of the microcosm."[101] Secrecy, reserve, cultivation of an "enigma of a manner," incuriosity, and an ineradicable egotism that imagines itself the center of universal purpose: the basic elements of the artist's image are already present. So is the enormous disdain for the multitude of men, "their Intensities" and "their Bullockships," but once he has lodged his single violent protest, cool self-control reigns: "His Nego therefore, written amid a chorus of peddling Jews' gibberish and Gentile clamour . . . was drawn up valiantly . . . but, that protest over, it was urbanity in warfare."[102] Just as solitude is the key to the transformation of Dantes, so the young artist finds that "Isolation . . . is the first principle of artistic economy,"[103] and actively pursues it.

Certainly there is irony in the presentation even of this artist, and increasing irony in the presentation of the Stephen of *Stephen Hero* and of *Portrait*. But the irony is also increasingly directed toward the young man's own "intensities," never toward his disdain and coolness. This aspect of the romantic heroic image apparently was the last to become the object of Joyce's distancing irony, perhaps because he never quite abandoned it himself. Eugene Sheehy has testified that "Joyce, the schoolboy, was as icy, aloof, and imperturbable as . . . Joyce the man."[104] Thomas F. Bacon describes him reading a paper before a college society: "Joyce, thin and pale, stood erect, scarcely moving, cold and undisturbed by interruptions (and he had many), and seemed in passionless tones to wither the opposition by his air of indifferent disdain."[105] Padraic Colum was well aware that, like Wilde, Joyce on his return from France was busy establishing a public persona as artist. The social chill Joyce was fond of utilizing, Colum remarks, was a fairly popular technique: "All of us used the cold approach from time to time, of course—the 'frozen mitt' was often proffered." But Joyce seemed to take artifice a step further. "The gestures he made with the ashplant he now carried, his way of making his voice raucous, was surely part of an act."[106]

And as the Count of Monte Cristo sends young Franz to Paris ahead of him to spread the tale of this fascinating figure, Joyce could sometimes rely on companions to publicize and embroider his image. "It was solely as a 'character,' and that partly a Gogartian creation, that Joyce was known to Dubliners of that time."[107] Like Joyce (and like Dantes),

Stephen is never vulgar in direct speech, although at least in implication some of his remarks are as blasphemous as any of Mulligan's more obvious shockers. But the key to Stephen's artistic persona is the whiff of brimstone floating about his fastidious and composed demeanor. Unlike the Count, Stephen does not have the enormous wealth that will insure that his reputation will proceed him, and so he must sometimes hint at the extent of his private degradation. "When you told me that night in Harcourt Street those things about your private life," admits Davin, "honest to God, Stevie, I was not able to eat my dinner. I was quite bad. I was awake a long time that night. Why did you tell me those things?" (*P*, 202). "That he was an intellectually exceptional young man anyone who met him could tell," Colum asserts, adding, "but they also knew he had frequently been in the gutter."[108] Joyce would make sure of both impressions.

While the image of Stephen and the Count draws energy from the creative tensions between propriety and degradation, or between Christian and Satanic motifs, it also relies on a final contradiction between freedom and fatality. Both men, relying on stock romantic imagery, equate freedom with the flight of birds. In his island cave, "Sinbad" explains to young Franz, "I am as free as a bird, and have wings like one."[109] So does Franz, once he has indulged in the Count's hashish, and the Count must reassure him that there is no danger in *this* flight: "If your wings, like those of Icarus, melt before the sun, we are here to receive you."[110] Dantes is no Icarus; he has already followed the "Daedalian labyrinth of probabilities"[111] to hunt down the treasure, and has emerged as a fullfledged artificer. But the Count's bursts of elation in his own powers are sometimes followed by bouts of depression wherein he sees himself victim of a terrible fatality. He has, after all, already lost Mercedes before he begins his career as nemesis. At the end of the book he admits, "I have become revengeful, cunning, and wicked,"[112] and wonders whether he has traced a false path throughout the last ten years. As he explains to Villefort in his parable, he has struck a devil's bargain to become the agent of Providence, and at the book's end neither he nor the reader is sure whether he has been the embodiment of perfect human freedom or has merely been acting out his own doom.

Stephen, once he has recognized himself as Artist, invariably articulates the ideology of romantic freedom, but of course his self-doubt is equally apparent in *Portrait*. If the prophecy of "his own strange name" fills him with elation when he realizes his vocation (*P*, 168), not long afterward when he broods on the image of the hawklike man "a sense of fear of the unknown moved in the heart of his weariness" (*P*, 225). As he rather grandly explains to Cranly at the end of *Portrait*, the magnitude of his ambition will demand equally great self-denial and suffering. In *Ulysses* his self-doubt, even self-contempt, is a running unspoken obbligato to his public self-assertion. Unlike Dantes, his fear has become less the terror before an unknown fate and more a sinking suspicion that he may be neither superlatively successful nor magnificently doomed. Doubting and mocking voices, like his father's, frequently sound in his imagination: "Sure he's not down in Strasburg terrace with his aunt Sally? Couldn't he fly a bit higher than that, eh?" (*U*, 32/38). Yet the more he is assailed by self-doubt, the more imperviously polished his image grows. Even drunken and exhausted, in "Eumaeus," he treats Bloom to a sequence of perverse epigrams and "dagger definitions." It is not the fault of his scrupulously maintained image if Bloom is the single character in the book who is immune to this sort of cold wit, and thus able to render it impotent.

> —You suspect, Stephen retorted with a sort of a half laugh, that I may be important because I belong to the *faubourg Saint Patrice* called Ireland for short.
> —I would go a step farther, Mr Bloom insinuated.
> —But I suspect, Stephen interrupted, that Ireland must be important because it belongs to me.
> —What belongs, queried Mr Bloom bending, fancying he was perhaps under some misapprehension. Excuse me. Unfortunately I didn't catch the latter portion. What was it you? . . .
> Stephen, patently crosstempered, repeated and shoved aside his mug of coffee or whatever you like to call it none too politely. (*U*, 527/645)

From the perspective of Stephen's image, the real significance of his meeting with Bloom is that, like a father, Bloom ignores the young man's pose. He ruins Stephen's timing with his interjections and destroys his mots by asking to have them repeated. His reaction to Stephen's romantic egotism here is to assume some failing in "the home life" and to remind himself in extenuation that the boy has recently returned from Paris. From a dialogical perspective, Stephen's aggressive language has been rendered meaningless by Bloom's refusal to participate in the social sparring to which the intellectual is accustomed. Stephen's "offensive" language has hitherto been his best defense; he is disarmed by Bloom's unwitting but effective refusal to take offense.

Since his childhood discovery of the Count, Stephen has partially successfully and wholly unconsciously attempted to adapt that persona to his own situation. Like Dantes, he has gone to the brink of madness and has undergone a regimen of prayer and self-mortification. When his situation grows too obviously dissimilar to Dantes's, he modifies it by brute force, seeking out solitude in the midst of his crowded family life, manufacturing betrayals by those who owed him no allegiance and exiling himself from a country that tries to persuade him to stay. Although he cannot purchase a patent of nobility like Dantes, he persuades himself that he is a Milesian among Firbolgs. His guilt and horror at his own sexual excess is certainly psychologically real, but his careful interweaving of the *poète maudit* into the fabric of his image is no less real. No doubt he is genuinely outraged that E. C. should speak informally to a young priest when she might have been speaking to a young poet, but the violence of his reaction indicates that he needs a traitorous Mercedes even more than a faithful one (*P*, 219–20). Indeed, the lingering remnants of the chivalric-romantic ideology, the search for a "pure" woman who by purely reflecting the hero's ego can transform it, is all that restrains Stephen from transforming himself into a creature of pure vengeance.

Romantic Precursors

If, as Bakhtin has argued, the novel is a genre which feeds upon itself, this is even more true of romantic narrative. Certainly Joyce's *Portrait* echoes *The Count of Monte Cristo* in theme, image, and language; but the elder Dumas's book is itself a farrago of allusions, adaptations, and borrowings from earlier romantic literature. Indeed, the situation is complicated by the fact that Edmond Dantes as Count becomes a self-conscious artist whose basic mode is the conventional romantic dramatic tableau: for all the talk of his uniqueness, he works upon his victims most powerfully through their shocked recognition that they have been cast as the victims of poetic justice. Perversely, they only know the Count is unique when they recognize in him the stock figure of Nemesis. Further, he is paradoxically recognized as an "original" primarily because he employs signs belonging to an established repertoire: he is a pirate, a superior sort of outlaw; he is mysteriously associated with the East; he has no ordinary communal or familial ties; his demeanor is cold and polite. Byron, whose works themselves became popular literature during the nineteenth century, is the immediate source of this repertoire, in narratives such as *Childe Harold*, *The Giaour*, *The Corsair*, *Lara*, and of course *Don Juan*. But then Byron himself is indebted to the popular Gothics and other ephemeral literature. Peter Thorslev notes that he "was quite well-read, perhaps especially in the contemporary popular literature which seems no longer of much importance to us. . . . He devoured Gothic novels by the score."[113] The heritage of romantic narrative up through the twentieth century is a particularly tangled tapestry of literary and subliterary elements. Still, Dumas's direct reliance upon Byron is undeniable, nor does he attempt to hide it: on several occasions characters refer to the Count as "Lord Ruthven," the name of a satiric and sinister portrait of Byron in Lady Caroline Lamb's *Glenarvon*,[114] while Haidé, his Greek slave/princess, shares her name and physical description with the Greek princess Don Juan encounters in the Cyclades (canto 3, stanzas 70–76). Nor are these merely casual allusions; Byron himself was so closely identified with his ambiguous heroes that his eulogy by Scott can serve as the standard description: "That mighty Genius, which walked among men as something superior to ordinary mortality, and whose powers we beheld with wonder, and something approaching to terror, as if we knew not whether they were of good or ill."[115]

The central sinister/heroic figure is the most significant of Dumas's Byronic echoes, in that it is adapted most directly by Joyce. But Joyce, of course, also had direct access to Byron's work and to Byron's precursors and imitators, so that there is no hope of establishing a direct chain of influence. Varieties of the dark romantic hero were important elements of the general cultural repertoire of the late nineteenth century. The figure of the "noble outlaw," naturally, predated Byron's writing; Thorslev points to Goethe's *Götz von Berlichingen* (1771), Schiller's Karl Moor in *Die Räuber* (1781), and Scott's *Marmion* (1808).[116] He has elements of the Gothic villain and of the ballad outlaw in his makeup, but is ostensibly a more serious figure than either. Wronged by his intimates or by society in general, he is compelled to a rebellion that is essentially solitary, whether or not he is surrounded by cohorts. He loves one woman, who is denied to him. He is possessed by *Weltschmerz*, which Thorslev acutely analyzes as a tension between the drive to lose the self in a vision of the absolute and the drive to assert the self as individual.[117] Put in these terms, the relevance to Stephen Dedalus's character is clear. The Byronic hero's interpersonal aspect is forbidding but paradoxically attractive. The description of Conrad "The Corsair" fits Monte Cristo perfectly and, softened somewhat, suggests Dedalus as well:

> And oft perforce his rising lip reveals
> The haughtier thought it curbs, but scarce conceals.
> Though smooth his voice and calm his general mien,
> Still seems there something he would not have seen:
> His features' deepening lines and varying hue
> At times attracted, yet perplexed the view,
> As if within that murkiness of mind
> Work'd feelings fearful and yet undefined.
>   (canto 1, stanza 9)

With archetypal elements of Faust, Cain/Ahasuerus, and Satan/Prometheus in his constitution, the Byronic hero is driven by an overriding but somehow illegitimate purpose. He is uneasy within the repellent sphere of ordinary men, yet—sometimes against his own wishes—is fated to play their benefactor. He brings a transfusion of energy from beyond the social bounds, and thus becomes both savior and pariah, a fate he faces with accustomed arrogance. His isolation is the source of his strength, and the individuality of his selfhood must be preserved at all costs:

> He would not yield dominion of his mind
> To Spirits against whom his own rebelled,
> Proud though in desolation.
>   (*Childe Harold*, canto 3, stanza 12)

Pirate or poet, he is preeminently a sensual figure, yet the very intensity of that sensuality seems to point to a source of energy or inspiration that is supramundane. The Romantic sensual vocabulary is filled with swooning languors and ecstasies primarily because even the swollen Romantic ego cannot contain its own sensual impulse. Indeed, the defining (and self-defeating) characteristic of his sensuality is that it overpowers any possible worldly object. Nothing is fit to receive it, and so the sensual impulse inevitably moves toward death, frustration, or a major displacement into politics, personal intrigue, or art.

With Stephen this latter is the case, and we should note that the "birdgirl" is primarily a sensual image, which for him embodies the intersection of art and life. So overwhelming is the role of the church in his psyche that it is easy to overlook the possibility that the boy's enormously charged sensual impulses might have driven him to desperation even in the absence of institutionally imposed guilt. As a child, he "wanted to meet in the real world the unsubstantial image which his soul so constantly beheld" (P, 65), and as a youth he so hypostatizes the image of E. C. that she could never serve as an adequate object for his dangerous adoration. Like the Byronic hero, Stephen emerges from Portrait in a frozen attitude of defiance toward those who would impose their will upon him, disgusted disdain for the mass of men, and resolution "to express myself in some mode of life or art as freely as I can and as wholly as I can" (P, 247).

There is nothing very surprising in the idea of Stephen Dedalus as romantic hero; to some extent, this was how he was viewed during the first phase of the book's reception. Yet two important qualifiers were always added in mitigation of the book's romanticism: the presence of irony and the abundance of realistic detail. We should realize that both of these are in fact aspects of the Byronic narrative that were often carried over into its novelistic reflections, even on the popular level. Admittedly Don Juan's irony probably kept it from the massive popularity of the "Turkish Tales" during the nineteenth century, and Byron's interjection of "realistic" detail never approached the naturalism of Joyce's narrative, but with these qualifications in mind it is not difficult to see the debt of Portrait to the general tradition of the Byronic narrative.

Even in its formal aspects Portrait suggests the Byronic narrative more closely than it does the mainstream of the Victorian novel. Joyce's novel is immediately experienced as a mixture of literary modes, with exaggerated passages of naturalistic description (Stephen's grotesque "epiphanies" while visiting relatives [P, 67–68]), dream-visions (the capering goat-like creatures, [P, 137]), external narration, internal narration verging on stream-of-consciousness, and even diary notations of a variety of modes. Karl Kroeber has pointed out that a defining characteristic of romantic style is "the way in which it combines hospitality to a wide

variety of literary traditions with insistence upon original, strongly indi-
vidualized expression."[118] Like the romantic story-poem, *Portrait* is
catholic in its literary posture, suggesting at times *Young Werther*, at
others *New Grub Street*. But it is in narrative movement, not narrative
texture, that the book is most indebted to romantic narratives. Even the
most action-centered of Byron's story-poems move from tableau to tableau, alternating meticulous description, inward reverie, and outward
action virtually without transitions; the effect, muffled somewhat by the
poetic form, is of Joycean juxtaposition. Joyce's "metonymic method,"
which struck early readers as unnovelistic, had a clear precursor in romantic narrative.

   While the romantic narrative had minimal influence on the main
course of the Victorian novel, appearing mainly in debased popular novels of the 1830s and 1840s, the work of the Brontës, and the early works
of Bulwer-Lytton, it flourished on the Continent—in the novels of Dumas *père* and *fils*, of course, but in Hugo as well. Still, an argument can
be made that, having skipped sixty years, the influence of the romantic
aesthetic on prose narrative made itself felt around the turn of the century in England. As John Bayley put it, "It is arguable that the novelists
rather than the poets of the nineteenth century are the real beneficiaries
of the great Romantic endowment. . . . Those who deplore the plight of
contemporary poetry often ignore the fact that many of the former functions of the poet have been taken over by the novelist: the change is
simply one of form."[119] Charles Schug develops this thesis in *The Romantic Genesis of the Modern Novel*, stressing the "discontinuous, nonnarrative structure" of Romantic fiction and citing its appearance in
James, Conrad, and Woolf.[120] On purely formal grounds, the early
Joyce is an equally appropriate example.

   But from a Bakhtinian perspective, much of this literary history is
beside the point:

> Unfortunately, historians of literature usually reduce this struggle
> between the novel and other already completed genres, all these as-
> pects of novelization, to the actual real-life struggle among
> "schools" and "trends." A novelized poem, for example, they call a
> "romantic poem" (which of course it is) and believe that in so do-
> ing they have exhausted the subject. They do not see beneath the
> superficial hustle and bustle of literary process the major and cru-
> cial fates of literature and language, whose great heroes turn out to

be first and foremost genres, and whose "trends" and "schools" are but second- and third-rank protagonists. (*DI*, 7–8)

Bakhtin's "novelization" process automatically embraces romantic narrative, in great measure because in the Byronic story-poem there is a mutual interpenetration of the languages of author and protagonist: as he observes of *Eugene Onegin*, "the hero is located in a zone of potential conversation with the author, in a zone of *dialogical contact*" (*DI*, 45).

There is a close connection between this linguistic positioning of author and protagonist and the image of the Byronic hero (which after all is a matter of language as well). For the Byronic hero, most especially in his purest novelistic form—the Count of Monte Cristo—occupies a space within the parameters of the surrounding fictional world and characters that is directly analogous to that occupied by the author. He is central; he encounters only forms of his desire and imagination, all of them in some manner bearing his signature. He is the motive force of the narrative, which nonetheless impedes him, like a viscous fluid, from the full realization of his desire. And it is his very centrality and energy that creates the sense of his own "otherness," his partial removal from the sphere of his action. Like the author faced with his text, he cannot avoid a stance of arrogant disdain before a world entirely composed of reflections, permutations, and perversions of his desire; like the author, he is continually impelled toward a consummation that is unreachable simply because it lies beyond the textual world. The dialogue of author and protagonist, in *Portrait* as in the Byronic narrative, is a semiotic necessity; on this level, at least, neither has anyone else who could understand his speech.

Within a larger context, both author and protagonist are engaged in continuous dialogues with literary precursors. If the language within which Stephen is embedded echoes that of the Byronic narrative, popular French responses to that narrative such as *The Count of Monte Cristo*, and even less literary avatars of the form like *A Modern Daedalus*, this is not to say that nothing essential is altered in the course of the dialogue. Stephen is not simply a Byronic hero, a Monte Cristo, or an O'Halloran; he is that figure trapped within a world that offers resistance to his desires in forms other than those he is able to assimilate. The lips of the prostitute he encounters "pressed upon his brain as upon his lips as though they were the vehicle of a vague speech" (*P*, 101), and this image can serve as an emblem for his ceaseless interactions with languages he does not know and cannot accept—that of his school-fellows, that of the church, and at another remove the language of grim banality he hears embodied in the watery tea and yellow dripping with which he must make his daily communion. And all of these are aspects of the incredibly protean authorial language, manifestations of the stunning literary ventriloquism that presides over Stephen's heroism. Stephen is not simply a Byronic hero, but unless that fundamental impulse of his image is recognized it is impossible to realize the extent and complexity of his plight.

· 5 ·

A PORTRAIT OF THE

ARTIST AS TEXT

Stephen's Reading: Allusive Dialogism

Peter Parley's Tales

If popular novels of the genre of *The Count of Monte Cristo* are the most significant formal precursors of *Portrait*, at least from the perspective of the artist's developing image, countless other evanescent works also come into dialogical interaction with Stephen's consciousness as its verbal structures evolve within the novel. Paramount among the texts which offer a structure and a repertoire of images to the mind of the young Stephen are his schoolbooks. The few of these which are specified in *Portrait* include Doctor Cornwall's *Spelling Book* (*P*, 10), the nameless geography text whose illustration of the earth among clouds Fleming colors green and maroon (*P*, 15), Richmal Mangnall's *Questions* (which Joyce spells "Magnall"), and Peter Parley's *Tales* about Greece and Rome (*P*, 53). In addition, a few texts are suggested by internal evidence: for instance, the sentence "Balbus was building a wall" (*P*, 43), which Atherton has traced to *Kennedy's Latin Primer*.[1] Clearly, not all these books are especially significant, although each plays some part in Stephen's developing consciousness. Cornwall's Speller and the Latin text are probably most fruitfully approached precisely as Joyce does in *Portrait*, as sources of gnomic, detached phrases which catch Stephen's imagination:

Wolsey died in Leicester Abbey
Where the abbots buried him.
Canker is a disease of plants,
Cancer one of animals.

These "nice sentences," as Stephen notes, "were like poetry but they were only sentences to learn the spelling from" (*P*, 10).

Certainly in the context of the chapter, the sentences underline the imagery of death and illness, which culminates in Stephen's delirious vision of Parnell's funeral ship. But for Stephen at the moment, they are parallel to the nonsense rhymes of childhood games or the more complex phrases of the catechism he must learn; they are form with minimal content, or a content whose context is mysterious to him.[2] Like "Balbus was building a wall," they suggest an actor and an action, but no grounds for evaluation, no background against which the action is perceived. As such, they are unique in that they carry with them no ideology. Stephen as the young poet reacts to the rhythmic phonemes before he has any idea of their meaning. They are a sort of language that, because it appears "unclaimed" by any authoritative context, might be available for Stephen's dialogical appropriation. Yet this is not really the case; the boy already suspects that the sentences carry a coded meaning to which he has no access. Each sentence stands isolate, pregnant with a mysterious, ritual significance that defies exploration. No doubt Stephen, like other schoolchildren of the time, studied the random sentences for translation at the end of each chapter in Kennedy's *Primer* in a baffled attempt to connect them in a meaningful narrative. In this respect such texts mimic the specialized languages of the adult world, for example the language of political rhetoric Stephen hears uncomprehendingly at Christmas dinner. They defy connection or logic and persist as unassimilated linguistic bits, floating free on the surface of consciousness.

Mangnall's Questions is a different case; with its strict catechistic form it is more important for the structuring of consciousness than these early texts, but since Joyce kept the book in his personal library and used it as a major model for the "Ithaca" episode of *Ulysses*, it might more usefully be examined in that context. The Peter Parley books, on the other hand, resemble the line of school stories since *Tom Brown* in that they come close to furnishing a structure for the final episode of

Portrait's Chapter 1. This is made quite explicit as Stephen is contemplating appealing Father Dolan's unjust punishment to Father Conmee:

> He would go up and tell the rector that he had been wrongly punished. A thing like that had been done before by somebody in history, by some great person whose head was in the books of history. And the rector would declare that he had been wrongly punished because the Senate and the Roman people always declared that the men who did thta had been wrongly punished. Those were the great men whose names were in Richmal Magnall's [*sic*] Questions. History was all about those men and what they did and that was what Peter Parley's Tales about Greece and Rome were all about. Peter Parley himself was on the first page in a picture. There was a road over a heath with grass at the side and little bushes: and Peter Parley had a broad hat like a protestant minister and a big stick and he was walking fast along the road to Greece and Rome. (*P*, 53)

Peter Parley is the authority for history; his concrete presence on the title page lends verisimilitude to the Greeks and Romans. He is the thoroughly mythical point of origin of the text, whose presence is attested to by his speaking voice. A benevolent, avuncular deity, he narrates and evaluates historical events and directly addresses his young readers. Far from a nightmare, history according to Peter Parley is a series of repetitive, personal narratives exemplifying moral points.

The Peter Parley persona, adopted by the American Samuel Griswold Goodrich and his stable of writers, narrated many texts for school use, of which the volumes on Rome and Greece were two of the most widely used. During a thirty-year period some seven million copies of 120 genuine Parleys were sold, not counting a flood of imitators and spurious Parleys, particularly in England. Having been severely frightened by fairy tales in his childhood, Goodrich dedicated himself to producing factual texts for children that would counteract these "atrocious books," and indeed the matter-of-fact style of narration of his histories and geographies tends to flatten the most romantic of events. Aside from school texts, *Peter Parley's Annual* (1840–92) and *Peter Parley's Magazine* (1840–68) appeared in several rival sets during the period and characteristically injected factual information into the most romantic of narratives. The themes of the stories could be dampening, as well; a story in the 1871 *Peter Parley's Annual* entitled "Found Wanting; or, He Would

Be a Traveller" tells of a young boy with the sea in his blood who resists his grandfather's wish that he enter the counting-house. When the grandfather relents and accompanies him on a voyage to India the boy falls down stairs and is crippled for life, an event both agree is just punishment for his willfulness.[3]

In a preface, "Parley" explains the approach of his persona: "I have imagined myself surrounded by an audience of boys and girls about ten or twelve years of age." He plans to tell the "story" of history much as he would aloud. He stresses that he speaks "not as a scholar . . . but as a plain man," but on the other hand, "while it is my endeavor to amuse, I would not let any opportunity escape to communicate knowledge, and implant principles of virtue in the hearts of my young listeners."[4] The style and posture is colloquial and dramatic: "Would any of my young readers like to take a long voyage with their old friend Peter Parley? I suppose they would first wish to know where I am going; I will tell them that by and by. Suppose that we enter a ship at Boston, and when all things are ready, proceed to sea."[5] Clearly the narrator is striving for an effect of intimacy and immediacy. This effort is underlined by the wealth of contemporary "homely comparisons" furnished for historical personages and events. Parley admits he has "subjected even Jupiter to the test of our Yankee morality."[6] Morality aside, Parley seems to delight in contemporary comparisons that do less to elevate modern history than to demystify the mythic. For example, the tale of Hercules strangling the lion he relates not only to the Biblical tale of Samson but also to "that which is told of General Putnam of Connecticut, who followed a wolf into his den, and after looking him in the face, shot him dead."[7] The constant appeal to rather bathetic contemporary parallels for mythic actions and characters has obvious relevance, not only for Stephen, who sees himself as a vindicated martyr of the Roman people, but for the entire expanding set of Joycean mythic parallels through *Ulysses* and the *Wake*.

Unsurprisingly, given Parley's approach, each book is organized around famous figures, their adventures and their personal qualities—a diluted, simplified version of Petrarch. Greek myth is represented mainly by the "Story of Helen" and a series of stories about Hercules. Other myths are scattered through the text, such as the story of the Minotaur and the Labyrinth—no doubt Stephen's first exposure to this legend—as Parley rather awkwardly but suggestively attempts to integrate Greek mythology into Greek prehistory. Greek history is represented by chapters on Aristomenos, Darius, Miltiades, Xerxes, Ataxerxes, Alcibiades, Philip of Macedon, and of course a concluding section on Alexander divided into "Youthful days of," "Generosity of," "His gloomy state of mind," Intemperance," "Character of," and so forth. The vivid illogic of Parley's subdivisions recalls Borges's descriptions of an ancient Chinese encyclopedia, but of course Parley is far more interested in the striking detail than in anything approaching analysis. A brief section on modern Greece focuses on "Lord Byron's view of Greece"; it is entirely likely that Stephen's early fascination with Byron was spurred by Parley's assertion on the book's final page that "he was a man of wonderful genius, and as a poet, he ranked above all other living men."[8]

Wherever possible a figure's notable sayings are stressed: "Pyrrhus the conquerer exclaimed that one more such victory would be his ruin."[9] Years later, teaching history himself, Stephen realizes that he is drilling students on the battle of Asculum in order to climax the lesson with that famous phrase. This involuntary reiteration of Peter Parley bothers him, and he dismisses the battle as "fabled by the daughters of memory," Blake's denigrating phrase for mere factuality, as opposed to the fables of the daughters of inspiration. Yet, he reminds himself, "it was in some way if not as memory fabled it"—Blake notwithstanding, history is still there; and Pyrrhus's comment was indeed "a phrase, then, of impatience, thud of Blake's wings of excess." Pyrrhus himself spoke in an imaginative leap, transcending the conventional categories of victory and defeat in a Wildean paradox. The deathly, anti-imaginative aspect of history, Stephen realizes, is not a property of history itself, but of its conversion into reiterated cliché and repetitive pattern: "That phrase the world had remembered. A dull ease of the mind" (U, 20/24). Stephen's critique of the teaching of history through inculcating famous phrases is immediately underlined by his encounter with Deasy, who manifests his own "dull ease of the mind" by addressing Stephen with a series of inapposite quotations wrenched out of context. For Deasy, classical quotations are the requisite insignia of upper-middle-class discourse, nothing more, and he is prepared to quote Iago in support of his own mercenary outlook.

More relevant to Stephen's position as he broods on the Parley books in *Portrait* is that text's narratizing of history and its concomitant emphasis on repetitive pattern. Like a book in Joyce's Trieste library,

Georges Polti's *Les Trente-six situations dramatiques* (Paris: Mercure de France, 1912), Parley offers a limited repertoire of dramatic situations endlessly repeated: the trust betrayed, the dedication rewarded, the innocence triumphantly revealed, the heroism theatrically enacted, and so forth. In his decision to appeal to the rector, Stephen is merely reenacting the appeal to the Roman senate of a wronged citizen; he approaches it in this way, and so do his classmates. Their joy at his success is an enthusiasm for what they perceive as the simple narrative patterns of experience as well as pleasure in the vindication of a classmate over a figure of authority. For a brief moment, Stephen is caught up in a simple schoolboy narrative, complete with improving moral. His later revulsion when he discovers that his father and Conmee found the episode a great joke is also a revulsion against the reduction of history to easy tales. Stephen's appeal to school authority has been inspired by Parley's narrative authority, and he soon discovers the groundlessness of each. Peter Parley's ingratiating personalism is at root as heavily ideological as the most vulgarly reductive of Marxist historical texts. Parley is at ease among the Greeks and Romans simply because he has never left home; and he is as dangerously smug about this as is Deasy: "Such was the religion of the ancient Greeks. The gospel had not yet dawned on mankind, and these heathens were left to build a system for themselves. However ingenious and poetical it may be, we cannot but remark its gross absurdity, and its utter inability to mend the heart, and correct the manners of mankind."[10]

Ingomar the Barbarian *and* The Lady of Lyons

After Stephen has won the prize competition and collected his thirty-three pounds, "every night [he] led a party of three or four to the theatre to see *Ingomar* or *The Lady of Lyons*" (P, 97). The chances are that specifying these two plays is not a casual metonymy, but full documentation: for a major city known to be receptive to theater, Dublin's offerings in the late nineteenth century were severely limited. In 1892 a select committee investigating entertainment opportunities in Ireland was shocked to learn that there were only two theaters in Dublin, while in London alone there were about forty, and an equal number of large music halls. By 1900 there were three theaters—the Gaiety, the Queen's, and the restored Theatre Royal—and two music halls.[11] Still, during the brief period of his wealth, Stephen must have sat through innumerable performances of these staples of bourgeois drama. *Ingomar* was a translation and adaptation by Maria Anne Lovell of *Der Sohn der Wildnis* (1843) by Friedrich Halm, pseudonym of the Austrian dramatist E. F. J. Baron von Münch-Bellinghausen. Lovell's version was first produced at several theaters simultaneously in late 1851, and continued to be popular until the close of the century; the editor of French's Standard Drama series remarks that "The language, poetry, and dramatic action of this Play, have not been excelled, if equalled, in the history of the Modern Drama." Lord Bulwer-Lytton's *Lady of Lyons: or Love and Pride: A Play in Five Acts* is of even earlier vintage, having first been produced anonymously at Covent Garden in 1838. The anonymity was probably an attempt to disarm the critics and public who had rejected his *Duchesse de la Vallière*, but Bulwer-Lytton need not have worried; his play was a rousing and continued success both in England and America.

The remarkable aspect of these two plays is their structural similarity, despite enormous superficial differences. As Magalaner and Kain have suggested, both articulate a form of popular romantic ideology that relates closely to the Byronic/Monte Cristo pattern Stephen found so irresistible, and thus both articulate an embryonic drama Stephen attempts to embody in his own life.[12] *Ingomar* is set in the Greek town of Massilia during a period when the citizens are menaced by the incursions of barbarians such as the Allemani. The female lead, Parthenia, is urged by her mother Actea to wed the wealthy Polydor; Actea's husband, the armorer Myron, is old and in debt. When Parthenia refuses, appalled by her suitor's mercenary approach, both he and her mother are enraged. Parthenia explains to her mother that she believes the tales of romantic love she was told as a child. Meanwhile news comes that Myron has been captured by the Allemani and is being held for ransom. When Polydor and the rest of the townspeople refuse to gather the funds, Parthenia sets off alone to negotiate with the barbarians. This apparently suicidal venture is true to her madly independent and romantic character.

On her arrival at the camp as a captive, she confronts the noble but untutored Ingomar, leader of the Allemani, and captivates him by her saucy bravery. She convinces him to exchange herself as a willing hostage for her father, who can then work for her ransom. Soon she teaches him the concept of romantic love and, when he attempts to treat her as a slave, threatens suicide. The troops, disturbed by the obvious change in their leader, grow restless, until Ingomar willingly gives up command and his portion of booty in order to follow Parthenia, whom he sets free. Soon he is escorting her back to Massilia, carrying her basket, while she carries his treasured weapons. He makes a painful decision to become a Greek citizen and is grudgingly accepted by the townspeople; he soon distinguishes himself helping Myron at the forge and performing general acts of heroism. But when the Allemani are sighted near town Polydor and Actea seize the occasion to denounce Ingomar as a traitor. When Ingomar refuses the Timarch's offer of citizenship and wealth if he will spy on his former friends, he is banished, and Parthenia reverses their previous roles by offering to follow him. Before they can leave, Polydor announces that he has bought up all of Myron's debts and demands Parthenia as his slave; Ingomar somewhat menacingly offers himself as slave in her place, thus making the final sacrifice. All is resolved when the Allemani arrive peacefully, demanding only to know whether their former chief is enslaved by the Greeks. The Timarch, horrified to learn that this is indeed the case, pays off Polydor, then banishes him, and asks Ingomar to act as Timarch of a new city to be founded nearby.

The only explicit theme of the play is probably found in the couplet repeated throughout it at crucial moments: "Two souls with but a single thought, / Two hearts that beat as one." Ingomar and Parthenia are fated lovers, and the vast gulf between them vanishes in the face of that transcendent truth. Ingomar's barbarian ethic dissolves almost immediately at the touch of Romance; he is allowed to keep only his barbarian love of freedom and relinquishes even that for Parthenia. The confrontation between Greek and barbarian cultures seems mostly a matter of Ingomar cutting his hair short and changing his skins for a toga. Both Greeks and Allemani generally act out of pure self-interest, with the exception of the Allemani's inexplicably peaceful mission at the play's end, while Ingomar's and Parthenia's "spontaneous" values are affirmed against both cultures. Social movement in the play consists in huge leaps from autonomy to slavery and back, which of course makes for satisfyingly dramatic reversals at regular intervals.

Superficially, *The Lady of Lyons* is very different. It is set in France under the Directoire and centers on Claude Melnotte, a gardener's son known locally as "The Prince" because of his unusual physical and scholarly attainments and his "natural" nobility. Since youth Claude has loved Pauline Deschappelles, a young lady of the haute bourgeoisie whose mother intends her to make a spectacular marriage. As the play opens Pauline is refusing the offer of the noble Beauséant, who is enraged that she does not seem to recognize or value his condescension and swears revenge. Meanwhile, Claude has sent Pauline a sonnet he has written for her, and his servant is beaten and turned away for the peasant's presumption. Beauséant and a friend, hearing about this rejected "Prince," decide to take an expensive and elaborate revenge by outfitting and introducing him as the Prince of Como, in hopes Pauline will marry him. In a fit of wounded pride, Claude promises to play his part in the charade. He plays the princely role excellently so that, despite the suspicions of Pauline's cousin, the blunt Colonel Damas, the two are hastily married and depart immediately because the Directoire has taken a dangerous interest in the foreign nobleman. Claude marries in a feverish state, torn between his reborn love for Pauline and his oath.

Once the marriage has taken place, Beauséant withdraws his servants and financial support, and Claude is driven to lodging at his mother's, where he confesses all to his appalled wife. Determined to make amends, he signs a full confession and explains that the marriage can easily be annulled, since he will make no conjugal claims. Beauséant enters to gloat and make advances to Pauline, but is thrown out by her husband. Gradually it becomes clear that Pauline, who was originally horrified to discover she has married a peasant, is nonetheless deeply in love with him. Claude then leaves with Damas, whom he has impressed with his swordsmanship, to make his fortune in the army and become worthy of his wife. In Act 5, two and a half years have passed; Claude and Damas return to Lyons, the former under a false and famous name, to find that Pauline is to marry Beauséant. Much talk of woman's inconstancy ensues, but they soon learn that Beauséant is forcing the marriage because of debts her father owes him, while Pauline, still in love with Claude, assents only to save her father from jail. Claude, throwing off his disguise, reveals himself as the famous Colonel Morier, hero of the Republic. He pays her father's debts and claims his enraptured bride.

Bulwer-Lytton's play fairly resounds with folk motifs such as the marriage of the peasant and noblewoman, and in the final act clearly anticipates the Monte Cristo scenario where the betrayed lover returns, disguised, in a position of wealth and power. The difference, of course, is that Melnotte's faith is rewarded, while Monte Cristo's is not, and this is why, when "the image of Mercedes traversed the background of [Stephen's] memory," he is reassured by "the soft speeches of Claude Melnotte" (*P*, 99). For Stephen, Melnotte's romantic rhetoric magically makes the difference between the loved one's betrayal and her constancy; later, he will find Monte Cristo's proud silence preferable, even though—or perhaps because—it is associated with the lady's betrayal. Like *Ingomar*, *The Lady of Lyons* affirms spontaneous love against social distinction, and like the later play it also assumes that the lover of lower rank must rise in society in order to merit the high-born bride. Both plays invoke the concept of a "natural" aristocracy in the hero that need only be brought to the level of social recognition, an idea that is never quite articulated but nevertheless pervades *Portrait*.

But at a slightly greater level of abstraction, the similarities between the plays are more striking. In each an aggressively proud woman rejects a wealthy, older, and more powerful suitor favored by her mercenary mother; she then meets a social outsider whose status is ambiguous or disguised and cannot be effectively evaluated. The outsider has power over her that is not underwritten by her own social codes, and she responds erotically but within narrowly fixed parameters. The two enact a charade of marriage, but without the essential sexual connection. In the first major reversal the outsider is stripped of his power and brought within the woman's governing codes, a process that emasculates him and allows the original suitor, in league with the mother, to gain power over both. The powerless father is threatened by him, which seems to deliver the woman into the hands of the older suitor, but before this can transpire the outsider has gained social power through successfully confronting groups of outsiders who threaten the social order itself. Ironically, in each case the older suitor stands for an extension of social norms that threatens to destroy the social fabric by revealing the contradictions inherent in it, while the outsider, who apparently threatens that society merely by interacting with it, winds up reaffirming its values. In Freudian terms, this is obviously a drama of incest threatened and defeated, wherein the older suitor holds the position of the negligible father and is supplanted by the exogamic youth. But in both plays this dangerous theme is defused, not only by the variety of substitutions, disguises, and metamorphoses that mystify the underlying structure, but also by the thematic stress on a romantic value system which apparently—and *only* apparently—triumphs over a bourgeois system based upon class and money.

Stephen's infatuation with these texts and his wish to inscribe himself within them is a consequence of his initiating sense of difference. Virtually his first statement of self is an articulation of his distinction from father, from mother, from schoolfellows, from any social model available to him: "He saw clearly too his own futile isolation. He had not gone one step nearer the lives he had sought to approach nor bridged the restless shame and rancour that divided him from mother and brother and sister. He felt that he was hardly of the one blood with them" (*P*, 98). Only literary figures clearly defined as outsiders, such as Monte Cristo, Ingomar, or Claude Melnotte, hold out any hope for his participation in a pattern of social triumph. Because each of these is at root a bourgeois drama, where apparent difference can be subsumed within a social order that appropriates whoever comes within its sphere, Stephen can indulge his fantasies of difference without having to face the possible radical consequences—ostracism, exile, or simple nonrecognition of his selfhood. Both dramas, like Monte Cristo, feature heroes who are simultaneously prince and slave, natural aristocrats unfairly deprived of their appropriate social position.

Reassuringly for Stephen, who is painfully driven by lust during this period, both heroes are driven near madness by erotic attraction to their women; Melnotte during his false marriage and Ingomar at his decision to become a Greek and follow Parthenia are both reduced to babbling. Yet, magically, having ceded their manhood to the women in grand gestures of self-abnegation, both are then reempowered and awarded the social recognition that had been denied them. Because both seem to gain that recognition almost instantly—Melnotte's military career is offstage, while Ingomar's triumph is a sort of political accident—the implication is that each hero is socially validated by a short burst of rhetoric, something Stephen feels himself quite capable of delivering: "At those moments the soft speeches of Claude Melnotte rose to his lips and eased his unrest. A tender premonition touched him of the tryst he had then looked forward to and, in spite of the horrible reality which lay between his hope of then and now, of the holy encounter he had then imagined at which weakness and timidity and inexperience were to fall from him" (*P*, 99). Stephen fears that his lust has betrayed his image of Mercedes, that the "horrible reality" of his physical extremity and his family's squalor will make impossible the scene of erotically charged abnegation that was his first image of consummation. But at this stage in his development that image could not satisfy him anyway; a more direct erotic fulfillment is now necessary. *Ingomar* and *The Lady of Lyons* hold out hope of that magical consummation and transformation in which his difference, like his timidity, will "fall away." Both dramas allot him the gesture of "proud refusal"—Ingomar's failure to take advantage of Parthenia when she is his captive, Melnotte's refusal to exercise his husbandly rights—but both lead inexorably toward a further consummation in which the outsider finally finds the right language and is welcomed home at last.

Joyce's Reading: Elusive Dialogism

The Ideology of an Aesthete: Havelock Ellis and The New Spirit

Fundamental to Stephen's public persona as artist is his set of public enthusiasms and semiprivate preoccupations. He is known as the Irish acolyte of Ibsen and a defender of Zola. He goes through a socialist phase, emerging on the other side with a vague distrust of capitalism and a sense of personal aristocracy; there is a Nietzschean element to his politics and a dislike of nationalism. By the time of *Ulysses* he has studied medicine and even in *Portrait* sometimes speaks pseudo-scientifically in discussing mental, moral, or aesthetic events: he quotes Luigi Galvani's phrase "enchantment of the heart" (*P*, 213) and sounds like Dreiser at his most naturalistic when he tells Cranly that he fears "the chemical action which would be set up in my soul" by taking an insincere communion (*P*, 243). Yet in *Ulysses* he is clearly repulsed by the materialism of clinical types like Mulligan. Eventually, whether ostensibly discussing philosophy, morality, history, or psychology, he will lead the discussion into aesthetic terminology. In *Stephen Hero* his guarded discussion with Emma Clery (*SH*, 66–67) suggests that she expects him to have some sympathy for her proto-feminist perspective, if only because his views on women and sexuality are known to be unconventional; yet for all his rejection of the Victorian stereotype of femininity he still finds the female principle utterly alien. At least in *Portrait*, his most enthusiastic social vision is a sort of millennial modernism, a conviction that he and some "kindred spirits" represent the dawning of a new age of freedom from hypocritical moralism, small-mindedness, and exhausted art.

Much of Stephen's reputation for originality among his peers is simply a reflection of Irish insularity; Ibsen, for example, had long been championed by progressive British critics like William Archer by the time Stephen (or Joyce) discovered him. Ironically, because of our relative ignorance of the popular intellectual ferment of the British Isles in the late Victorian and early Edwardian periods, the contemporary reader also tends to give the young artist inflated credit as a rebel. We take Stephen's presumption of uniqueness at face value and ignore the degree to which his conversation and thoughts are dialogical participants in— or even products of—a series of culturally mandated discourses of his time. All of the themes suggested above, and much of the tone of Stephen's pronouncements, can be found in a well-known book of the period that was in Joyce's library, Havelock Ellis's *The New Spirit* (1890). Indeed, many of Joyce's own interests that are not specifically reflected in Stephen suggest either that Joyce had a broad knowledge of Ellis's work or else that his intellectual concerns are an example of parallel development.

In *The Edwardian Turn of Mind*, Samuel Hynes describes Ellis as "a sort of all-purpose prophet, defending Zola and Ibsen, supporting socialism and the women's movement, speaking always for what he called The New Spirit."[13] Ellis's major claim to fame rests upon the monumental *Studies in the Psychology of Sex* (six vols., 1897–1910). There can be no doubt that Ellis as sexual theoretician had an impact upon Joyce's thinking; Richard Brown has discussed Joyce's indebtedness to Ellis within the sphere of sexual ideology.[14] But Ellis's current reputation as a pioneering "sexologist" has obscured his earlier reputation as a literary critic with a strong socio-philosophical orientation. Born in 1859, Ellis belonged to the generation before Joyce, and had already followed a similar course of intellectual development. He had been a nervous, sometimes sickly, child and combined an early passion for reading with intense Christian spirituality. By the time of his adolescence, however, he had experienced the usual Victorian crisis of faith, and had begun to see the church as a force opposed to the principle of free inquiry that his scientific and philosophical side valued most. In the 1880s Ellis was a member of the Fellowship of the New Life, whose progressive, idealistic membership included Edward Carpenter and Bernard Shaw; Shaw later led a group of dissidents away to form the Fabian Society, while Carpenter became even more notorious, as a defender of homosexuality. Two other Fellowship members were on the staff of the Walter Scott Publishing Company and recruited Ellis to edit Ibsen's *Pillars of Society* and other plays.[15]

Like Joyce later, Ellis had read Shelley, Spinoza, and Schopenhauer. Also like Joyce, he had begun training in medical school, but despite his difficulties with hard science and his squeamishness, Ellis actually managed to complete the course of study. By the time he had begun an abbreviated medical career, Ellis had already determined that a study of sexuality would be one of his major undertakings, but in his first collection of essays sex is present mainly as metaphor. Still, under the influence of a somewhat dubious "free-love" philosopher named James Hinton, Ellis had become convinced that free erotic expression was fundamental to the grand revolution in art, life, and the "human sciences" that he felt brewing. Like Joyce, Ellis began referring to himself as a socialist, though again like Joyce "there is no evidence of his practical advocacy of any single measure."[16] Like Joyce, he had a flirtation with fin-de-siècle decadence. In an essay on *Jude the Obscure* published in Symons and Beardsley's *Savoy* he argued that the artist has not only a right but a duty to treat subjects generally considered immoral; echoing Flaubert and anticipating Stephen, he asserted that "the artist is god in his own world."[17] Meanwhile, in the social sphere, he was developing an intuitive form of radical feminism that would lead him to speculate that women were not merely equal, but inherently superior to men.

The New Spirit brought together somewhat artificially most of Ellis's concerns and those of the radical edge of his time: a spiritual Darwinism and an enthusiasm for science, an emphasis on frank sexuality as an integral part of human experience, a desire for a new, "freer," and more equitable social organization, an interest in writers and philosophers who dealt with the dark, perverse, or unconscious side of human nature, and a tendency toward aestheticism, internationalism, and feminism. Ellis's tone is millennial, even apocalyptic at times, and has the arrogant prescriptive confidence of Joyce's "Rabblement" essay. Ostensibly the book is a survey of "representative" literary figures: Diderot, Heine, Whitman, Ibsen, Tolstoy, and Huysmans. What these figures represent, it soon emerges, is the growth of the New Spirit, a radical tradition of "enlightenment," which he evokes in a prefatory note: "The present is in every age merely the shifting point at which past and future meet, and we can have no quarrel with either. There can be no world without traditions; neither can there be any life without movement. . . . In the moral world we are the light-bearers, and the cosmic process is in us made flesh. For a brief space it is granted to us, if we will, to enlighten the darkness which surrounds our path."[18] The book was received with surprising fury in the mainstream periodicals. The *Spectator* opened its review by doubting Ellis's masculinity and culminated with the words, "We cannot imagine anything of which it would be more necessary for human nature to purge itself than of the New Spirit of Havelock Ellis."[19] Nevertheless, the book was popular enough to run quickly into a second edition, and eventually into a third and fourth, so it is unsurprising that it should have appeared in Joyce's library. In his introduction Ellis launches a disguised attack on organized religion, all the better disguised because his vision is essentially religious. "To drink deep of that cup [religion]," he asserts, "is to have all the motor energies of life paralyzed. Art remains to give us the same joy and refreshment, in more various, wholesome, and acceptable forms." Yet "the fanatical commercialism that has filled so much of our century made art impossible," and "the satisfaction of the art-instinct is now one of the most pressing of social needs."[20] Aside from the appeal to "health"—an appeal which in other contexts Ellis hypostatizes into a spiritual imperative—the argument is Joycean, down to the diagnosis of "paralysis" and the invocation of a priesthood of art.

Notes from Ellis's section on Ibsen are sounded through both of Joyce's juvenile essays, "Ibsen's New Drama" (1900) and "The Day of the Rabblement" (1901), and through his review "*Catilina*" (1903). Ellis cites Ibsen's "insistence that the social environment shall not cramp the reasonable freedom of the individual, together with a passionate hatred of all those conventional lies which are commonly regarded as 'the pillars of society.' "[21] Ellis and Joyce both stress Ibsen's aristocratic reticence and his silence in the face of criticism or outrage (CW, 48). Both are struck by the extraordinary conciseness of his plays: "There is from first to last hardly a superfluous phrase" in *When We Dead Awaken*, notes Joyce (CW, 49), while Ellis observes that in the late dramas "every word tells, and none is superfluous."[22] Both commentators are struck by Ibsen's portrayal of women, Joyce claiming that "he seems to know them better than they know themselves" (*CW*, 64), Ellis more programmatically affirming that they are "actually or potentially, the representatives of freedom and truth; they contain the promise of a new social order."[23] Both men, though in different terms, praise his bravery in the face of difficult subjects, his opposition to social hypocrisy, and his union of spirituality with naturalism.

Joyce used his review of *Catilina* as an occasion to elaborate his famous contrast between the "classical" and "romantic" tempers, concluding that "posterity will probably forget Ibsen the romantic as completely as it forgets Goethe and his athanor" (*CW*, 99). This division between an early romantic style and a late classical one is not emphasized in Ellis's survey, but the "classical" qualities Joyce admired are indeed stressed. Joyce defends Ibsen's objectivity against "commonsensical" critics who are dismayed by the confusion they find. He argues that Ibsen writes "a clear work of art that reflects every obscurity like a mirror" (*CW*, 99–100). In "Ibsen's New Drama," Joyce writes that "his genius as an artist faces all, shirks nothing." He refuses to "cast a spiritual glamour" over unpleasant facts (*CW*, 62–63). Apparently this unshrinking gaze, along with a certain aesthetic calm and detachment evidenced in irony, is the heart of Ibsen's classical dimension for Joyce. Ellis praises much the same qualities under a different rubric: in *Ghosts*, he asserts, "Ibsen has absorbed the scientific influences of his time, the attitude of unlimited simplicity and trust in the face of reality." There is in late Ibsen always "the absolute acceptance of facts, however disagreeable."[24] Ellis's "science" is as metaphorical and idiosyncratic a conception as Joyce's "classicism" here; in a literary context, both mean something like "naturalism."

Perhaps more significant is the group of themes scattered throughout *The New Spirit* that Joyce would have found attractive. First is the primacy of art: "The work of art," he asserts, "succeeds in being what every philosophy attempts to be. Neither change nor death can touch it; also it is immeasurable; we feel that we are in the presence of the infinite."[25] And for Ellis, more radically, art is joined to life and to sexuality: "When the youth awakes to find a woman is beautiful, he finds, to his amazement, that the world also is beautiful," and this is the wellspring of art. "Who can say in what lowly organism was stored the first of those impressions of beauty, the reflections of sexual emotion, to which all creators of beauty . . . can always appeal, certain of response?"[26] Although Ellis sounds a bit more like Lynch here in his appeal to physiology, surely Stephen's climactic epiphany with the wading girl is meant to illustrate exactly this realization. Paradoxically, although Ellis generally defends art on social and even hygienic grounds, in his discussion of Huysmans and the Decadents he takes a more formalistic approach. Why be offended by the repulsive aspects of experience these writers treat, he asks, when "we are not called upon to air our moral indignation over the bass end of the musical clef"?[27]

It is probably useless to speculate upon the precise influence of Ellis's volume upon Joyce's developing ideas; after all, Joyce had certainly consulted Shaw's *Quintessence of Ibsenism* (1891) before writing his essay, and although his tone and imagery is closer to Ellis's than to Shaw's, many attitudes toward the dramatist's importance are common to both earlier writers. Perhaps the complex of interests and attitudes shown in *The New Spirit* corresponds more closely to those of the protagonist of *Stephen Hero* than to those Joyce chose to stress in *Portrait*. Like socialism, feminism may have been a movement with which Joyce had an early sympathy, later distanced by his dislike of being identified with movements. Certainly Joyce was not above publishing his broadside on the Irish Literary Theatre alongside that of his friend Francis Skeffington (later Sheehy-Skeffington), which was a fervent plea for woman's education. Emma Clery does not hesitate to appeal to Stephen to "persuade the President of his College to admit women to the college" (*SH*, 66). Emma appears to regard Stephen as at least potentially sympathetic and drops her guard sufficiently to speak to him without a coy pretense of mindlessness: "She treated femininely everything that young men are supposed to regard as serious but she made polite exception for Stephen himself." (*SH*, 67).

Indeed, Stephen is amused that his contemporaries, who are so quick to belittle the intellectual abilities of women, are terrified at the competition for prizes they face with women students (*SH*, 130–31)—a point Skeffington makes in his essay.[28] If not a feminist, Stephen in this book is associated with feminism. He is also something of a sexual liberationist, as witnessed by his attempt to persuade Emma to "live one night together . . . and then to say goodbye in the morning and never to see each other again!" (*SH*, 198). In like fashion, he is far franker about his individualistic socialism and his "modernism" than in *Portrait*, where perhaps Joyce had begun to feel some of the pretentiousness and banality of these attitudes, unaccompanied by actions. Yet even in the later book there is an intuitive interconnection among sexual self-expression, social rebellion, literary naturalism, and art that is surprisingly congruent with Havelock Ellis's argument. Stephen subscribes to the New Spirit, or would like to do so; he is franker than Ellis about the lingering guilt which complicates an implementation of this new ideology, but then unlike Ellis in *The New Spirit* he is not only an authoritative voice but a fictional character.

Portraits of Artists and Others

The Increasing Purpose and The Mettle of the Pasture

One of the few positive newspaper reviews Joyce wrote was of James Lane Allen's novel *The Mettle of the Pasture* (1903). The review begins with a clear indication that Joyce had read and respected an earlier novel of Allen's: "A book written by the author of 'The Increasing Purpose' is sure of a kind hearing from a public which can be thankful to those who serve it well." In both novels, as Mason and Ellmann note, "Allen . . . had hit upon themes that were of extraordinary interest to Joyce, even when treated in Allen's old-fashioned manner" (*CW*, 117). Allen, a Kentuckian, was taken rather seriously as a novelist around the turn of the century; his most popular books were *A Kentucky Cardinal* (1894), *Aftermath* (1896), and *The Choir Invisible* (1897). By the time of his death in 1925, however, his growing mysticism and obscurity, along with a latent sentimentality in his writing, had caused both his popularity and critical esteem to slip considerably. Among his later works is *The Last Christmas Tree* (1914), a prose-poem on the ultimate glacial conquest of the earth.

The Increasing Purpose (1900) takes its title and epigraph from Tennyson: "Yet I doubt not thro' the ages one increasing purpose runs, / And the thoughts of men are widen'd with the process of the suns." What this increasing purpose is, is made no more clear in the novel than in Tennyson; Allen has a lyrical, somewhat mystical belief in progressive enlightenment in the world. His writing sometimes leaves the reader with the sense of an ill-defined deism, but working against this is his belief in inevitable tragic decay. The initial chapter begins with a lyrical passage on the cultivation of hemp, once a staple of the region's economy and now falling into disuse. The passage seems to cast a metaphorical shade over the following action, as if the drama were to be played out in some pantheistic *Götterdämmerung*. Still, Allen's stress is upon the excitement of the young growth:

> Lightly covered over by drag or harrow, under the rolled earth now they lie, those mighty, those inert seeds. Down into the darkness about them the sun rays penetrate day by day, stroking them with the brushes of light, prodding them with spears of flame. Drops of nightly dews, drops from the coursing clouds, trickle down to them, moistening the dryness, closing up the little hollows of the ground, drawing the particles of maternal earth more closely. Suddenly—as an insect that has been feigning death cautiously unrolls itself and starts into action—in each seed the miracle of life begins. Each awakens as from a sleep, as from pretended death. It starts, it moves, it bursts its ashy woody shell, it takes two opposite courses, the white, fibril-tapered root hurrying away from the sun; the tiny stem, bearing its lance-like leaves, ascending graceful, brave like a plum.[29]

This passage illustrates clearly both the ambivalence of Lane's vision, in his metaphor of the hemp-seed sprouting, and the erratic quality of his writing: the first half of the paragraph shows the wooden, perfunctory lyricism to which he often stoops, while the last long sentence is comparable to Lawrence's best natural descriptions.

The novel's action is extremely simple, as the focus is mostly internal. David, a Kentucky farm boy who is naturally religious and has a "seeing eye," decides to attend the newly opened Bible College of the State University. Once in the city, his fundamentalist faith is shaken by his exposure to a number of creeds in the various churches he seeks out. "He had commenced by being so plastic a medium for faith, that he had tried to believe them all. Now he was in the intermediate state of trying to ascertain which."[30] The climax of his doubt is reached in an interview with his supervisor, a bigoted pastor, which takes place in catechistic form, with David ironically quizzing his superior. Although it is far more melodramatic, the scene recalls the episode in *Portrait* in which Stephen and the Dean of Studies catechize one another (*P*, 185–90). Meanwhile, David has been reading Darwin and Spencer, and his college has begun to view him with increasing suspicion. The moment of his decision arrives in an epiphany that is laboriously written but clearly parallel to Stephen's moments of realization in *Portrait*, both in technique and in psychological significance. David has seen out his window a locust tree covered with washing all winter, and though it had appeared dead it has burst into blossom with the spring. "A certain homely parallel between the tree and himself began to shape itself before his thought"[31]: he will cast off the worn-out dogmas that have clung to him. The narrator explains the epiphanic process: "The moment for the lad may have been one of those in the development of the young when they suddenly behold familiar objects as with eyes more clearly opened; when the neutral becomes the decisive; when the sermon is found in the stone."[32] His elation and determination are like Stephen's following his experience of the girl wading, and his interior monologue is equally heroic: " 'No,' he cried, 'into whatever future I may be driven to enter, closed against me is the peace of my past. Return thither my eyes ever will, my feet never!' "[33]

At the end of term David is examined by the college authorities and, asked about his faith in God, replies, "Lord, I believe; help Thou my unbelief!"[34], the passage Stephen chooses to epitomize his own state of doubt in *Ulysses* (U, 176/214). Expelled by the college, he returns to a home where he is rejected and misunderstood by his ignorant and closed-minded parents. His mother keeps a slovenly home and has evidently entered a sort of mental and moral paralysis. "And few causes age the body faster than such wilful indolence and monotony of mind as hers. . . . [She] lived in her house with the regularity and contentment of an insect in a dead log."[35] David, a tall, healthy, intelligent, and spiritually ambitious boy, finds it hard to believe that he is the child of these parents, as does the narrator:

> That from so dark a receptacle as this mother there should have emerged such a child of light, was one of those mysteries that are the perpetual delight of Nature and the despair of Science.[36]

> The father never felt at home with his son; David, without knowing why—and many a sorrowful hour it had cost him—had never accepted as father the man who had brought him into the world.[37]

David goes on living with his parents, picking hemp in their fields, a natural aristocrat among peasants. His thoughts are lofty, though confused, but the narrator does not flinch from noting the degrading naturalistic details of the boy's environment: "[Before him were] two partly-eaten dishes: one of spare-rib, one of sausage. The gravy in each had

begun to whiten into lard. Plates heaped with corn-bread and with bis-
cuit, poorly baked and now cold, were placed on each side. In front of
him had been set a pitcher of milk; this rattled as he poured it, with its
own bluish ice."[38] Although this American country meal would doubtless appear a feast to Stephen, the passage obviously is meant to serve
the same function as his breakfast of watery tea and crusts of fried bread
at the beginning of chapter 5 in *Portrait*. But while Stephen's attempts to
rise above the repulsive facts of his physical surroundings are the object
of some irony in that book, in *The Increasing Purpose* David's noble
indifference to the squalor is underwritten by the narrator: "the first and
last proof of high personal superiority is the native, irrepressible power
of the mind to create standards which rise above experience and surroundings; to carry everywhere with itself, whether it will or not, a
blazing, scorching censorship for the facts that offend it."[39] Meanwhile,
David labors on the farm, his only relief being the time he can pass with
his trunkful of books, which he calls "his treasury,"[40] recalling Stephen's
treasury of phrases.

This stagnation is broken by the appearance of a young schoolteacher,
Gabriella, with whom the boy falls in love more or less at sight.
Throughout the book David's aspiration has been imaged as light; while
he watches a sunset, "on his rugged face an answering light was kindled,
the glory of a spiritual passion, the flame of immortal things alive in his
soul." The narrator contrasts the flickering lights of the farmhouse to
the beacon in the sky and observes that "that distant road and gateway
to the Infinite" appears "more nearly his real pathway."[41] As soon as
Gabriella appears she shares in that imagery and is also immediately
associated with the world of ideas. David puts down his book, and
"now, floating to him through that mist in his brain, as softly as a
nearing melody, as radiantly as dawning light, came the image of Gabriella: after David had pursued Knowledge awhile he was ready for
Love. . . . [She was] the only being he had ever known who seemed to
him worthy of a place in the company of his great books."[42] The two are
mutually attracted, but David worries that her strong faith may keep
them apart. A plantation girl displaced by the South's defeat, Gabriella is
a Protestant devotee and, "had she been a Romanist, she would long ere
this have been a nun."[43] Nevertheless, she nurses him through a serious
illness, and when he confesses his love and his doubt she embraces him
without question. When he tells her he has decided to attend a northern

university to study the physical sciences and to become a teacher, she is delighted and furthermore offers to support him by teaching while he studies. She realizes that he "could not forget Truth for her. And so, she said to herself with a hidden tear, it would be always. She would give him her all, she never could be all to him."[44]

Although David and Gabriella will be married, their relationship will be unconventional in the extreme, given the time and place; it is almost as if Emma had proposed to join Stephen in his exile, without conditions or thought for the future. And yet the narrator makes it clear that these are two pure, highly spiritual beings. David's rather formless aspiration, which prefers physics to theology, is made to appear superior to Emma's simple but strong faith, and she acknowledges this by her unconditional surrender. Allen seems to want to elevate David's doubt to a sort of affirmation and closes with a peroration both affirmative and tragic, invoking the hemp once again: "O Mystery Immortal! which is in the hemp and in our souls, in its bloom and in our passions; by which our poor brief lives are led upward out of the earth for a season, then cut down, rotted and broken—for Thy long service!"[45]

Although the book has some good moments and a few fine passages, it is essentially spiritual melodrama, and the tragic note at the end cannot balance the easy wish-fulfillment of the plot, in which difficulties and ideological contradictions simply drop away. Yet it had much to offer Joyce, struggling with *Stephen Hero*'s formlessness. In the first place, Allen's novel is strongly and simply constructed around the boy's spiritual crisis and romantic involvement, two thematic elements that intertwine because of Gabriella's faith. In recasting his novel as *Portrait*, Joyce chose the same route, reducing the incidental characters and episodes to a minimum. Perhaps more important, Allen's novel is an unusual blend of naturalistic description and lyrical meditation, with relatively little "middle-ground" social or action-centered narrative for connective tissue. Allen has no fear of the book's action becoming overly internal; his lyricism disguises and, to a degree, justifies the frequent transitions inward. Joyce's comment on *The Mettle of the Pasture* is equally true of the earlier novel: "The method is psychological, very slightly narrative, and though that epithet has been used to cover a multitude of literary sins, it can be as safely applied to Mr. Allen as *longo intervallo* to Mr. Henry James" (CW, 118). The narrator is extremely close to the protagonist—indeed, there is even less irony directed toward the young man in *The Increasing Purpose* than in *Stephen Hero*, let alone *Portrait*. But Joyce must have felt the book redeemed by the numerous themes with which he was immediately in sympathy: the rebellion of a spiritually ambitious youth against a stultifying family and community, the confrontation with closed-minded representatives of the church, the young woman who is somehow bound up with the protagonist's spiritual ambitions but whose social and religious convictions are in conflict with his, and the open-ended climax in which the young man deserts his family and friends in search of a vaguely imagined goal.

The Mettle of the Pasture is of more tangential relevance to Joyce's own work, although there is evidence that he was at the time interested in the novel's central theme, mutual honesty regarding the sexual relations of an engaged couple. Ibsen had treated the question most notably in *The Wild Duck*, and indeed other Scandinavian dramatists, such as Edvard Brandes and Bjørnstjerne Bjørnson, had attempted ambitious treatments of the theme. Allen's novel begins with a painful meeting between Rowan Meredith and Isabel Conyers, who are soon to be married; with great difficulty Rowan confesses that he has fathered a child by another woman. The woman had refused to marry him because of her lower social rank and soon married a man of her own class who was convinced the child was his own. Rowan's confession to Isabel is not made explicit until near the end of the novel, however, so that at this point the reader only knows that Rowan has somehow sinned and that, despite his hopes of forgiveness, Isabel rejects him in horror. Both characters are portrayed by the narrator as superior, noble people, and the reader's sympathies are somewhat divided. In the novel's succeeding action, Isabel goes on a journey with the intention of returning much later and allowing the engagement gradually to lapse, so as to avoid scandal, but upon learning that Rowan is being accused of nameless sins she returns and defends him. Eventually, when he becomes seriously ill, she marries and presumably forgives him.

In fact, although Isabel and Rowan are at the center of the novel, they are seldom directly involved in the greater part of the action, which turns about a series of minor courtships and relationships among hopeful or failed lovers. The novel is more clearly social than most of Allen's work and deals almost exclusively with the upper and upper-middle class in a small town. The most successful and interesting character study is Isabel's grandmother, Mrs. Conyers, an attractive lady of good social standing who is gradually revealed as a venal and subtle mocker and plotter whose major interest is malicious gossip. She was responsible for spreading a baseless slander about Ravenel Morris, Rowan's guardian, and thus preventing his marriage to the noble-hearted Mrs. Meredith. Ironically, he and Mrs. Conyers have struck up a guarded sort of friendship, although he suspects her role in the destruction of his romantic hopes. Rowan's brother Dent becomes engaged to a farmer's highly intelligent daughter, Pansy, and Mrs. Meredith's painful adjustment to this is the occasion for some light social satire. Similarly, the love of Judge Morris's nephew Barbee for a light-headed girl named Marguerite provides a mild comic relief, especially when she forms a hopeless passion for Rowan. These minor romances furnish a Shakespearean counterpoint to the central romance and help disguise the fact that there is virtually no plot involving the main characters. The unhappy marriage of Isabel's sister meanwhile reminds Isabel of the danger of marrying a conventional man who, conventionally, confesses nothing to his bride.

Allen has some difficulty handling his bold theme. Certainly malicious gossip emerges as a central evil in the book, but then this is slightly beside the point, considering the fact that, while the people who discuss Rowan are ignorant of his actual crime, they are correct in presuming he has committed one. Although Isabel could never put it to herself in these terms, it seems that she is infuriated by people's lack of appreciation of just how noble are both Rowan's passion and her renunciation. Certainly Allen wants to defend Rowan's truthfulness. Judge Morris, who serves as a moral touchstone, asks toward the end of the book whether there is a characteristic American virtue, or "mettle," and expostulates, "I wish to God that some virtue, say the virtue of truthfulness, could be known throughout the world as the unfailing mark of the American—the mettle of his pasture."[46] But at the novel's close, Rowan has grown too ill, presumably from heartsickness, to be saved even by his marriage to Isabel. He dies shortly after addressing his infant son, begging him to have no stain upon his purity to confess to his fiancée when his time comes to marry. Rowan dies in a state of Victorian melodrama, whispering to Isabel, "I am tired of it all. . . . Love has been more cruel to me than death."[47] It was admiration for Rowan's stoical suffering, pity for his illness, and the simple passage of time that changed Isabel's mind, not any moral revelation. Nor does Allen really sound Ibsen's note of moral outrage at the hypocrisies of society. He gives the impression of having begun his book in the twentieth century and finished it in the nineteenth, when a conventional sacrificial death could efface moral ambiguities. The only surprising aspect of the conclusion is that, within the context of Victorian domestic melodrama, it is Rowan who plays the conventional female role while Isabel plays the male one, asserting her principles in the face of family and societal pressure.

If Joyce echoes *The Mettle of the Pasture* anywhere, it is certainly in *Exiles*, where he borrows the hero's Christian name for his protagonist's patronym. He may allude faintly to Allen's structural device of setting a group of "minor" romantic relationships against a single large, tragically flavored one when he counterpoints Richard Rowan's relationship with Beatrice to Robert Hand's with Bertha. But the relationships are quite different, though all deal with fidelity. And Joyce is struggling, however unsuccessfully, with genuine moral ambiguities, while Allen seems to invoke them only to abandon the battle. Perhaps a more suggestive aspect of Allen's book is a speech Judge Morris makes in defense of the eternal verities of human nature, hinting rather broadly that the romance of Rowan and Isabel is of literary proportions: "You may think I have not seen Paris and Helen, but I have. And I have seen Orestes and Agamemnon and Clytemnestra and Oedipus. Do you suppose I have not met Tarquin and Virginia and Lucretia and Shylock—to come down to nearer times—and seen Lear and studied Macbeth in the flesh? I knew Juliet once, and behind locked doors I have talked with Romeo. They are all here in any American commonwealth at the close of our century: the great tragedies are numbered—the oldest are the newest."[48] Certainly the rebirth of classical heroes in modern guise was a common theme in the late nineteenth century, as witness Greer's *A Modern Daedalus* (1885) and Charlotte Yonge's *A Modern Telemachus* (1886), but Allen's treatment of a classically tragic couple is subtler than any of these, if only because Rowan and Isabel are not identified with any specific classical figures.

The passage from the novel that Joyce quotes approvingly in his review is a meditation of Mrs. Meredith immediately after she learns that Rowan no longer plans to marry Isabel and that her younger son intends to marry a farmer's daughter:

For her it was one of the moments when we are reminded that our lives are not in our keeping, and that whatsoever is to befall us originates in sources beyond our power. Our wills may indeed reach the length of our arms or as far as our voices can penetrate space; but without us and within us moves one universe that saves us or ruins us only for its own purposes; and we are no more free amid its laws than the leaves of the forest are free to decide their own shapes and season of unfolding, to order the showers by which they are to be nourished and the storms which shall scatter them at last.[49]

Although Mason and Ellmann claim that Joyce is quoting from memory, he makes only two trivial emendations, "seasons" for "season"—more euphonious but less accurate—and an added unnecessary comma after "nourished." These are probably errors of transcription, and help demonstrate the truism that Joyce was usually more attracted by the sound of quotations than by their sense. The passage as a whole is better out of context than in context, since the failure of Rowan's engagement is a result of his own conscious action, rather than the work of an immanent and alien universe. Nevertheless, it is a powerful enough statement of Allen's overriding belief, a spiritualized naturalism that had considerable appeal for Joyce. And perhaps this passage is the key to the resonance of Allen within Joyce's work, for both writers were struggling with a mingled romantic heritage and naturalistic conviction. Allen was sufficiently an exponent of regional realism to find heroism in a Kentucky farm boy, and enough of a romantic to presume that the boy is significant only insofar as he "rises above" his station. But the romantic and naturalistic strains are uneasy together in his writing, while Joyce manages to blend them in a vision which gives the impression of remarkable unity.

Dujardin's *L'Initiation au péché et à l'amour*

A treatment of the conflict between the religious and erotic impulses that was more serious and more ambitious than that of James Lane Allen was available to Joyce during the composition of *Portrait*; this novel, Edouard Dujardin's *L'Initiation au péché et à l'amour* (1898), had the further advantage of employing a unique structure strikingly similar to the one Joyce was to adopt for his own *Künstlerroman*. Joyce's debt to Dujardin, the minor French novelist now generally credited with the first sustained use of interior monologue in fiction, is well known. Because of Joyce's oddly scrupulous insistence on drawing the attention of friends and critics to Dujardin's *Les Lauriers sont coupés* (1888), a book which until then had been virtually ignored, Joyceans are all familiar with the outlines of this literary relationship.[50]

Most commentators are agreed that, whatever Joyce's degree of sincerity in professing admiration for Dujardin's book, his compliments were somewhat *de haut en bas*, a situation the French writer fully appreciated. Despite Larbaud's later effusions, *Les Lauriers* is a slight work whose technical significance could be appreciated only in hindsight—or by a brilliant writer immediately alert to the form's possibilities. Joyce, ever the Pygmalion, must have delighted in inventing Dujardin, a delight intensified by the opportunity to teach French literati their own literary heritage and the chance to engage in another of his notorious campaigns. Nevertheless, the evidence is irrefutable that Joyce at any rate believed that the book would be useful to him when in 1917 he wrote Dujardin in search of another copy. Indeed, there is hard evidence of his continued early interest in Dujardin: by the time he left Trieste in 1920 he had acquired a copy of Dujardin's more successful—and some ways equally interesting—second novel, *L'Initiation au péché et à l'amour*. Neither Joyce nor Larbaud discussed his interest in this book. With the exception of Richard Brown, who mentions it briefly in passing, Joyce's critics have ignored the novel.[51] Yet there is a good possibility that it played as significant a role in the development of *Portrait* as did *Les Lauriers* for *Ulysses*.

At first glance, *L'Initiation* appears to be a retrenchment after the highly experimental *Les Lauriers*, published ten years previously. Where the earlier book follows Daniel Prince through a single day, *L'Initiation* recounts the development of Marcelin Desruyssarts from birth through his early manhood. Where Daniel Prince's experience is narrated almost entirely through an interior monologue of the protagonist, Marcelin Desruyssarts's story is told through a conventional third-person retrospective narration. Kathleen McKilligan describes it as "a conventional tale of a young man's introduction to life in the capital" and notes that it is "remarkably similar in theme to *Les Lauriers sont coupés*."[52] The narrative—some 40,000 words—is divided into three major *parties*; the first *partie* is subdivided into three sections, the second into four, and the last into two. Each section is further subdivided into anywhere from four to twenty-six shorter units, separated by asterisks; the units may be as short as a single paragraph or as long as twenty pages. The relationship between these narrative units varies widely. Occasionally a unit will simply continue the narrative with only a slight change in tone or emphasis; more frequently, there is a substantial break in chronology or in *mode de récit*. Years may pass in the life of the protagonist, who was left in an unresolved situation in the last unit, without Dujardin making any attempt to maintain continuity of action.

Portrait, of course, is divided into five chapters, the first, second, and fifth of which are subdivided into four sections separated by asterisks, the third and fourth into three. But in fact there are far more subdivisions than these; an obvious example is the second part of the second chapter, which deals with Stephen's growing embitterment after the move from Blackrock. The section includes a series of negative epiphanies dealing with various visits of Stephen to his relatives, each beginning "He was sitting . . . " but separated by no transitional markers (*P*, 67–68). *Portrait*'s division into five chapters of course suggests the acts of a drama—as does *L'Initiation*'s division into three—and the further subdivision of each suggests dramatic "scenes." Indeed, both Joyce and Dujardin were preoccupied with the idea of drama during the composition of their respective novels. But the final effect of the fragmentation of narrative in both books is less to evoke the stage than to frustrate the expectations of the novel reader. Joyce and Dujardin shatter what Barthes terms the proairetic code, the text's matrix of sequentiality.[53] As a result, the reader's awareness of direct causality within the narrative is lessened; scenes and events, insofar as they are patterned, appear to rely less on events immediately preceding them than upon some overriding theme or original, tacit cause. When, as happens in the third *partie* of *L'Initiation*, an extended dialogue is subdivided, a further effect is the foregrounding of the discourse itself: passages we would otherwise be inclined to view as incidental conversation in an ordinary novel take on a "framed" quality, a solidity and lack of narrative transparency that we ordinarily associate with poetry.

As its title suggests, the subject matter of *L'Initiation au péché et à l'amour* is a boy's struggle with love and sensuality and with religion. Indeed, Dujardin explains in the preface that "love" in the book's title is meant in a Christian sense, which he interprets rather romantically as "devotion to some dream of goodness" while sin is "the work of an egotism, be it noble or vile . . . which is the opposite of sacrifice."[54] The novel opens on Christmas Day in a church where Marcelin's mother has gone to pray despairingly for the return of her husband, who has abandoned her. On feeling her son move within her for the first time she faints and is revived with holy water. Sometime later she gives birth and dies as her son is born; the father returns, remorseful, to raise his son in a distant, defensive fashion. Marcelin Desruyssarts has a few childhood friends, notably his cousin Paul, an energetic, thoughtless boy, and the more meditative and serious Henri, the son of the local doctor. His childhood in the château is solitary and marked by great natural piety; when he first takes communion at eleven he is moved to tears, and the priest singles him out for special attention. Although the theme of religion is sounded clearly in this section, we do not realize until a series of extended dialogues near the book's end how profoundly Marcelin has been affected; there we learn that up to the age of fifteen, while he is attending a *collège* in Paris, he continued to take communion regularly until "one day I asked myself . . . whether I ought not become a priest."[55]

As with Joyce's Stephen, this desire of Dujardin's protagonist reflected the author's life. At the age of nineteen, Dujardin wrote his mother concerning his desire to become a priest[56] and Dujardin's widow has commented, "He always treasured his memory of the appearance of the Archbishop of Rouen at the time of his first communion, for whom he had written and delivered the address of welcome. He admitted to me that he would have liked to be a prelate blessing the faithful and giving them his ring to kiss in a dignified and unctuous gesture; it would have appealed to the 'ham' in him."[57] Stephen Dedalus's ambition is completely parallel in its stress on form and ritual: "He longed for the minor sacred offices, to be vested with the tunicle of subdeacon at high mass, to stand aloof from the altar, forgotten by the people, his shoulders covered with a humeral veil, holding the paten within its folds, or, when the sacrifice had been accomplished, to stand as deacon in a dalmatic of gold on the step below the celebrant, his hands joined and his face towards the people, and sing the chant *Ite, missa est*" (*P,* 158–59).

But just as Stephen Dedalus's religious aspirations are mingled confusedly with his chivalric and romantic feelings, Marcelin's piety is directed as much toward the image of his mother as toward God. At the age of fourteen he discovers a pastel portrait of his mother, and from that moment she becomes the focus of his vague, romantic adolescent longings. Indeed, he attempts to redefine "love" so as to include his obsession: "It seems to me that what I miss is a heart in which to confide, arms to which to offer myself, a spirit which might hold me, to be no more alone, to be a friend and to hear and speak words."[58] As his absorption in the image of his absent mother grows, his distrust of his father begins to turn to hatred, until a climactic moment when his father discovers him staring at the portrait in the middle of the night, and he feels both like a lover surprised in his courtship and like the keeper of a shrine that is suddenly profaned. He is speechless with rage and shame, and starts to hurl the lamp in his father's face, but breaks into tears instead. As Dujardin notes in his preface to the 1925 edition, this highly explicit dramatization of the Oedipal complex is one of the more unusual features of the novel, written before Freud's ideas had gained any currency in France. Although no such identification of the mother with religious aspiration is explicit in *Portrait*—Stephen's mother, after all, is alive—the young boy certainly associates spiritual aspiration with a feminine principle and believes that his abandoning the church is a betrayal of his mother. He addresses his prayers to the Virgin rather than to any member of the Trinity. Eileen's hands and hair give him his first understanding of "Tower of Ivory" and "House of Gold," and he imagines himself and Emma brought together under the Virgin's auspices (*P*, 42–43, 116). Even after his experience with the prostitutes, he is drawn to the Virgin, and when he feels the desire "to cast sin from him and to repent the impulse that moved him was the wish to be her knight" (*P*, 105).

Soon after this episode, in the second major part of the book, Marcelin leaves to study law in Paris and his father dies. His religious vocation and his mother-fixation seem to vanish mysteriously, but again his dialogues with Henri later in the book shed light on the process, which the narrative proper elides. As he explains to his friend, under the influence of Pascal's *Pensées* he became absorbed in the notion of Christian renunciation and sacrifice. But his desire to become a priest conflicted with his repulsion for the actual priests around him, whom he saw as mere timeservers, "professionels du culte," just as Stephen grows disillusioned by the slow-witted, mundane, and unexalted priests who must be his model. When Marcelin discusses his religious passion with his confessor, the priest disgusts him with his counsel of "Pas d'exagération!

pas d'excès! pas de zèle!"[59] Marcelin discovers that he is, effectively, the last of the true Jansenists. Disappointed in his religious aspirations, he turns to the poets—Lamartine and Hugo—and finds that "their lyrics filled up the emptiness in my heart and by fall, when I had established myself in Paris, I had nearly forgotten my religious crisis." Or, as Henri acutely puts it, "That is to say . . . that in your eyes religion no longer took the form of love."[60] For Stephen, likewise, his period of religious vocation is one of exaltation. He indulges in Jansenist-influenced exercises in self-mortification and is convinced of the uselessness of mortal life. "So entire and unquestionable was this sense of the divine meaning in all nature . . . that he could scarcely understand why it was in any way necessary that he should continue to live." His imaginative icon is the "attitude of rapture in sacred art," symbolizing renunciation and sacrifice: "the soul in prayer, humiliated and faint before her Creator" (P, 150). It is only in "vague sacrificial or sacramental acts" that "his will seemed drawn to go forth to encounter reality" (P, 159).

Once the conscious phase of Marcelin's religiosity has ended, along with his obsession with his mother, he sets up an establishment in Paris. Romance quickly takes the place of religion in his inner life. He becomes infatuated with an actress he has seen upon the stage and conceives a platonic passion for the daughter of a former teacher. He is accosted by a prostitute who initiates him into the mysteries of sexuality; but, like Stephen, he is reluctant to yield and afterwards disgusted by his indulgence: "Marcelin experienced . . . the horror that followed the satisfaction of desire. . . . He had held in his arms nothing but the corpse of the poor creature, bereft of every charm."[61] A more serious infatuation is formed with a young woman of good family, Amélie, whom he meets at a cousin's wedding. But like Stephen on the steps of the tram—and, we can presume, elsewhere—Marcelin is both too shy to make serious advances and too serious to maintain a flirtation. During their first dance at the wedding festivities they are both transported with pleasure in their mutual grace of movement; but afterward, he and Amélie, his cousin Paul, and another girl go out walking. An epiphany of this period in Marcelin's romantic life occurs when the two couples discover a dark, abandoned theater and decide to explore it. Marcelin takes a wrong turning and they find themselves alone in the darkness. But, although Amélie seems willing, Marcelin fails to take advantage of their solitude. After they have returned to the party, Amélie seems friendly enough, but no longer concentrates on Marcelin. "But they danced more decorously. They spoke of one thing and another. He partnered several other young ladies; once he caught sight of Amélie dancing with Paul. So he was back? Amélie was blushing. What was he saying to her? Marcelin felt fury."[62] The passage, and the experience, parallels that which Stephen remembers when Emma, "dancing lightly and discreetly, giving herself to none" (*P*, 219), infuriated him by moving off to talk with a priest instead of with him. In both relationships the boy is too shy or fastidious to make the conventional gestures of courtship, yet too infatuated to accept the ritualized changing of partners and social circulation of the girls.

Like Stephen's, Marcelin's romantic difficulty takes the form of an inability to bring together the spiritual and physical aspects of love in a single woman. Unlike Stephen, he experiences a wide variety of relationships in his late teens and early twenties, but to a great extent these women are interchangeable. He becomes interested in another cousin, but when he visits her household she is entertaining a "fast," rather vulgar group of friends. Marcelin is too stiff to take part in the entertainment, like Stephen at the children's party at Harold's Cross (*P*, 68). He falls for a "cocotte," who dances and sings in music halls, but when she convinces him to send her money and then fails to keep their appointment, he feels romantically betrayed, and writes in his diary with something of Stephen's lyrical egotism and passion: "You have made a game of me, very banally. You never glimpsed the life that was being offered to you. . . . My soul filled with tenderness, my soul of springtime and fresh essences—you might have had this, this soul possessed by no woman but promised to you, O foolish consort of an evening!"[63] He begins a campaign to find a woman or a mistress, and with the aid of Charles embarks on a career of picking up factory and shop girls, or "trottins." It is this period that corresponds most closely with Stephen's secret life among the Dublin prostitutes. The narrator describes Charles and Marcelin as walking Paris "solely occupied by their vice, blind and deaf to anything beyond the flesh," and as mirthless as "momomaniacs."[64] Eventually he finds one with whom he believes happiness is possible, but just as he is congratulating himself on the end of his search he discovers that she has infected him with a venereal disease. The final phase of Marcelin's youth thus begins with a period of medically enforced asceticism.

The last section of the book occurs after Marcelin has traveled abroad extensively and returned home to his father's château. Here he becomes reacquainted with his boyhood friend Henri; much of the book's final section is composed of their dialogues, which center on the question of religion. This is the most obvious formal element the novel shares with *Portrait*: both books largely abandon their fragmentary narration in the final section in favor of extended dialogues and quotations from the protagonist's journal. There is one important difference from Joyce's book, however, which is that in Dujardin's novel, aside from passages where Marcelin recounts his early religious phase, Henri is the main speaker. Indeed, he comes to represent Marcelin's serious, spiritual, and intellectual aspect just as Marcelin's *fidus Achates*, Charles, represents his physical, sensual side. Henri believes in a radical Christianity whose main elements are a Manichaean worldview and a hatred of conventional, bourgeois Catholicism with its "modern" attempts to reconcile science and faith. He adjures Marcelin, "Hate, learn to detest that conciliatory Christianity that dresses up in modernity and leaves on the latest boat of the stylish philosophers."[65] The theme of a radical Christianity, rather tentative and undeveloped here, would later become the central direction of Dujardin's work. In a 1936 interview Dujardin explained that his major interest was in primitive Christianity: "For me, Christianity is a revolution, a most important revolution—much like, in our time and *mutatis mutandis*, the advent of Leninism."[66] Although Dujardin claimed merely to be a historian, from the beginning his work was opposed by the Catholic church.[67] Quite accurately, the Church detected the heretical thrust of a sensibility like that of Henri.

Marcelin is seized with regret for the "pure soul" that he had possessed in his youth, yet finds the powerful religious and spiritual impulse lacking now. Returning to Paris, he takes up once again with a society woman who has captivated him, but with whom he has not yet consummated the relationship. At last she agrees to receive him as a lover. In a journal entry that parallels Stephen's inner monologue following the "bird-girl" epiphany, Marcelin effuses, "O joy of entering into life! Joy, O joy of living!"[68] Yet he cannot decide whether to keep their appointment. In the book's final pages he agonizes over the choice he has come to see as central in his life, between religion and self-sacrifice on the one hand and a sensual, sexual life on the other, between "l'amour" and "le péché." Yet the more he interrogates his soul over the choice, the more confused he becomes: "Then, little by little, the terms of the question became clouded; he repeated to himself words whose meaning grew more and more shrouded in a fog; and now he carried on almost thoughtlessly in a swarm of confused ideas."[69] At last, in an anticlimactic moment of indecision he stumbles toward her door and the narrative breaks off. Several days later, in a comment that is ludicrous in its colloquial dismissal of the book's essential problem, he explains to Henri, "What do you want? . . . I haven't the stuff to make an ascetic, even if I'm thoroughly sick of being a playboy . . . Like everybody, I'm just a poor sap trying to live his life."[70]

Marcelin Desruyssarts does not think of himself as an artist; but, like Daniel Prince—indeed, more emphatically—he has the artist's temperament.[71] He feels intensely, is involved however sporadically in a life of ideas, and frequently expresses himself lyrically and passionately in his journal or even in his conversations with Henri. At the novel's end he is left dangling. He has failed to devote himself to a religious life yet is unsatisfied with a life of sensuality. He expects imminently to be drafted and has no idea how he will cope with that. In this respect, as well as structurally, the novel is curiously modern. It resists closure. Less obviously experimental than *Les Lauriers*, it is nonetheless quite unusual in the context of turn-of-the-century French (or English) novels. There is no single central romance, as there is in a novel otherwise rather similar, Marcelle Tinayre's popular *La Maison du Péché* (1902); instead, as in *Portrait*, the focus is so completely upon the protagonist's feelings that the figures of the women with whom he is involved are blurred and indistinct, or even wholly absent from the narrative. The protagonist is neither clearly heroic nor a butt of satire, but at times the narration, usually so close to Marcelin's consciousness, allows an ironic reading of his enthusiasms. Indeed, the bathetic and open-ended conclusion casts an ironic light over the entirety of Marcelin's experience; if this is only "un pauvre bougre qui vit la vie," then there has been much ado over little.

Edouard Dujardin was certainly no "congenital novelist," but then this is undoubtedly responsible for his novelistic innovations that so intrigued Joyce. Because critics have ignored the highly unusual narrative structure of *L'Initiation* ever since its first publication, Dujardin never felt encouraged to discuss the aesthetic background of that book; but in fact his extensive commentary on *Les Lauriers* has considerable relevance for the later book as well. Dujardin began his career as a composition student and a Wagner enthusiast, founding the *Revue Wagnerienne* in 1885 in partnership with H. S. Chamberlain. Soon thereafter he became associated with Mallarmé's group and in 1886 became director of the *Revue Indépendante*, which published Verlaine, Laforgue, and Verhaeren as well as Mallarmé and a symbolist theoretician who had great influence on Dujardin's thought, Teodor de Wyzewa. A flamboyant dandy, Dujardin was better known for his social and administrative roles than for his own poetry, drama, and stories; Jean Ajalbert called him "le *manager* de la génération."[72] Something of a literary dilettante, Dujardin also tried his hand at a collection of stories in 1886; entitled *Les Hantises*, they dealt with unusual and obsessive states of mind of a group of protagonists, but from a more or less conventional third-person narrative stance.

In the same year, however, while working on a draft of *Les Lauriers*, he published a prose-poem entitled *A la gloire d'Antonia*. Antonia, a figure of the ideal woman who recurs in Dujardin's work, is the beloved of the central consciousness; the poem is an extended experiment in the presentation of subjective consciousness, divided into eight parts of varying length and a variety of narrative techniques. Some "objectively" advance the narration, while others are inner meditations, and still others use a disjointed and dreamlike direct speech reflecting an imagined dialogue between the protagonist and Antonia. There are also short, nonnarrative evocations of the beloved that strongly recall some of the "epiphanies" from which Joyce was later to begin his progress toward *Portrait*: "O visions of times, things which were in the centuries of my childhood, sweetest joys of childhood, false loves, tears of dreams, cries of aspiration, pities for God, O most deep and ancient pieties, former life, O that which was my days, bare rocks and shiverings of hidden winds."[73] Certainly Joyce is unlikely to have had any knowledge of this early work of Dujardin; more probably, his experiments in lyrical inner narrative were inspired by a far greater figure, Rimbaud.[74] But the point is that Dujardin approached the novel as a symbolist poet, who thought naturally in terms of discrete short passages whose narrative stance might vary enormously, but whose point of view was more likely to be radically subjective than naturalistically objective. In this respect he is clearly Joyce's predecessor.

Discussing the aspects of his own aesthetic that led to his use of internal monologue, Dujardin cites his Wagnerian interest in leitmotif, which tended both to emphasize the musical aspects of prose over the denotative aspects, and to minimize the importance of rational continuity.[75] Insofar as the "rational" element is dominant in a work of prose, he asserts, the "poetic" element, linked to the subconscious, suffers. The entire thrust of the movement of 1885, he asserts, with its stress on a "musical, that is to say de-intellectualized, conception of poetry" helped lead toward internal monologue;[76] but it led equally toward the experimental narrative of *L'Initiation*, with its fragmentary, subjective narration, frequent lyrical interpolations by the protagonist, and its emphasis on the emotional life rather than the mundane experience of Marcelin Desruyssarts. Similarly, while in *Les Lauriers* Dujardin's enthusiasm for leitmotif takes the form of frequent fragmentary verbal echoes, in *L'Initiation* it is betrayed by the emphasis on the interplay of a few emotional themes throughout the protagonist's experience. Just as, in a more sophisticated way, the disjointed narrative of *Portrait* is held together by major themes of poetic vocation, religion, sexuality, and rebellion as well as the famous multitude of motifs that includes water, hands, and birds, so Dujardin's *L'Initiation* is unified by the major themes of religion, the mother, sexuality and love, and a group of motifs including solitary walking, dance, paintings, and music. To a degree, Dujardin also anticipates Joyce's metonymic method, wherein a single vivid scene replaces the narration of an entire phase of experience. Scenes such as Marcelin's confrontation with his father before the portrait of his mother or his sexual failure with Amélie in the darkened theater, have some of the power and concentration of Joyce's epiphanies in *Portrait*. David Hayman has pointed out Joyce's debt to the structure of d'Annunzio's *Il Fuoco*, with its blend of symbolist and realist techniques and its de-emphasis on transition.[77] *L'Initiation* provides these in even clearer fashion, and within the context of themes more closely related to those Joyce meant to explore.

The question remains, at what point Joyce encountered Dujardin's second novel, and how much influence it could have had in the construction of *Portrait*. Unfortunately, unless further evidence comes to light, the problem is probably unresolvable. Ellmann identifies Joyce's edition of *L'Initiation* as published by Mercure de France in 1912.[78] If Joyce acquired and read the book in 1912, then the potential for its influence upon the shape of *Portrait* is great. Hans Walter Gabler has argued that

Joyce during the period 1912–14 engaged in far more creation and substantive revision than has generally been assumed:

> Joyce's post-1911 labors were threefold. He composed all of chapter 5, or approximately the last third of the book, in its final form. From it, he devised an essentially new structural plan for the entire book, and, consequently, he revised and recopied chapters I–III. The operations were interrelated and interdependent, and the creative achievement, one may well believe, was on a scale that would have required the best part of two years' work. . . . The sections of text which from bibliographical evidence were last included in the manuscript, such as the end of chapter IV and the revised villanelle episode, may not have reached their final form before they were required as copy for the Trieste typist in, presumably, the summer of 1914. But . . . in essence, the novel attained the shape and structure in which we now possess it during 1912 and 1913.[79]

If Gabler is correct, and if Joyce indeed purchased and read Dujardin's novel in 1912, then at the least he must have been encouraged to find a kindred soul wrestling with the structure of the novel in so similar a fashion. But it is difficult to resist the speculation that *L'Initiation au péché et à l'amour* was a critical influence upon the structure of *Portrait* that Joyce chose not to acknowledge; for that would make it one of the great Purloined Letters of literary history, invisible not despite but because of the attention Joyce so generously drew to *Les Lauriers sont coupés*. If there is in fact direct causal intertextuality between the two books, then surely *L'Initiation* has been an especially elusive example of Joyce's dialogism.

CHAPTER

· 6 ·

SEX/LOVE/MARRIAGE:

PORTRAIT, STEPHEN HERO,

AND *EXILES*

The Discourse of Sexuality and Marriage

Roughly between 1900 and 1915, Joyce apparently gave a great deal of serious thought to the problem of sexuality and marriage. In this he was entirely representative of "advanced" thought of the period in the British Isles. Perhaps, as Foucault has argued, this was not a radical break with Victorian repression; according to Foucault, sexuality had been encouraged as a topic of discourse since the seventeenth century: "A first survey . . . seems to indicate that since the end of the sixteenth century, the 'putting into discourse of sex,' far from undergoing a process of restriction, on the contrary has been subjected to a mechanism of increasing incitement."[1] But even Foucault admits that there were significant alterations in the discourse of sexuality following this; first in the gradual replacement of the "deployment of alliance," or marriage and kinship ties, by the "deployment of sexuality" from the eighteenth century onward; and then, among the bourgeoisie toward the end of the nineteenth century, in an alteration in the deployment of sexuality itself:

> Somewhat similar to the way in which, at the end of the eighteenth
> century, the bourgeoisie set its own body and its precious sexuality
> against the valorous blood of the nobles, at the end of the nine-
> teenth century it sought to redefine the specific character of its

sexuality relative to that of others, subjecting it to a thorough dif-
ferential review, and tracing a dividing line which would set apart
and protect its body. This line was not the same as the one which
founded sexuality, but rather a bar running through that sexuality;
this was the taboo that consitituted the difference. . . . It was here
that the theory of repression—which was gradually expanded to
cover the entire deployment of sexuality, so that the latter came to
be explained in terms of a generalized taboo—had its point of
origin.[2]

Social and historical events certainly testify to a growing ferment over
the issue of sexuality in marriage; numerous commissions investigated
divorce, the falling population, prostitution, and related areas. In this
period Freud's work was first published and began to be disseminated,
and the first five volumes of Havelock Ellis's *Studies in the Psychology
of Sex* appeared. Both of these theorists were important in articulating
the "repressive hypothesis," but Foucault is probably correct in refusing
to ascribe this shift in the sexual episteme to any single factor.

From a somewhat different perspective, concentrating upon the problem of literary representations of adultery, Tony Tanner finds that during
the nineteenth century this illicit sexuality already constitutes a radical,
problematic sort of absence within the novel: "The invisible, inaudible
deed becomes a silence and an absence in the text that gradually
spreads, effectively negating what *is* made audible and present."[3] After
the Edwardian period, the novel dealing with sexual matters either
moves toward Lawrence's vision, in which sexuality tends to *replace* the
social considerations it traditionally played against, or toward the vision
of *Ulysses*, in which according to Tanner "there is no example of what
might be called normal sexual intercourse and perversion is the usual
mode of procedure."[4] However dubious this last description, it is apparent that in novels such as *Ulysses* and its progeny sexuality and marriage
play vastly different roles—both with respect to the representation of
society and with respect to the text—from those prescribed by nineteenth-century literary norms. Indeed, it might be argued that where the
problem of sexual fidelity and marriage was given the sort of subtle
exploration Tanner reveals during the nineteenth century, during the Edwardian period that exploration was foregrounded, made explicit, and
during the Modernist period it either dissipated throughout the back-

ground of the text or swelled to fill completely the available textual space.

For the Edwardians, the major difficulty in addressing the problem of marriage and fidelity was in knowing where to stop, for at each point this central social institution was connected to a multitude of other institutions. When Edward Carpenter and Laurence Housman—both, significantly, literary figures—organized the British Society for the Study of Sex Psychology in 1914, Housman proposed for discussion: "the admitted evil of prostitution, male and female; . . . the lack of proper safeguards for consent in sex-relations, free from all compulsion social, economical, or physical; the unsatisfactory conditions of marriage and divorce; the failure to deal equitably and soundly with the spread of venereal disease; the almost total absence of sex-training from education."[5] The terms of the discourse greatly determined the discourse itself. The specters of feminism, socialism, and sexual education arise almost automatically from such questions, so it is hardly surprising that Carpenter, Housman, and Ellis were all campaigners for women's rights and all sympathetic to socialism.[6] Others concentrated upon reform of the antiquated divorce laws, which seemed to underline bourgeois sexual hypocrisy by producing scandalously explicit divorce trials of the sort that ruined Parnell. These trials were followed assiduously by a public that professed shock at the idea of reading Zola's yellow-backed novels. Some of those whose uncomfortable marital situations had become public property, such as H. G. Wells, actively campaigned for reform of the divorce laws, or even for a sweeping alteration in the institution of marriage. Lord Russell's famous divorce reform bill of 1902 failed, but within seven years it had led to the founding of two influential societies for promoting divorce reform and a Royal Commission to investigate the issue. Others concentrated upon investigating prostitution—usually as a symptom of some other social ill—or upon reforming the 1857 Obscene Publications Act, which to some extent regulated the terms of all the other debates.

For Joyce, of course, both of these latter issues were especially important. His eight-year struggle with Grant Richards over the publication of *Dubliners* was, at least in retrospect, one of the most notorious examples of the "passive censorship" created by the Bill and the libel laws, while the case of *Ulysses* rewrote American law as well. Prostitution is an issue in *Portrait*; the fact that Stephen's encounters with prostitutes are subsumed within a set of complex structures involving woman, spirituality, and guilt somewhat muffles the realization that we are reading about an objective social problem in turn-of-the-century Dublin. During the latter part of the century Dublin became famous throughout the Empire for the quantity of its streetwalkers; in 1870 records show 3,255 arrests for prostitution in Dublin as compared to 38 for Belfast and 301 for Liverpool. By 1900 the situation had improved somewhat—or the police were more lenient—but the number of women identified as prostitutes among those arrested for general offenses was still 1,907. In the early 1890s between 75 and 82 houses of prostitution were on record in Dublin, more than the number of licensed *maisons closes* in "decadent" Paris. Stephen would hardly have to seek out prostitutes on the streets, since contemporary accounts testify to some 1,500 "well-known prostitutes" slowing the traffic on Grafton Street.[7] The irony of this situation in Catholic Dublin certainly did not escape Joyce, and it encourages a reading of *Portrait* that sees Madonna and Whore as two sides of an Irish coin. Stephen obviously suffers from his bouts with prostitutes; he is, in fact, driven near madness by guilt.[8]

Yet, as the intense lyricism of the concluding epiphany of chapter 2 testifies, the erotic experience with a prostitute cannot simply be dismissed. In *Stephen Hero* this ambivalence is made more explicit; Stephen remarks to Cranly that people when they love give their bodies, and "it is something to give one's body even for hire. . . . In a way they love too" (*SH*, 175). In *Ulysses* Stephen maintains his sympathy for prostitutes, arguing that their "sin" is relatively minor: "Fear not them that sell the body but have not power to buy the soul. She is a bad merchant. She buys dear and sells cheap" (*U*, 517/633). Joyce himself suffered more directly and physically from these transactions, although he apparently was cured satisfactorily by medical friends; but if John Garvin's speculation is correct, and Joyce's father suffered from advanced syphilis, then Garvin may also be correct in asserting that syphilitic paralysis runs as an unspoken theme through Joyce's work.[9]

In Catholic Dublin, if only because of the inordinate length of time young Irishmen felt they must wait before marrying, prostitution appeared an inevitable recourse. But throughout late nineteenth-century Britain young men faced the explicit injunction to remain pure before marriage and the tacit injunction to gather sexual experience where they must. The single practical outlet for the sexual drive before marriage was masturbation: Stephen "Hero" observes that the Irish are relatively chaste "because they can do it by hand" (*SH*, 55). Yet masturbation had by this period been castigated by the leading medical authorities as a pernicious habit more serious in its immediate and eventual consequences than an addiction to opium.[10] To some degree this double-bind situation had obtained since medieval times, but in the nineteenth century it became more acutely felt.

The Victorian pragmatizing of the Romantic cult of sincerity with its concomitant ritualization of confession helped to create a subgenre of literature addressing and sometimes questioning the institution of marriage within the context of sexuality.[11] Should a man—or, indeed, a woman—have sexual experience before marriage, and if so, should he or she confess it to the prospective partner? What is the essential difference between sexual relations with a wife and with another partner? Under what circumstances is divorce appropriate? What are the respective claims of sexual enjoyment and social responsibility? Such questions were central to a substantial group of "problem" novels and plays during the Edwardian and late Victorian periods. Among the more serious writers treating such questions were Hardy in *Jude the Obscure* (1896), Shaw in *The Philanderer* (1895), *Getting Married* (1908)[12] and *Misalliance* (1909), Bennett in *Whom God Hath Joined* (1906), Ford Madox Ford in *A Call* (1910) and much of his later work, Wells in *Ann Veronica* (1909), and of course Ibsen throughout his later period. The Italian dramatist Marco Praga explored marriage and adultery in much of his oeuvre; three of his works in Joyce's library were *L'Innamorata* (1893), *La Moglie ideale* (1891), and *La Porta chiusa* (1914).[13] Wilde's *An Ideal Husband* (1895) treats the theme more lightly, but with equally serious implications.

But perhaps more significant of perceived social change were the group of ephemeral novels and plays, ranging from farce and melodrama to works of some literary respectability, which captured the public imagination while dealing with—or capitalizing upon—these issues. Samuel Hynes discusses at length several plays of the nineties dealing with the "Woman Question" in the context of marriage and fidelity, such as Henry Arthur Jones's *The Case of Rebellious Susan* (1894) and Arthur Wing Pinero's *The Notorious Mrs. Ebbsmith* (1895);[14] other plays in this category include Pinero's *The Second Mrs. Tanqueray*

(1893), Stanley Houghton's *Hindle Wakes* (1913), and Harley Granville-Barker's *The Madras House* (1910). But while the Woman Question upon the stage often elicited farce even from dramatists like Shaw and Wilde, let alone Pinero, it tended to produce self-consciously serious, even turgid novels. Joyce's Trieste library included a representative sampling of these, including Grant Allen's *The Woman Who Did* (1895), James Lane Allen's *The Mettle of the Pasture* (1903), Compton Mackenzie's *The Passionate Elopement* (1911), Karin Michaëlis's *The Dangerous Age* (1912), and Filson Young's *The Sands of Pleasure* (1908?).[15] Outside the genre, but of closely related interest, were Charles Albert's *L'Amour libre* (1910), St. John Ervine's *Mixed Marriage* (1911), Edouard Dujardin's *L'Initiation au péché et à l'amour* (1912), and J. M. Barrie's *The Twelve-Pound Look* (1910). These were, of course, additional to his large collections of Shaw, Wilde, George Moore, and Ibsen, not to mention earlier classics on the marriage question such as *Madame Bovary* and a 1910 edition of Balzac's *A Woman of Thirty*, which he presented to Nora.

Charles Albert: *L'Amour libre*

Before examining several of these works of popular fiction, it may be useful to discuss the major theoretical work on the marriage question that we know to have been in Joyce's library, Charles Albert's *L'Amour libre*.[16] A socialist who wrote numerous books on art and society, anarchism, and European politics around the turn of the century, Albert never again achieved the popularity of *L'Amour libre*, which was quickly translated into English, Spanish, and German. His arguments closely parallel those of Havelock Ellis and of Bernard Shaw, with somewhat different emphases, and thus are fairly representative of "enlightened" thought of the time. Like Ellis, Albert is a believer in "spiritual evolution" who relies on the mechanism of evolution of species to bolster his arguments regarding social structures. He begins by discounting vague metaphysical talk of love; love among men and women is simply the next evolutionary step beyond the sexual relationships of the lower orders. And even in human history the same evolutionary process is apparent, as brute sexuality is gradually replaced by love: "At the limits of the human species we shall find again that evolution of sexual relationships toward love which we have seen traced across the entire spectrum of living beings."[17] But poetic talk of ideal love has blinded us to the real situation of love and sex in history, Albert continues. In contemporary society, love and sex have become artificially separated, and both have been degraded, by the operation of bourgeois capitalism and the harnessing of the marriage relationship to patriarchal legal codes. The domination of capital has had a terribly destructive effect upon both sexes, but most especially upon the woman, who is "twice a slave of this exploitation": she is financially and socially dependent upon the man, who is himself a slave of the capitalist system.[18] Thus, Albert summarizes, "We can say that there is in bourgeois society a kind of force that tends to maintain the sexual instinct at the level of simple, brutal coupling and to halt its natural evolution toward its superior form."[19]

Albert devotes an extensive chapter to prostitution, which he regards as the chief symptom of the sickness of bourgeois culture. "Prostitutes are the kind of lover typical of the capitalist regime," he pronounces. Including the "prostituées clandestines," he cites a recent estimate of three hundred thousand operating in Paris alone.[20] Albert makes the familiar comparison between prostitution and marriage as similar sorts of economic exchange, but also shows the intimate involvement of the state administration with the maintenance of this "necessary evil." Prostitution, he concludes, is actively encouraged under the regime of Capital, because it demonstrates that even the mechanics of love can be reduced to an instance of monetary exchange. His chapter on "Le Mariage bourgeois" is equally unforgiving and equally based upon Marxist-feminist analysis. Love, he asserts, is fundamentally dependent upon equality, whereas the legally constituted marriage relationship establishes a grossly unequal partnership. Adultery, which he describes as the revolt of love against marriage, is punished with incredible severity, so that a person whose marriage is dissolved on the grounds of adultery is legally prohibited from then marrying his or her lover. Indeed, if the lover is killed by the cuckolded husband, this "crime passionel" is generally unpunished. Fundamentally, marriage in bourgeois society is an economic transaction, whose laws thus supersede any considerations of love. The institution of the arranged marriage clearly demonstrates this fact. Albert quotes approvingly from the book Joyce gave Nora, Balzac's *Femme de trente ans*: "You cry shame on the poor creatures who sell themselves for a few crowns to a passer-by. Hunger and need justify

emphemeral unions, while society tolerates, even encourages the immediate union—which is otherwise despicable—of an innocent young girl
and a man she has hardly known for three months; she is sold for life.
Truly, the price is high!"[21] Albert also discusses approvingly the couples
who (like Joyce and Nora) rebel against the institution of marriage:
"Indeed, numbers of couples have undertaken this urgently needed reform. They live in free unions beyond and above the despicable law. And
certainly this rebellion is not useless in the progress toward our ideal. It
is an act of good will and of revolt that enormously benefits the cause of
free love. But it is not sufficient."[22]

What will suffice, he argues, is nothing less than replacing bourgeois
society with "la solidarité, l'egalité communiste."[23] Most of the remainder of his book is devoted to an expansion on this theme, treated upon a
level of grand generalization. The reader who opened *L'Amour libre*
hoping for titillation or even erotic illumination would be sorely disappointed; Albert seldom descends to cases, except when demonstrating
the failures of bourgeois society. Nor does he investigate the difficulties
of the state of free love to which he points as an ideal. His philosophy of
love is at root quite simple: love is defined as choice—a definition with
which Richard Rowan of *Exiles*, and probably Joyce, would be in sympathy. A couple should stay together while love is present and separate
once it is gone. Any practical difficulties ensuing from this practice will
be swept away by the establishment of a communist state. A final chapter, almost an afterword, returns to the Woman Question, this time to
clarify his feminism. Woman's special province is indeed the home, he
asserts, and in a just society she will be suitably rewarded for her necessary and important role as homemaker and educator of children. Those
feminists who deny woman's essential maternal role are mistaken and
should turn their efforts toward the revolution without which any liberation would be illusory; once the revolution is accomplished, and
woman is no longer the economic vassal of man, a true equality will be
possible.

L'Amour libre is obviously something of a Trojan horse; Albert's
Marxist orientation may be implicit in his analyses of bourgeois society,
but he does not explicitly invoke communism until very late in the book.
Indeed, he joins to his dialectical materialism a good deal of rhetoric
with which Lawrence might feel comfortable, all loosely based on Herbert Spencer's idealist evolutionary arguments. Certainly he was not the

only writer of the period to harness together the dialectical progress of society and the upward thrust of evolution—Shaw's materialist stress upon economic realities along with his spiritual invocation of the Life Force is a parallel example—but, given the general prudishness of communist theoreticians, Albert's millennial goal of sexual liberation may appear to be among strange bedfellows. From the young Joyce's perspective, however, this would not be the case.

As Richard Ellmann and Dominic Manganiello have shown, Joyce's anarchic socialism was essentially a matter of personal liberation.[24] This would include sexual, social, and aesthetic dimensions and would stress above all freedom from the power of institutions and conventions: "He wished to express his nature freely and fully for the benefit of a society which he would enrich and also for his own benefit, seeing that it was part of his life to do so. It was not part of his life to undertake an extensive alteration of society but he felt the need to express himself such an urgent need, such a real need, that he was determined no conventions of a society, however plausibly mingling pity with its tyranny, should be allowed to stand in his way" (SH, 146–47). Certainly Joyce would have admired the demythifying social analyses of Albert's book, which exemplify so clearly the "vivisective spirit" Stephen found to be characteristic of modern criticism (SH, 186). Indeed, Richard Brown's argument in James Joyce and Sexuality presents Joyce as a somewhat less romantic ideologist of "free love." "Free love, in this sense of the recognition of the matrimonial formulation of the sexual relationship and the representation of individuals as fundamentally separate from each other, though Joyce makes little attempt to argue directly for it, runs through the understanding of relationships in all his works, whether those relationships be formalized by marriage or not."[25]

Certainly this characterization fits Stephen, who scorns Emma's "burgher cowardice" (SH, 210) in rejecting his erotic proposal. He specifically despises her "middle-class affectations" (SH, 67), thus demonstrating at least a familiarity with the techniques of socialist obloquy. Stephen also echoes Albert's denunciation of conventional marriage (SH, 201), as indeed Joyce would do in his life. There can be no doubt that in refusing to marry Nora, Joyce felt he was making a moral statement upon the simoniacal nature of that institution. Indeed, he was embracing a higher morality, as he assured Stanislaus that his goal was "to live a more civilized life than my contemporaries," a "struggle against conventions" that would be "in conformity with my moral nature."[26] Nor was Joyce above calling for a vague revolution to which he was willing to lend a certain historical inevitability: "Already the messages of citizens were flashed along the wires of the world. . . . To those multitudes, not as yet in the wombs of humanity but surely engenderable there, he would give the word: Man and woman, out of you comes the nation that is to come, the light[e]ning of your masses in travail; the competitive order is employed against itself, the aristocracies are supplanted; and amid the general paralysis of an insane society, the confederate will issues in action."[27] As he was to demonstrate in *Exiles* and *Ulysses*, Joyce had a far greater appreciation of the complexities of love and lust than Albert allows. Nonetheless, Albert surely deserves a place alongside Bakunin and Benjamin Tucker in the development of Joyce's political thought.

The Example of *Exiles*

Hugh Kenner is one of several critics who have pointed out that, especially in *Ulysses*, Joyce characteristically omits certain scenes that in an ordinary novel sharing the same general plot would be not only crucial but climactic: for example, Bloom's conversation with Molly before leaving for the funeral, during which he makes it clear that he will not be home to interfere with her tryst.[28] In part, no doubt, this results from Joyce's ambivalence about melodrama and sentiment. Joyce delights in invoking the material of cheap Victorian cliché—such as the disappearing child's funeral, the mysterious thirteenth mourner at Dignam's funeral, or Bloom's watch stopping at what he assumes to be the hour of his betrayal—and then so embedding and enmeshing it in a complex text that its dramatic (or melodramatic) impact is lost to the reader. Similarly, we learn about Bloom's and Molly's parting on Bloomsday morning as indirectly as we learn about their final conversation that night. Both are scenes simply too highly charged with drama for a naive, conventional presentation. This was precisely Joyce's dilemma with regard to the treatment of sexuality and marriage, whether in drama or in the novel. The established "advanced" discourse in both genres was revelatory, millennial, and painfully foregrounded theme, while his own romantic, visionary side was always undermined by a skeptical objectivity and a disinclination for explicit, unironic thematic statement. Stephen makes a similar point about the difficulty of writing modern love-poetry: "But in his expressions of love he found himself compelled to use what he called the feudal terminology and as he could not use it with the same faith and purpose as animated the feudal poets themselves he was compelled to express his love a little ironically. This suggestion of relativity, he said, mingling itself with so immune a passion is a modern note: we cannot swear or expect eternal fealty because we recognize too accurately the limits of every human energy" (*SH*, 174).

It has escaped few readers that the natural autobiographical conclusion of *Portrait* would be the equivalent of Joyce's departure with Nora, a woman with whom he would live in an ongoing experimental protest that finally became indistinguishable from marriage even while attempting to redefine it. This is the pattern of James Lane Allen's *The Increasing Purpose* and of many other Edwardian novels of rebellious youth. Instead, Stephen firmly bids E. C. goodbye, while the only sign of her successor is the lower-class girl he spies wading but never approaches. In *Stephen Hero*, despite a relatively diffuse focus, the direction is even clearer; Stephen, who at least at times is an Albertian exponent of "free love," attempts to have Emma join him for a single night together. In neither book does Stephen show any signs of retreat toward a stance of monk-like abstinence. "We must have women," he tells Lynch during a conversation touching on Emma and on prostitution, and Lynch points out that Stephen could "get" Emma by marrying her, in the accepted economic exchange (*SH*, 191–92). Obviously, at least to Stephen, this too is unsatisfactory; like Balzac, he might well observe that "Il est vrai que le prix est élevé!" Instead, the sexual current of the plot moves toward a rebellious climax that may never have been written, and which in *Portrait* is withheld or displaced.

Of course Joyce did make his attempt at this ultimate Edwardian topic, his own contribution to the genre of Ibsen, Shaw, Grant Allen, and Filson Young, in the relative failure of *Exiles*.[29] Richard Rowan and Bertha, who left Ireland together unmarried and had a son out of wedlock, live together in "freedom"—and the definition of that state forms much of the substance of the play. Elliott M. Simon has argued convincingly that *Exiles* must be seen within the specific formal generic context of the Edwardian "problem play," although he does not appear to recognize the extreme conventionality of the particular "problem" within Edwardian dramatic discourse. He concludes that what is often seen as the play's dramatic failure is deliberate theatrical technique: "Joyce not only borrowed his metaphor of marital infidelity and spiritual liberation from the Edwardian problem-play, but also adopted the theatrical technique of the indeterminate ending which forced his audience to become part of the dramatic experience by having them resolve the thesis of the play. Joyce demanded that his audience suspend their disbelief in the moral conflict on stage to appreciate the symbolic dimensions of his characters and the philosophical statement implicit in his aesthetic development of their personalities."[30]

But despite Simon's Brechtian defense, the problems of this problem play are many. The characters do not readily reduce (or ascend) to ideas and often do seem to embody a character-based appeal to the audience's sympathy. As many readers have observed, Richard is too complicated, while Robert, Bertha, and Beatrice are too simple. And it is just the complexity of Richard's stance that best shows Joyce's difficulty in writing within a genre challenging sexual fidelity. In an ironic description of Judgment Day, the "betrayer" Robert Hand puts forth a position reminiscent of the Stephen of *Stephen Hero*: "And He will say to us: Fools! Who told you that you were to give yourselves to one being only? You were made to give yourselves to many freely. I wrote that law with My finger on your hearts" (*E*, 64–65). As Robert, a cut-rate romantic, argues for "the blinding instant of passion alone," Richard admits that he recognizes "the language of my youth," and it is this realization that most disheartens him. He recognizes his own youthful rebellion against the ideology of conventional marriage in what seems to him a distorted form—distorted, perhaps, only because it is now made concrete and immediate. Indeed, Robert is not only Richard's "disciple" but something of a Grant Allen, in that he argues an equal right to sexual experimentation for women and claims to have begun writing a book about such a woman.

Richard's position, at first glance, is equally simple: he wants Bertha to *choose* to be faithful, free from any social or legal compulsion—even free from the force of his own desire. But he admits to Robert that he has a positive need for betrayal, parallel to his own need to confess to her his episodes of unfaithfulness. As he tells Robert, he is terrified at the possibility that he will have been responsible for restricting her experience; and as both Robert and Bertha recognize, he is equally terrified that she will choose to sleep with another man. Like Charles Albert, Richard scornfully rejects the ensurance of fidelity provided by the bourgeois code. Fidelity without choice is meaningless—just as, in the parallel problem of free will in a Christian universe, man's obedience to God would be meaningless had he been created unable to sin. Yet, on the other hand, for Bertha to exercise a meaningful choice, she must be meaningfully tempted, an event Richard naturally fears. But Richard is brought to a state of moral paralysis by more than this simple paradox of desire.

Once he is involved in Bertha's "betrayal," Richard finds that the straightforward drama of fidelity he has imagined has become infinitely more complicated. If Bertha chooses to sleep with Robert, will she be doing so only in order to revenge herself on her manipulating husband? And if so, will she be acting "freely"? Will she do so out of jealousy of Beatrice, with whom Richard has a "spiritual" relationship, and if so, does she have a right to be jealous? What is the importance of the fact that Bertha is not seen as Richard's "equal"? Admittedly, the play has too many themes—Richard's "genius" and its rights, his "unnatural" rebellion against his mother, the question of returning to Ireland or living in exile, the problem of Robert's friendship, the rather fruitless relationship between Beatrice and Richard; but from an ethical point of view rather than an aesthetic one, this chaos of circumstance is precisely the point. Richard cannot have his experiment in marriage conducted in a pure state, because there is nothing pure about a real quotidian marriage relationship. Indeed, even were his circumstances less muddled, his experiment in fidelity would be a failure because he cannot play the disinterested observer. He cares; and even if he did not care, his mere presence would affect the outcome. Richard is forced to realize the dramatic equivalent of the Heisenberg Principle. Like the rest of the world, he is one more element of contigency muddling the clear drama in his mind.

The ending of *Exiles* is somewhat strenuously ambiguous. We are left unsure of whether Richard has been cuckolded (probably not, but we can be no more certain than Richard); whether Richard and Bertha will, in some sense, recover from their experience; whether Robert meant to betray Richard with his double-edged newspaper article; whether Beatrice had anything to do with the plot; and especially whether the boy who keeps dashing meaningfully through the play can do anything to give the action some kind of unity. All we can be sure of is that everyone involved seems to regret the whole experience—an honest conclusion from Joyce's point of view that also conveniently satisfied conventional morality, so that there was no problem in publishing the play. The general movement of the play from sharp-edged choices toward muddle is greatly responsible for its dramatically unsatisfying quality, but it is important to realize that the same movement represents Joyce's best attempt at the moral analysis of marriage.

In *Exiles* Joyce is midway between *Portrait*'s urge toward a millennial solution, perhaps something along the lines suggested by Albert, and *Ulysses*'s scrupulous backgrounding of the problem while offering only the stoic sort of situational ethics that loosely guides Bloom. From a Bakhtinian perspective the relative static failure of the play may be a consequence of Joyce's refusal of dialogism; this is the only major work of Joyce in which there is no true interplay of voices. Raymond Williams has noted this unique feature of *Exiles*:

> In effect none of the devices of disturbance, dislocation or limitation of speech, none of the indications of unarticulated modes of being and desire beyond its specific and structurally limited forms, is attempted. Of course Joyce does not then rest on the representation of everyday speech as itself. He moves, instead, in a quite different direction, to forms of mutual self-presentation, in a rhetorical and even declamatory mode. Standing right back, we can observe the cold clash of egos which such a mode sustains. . . . It is a linguistic mode of enclosure and presentation, not of exploration.[31]

As Williams observes, this language of the predominant "actor-manager" is one that Ibsen, Strindberg, and Chekhov had both rejected and complicated. Yet Joyce, while obviously indebted to Ibsen in theme, fails to capture his model's linguistic innovations. Bakhtin himself suggests that there are built-in limitations to the polyphonic richness of dramatic language, regardless of the playwright. He feels that drama is, more or less by definition, monologic: "The whole concept of a dramatic action, as that which resolves all dialogic oppositions, is purely monologic. A true multiplicity of levels would destroy drama, because dramatic action, relying as it does upon the unity of the world, could not link those levels together or resolve them. In drama, it is impossible to combine several integral fields of vision in a unity that encompasses and stands above them all, because the structure of drama offers no support for such a unity" (*PDP*, 17). However limited its value as a general observation, Bakhtin's comment does seem to apply precisely to Joyce's work. Only in *Exiles* does Joyce enter directly into the frantic Edwardian discourse that framed marriage, and the failure of this attempt may have helped to precipitate the radically different, dialogical approach to sexuality in *Ulysses*.

Grant Allen: *The Woman Who Did*

Before exploring the failure of sexual discourse in *Exiles* and the parameters of Joyce's participation in that discourse in his early work as a whole, it may be useful to sketch the outlines of the enterprise in a few representative popular works from Joyce's library. The best-known of these was Grant Allen's *The Woman Who Did* (1895). A serious novel of inevitably prurient interest at the time, it presented a case for love without marriage and remained for years the most notorious example of the "advanced" or "daring" novel which should be kept from the hands of wives and children. Joyce gives the book a backhanded tribute in the "Cyclops" episode of *Ulysses* when "The Woman Who Didn't" appears in the list of "tribal images of many Irish heroes and heroines of antiquity" adorning the Citizen, immediately preceded by The Man in the Gap and followed by Benjamin Franklin (*U*, 244/296–97).[32] A note of preface by Allen characterizes the book as "Written at Perugia / Spring 1893 / For the first time in my life / Wholly and solely to satisfy / My own taste / And my own conscience."

The action is quite simple: Herminia Barton, daughter of the Dean of Dunwich, becomes involved with handsome young Alan Merrick. "Freedom" is apparently part of her identity, an inner grace immediately obvious to observers:

> But it was her face particularly that struck Alan Merrick at first sight. That face was above all things the face of a free woman. Something so frank and fearless shone in Herminia's glance, as her eye met his, that Alan, who respected human freedom above all other qualitites in man or woman, was taken on the spot by its perfect air of untrammelled liberty. Yet it was subtle and beautiful too,

undeniably beautiful. Herminia Barton's features, I think, were even more striking in their way in later life, when sorrow had stamped her, and the mark of her willing martyrdom for humanity's sake was deeply printed upon them. But their beauty then was the beauty of holiness, which not all can appreciate.[33]

Herminia has attended Girton, but left on discovering that the freedom offered there was purely intellectual; her own interest is not so much in political equality as in "social and moral emancipation."[34] She is now self-supporting and living in London. Further, she sees herself as part of an ideological group opposed to the "unthinking mass," and immediately gathers that Alan is "with us," as she puts it.

The two fall in love, but Herminia is unalterably opposed to the terms of legal marriage on grounds that are partly purely feminist, partly identical to those of the young Joyce: "I deny and decline those terms; they are part and parcel of a system of slavery. . . . I will not palter and parley with the unholy thing. Even though you go to a registry-office and get rid as far as you can of every relic of the sacerdotal and sacramental idea, yet the marriage itself is still an assertion of man's supremacy over woman. It ties her to him for life, it ignores her individuality, it compels her to promise what no human heart can be sure of performing; for you can contract to do or not to do, easily enough, but contract to feel or not to feel—what transparent absurdity!"[35] Alan cannot let that conviction terminate their relationship because, the narrator asserts, a "man with an innate genius for loving and being loved cannot long remain single. He *must* marry young; or at least, if he does not marry, he must find a companion, a woman to his heart, a help that is meet for him."[36] Alan, the narrator makes clear, is not quite of Herminia's stature and purity; among other things, he is near thirty and still prudently unmarried, a situation that the narrator suggests is almost depraved. They plight their troth in a setting reminiscent of the Hill of Howth, at the crest of a meadowed hill rising steeply over the fields of Sussex:

> He folded her in his arms. Her bosom throbbed on his. Their lips met for a second. Herminia took his kiss with sweet submission, and made no faint pretence of fighting against it. . . . She quickened to the finger-tips.
> . . . "So Herminia, you will be mine! You say beforehand you will take me."

"Not *will* be yours," Herminia corrected in that silvery voice of hers. "*Am* yours already, Alan. . . . I am yours this moment. You may do what you would with me."[37]

Alan dutifully proposes marriage, and she of course is horrified. She proposes "simply that we should be friends, like any others, very dear, dear friends, with the only kind of friendship that nature makes possible between men and women."[38] Like a far stronger and more articulate Mrs. Sinico, Herminia suggests a paradoxical inversion of Mr. Duffy's maxim that "friendship between man and woman is impossible because there must be sexual intercourse" (D, 112). She is far more unconventional than Mr. Duffy, although her remark is rooted in the same cynical reductionism; she merely wishes to redefine "friendship."

Naturally Herminia is intelligent enough to realize that she is courting martyrdom, and she nobly embraces this fate for the sake of "Truth." Throughout, the narrator chimes in, echoing the heroine's sentiments about marriage, affirming her superhuman strength and conviction. The only possible distancing is lent by Alan's practical arguments against the arrangement—he agrees with her in principle but is reluctant to see her martyred and to be the agent of that martyrdom. Herminia's rooms are lined with Shelley, Keats, Morris, and Rossetti, but the narrator gives no indication that this may be an ironic detail; perhaps the woman is an idealist, but the narrator seems to feel that her idealism simply underlines the hypocrisy of society. "In the topsy-turvy philosophy of Bower Lane and of Belgravia, what is usual is right; while any conscious striving to be better and nobler than the mass around one is regarded at once as either insane or criminal."[39]

There is a clear element of Nietzscheanism here which is strongly reminiscent of many of Stephen's pronouncements regarding genius and its defining distance from the "rabblement." At one point, Herminia hears a clergyman making the conventional apologies for Shelley's moral conduct, on the grounds that genius is allowed lapses. She protests vigorously, "Not less but more than most of us is the genius bound to act up with all his might to the highest moral law, to be the prophet and interpreter of the highest moral excellence."[40] Like the protagonist of *Stephen Hero*, Herminia and Alan are constantly confronted with exemplars of bourgeois moral obtuseness whose function is to elicit the heroine's brilliant response without seriously challenging it. When Alan explains the situation to his father, a Harley Street physician, the man is utterly outraged and casts his son out; the narrator expands upon the conventional alternative Dr. Merrick would have preferred for his son:

> If he had continued to "live single" as we hypocritically phrase it, and so helped by one unit to spread the festering social canker of prostitution, on which as basis . . . the entire superstructure of our outwardly decent modern society is reared, his father no doubt would have shrugged his shoulders and blinked his cold eyes, and commended the wise young man for abstaining from marriage till his means could permit him to keep a wife of his own class in the way she was accustomed to. The wretched victims of that vile system might die unseen and unpitied in some hideous back slum, without touching one chord of remorse or regret in Dr. Merrick's nature.[41]

The lovers leave for Europe, and after an idyllic period Alan grows ill in Perugia. He dies there, after offering marriage one last time to legitimize the child Herminia is carrying. Dr. Merrick, who arrives just after the death, refuses to offer any support, and Herminia and her daughter return to a life of poverty in London. She writes an "advanced" woman's novel, but it fails with the public, "for her novel was earnestly and sincerely written; it breathed a moral air, therefore it was voted dull; therefore nobody cared for it." Or perhaps it is not the seriousness of tone but the originality of ideas that is responsible for its failure: "People said to themselves, 'This book seems to be a book with a teaching not thoroughly *banal*, like the novels-with-a-purpose after which we flock; so we'll give it a wide berth.' "[42] Both of these are positions that Joyce held regarding popular taste, and it is unsettling to see them passionately avowed by a bestselling novelist such as Grant Allen; but then, they were equally passionately held by Marie Corelli, who was even more popular than Allen. The rest of Herminia's career, when she abandons her standards and convictions to turn out hack-work, is perfectly successful, however, and if we recall that Allen announced *The Woman Who Did* as the first book he had written according to his taste and conscience, the paradox is resolved. The novel may not have been Joyce's—or any modern reader's—idea of literature, but its sincerity is apparent.

The remainder of Herminia's life is a succession of melodramatic encounters, such as the one with her father the Dean where he offers to forgive her if she will repent but spurns her and his granddaughter when she refuses. She is tempted to marry a fellow Fabian in middle age, but rejects his proposal less out of passionate conviction than a desire to remain consistent. Thus she consciously refuses to mimic George Eliot, who she believes betrayed her own principles. A final essay by the narrator relates marriage to monopoly capitalism, as an unethical avarice of the heart, and then the inevitable tragic denouement is recounted. Herminia's daughter, a conventional girl of average talent and intelligence appropriately named Dolly, rejects her mother. The narrator puts this in the pseudo-Darwinian perspective of degeneration theory: "She had reverted to lower types. She had thrown back to the Philistine."[43] When her mother tells Dolly of her illegitimacy the girl feels she must reject the attractive proposal of marriage she has received. She goes to live with Dr. Merrick and informs her mother that she can never marry while Herminia lives to shame her. Obligingly, Herminia commits suicide and is discovered by her daughter dressed as for a wedding.

Despite its *succès de scandale*, *The Woman Who Did* clearly fails as literature. The hectoring, lecturing narrative intrusions are only part of the problem; the heroic character of Herminia is for the most part unconvincing, only gaining some credibility when in middle age she contemplates compromise and begins to feel the measure of her defeat. But probably the central weakness of the book, the one ironically responsible for its popularity, is that by the story's end Herminia has been transformed into the conventional sacrificial heroine of Victorian woman's fiction. During most of the final chapters she begs Dolly to understand that everything she has done has been for her daughter, who was to be the first of a new breed of free women. Her suicide, allowing Dolly to marry, is the logical extension of this sacrificial mode. But Herminia's strength at the opening of the story is much like that of Stephen Dedalus: she is the heroine in pure opposition who is admirable because she will not compromise with the opinions of others. This is a variety of Romantic egotism, and all of the narrator's talk about her dedication to Truth cannot disguise the fact. Certainly she is embracing a martyrdom, as is Stephen, but a martyrdom that is a perfect fulfillment of self rather than a sacrificial negation of it. Herminia's apologia to Dolly is unconvincing because the daughter in whose name she refused marriage is wholly her own creation, an ideal second self; she needs to justify her actions—if at all—through an assertion of selfhood, not by playing the lead role in a masochistic scapegoat ritual. When Grant Allen throws her into a protracted deathbed scene, complete with posthumous letter and white flowers, he is turning the Count of Monte Cristo into Camille.

Filson Young: *The Sands of Pleasure*

Another book of some importance in the popular discourse of marriage and sexuality is Filson Young's *The Sands of Pleasure* (1905). Alexander Bell Filson Young was Grant Richards's reader for *Dubliners*, a fact of which Joyce was aware, and Joyce probably purchased or was sent the book for this reason.[44] Richards took some pride in publishing advanced writing—within his own very limited perspective—and Young's book is gratefully dedicated to Richards, the book's original publisher. Young's career would have had a certain bitter appeal to Joyce. His earliest work is *A Psychic Vigil*, signed "X-Rays," which appeared in 1896, and *The Sands of Pleasure* was followed by a collection of poems in 1907 and by another novel, *When the Tide Turns*, in 1908. But Young soon discovered his literary limitations, and the latter, more successful portion of his writing career is dedicated to journalistic works on flying, music, the political situation in Ireland, and an extrememly popular guide to motoring, which went into new editions well into the 1920s. Still, there is no reason to doubt Young's original literary commitment. Like Grant Allen's novel, *The Sands of Pleasure* is undeniably serious in its approach to "dangerous" material. It, too, is both self-consciously advanced and unconsciously bourgeois. The subject is the relationship between Richard Grey, an Ibsenesque lighthouse-builder, and Toni, a German-born Parisian demimondaine whom he meets while slumming in Montmartre. In an introduction, Young defends his right to portray the Parisian "half-world" objectively: "there is every reason why mature people should read about it, not bitterly or unpleasantly, but as pleasantly as possible, in the mirror of a page written without moral preoccupations." Clearly, Young has read his Flaubert. There *is* a moral to the book, he admits, but "it comes assuredly from the incidents themselves, and not from my view of them."[45]

The novel is mostly a character study, not so much of the protagonist Richard Grey, an intelligent and ambitious young man who is greatly attached to his work but otherwise seems to have no very strong beliefs, but rather of Toni, the expensive demi-prostitute. Richard is taken to

Paris by his sophisticated friend John Lauder, an aristocratic former artist with an interest in the young man's education and amusement. The
Paris they see is very much the mythical topos to which Henry James
refers in his preface to *The Ambassadors*: "There was the dreadful little
old tradition, one of the platitudes of the human comedy, that people's
moral scheme *does* break down in Paris; that nothing is more frequently
observed; that hundreds of thousands of more or less hypocritical or
more or less cynical persons annually visit the place for the sake of the
probable catastrophe."

Richard has no particular conscious reason for visiting Paris, although
it is suggested that he has been devoted exclusively to his work up to this
point and now is growing interested in personal development, a concept that turns out to embrace sexuality and sensuality in general.
Lauder first shows him an area frequented by well-dressed streetwalkers.
"That's what I call vice," says Lauder, "it shocks and frightens me. It is
so hideous and cruel, there is so little happiness in it for anybody; there
is only courage and the keeping up of appearances."[46] Lauder attempts
to make a distinction between the "immoral," about which he is relatively neutral, and the "indecent," which he views as an assault upon the
human spirit. The unremitting, businesslike Parisian pursuit of sex he
finds indecent: "Paris thinks of only one thing, exists for only one thing.
All day it toils and earns money, and builds houses, and prepares food,
in order that at night it may devote itself to its one interest. . . . Paris has
the most perfect system of passenger transport in Europe—in order that
Jacques may get to Marie as quickly and as cheaply as possible. Paris
invented the *petit bleu*—in order that for twopence Marie might tell
Jacques not to come, as her husband has returned. . . . It's damned
funny; but it's something else as well: it's frightful!"[47]

Apparently the frightfulness does not extend to the area of expensive
nightclubs in Montmartre where the better class of demimondaines are
to be found, presumably because there the "businesslike" aspect of the
traffic is muted, or has been mystified by the mythology of Bohemia.
Richard, for his part, is not repelled so much as fascinated, with a curious sensation of detachment; this is all strange to him, and he feels in
some way immune to its siren call. However, in Montmartre he meets
Toni, Lauder finds a companion of his own, and the foursome spend
some weeks in various carefree pleasures. Richard gradually finds himself increasingly fascinated by Toni, unable to give her up—essentially,

addicted to her. His fascination is partly sexual, of course, but to a degree he is also mesmerized by her contradictory character. She is a "child of nature," completely at home in a rural setting, and in some undefinable way innocent; yet she is also a thoroughgoing materialist, or a materialist with an acute bourgeois social consciousness, who is only interested in the "best" and most stylish of everything. When Lauder, late in their relationship, presents her with a gorgeous and valuable antique ring she is insulted because she feels he is fobbing her off with used goods. He thinks he is in love with her; she refuses to consider the possibility of love, at least for someone in her situation, but is amenable to "pretending" love. Eventually their quarrels and misunderstandings grow acute, as much under the pressure of their genuine attachment as from their deep differences, and he is able to tear himself away. After a prolonged absence he returns to see her once more, to prove to himself that he is "cured." Unobserved, he watches her with a client and is filled with disgust, but when a song he and Toni had considered their own song is played he sees her weeping. He returns to England somewhat satisfied and plans respectable marriage with Lauder's sister.

There are a number of surprising facets to this book, which is less remarkable for its explicit subject than for its silences and gaps—the "rifts and discontinuities" which Fredric Jameson, following Althusser, sees as the locale of a work's "privileged content."[48] Young means to treat the intersection of eroticism and romantic love within a proscribed context. At one level, the book is an attack upon the Victorian schism between eros and agape, or in Denis de Rougemont's expansion of this opposition, between the systems of Christianized society and of heretical courtesy.[49] Yet, although Richard Grey is the battleground of these conflicting systems, he is curiously unaltered by the campaign; when he has thrown off Toni he is able to devote himself to the prospect of a marriage that is wholly Victorian in conception, without a qualm. He has "conquered himself." The reader must feel that, if this is to be the conclusion, Richard's relationship with Toni, for all its obsessive power, must boil down to little more than an updated Bower of Bliss. And yet this is not felt to be the case as we read of his infatuation. Toni certainly offers an arena of erotic free play that is alien to the upright, enlightened Edwardian lady Richard will marry. But her appeal is more complex than this. It is founded partly upon her baffling "innocence," which coexists with what her society would find the very definition of corruption. Toni is also a frank and thorough materialist who expects to be paid for her company, not in cash, but in ornaments, entertainment, and consumables. She is, in fact, the distorted mirror-image of the Wife. The main factor that keeps this realization from dawning upon Richard— and one of the great areas of silence of the novel—is her lower social class. Simply because she is of another class, a quality underlined by her exotic nationality and setting, Richard is incapable of evaluating their relationship from a social perspective. She may possess him and obsess him, but she is also invisible to him.

Richard's solitude, his unmoving, untouched quality, is emphasized by the dominant image of *The Sands of Pleasure*, which is the lighthouse. At the book's end Richard waits out a violent storm in his newly completed lighthouse; at the end of the storm, in a scene that recalls the end of "After the Race," the lightkeeper enters with his watch in hand and announces simply, "Sunrise, sir."[50] Richard realizes that his lighthouse has been built upon rock and so, unlike the Biblical house built upon sand, it will endure. The moral is hardly as indirect as Young advertises. He has successfully avoided founding his life upon the "sands of pleasure" and in leaving Toni has emerged from a dangerous storm, his beacon still bright. When he returns to Paris to see Toni cry at "their song," his ego is further bolstered by the realization that the love at which Toni had played had not been total pretense. As Joyce's Stephen observes of prostitutes in general, hers too is a "sort of love"; but because her class, profession, and nationality brand her as wholly other, it is not finally an important sort for Richard. His own emotion toward her, whose power and complexity Somerset Maugham would explore somewhat more intelligently fourteen years later, is simply dismissed as an aberration, a storm that ends in silence.

Certainly Filson Young is tackling a subject of significance, but his effort is undermined throughout by his inability to face its implications. Toni constitutes a critique of marriage more powerful than that posed by Herminia Barton, although less articulate. The distant, insubstantial relationship between Richard and Margaret Lauder, his wife-to-be, suggests that their marriage will be a pale image indeed of his relationship with Toni, although he will similarly provide Margaret with shelter, entertainment, and consumables in exchange for her less polished erotic favors. Margaret's ungrounded love for this totally "suitable" suitor, which the reader must assume, balances Toni's "pretended" love. Both partners will repress and disguise the terms of this exchange; Margaret as a bourgeois wife cannot afford Toni's frank "innocence," even within her own mind. Hovering in the novel's background, of course, is the sense that Richard has successfully, even romantically, completed his period of erotic training and is now prepared for a serious emotional commitment. Margaret will never ask him about his experience, of course, although she cannot help being aware of it, and he will never volunteer to discuss it. These implications are tacitly underwritten by the narrator, who has none of James Lane Allen's passion for truthfulness in relationships. All of these silences between characters are subsumed by the silence at the novel's end. Young's narrator deals with none of this, which makes his novel more symptom than diagnosis; and yet the book's central experience testifies to his reluctant recognition that eros and agape inextricably intertwine in ways that institutionalized marriage cannot resolve.

In an essay on *La Dame aux camélias* (1852) by Dumas *fils*, Barthes makes the somewhat paradoxical argument that while Armand's "classical" love for Marguerite is founded in bourgeois essentialism, as an act of ownership and appropriation, Marguerite's love for him is simply a demand for *recognition* from the world of the masters and is in fact an authentic existential act embodied as cynicism. Had Dumas allowed her to die as the object she is, mute and unintelligent, she might have achieved a Brechtian critique of the society responsible for her situation. Instead, she becomes noble and "touching" in death, and thus her death too can be appropriated by the bourgeois audience.[51] There are elements of Marguerite Gautier in Toni—her collapse in tears while hearing the song parallels the earlier courtesan's indulgences in sentiment—but in Young's novel it is ironically the bourgeois lover who suffers at stage center, who "dies" during the dark night of his soul as he tries to extricate himself from the relationship, a scene dramatically set within the storm-buffeted lighthouse he has built. To echo Barthes, had Toni shown herself unaffected by the relationship with Richard, she might have escaped the world of petit-bourgeois sentimentality, although the novel itself, in its return to focus on Richard's travail, virtually bathes in it. Once the protagonist emerges from the bath, of course, all is forgotten; paradoxically, nothing essential has happened to this man who inhabits a world of essential love. His life with Toni has been, for him, merely literary; it has happened between the parentheses of his genuine life of work and marriage.

Karin Michaëlis: *The Dangerous Age*

A book of far more literary merit than either Young's or Allen's that treats the conflict of marriage and freedom is Karin Michaëlis's *The Dangerous Age: Letters and Fragments from a Woman's Diary*. Joyce may have been attracted to Michaëlis as a Danish writer working somewhat the same territory as Ibsen; in any case, the book was extremely widely known, so it is hardly surprising that it found its way to Joyce's library. Published as *Den farlige Alder* in 1910, within two years it had been translated into most major European languages. Marcel Prévost asserts in his introduction that "in all the countries of Central Europe, the most widely read novel at the present moment is *The Dangerous Age*."[52] Much of its fame and notoriety was due to its explicit subject, the emotional dislocations in the life of a menopausal woman who leaves her husband, but as Prévost notes, Michaëlis's extreme frankness in presenting unromantically the thoughts of a woman about men was equally shocking: it is "one of those rare novels by a woman in which the writer has not troubled to think from a man's point of view," and "the outcome is astonishing."[53] Michaëlis did not anticipate Joyce and Lawrence in their direct portrayals of physical sexuality, but her portrayal of a woman's emotional and erotic attitudes was nearly unprecedented. As becomes clear in the course of the book, those attitudes permeate a woman's entire experience, and to this extent the theme of a "dangerous age" is a red herring, merely a dramatic device for bringing to the surface tensions always present in women's sexual relationships. The protagonist, Elsie Lindtner, at the age of forty-two has decided to divorce her husband and live in relative solitude on an island; the novel is composed of her letters to friends and of passages from her intimate journal. As she explains to an apparently happily married woman friend, "There is no special reason for our divorce. None at least that is palpable, or explicable, to the world."[54] The book, in a sense, is in place of that impossible explanation.

In some respects the book belongs in a library of early twentieth-

century feminist writing. Lindtner stresses the vast physical, social, and
mental gulf between the sexes. "Between the sexes reigns an ineradicable
hostility," she writes, which is concealed only "because life has to be
lived."[55] "What is the use of all these discussions and articles about the
equality of the sexes, so long as we women are at times the slaves of an
inevitable necessity?"[56] she asks, and indeed later in her self-exile she
herself is enslaved first by the need she feels for a man to protect the
house and then by her growing erotic and emotional need for the lover
she has longed for or even the husband she has rejected. She asserts that
the inner life of most women would be appalling to most men: "If men
suspected what took place in a woman's inner life after fifty, they would
avoid us like the plague or knock us on the head like mad dogs."[57]
Luckily, there is little danger of this, because "it may safely be said that
on the whole surface of the globe not one man exists who really knows a
woman. . . . If a woman took infinite pains to reveal herself to a husband or a lover just as she really is, he would think she was suffering
from some incurable mental disease."[58]

Yet it is not at all clear that Lindtner regards woman's difference as a
hidden superiority. She is unsparing about what she sees as women's
vanity and jealousy. Speaking of a friend, she writes, "Lillie must never
have the vexation of learning that I detested her girls simply because
they represented the youthful generation which sooner or later must
supplant me." While she reveals herself as a woman who in her youth
was obsessed by vanity and a desire to "succeed" by marrying well—
even against her own inclinations—she nonetheless feels that she is a
fairly representative case. "If women could buy back their lost youth by
drinking the heart's blood of their children, many murders would be
committed in secret."[59] And following one of her many attacks on the
stultifying effect of marriage, she observes, "Any one might suppose that
I was on the way to become a rampant champion of Woman's Cause.
May I be provided with some other occupation! I have quite enough to
do to manage my own affairs."[60]

In Michaëlis's sexual ideology there is indeed a distinction between
spiritual and physical relationships, and women may need both; often
the same man cannot satisfy the two sorts of need. Elsie Lindtner apparently has been more or less satisfied physically by her husband—or at
least she admits that "for many years he dominated my senses, which
gives him a certain hold over me still."[61] Yet she has for years had a

spiritual passion for the young architect Joergen Malthe, which she has never admitted to him because she fears that as an older woman she would be a figure of ridicule. Similarly, her "happily married" friend in the course of the book leaves her husband to sit by the deathbed of a man she has worshipped for years without ever letting him know of her feelings. On the other hand, a recently widowed friend of hers has earned the enmity of the late husband's family by a series of poorly disguised affairs with unsuitable men; Lindtner points out to her that she has in each case convinced herself that the new lover is an "ideal" love, whereas her attraction to him is obviously sensual. In fact, Lindtner asserts that the original problem was the unimaginative man her friend married: "Better have a lover than torment this poor man whose temperament is so different to your own."[62] Coldly practical, Lindtner points out that the woman does not have free choice as to her behavior because she is dependent upon her husband's family. She offers to support her until she can learn a trade. For Michaëlis, sensual attraction is neither rational nor decorous; her protagonist finds herself attracted to the ugly gardener she hires because of the way he walks and moves —and, probably, because he is the only man around. At another point, Lindtner writes in her journal, "I am almost ashamed to confess that men are almost the same to me as flowers; I judge them by their smell."[63]

Like Ibsen, Michaëlis finds that the most damaging aspect of sexual relationships comes through social hypocrisy. Elsie Lindtner's maid and companion Jeanne had a shattering experience in her youth, when she accidentally discovered that her mother, whom she had always thought happily married, was carrying on an affair with a family friend. In reaction to this trauma, Jeanne then began a life of casual liaisons, at one point selling herself for a pair of green silk stockings. When Lindtner asks her whether she regretted the act, Jeanne replies, "I don't know. I only thought about my stockings."[64] Jeanne is one of several victims of sexual hypocrisy in the book. Lindtner's "happily married" friend is another; when she leaves her husband to stay with the man she admires while he lies dying, the husband is unable to conceive that she is not having a sexual affair or indeed that she could still have any feeling for himself. Lindtner points out in a letter to him that his wife is simply in love with two men at the same time; one love is sexual, the other not. Obviously the husband will be unable to accept this analysis; in his bourgeois ideology, mature love, marriage, and sex are mutually bounded, and each is evidenced through the husband's complete possession of his wife.

Elsie Lindtner's experiment in seclusion ends in failure all around, although it is difficult to pinpoint the reasons for the failure. First, she discovers that she is not suited to life without men. She finally writes Joergen Malthe, confessing her love for him; but when he comes to visit she immediately perceives that although, as she knew, he had loved her for years in silence, he no longer does so. Humiliated and desperate, she then writes her husband hinting at a reconciliation and learns that he is engaged to a nineteen-year-old girl. The book ends with Lindtner's chatty, catty letter of congratulation to her husband. "One of my first thoughts was: how does she dress? Does she know how to do her hair? Because, you know, most of the girls in our particular set have the most weird notions as regards hair-styling and frocks."[65] The rage and jealousy are painfully obvious in the breezy, barely disguised dire warnings to her husband. Elsie Lindtner will join the emotionally cauterized Jeanne in a trip around the world. From one point of view, she is the victim of her own self-will; the world has not stopped while she has paused to come to terms with her chaotic feelings. Again, her cynicism about marriage comes back to haunt her. "The terrible part of home life is that every piece of furniture in the house forms a link in the chain which binds two married people long after love has died out—if, indeed, it ever existed between them,"[66] she writes, but then she is shattered when her boring, bourgeois ex-husband manages to break that chain.

Perhaps because the novel is somewhat more serious, in a literary sense, than most of those discussed in this section, it is difficult to determine the ideological stance of *The Dangerous Age*. Whatever Michaëlis's attitude toward her protagonist's actions, she appears to find in them an element of hubris which, at the book's conclusion, is thoroughly punished. But is this depressing denouement the natural result of any woman's independent action in a society that will not allow a woman time alone in which to reformulate her life? There is an element of hypocrisy in Lindtner's appeal to her husband, considering the coldness with which she has spoken of him through most of the book; we are tempted to feel that he is merely a last resort for her, once she has discovered that she cannot live happily without a man. Perhaps she is "justly punished" for her treatment of him. On the other hand, his marriage to a nineteen-year-old girl does nothing to establish him as a figure with claims to emotional dignity. Certainly Michaëlis means to confront Elsie Lindtner's utopian vision of solitude with the desire of women for men, which she reads as natural and overwhelming, and which surprises Lindtner in its intensity. And certainly she means to point to a pervasive unhappiness among married women, which is at least partly the result of the socially unacknowledged complexities of sexual and spiritual love.

Marcelle Tinayre: *The House of Sin*

Like Michaëlis's book, Marcelle Tinayre's *The House of Sin* (trans. 1903) has some claim to literary stature. Tinayre, who published her first book at the age of thirteen, was taken under the wing of Ludovic Halévy and was soon proclaimed a "nouvelle princesse des lettres." Her partisans compared her to George Sand; she was an outspoken feminist. Among her numerous serious novels she interspersed enough popular biographies and sketches to make her a wealthy woman. *La Maison du péché* (1902) is an intensely written meditation on the dichotomy of flesh and spirit, although it probably does not fully merit the enthusiasm of Joyce's review; as Mason and Ellmann show, even in transcribing a passage he found particularly charming Joyce was forced to edit the translation of Tinayre's florid prose (*CW*, 122). The reasons for Joyce's partisanship are obvious: the young hero, appropriately named Augustin, is torn between a love that is both physical and romantic on the one hand and his deeply embedded and narrow Catholicism on the other. There is very little action; as would be the case in *Portrait*, the bulk of the narrative is either internal *récit* or intimate dialogue, with occasional patches of lyrical description and even more occasional passages of social satire. The hero, Augustin de Chanteprie, is scion of an ancient provincial family with strong ties to Port-Royal and an almost unblemished record of Jansenist piety. The single blemish in the family annals is a gentleman named Adhémar who, as Joyce puts it, "assumed the excellent foppery of the world" (*CW*, 122) and had constructed a folly adjoining the family house where he lived in sin with a dancer named Rosalba-Rosalinde. Augustin is reared in the strictest piety and seclusion by his fanatical, impersonal mother and by a lay tutor appropriately named M. Forgerus. If Mme de Chanteprie in her total renunciation of the world and the flesh is a secular candidate for sainthood, M. Forgerus is a more sympathetic secular monk; she positively regrets her marriage and childbirth, while he simply has no experience of the lures of the flesh. Augustin learns to refer to Adhémar's folly as "The House of Sin." His only warm human contact is with the old family servant Jacquine, who is also a local herbal healer and who gradually comes to assume almost mythic proportions as a pagan proponent of Life.

Augustin is raised virtually without contact with the world beyond the village; his spiritual virginity is first disturbed when he is sixteen and during a visit of Jacquine's niece inadvertently spies her partly nude body. Still, he is severely tried only when Mme Fanny Manole purchases an outlying property of his family, a house known as "Trois-Tilleuls." During the negotiations he is mesmerized by her beauty and her air of sophistication. He is now in his early twenties, and Fanny finds the passionately devout youth fascinating. She is the illegitimate daughter of a well-known painter; raised in elevated but bohemian circles, she married another artist who abused her, ran through her inheritance, and died. Her own friends are drawn from the better class of artists and bohemians and include a wealthy and plausible playboy named Georges Barral who in a friendly way wishes to make her his mistress.

Slowly the relationship between Fanny and Augustin ripens. He attempts to convert her, but although she takes regular instruction her modern, skeptical mind is unable to manage the required faithful submission to doctrine. Although without genius, she is a competent artist with an entrenched independence of mind. She is, in fact, attracted to Augustin's Catholicism, but in an aesthetic way and as an aspect of the character of the man she has come to love deeply. Meanwhile, Augustin finds that his family and spiritual advisers are united in their opposition to Fanny, regardless of whether she converts; they wish him to marry a colorless young woman of a devout family whom he finds repellent. Mme de Chanteprie's antipathy to Fanny is almost instinctive, the repulsion an ascetic feels for the richness of life itself. Augustin, in whom the element of renunciation has been weakened, is nonetheless unable to bring himself to marry a woman against his mother's wishes.

Despite Augustin's strong moral qualms, Nature takes its course and Fanny becomes his mistress; their first night together occurs in the "House of Sin." Augustin has discovered a miniature of Adhémar hidden in the wall and presents it to Fanny, who is struck by his close resemblance to the portrait. Indeed, it is later revealed that Fanny herself closely resembles the mistress of Augustin's ancestor. As the lines of battle for Augustin's soul grow more distinct, Tinayre suggests that he is the point of intersection of two timeless, mythic principles: unworldly asceticism and abnegation, with all its spiritual strength, and worldly, sensual sexuality, with the added force of romantic love. The opposition is also between past and present, for Augustin realizes that the character instilled in him makes of him "a living anachronism." Near the end of the book, tortured by the choice he must make, he asks M. Forgerus,

—What did you wish to make of me?
—A Christian.
—Yes . . . a country gentleman of Old France, Catholic in the archaic mode, a good Latinist, a good gardener, a good hunter, fully
disposed to enter into a marriage "where neither love nor interest
should play the slightest part. . . ." But at the end of the nineteenth
century such a man must seem to be a character out of a novel.
Not a soul has understood me. . . . Once thrown into the world, I
have found the air there to be unbreathable.[67]

Fanny moves back to Paris, where Augustin visits her and finds himself awkward and silent among her friends. He also becomes acquainted with a right-wing Catholic politician who wishes to draft Augustin for the movement, but the young man comes to believe that the neo-Catholic movement has lost its spiritual authority through its involvement in the quotidian machinery of political action. His disillusionment here parallels Stephen Dedalus's disillusionment with the too-worldly Jesuits.

In the book's drawn-out denouement Augustin is torn between the claims of his family and religion, especially as embodied in his old tutor, who has been recalled for the emergency, and his attachment to Fanny, whom he has promised to rejoin. The two sides appear evenly balanced, the more so because his initial ardor toward Fanny has cooled somewhat. On the other hand, he is drawn to her in sympathy because since the situation of the lovers has become known to the village Fanny has been publicly reviled, in a demonstration of provincial petit-bourgeois vindictiveness that recalls the treatment of Kitty O'Shea in Ireland. Finally Augustin is convinced to make the break with Fanny, and shamefacedly sends M. Forgerus as emissary to her. Only here does the narrator's own moral stance become apparent, in the portrayal of Forgerus:

"He saw himself, judge and executioner, holding in his hands these two broken, bloodied souls. . . . But never did he ask himself whether he had the right to separate them, and whether he had not committed a kind of crime against nature in forcing the conscience of Augustin and substituting his own will for the will of the young man. The idea that Augustin and Fanny ought to dispose of their selves and destinies alone, in mutual agreement . . . this subversive and shocking idea never even faintly disturbed the mind of M. Forgerus."[68]

Following his rejection of Fanny, Augustin experiences first relief, then jealousy of Barral, who he assumes will be courting Fanny, and finally deepening depression. Romantically, he wastes away, tended by his mother and by Jacquine; he destroys unread the letters Fanny continues to send him, but the spiritual athleticism which allows him to maintain his stance of renunciation finally destroys him. The book closes with a hortatory, fanatical prayer spoken by Mme de Chanteprie as her son is dying, a prayer which lasts fully four pages. A dark crucifix hangs in the bedroom just as, in Joyce's words, "the writer has suspended over her tragedy, as a spectre of sorrow and desolation, the horrible image of the Jansenist Christ" (CW, 123).

From such an outline, it might appear that The House of Sin is a standard piece of anti-Catholic literature, contrasting the claims of a backward, life-denying superstition with the claims of love and life. But although there are elements of such a thesis in the novel, it is on the whole far more of a dialogue between ideologies, each of which has its own force and forceful spokespersons. In Bakhtin's perspective, the novel has strong elements of polyphony. Tinayre clearly is fascinated with the world of Jansenism; she published, among her other novels, Une Journée de Port-Royal. A great variety of Catholic apologists—even a great variety of conservative Catholics—speak in the novel and are allowed to speak with compelling eloquence. Fanny's secular faith in love and art, however attractive to a modern sensibility, is never allowed to dominate the discourse; indeed, it is the weakest of the voices in the novel, despite the narrator's bias toward it. Fanny's speech shades imperceptibly into that of Barral, who is essentially an opportunistic epicurean—a seducer-figure whose only redeeming trait is that he is frank about his aims. By contrast, the brooding language of the de Chanteprie family acquires a depth and solidity that makes Fanny's arguments appear weightless and ungrounded. Yet Fanny's language has the force of her immediate physical presence and that of the modern social world. Fanny, Augustin, M. Forgerus, Mme de Chanteprie are all, in Bakhtin's term, "idea-images," independent ideologues engaged in something approaching true dialogism (*PDP*, 91). In the conflict of these worlds the novel's basic values are thrown into question, especially the key value of love: Is what Augustin feels for Fanny genuine romantic love, or is it "merely physical"? Was the waning of his desire evidence that their relationship would eventually founder, or was it simply the reassertion of his familial training, a stage he might have transcended?

Here is where the strongest argument can be made for the resonance of *The House of Sin* within *Portrait*. While in *Stephen Hero* Stephen's antagonists are generally cardboard figures, with no true language of their own, in *Portrait* sections like the third chapter demonstrate the way in which the language of the church has a very considerable authority. Like Augustin's, Stephen's mind is permeated with Catholic dogma and its requisite language; he may subvert it through a gradual process of dialogue, but he can never simply deny or abandon it. On the formal level, Tinayre's novel may have provided a model similar to James Lane Allen's *The Increasing Purpose*: like Allen, Tinayre focuses unremittingly upon the protagonist's consciousness, exploring the subtleties of attraction and repulsion in his relationship to Fanny and to the church. In roughly the same degree as *Portrait*, the novel is internal and—as Joyce noted—attempts to suit the cadences of its prose to the progress of the drama: the "last chapters . . . show an admirable adjustment of style and narrative, the prose pausing more and more frequently with every lessening of vitality" (*CW*, 122).

Thematically, Tinayre's opposition of sexuality, art, and life to the church, of freedom to constriction, and of present to past are all echoed in *Portrait*. But Tinayre's example also shows clearly the differing terms in which Joyce saw the opposition. Tinayre's typical theme is Love; among her other novels are *L'Amour qui pleure* and *Avant l'Amour*. Certainly she would recognize the wading girl of *Portrait*, since Fanny represents much the same cluster of values. But Joyce has no intention of allowing his protagonist's struggle to be defined by a single love-relationship, or by an explicitly romantic ideology in which the love-relationship is identified with aesthetic achievement. In place of the single temptation of Fanny he invokes the prostitute, Mercedes, E. C., and the girl at the beach—all fragments of a courtly, physical, and aesthetic sexuality that

Joyce refuses to embody or define. To define it would be to limit it, whereas Joyce means for the Life/Love complex to center on an openness to experience; and to embody it would be to risk sentimentalizing it, whereas Stephen's passion must always be out of proportion to its object. Augustin is merely a lover whose upbringing has forbidden him to love, and so he is destroyed. Stephen is, or wishes to be, an artist as well, and it may well be the egotism in his nature that enables him to escape and, in his own fashion, to thrive.

Sexuality and Ideology

These convergent and divergent texts all participate in the popular discourse of marriage and sexuality at the turn of the century; they can hardly be called a random sampling, chosen as they are from Joyce's library and writings, but they cover a considerable span of attitudes and ideological presuppositions within the general parameters of "advanced" discussion. Joyce's own treatment of sexuality and marriage in *Portrait*, *Stephen Hero*, and *Exiles* is intertextual with these books—as, of course, with a huge number of other works that are beyond the scope of this examination, notably those of Shaw, Ibsen, and Wilde. An equally pertinent set of texts might be the extensive newspaper discussions of the issue. As Christopher Lasch notes, by the late nineteenth century "American newspaper and magazines brimmed with speculation about the crisis of marriage and the family," spurred by concern over the increasing divorce rate, the falling birth rate among the bourgeoisie, the changing position of women, and the apparent revolution in morals.[69] The same was true in Britain, with an additional emphasis on the possibility of racial degeneration following upon the disintegration of the family. Still, despite all the furor it should be remembered that the "marriage crisis" was almost exclusively a middle-class phenomenon; John R. Gillis's extensive research among the British working classes reveals no interruption in the Victorian mandate for marriage until well into the twentieth century.[70] Indeed, the tendency of the working classes to propagate in large families was one of the elements that lent urgency to bourgeois concern about the survival of bourgeois marriage.

"Marriage," writes Roland Barthes, "affords great collective excitations: if we managed to suppress the Oedipus complex and marriage, what would be left for us to *tell*? With them gone, our popular arts would be transformed entirely."[71] And it is precisely marriage as a narrative that is put into question in these books, which then may be regarded as narratives parasitic upon an understood cultural narrative; Joyce's works in this perspective are narratives at a second remove, narratives that question and destabilize those parasitic marriage-narratives. *Exiles*, the most coherent and complex of Joyce's early treatments of marriage, is an implicit response to the marriage debate on several levels. In a note to the play, Joyce shows that he is perfectly aware that *Exiles* will take its place in the European dialogue on marriage and adultery and indeed belongs to a particular subgenre within that narrative tradition:

> Since the publication of the lost pages of *Madame Bovary* the centre of sympathy appears to have been esthetically shifted from the lover or fancyman to the husband or cuckold. This displacement is also rendered more stable by the gradual growth of a collective practical realism due to changed economic conditions in the mass of the people who are called to hear and feel a work of art relating to their lives. This change is utilized in *Exiles* although the union of Richard and Bertha is irregular to the extent that the spiritual revolt of Richard which would be strange and ill-welcomed otherwise can enter into combat with Robert's decrepit prudence with some chance of fighting before the public a drawn battle. (*E*, 115–16)

There are several surprising aspects to this note, which as a whole indicates just how far Joyce as critic had come from the egotistical romanticism of the "Rabblement" essay. First, Joyce's assertion that the popular "displacement of sympathy" from lover to husband is economically grounded is one of the few overt instances in which he writes from a Marxist literary perspective. The waning of the popular romantic infatuation with the gay Lothario—the figure he pilloried in "Two Gallants"—is associated with the expansion of the reading public to include the lower middle class, and perhaps with the lowered economic expectations of the public in the later nineteenth century.[72] The last sentence of Joyce's note is ambiguous, but assuming that the clause "although the union of Richard and Bertha is irregular" is parenthetical, Joyce appears to be arguing that the new public sympathy for betrayed husbands will apply to Richard even though he is not legally married, and will also allow Richard's unusual views on man-woman relationships a hearing which they might not otherwise have had. The "decrepit prudence" of Robert's views—paradoxically, this apparently romantic "free love" advocate is characterized as prudent—will also make Richard's truly radical approach more attractive by comparison.

Joyce's first gesture is to distance his work from that of Ibsen and similar feminist ideologues: "Richard must not appear as a champion of woman's rights," he notes. "His language at times must be nearer to that of Schopenhauer against women. . . . He is in fact fighting for his own hand, for his own emotional dignity and liberation" (*E*, 120). This caveat is necessary only because the attack on programmatic fidelity in marriage was most powerfully articulated by narratives that posited the necessity of liberating women from their sexual bondage; for Joyce, as for some later feminists, to limit the problem to the respective rights of women versus men in marriage is to put a false emphasis upon the situation. Richard's objections to marriage, we may surmise, are like Joyce's: he refuses to subordinate the most important personal relationship of his life to the structures of church and state. Indeed, Richard's egotism demands that Bertha's commitment to him should be so strong as to override the objections of society; were she simply to marry him, he would never be certain that her commitment was not as much to the institution of marriage as to him personally.

However unsuccessful his attempt, Richard wants to make fidelity a matter of perpetual free choice for both partners; he is fully aware that his own indiscretions have left him vulnerable to Bertha's retaliation. Richard assumes equality of rights, but this does not begin to define the problem, much less to solve it. It is Robert who speaks in the voice of Grant Allen or Havelock Ellis in this play, defending the right of a woman, married or not, to take lovers, without regard to the consequences. Robert, hypocritically enough, is the sexual millennialist, while Richard struggles painfully with consequences and conclusions. In other regards, too, Joyce tries to displace the argument from its male-female bipolarity: he invokes and hypostatizes "the virginity of the soul" (*E*, 67) rather than the traditionally female virginity of the body, thus equipping both players in the marriage game with equally valuable counters. But although Richard's initial presumption is of equality between partners, this becomes increasingly difficult to assess or to implement as the play progresses. As Phyllis Rose eloquently puts it, "Equality is to sexual politics what the classless society is to Marxist theory: the hypothesis that solves the problem."[73]

The initial factor complicating Richard's experiment is that, however much he may believe in equal rights of sexual partners, he is far from imagining that man and woman—especially he and Bertha—are equivalent or interchangeable. Richard and Bertha are widely separated in education, birth, temperament, and interests; they speak different languages. Neither is ever wholly unconscious of the social gap separating them, and Bertha does not understand why Richard should not be drawn to a woman of his own social position. Thus even at their most dramatic confrontations they speak at cross-purposes, Bertha persisting in her jealousy of Beatrice when, from Richard's point of view, Beatrice is completely beside the point (E, 103). But concentric about this dilemma are a host of other complicating factors, many of them separately foregrounded as paradigms in the popular literature of the marriage crisis.

One of these is the opposition of Bertha and Beatrice, the sexual and intellectual loves of Richard's life; Michaëlis, for example, stresses that a woman is capable of such divided loyalties, while the same paradigm hovers about Filson Young's exploration of erotic fixation versus proper marriage. Bertha and Beatrice are, of course, a late avatar of the opposed dark and fair ladies of Victorian fiction who embody the principles of sensuality, anarchy, earthiness, and transgression on the one hand and those of ideality, rationality, abstraction, and conformity on the other. And just as Hardy had utilized and challenged this traditional dichotomy in *Jude the Obscure*, so in *Exiles* Joyce no sooner establishes the opposition than he begins to destroy it. Bertha may be uneducated, but she is articulate, even at times eloquent; she is by no means stupid. Beatrice is handicapped by having little real functional role in the action, but even aside from this technical problem her Beatrician nature is compromised. She is, somewhat paradoxically, a repressed Protestant; she yearns for a convent and, as Richard says, is unable to give herself freely and wholly (E, 22). Unlike the conventional figure, she is divided in her attraction and loyalty between spiritual Richard and worldly Robert. Perhaps most provocatively, she has suffered a mysterious illness and is now in some way "convalescent" (E, 22). Bertha in a moment of rage refers to her as "the diseased woman," and Richard replies, "Bertha, take care of uttering words like that!" (E, 54). Since the original discus-

sion of her illness follows immediately on Richard's recalling that Beatrice gave Robert her garter, there is some implication that she may
have a shameful sexual disease, just as her unofficial engagement with
her cousin Robert carries a certain burden of incest. By this point her
role as womanly spirit in opposition to Bertha's womanly body is severely compromised.

A minor popular paradigm invoked in *Exiles* goes relatively unex-
plored there, probably because it was too important in Joyce's own psyche. This is the bourgeois association of lower-class women with the
erotic. This paradigm is one of the "givens" of Filson Young's *The Sands
of Pleasure*, an important element in Dujardin's *L'Initiation au péché et
à l'amour*, in which Marcelin spends much of his youth in the pursuit of
trottins, and figures prominently in the upper-class Augustin's attraction
to bohemian Fanny in Tinayre's *The House of Sin*. In *Exiles*, Bertha
bitterly refers to Beatrice as "her ladyship" (*E*, 74) and makes it clear
that class antagonism is a great part of her jealousy: "She is everything I
am not—in birth and education" (*E*, 103). Richard, of course, thinks
that he regards the class distinction as irrelevant, but is continually confronted with the fact that for Bertha at least it is crucial. It may be no
less so for him. Steven Marcus has discussed the Victorian bourgeois
fixation on servants and working women as erotic objects, as exempli-
fied in *My Secret Life*. Marcus observes that for the protagonist of that
book the "relation of master and servant gives him the opportunity to
express that aggression which for him is the principal component in his
potency" and cites Marx's analysis of the process by which the objectification of human relationships is contingent on class distinctions.[74]

Freud also warned against the dangerous split between "objects of
desire" and "objects of respect," which arose from the Victorian male's
early association of sexuality with prostitutes and working women.[75]
Stephen Dedalus's neurotic combination of worship and contempt for
women is a textbook example of the dissociation of which Freud warns.
The class-based objectification of lower-class women coincided with the
structural objectification of women in pornographic fantasies to make
them an inevitable sexual prey for the Victorian bourgeois male. And
these psychological mechanisms were reinforced by the actual social circumstance that lower-class women, with their minimal expectations,
might indeed be more likely to respond to sexual overtures, either in
hope of monetary reward or because they simply had less to lose than
their bourgeois sisters. Emma haughtily rejects Stephen "Hero's" pro-

posal that they spend a night of love together, and Beatrice will not commit herself to Richard, but Bertha follows him into "exile" without being asked. The Victorian male rationalized and mythified his attraction in various ways, often by ascribing to lower-class women qualities of naturalness and childlike spontaneity, just as Richard Grey does for Toni in *The Sands of Pleasure*. Richard Rowan's obsession with his alleged destruction of Bertha's soul's virginity directly reflects this paradigm.

A final popular paradigm in *Exiles* is Richard's role, in which elements of the rebel, artist, iconoclast, bohemian, and the professor of a "higher morality" (which to conventional minds appears immoral) are mingled. Like The Woman Who Did, Richard is a Shelleyan figure who presents himself in opposition to a hypocritical society; like the protagonist of *The Increasing Purpose*, his opposition is most personally embodied in a painful relationship with his mother, who represents stultifying religious convention. Like both figures, his fundamental value is freedom. At the end of the play, like Grant Allen's Herminia, he assumes the martyr's role, telling Bertha, "I have wounded my soul for you" (*E*, 112). But although Joyce had far less distance upon this paradigm than upon those of bourgeois romances like *The Lady of Lyons* or *Ingomar the Barbarian*, he is not rewriting *The Woman Who Did* from a male standpoint. Allen's narrator explicitly confirms Herminia as the book's center of moral value; her sacrificial death is the demonstration that she is right and hypocritical society is wrong. The case in *Exiles* is far more complex and turns upon an exploration of the radical ambiguity in the term *freedom*.

Richard's insistence that he is giving Bertha her freedom is undercut throughout the play, first by her refusal to adopt his language—"what you call complete liberty" (*E*, 53) may be something very different—and then by their joint recognition that "freedom" means at least two different things:

> RICHARD, *bitterly*: I am in the way, is it? You would like to be free now. You have only to say the word.
> BERTHA, *proudly*: Whenever you like I am ready.
> RICHARD: So that you could meet your lover—freely?
> BERTHA: Yes.
> . . . .
> RICHARD: Bertha! *She does not answer.* Bertha, you are free.

BERTHA, *pushes his hand aside and starts to her feet:* Don't touch me! You are a stranger to me. You do not understand anything in me.

(*E*, 103–4)

Here freedom in the first instance means the equivalent of divorce—after all, Richard in theory has been giving Bertha her freedom all along. In the second instance it means what it has meant previously, the choice of fidelity or infidelity within their marriage-equivalent. Yet here, as throughout the play, Bertha refuses to make the choice because, as she realizes yet cannot articulate, it is a false choice and a sham freedom. The bulk of *Exiles* is a demonstration of the infinity of constraints upon the freedom Richard offers.

In her excellent analysis of a group of Victorian marriages, Phyllis Rose points to "the human tendency to invoke love at moments when we want to disguise transactions involving power." Indeed, she suggests that love might be defined as "the momentary or prolonged refusal to think of another person in terms of power."[76] There is much talk of love in *Exiles*, especially by Robert and Bertha, but the subtext is invariably power. Bertha feels that Richard has left her—abandoned her—at some point she will not specify (*E*, 111). It should be clear to everyone except perhaps Richard that for Bertha his insistence on her "freedom" is the equivalent of emotional abandonment. She fears she has nothing to offer him except her fidelity, which he rejects because it is tainted by institutional pressures. As she realizes, there is no way to show that she takes his offer seriously, and is thus free from the conventions of marriage, except to "betray" him. She does not wish to do this, but is tempted to do so because she suspects it is the only thing that will make him happy. Perhaps she even realizes, as Richard does, that his noble gesture also disguises a masochistic motive, which makes him long for his wife and best friend to betray him, and a homoerotic motive for union with Robert through Bertha. What Joyce terms Bertha's "mental paralysis" (*E*, 113) is at least partly a result of these two paradoxes: that Bertha can only show she is "free" by reluctantly obeying Richard's unspoken wish and that she can only be "loyal" to him by betraying him.

It is just as well that Richard is not presented as a feminist, because his effort to present Bertha with her own freedom is also an egregious exercise of patriarchal power. Like Rupert Birkin in *Women in Love*, he offers his reluctant mate a relationship of equality *on his own terms.*

Bertha responds by playing along—she has little choice, since she has little social support for her position and so must let Richard write the rules of the game. But as part of her play she tries to empower herself by evoking jealousy in her husband. Richard, of course, is both consumed by jealousy and unable ideologically to admit to it. When Richard appears at Bertha's assignation with Robert, she insists, "You had to come. You are jealous like the others" (*E*, 72). Richard claims that he has come merely to protect her against Robert's threat of violence—a dishonest enough defense that also makes little sense within the rhetoric of freedom he has established: he cannot both give Bertha her freedom and protect her from the possible consequences of it. Richard is a playwright whose characters are not wholly under his control; or, as was argued earlier, he is an experimenter involved in his own experiment. Robert perhaps willfully misinterprets Richard's position when he attempts to seduce Bertha, portraying Richard as a Nietzschean figure defined by his independence of society's laws and customs: "Every chain but one he has broken and that one we are to break" (*E*, 87). But Robert's interpretation is not really such a distortion of Richard's stance of romantic opposition. Richard's attempt at creating his own moral universe, however nobly motivated, is wholly destructive to those around him as well as to himself.

There are two main reasons for this. One is that Richard's notion of freedom within marriage even as theory is paradoxically self-defeating. To the extent that he and Bertha are committed to one another, they have limited their possibilities of action, and to the extent that they are "free" their relationship loses its importance. He cannot have it both ways. Rupert Birkin, otherwise as romantic an ideologist as Richard Rowan, argues this succinctly when Ursula Brangwen tries to equate love and freedom: "Don't cant to me. . . . Love is a direction which excludes all other directions. It's a freedom *together*, if you like."[77] A second reason for the painful denouement of Richard's experiment is that he has attempted to set up a closed moral system within a social universe that impinges upon it at every point. Here, Richard's romantic egoism is to blame. "I warn you that I don't take my ideas from other people," he insists to Bertha, ironically affirming the romantic ideology of originality, which descends to him from Byron and Shelley and which he shares with figures as diverse as Oscar Wilde and the Count of Monte Cristo. Like Herminia Barton, Richard assumes that his moral and imaginative integrity is guaranteed by his stance of opposition, and that, as Herminia argues, his genius obliges him to create a "higher morality," which, circularly, is one more proof of his superiority.

But the moral system Richard attempts to put in place is not closed and cannot be, a circumstance that the structure of *Exiles* makes explicit. Richard thinks he is involved in a classic triangle, in which Bertha will be forced to choose freely between "husband" and lover. But Bertha insists that they are involved in a romantic quadrilateral instead, with Beatrice an important element in the emotional dynamics of the situation. The child, Archie, certainly cannot be forgotten; whether Richard acknowledges the fact or not, his presence gives more weight to the marriage-equivalent of Richard and Bertha. Even absent persons, such as Richard's mother, lend their voices to the debate. Exile or not, Richard cannot convincingly pretend to be isolated. And his moral experiment is tangent at all points to a host of other issues that involve people other than himself, Robert, and Bertha: his taking up of a university post, his return to Ireland, the raising of Archie, and even the portrayal of Richard in the press all depend upon and in turn influence the romantic triangle.

Toward the end of the play Beatrice has reverently invoked Richard's ideas in her naive hero-worship, and Bertha testily replies, "Ideas and ideas! But the people in this world have other ideas or pretend to" (*E*, 100). For all his impatience with the other "people in this world," that is the world in which Richard lives, and as the play comes to a climax there are increasing indications that that world can no longer be denied. As Richard and Robert have their final confrontation over Bertha, for the first time an insistent voice from outside is heard, a fishwoman calling "Fresh herrings!" (*E*, 107). Like the voice from the street calling "Blocks, coal-blocks!" in O'Casey's *Juno and the Paycock*, the fishwoman's call represents the deflating reality of the surrounding community, a mockery of the protagonist's romantic egotism that may no longer be ignored. Most significantly of all, Archie, who for both Robert and Richard represents the future, appears with his face flattened against the glass, calling "Open the window! Open the window!" (*E*, 109). Throughout the drama Archie, with his passion for the milkman's horse, has represented a tie to the outside world. He comes and goes through the windows like a breath of fresh air; he has his father's unconventionality but none of his rejection of the world beyond the window. If Richard and his ideas are to survive, they must establish a dialogue with that world; it cannot be ignored or shouted down. The attempt to do so leads directly into the play's emotional maelstrom. As Joyce notes, "Critics may say what they like, all these persons—even Bertha—are suffering during the action" (E, 114).

That the play does not better succeed in its highly intelligent exploration of the marriage debate is probably due to the weakness and one-dimensionality of Robert; there is no voice within Exiles that represents humane sanity, and the "voice of society" within the play is mere caricature. Richard is admirable in his attack on institutionalized marriage, but fearfully wrongheaded in his application of a counterideology, while Robert is less a genuine antagonist than a smooth epicurean who uses society's arguments hypocritically. Even Richard's attraction to him seems unmotivated and arbitrary; Mulligan is a far more convincing friend and antagonist for Dedalus because he is at times both admirable and funny. In Exiles Joyce is in ideological transition. He is able to parody the sexual millennialism of Stephen by allowing Robert to voice it and Richard to recognize with pained embarrassment "the voice of my youth" (E, 71). Even Richard's more sophisticated endorsement of what became known in the 1960s as "open marriage" betrays its own limitations and contradictions in the play. But Joyce is still unwilling or unable to give voice to any strong, coherent opposition to Richard; he is so convinced that "the audience, every man of which is Robert" (E, 114) will necessarily be hostile to Richard that he allows him to speak unopposed and even to strike a bathetic pose of self-indulgent martyrdom at the play's end.

Sexuality is the most highly "naturalized" of social functions. Because the procreative urge is biological at root, it is easy to forget that among humans it is never manifested outside of a social context, and thus is never divorced from ideology. At various times, both Richard and Robert appeal to nature for justification of their sexual mores. Robert claims that the longing to physically possess the woman a man loves is "nature's law" (E, 63), to which Richard replies by denying that he is therefore bound by it: "What is that to me? Did I vote it?" (E, 63). Having thus implied that he is self-created, able to choose the laws that bind him, Richard then defends his disastrous experiment to Bertha by saying, "I did not make myself. I am what I am" (E, 103). Again, he wishes to have it both ways: to remake the conventions of sexuality according to his own desire, and to deny responsibility when the darker side of that desire surfaces.

In a cynical moment, Joyce described the play as "A rough and tumble between the Marquis de Sade and Freiherr v. Sacher-Masoch" (*E*, 124). And comically enough, as Joyce no doubt recognized, Robert satisfies his sadism by refusing to tell the masochistic Richard that he has been betrayed. But Richard and Robert cannot be explained by such simple psycho-sexual oppositions, nor are they "justified" by their natures. Like all of Joyce's characters, they are both bound and free: bound by their psychic architecture and by the encompassing structures of ideology, and free within those bounds to change the direction of their lives. Robert, the self-deluding egotist, is seemingly unaware of the problem, because he is so thoroughly the creature of popular ideologies. Richard, a far more honest egotist, finds that he cannot abolish by fiat either the constraints of his own nature or the society of which he is a reluctant member. Like the play *Exiles* itself, he is simply another voice in the polyphonic marriage debate of the early twentieth century. He cannot dominate that debate by closing his ears to the voices that surround him.

CHAPTER

· 7 ·

CONCLUSIONS

The implications of a Bakhtinian reading of Joyce tend to be expansive rather than narrowing; that is, unlike other, perhaps more rigorous critical methodologies—such as the vulgar Marxist or the unreconstructed Freudian—Bakhtin's questioning of texts produces widening circles of suggestion, instead of a reaffirmation of the tenets of the methodology by means of the text. There is no end to the dialogical interactions within a given text, nor to the intertextual relationships a book bears to its literary surroundings and antecedents. The final objects of Bakhtinian analysis might be said to be at one extreme the individual utterance, at the other the totality of discourse. Unfortunately, critical inquiry tends to disintegrate as it approaches either extreme; Bakhtin's concepts, however valuable their theoretical implications, seem to be most tangibly productive for the critic in a middle ground of inquiry, in analysis of the interactions of a small group of texts or voices.

In the case of Joyce, the force of Bakhtinian analysis is most evident in its reinsertion of the man's writings, protagonists, and—we must suppose—Joyce himself into history. As Bakhtin asserts, "Literature is an inseparable part of the totality of culture and cannot be studied outside the total cultural context" (SG, 140). That Joyce's writings have so seldom been studied from an historical perspective during the past half-century is a testament to the power of the overlapping ideologies of Modernism and of the New Criticism, as well as of the more formalist varieties of structuralism and poststructuralism. Joyce's writings invoke these ideologies, indeed sometimes furnish central articulations of them, but they also establish a space for their demystification and critique. Nevertheless, Stephen's voice has blanketed Joyce's texts to such an extent that we are mesmerized by the figure of the unique, self-generative artist whose outlawed language achieves total mastery and whose work is a self-enclosed, self-sufficient aesthetic unity. We are seldom drawn to ask simple questions such as, "How hard would it be for Stephen to find a prostitute?" or "How often is snow general over Ireland?" Yet if we ignore such trivial queries, which address the plane of two-dimensional realistic representation, we are all the more likely to ignore the participation of Joyce's characters and texts in a historically determined, multi-dimensional dialogical interchange.

In the course of the foregoing chapters our inquiry has gradually widened, from the specific interactions of dialogue within stories of *Dubliners* to the participation of *Stephen Hero*, *Portrait*, and *Exiles* in the discourse regarding sex and marriage, which was articulated in serious and ephemeral writing alike. Parallel investigations might be undertaken for any number of other discourses, or with a very different set of intertexts; Joyce's highly allusive writing is attached to the vast network of surrounding discourse at countless points. It echoes, contests, or adapts more voices than could ever be specified even by a perfect and perfectly informed reader. Of course, this is not to say that such investigations are useless; they may well prove illuminating, but they will never be *totalizing*. The entire thrust of Bakhtin's conceptual apparatus resists totalization. To a degree, it resists *interpretation* as well. Bakhtin does not offer a hermeneutics, because in Bakhtin's view meaning is never final and does not lurk "behind" utterance in however obscure or coded a form. Utterances, and especially literary utterances, offer a play of meanings. They affirm, contest, withdraw, court shyly, rebuff indignantly, contradict or subtly undermine themselves, speak with sidelong glances or deceptive frankness—in short, they act the way we do. The terrain of this play is partly linguistic, but wholly ideological. This is to say no more than that language is involved in the political—in its simplest form, the relationship to the addressee—from the very outset.

One of the implications of this is that the foregoing study has relatively seldom directly addressed questions of interpretation. Its focus, to put it crudely, has been upon *what the text is doing* rather than *what Joyce is saying*. The godlike author pronouncing enigmatically upon life, who lurks behind Joyce's work even for as sophisticated a reader as Kenner, is not a figure in Bakhtinian reading, nor in other postmodern readings. Nevertheless, there is some inevitable interpretive implication in such a reading. The readings of *Dubliners* stories in chapters 2 and 3 foreground the struggles of protagonists against the systems of discourse that surround them, and there is unavoidably an air of heroism to such struggles. It is natural to wonder to what degree the characters of the stories, from Gabriel to Eveline, are "free," and to what extent they have devised or are complicit in their own entrapment. The impersonal power in the operation of languages and ideologies, embedded as they are in the consciousness of the characters, suggests that Joyce's characters are nothing but hapless victims. There is an element of truth in this, but to see the Dubliners as merely doomed pawns of social forces is simply to restate in linguistic terms an interpretation implied by the most reductive of naturalistic readings. Even Eveline has choices and the capability of movement. If Bakhtin allows us to see her as her own narrator, hesitating among "ghost narratives," he does not conclude that her decisions and her fate have already been inscribed in social discourse. We may feel that going with Frank and staying with her father are equally disastrous alternatives, but the very multiplicity of texts in which these choices are inscribed assures that other alternatives exist—if she could only recognize them.

Similarly, there is a certain interpretive force to Bakhtinian readings of Joyce's later works, where the protagonist appears to be in a position of far greater mastery over his or her own fate. In *Portrait*, for example, an attention to the interplay of voices in the novel highlights the separation of narrator from protagonist and thus encourages an ironic reading of Stephen. Further, a reader sensitized to dialogical interplay will place more stress upon the voices that intrude upon Stephen's inner and outer monologues, such as Lynch's deflating quips, which punctuate Stephen's pronouncements on aesthetics, or the voices of the swimming rabble, who shout "O cripes, I'm drownded!" just as Stephen is trying to "cry piercingly of his deliverance to the winds" (*P*, 169). And certainly a reader alert to the turn-of-the-century discourse into which Stephen is a fictional insertion will be less likely to take seriously his claims of originality. Stephen is far more a creature of his own time and place than he is ready to admit and is greatly indebted to the reading he has put behind him.

This does not mean, however, that Stephen is not an artist or will not become one. Bakhtin is not about to pull this particular critical chestnut out of the fire, but his thoughts do bear upon the question. All artists, for Bakhtin, borrow ceaselessly, and in some regards they borrow best who borrow most. A great novelist, such as Dostoevsky, is one who allows such a vivid interplay of voices within his books that his own authorial voice is only one among them, without peculiar privilege even as the author's "self-expression." If anywhere, that expression is to be found in the cacophony of voices that constitutes the novel itself. Further, these voices, including that of the author, are all fundamentally social, linked to the history of a culture. Barthes makes a parallel point about style, which he says is less authorial signature than "a citational procedure, a body of formulas, a memory . . . , an inheritance based on culture and not expressivity."[1] For Bakhtin, an author is *someone who writes*. Despite Stephen's convictions—which are not so very different on this point from Little Chandler's—the problem has nothing to do with whether one has an artist's soul. Stephen will be an artist when, or if, he writes something more than a few flimsy verses. Until then, the question is meaningless.

The major interest Stephen's figure holds for us is in the peculiar, conflicting set of languages and ideologies he encompasses. He stands at an important point of literary transition, when the sentimentalized Victorian infatuation with romanticism is fading and the impact of Continental naturalism is beginning to be felt, when impulses from positivistic science, disturbingly turned upon society itself, mingle with the political inheritance of 1848 and, in Dublin, meet an occult brand of late literary romanticism marshalled to oppose the pragmatics of empire.[2] Complicating his image are a host of popular ideologies of heroism, such as those encountered in his childhood reading and playgoing, of which Stephen may be unaware. All of these are merely conflicting elements that contribute to the "self" which Stephen learns to oppose to the dominant ideologies surrounding him, primarily those of the church and of middle-class *doxa*. Each ideology, embodied in formal or popular discourse, registers as a language, and Stephen emerges as a walking, speaking compendium, or perhaps a battleground upon which these competing discourses clash ignorantly, by night. The clearest demonstration of this in *Portrait* is Stephen's journal, with its allusive fragments, disseminated topics, and vast variation in styles. Criticism has by and large avoided examining Stephen's journal entries as a whole, precisely because they cannot be seen as a whole: in their multitude of self-consciously competing voices they attest to fragmentation more clearly than to any coherent personal direction for the young man. And this may be the greatest sign of health we see in Stephen. His journal is witness to the dialogical vitality of his consciousness.

Still further complicating Stephen's portrayal is Joyce's own involvement in these systems of ideas, many of which have aesthetic implications and thus themselves influence the presentation of Stephen. Joyce is no more beyond ideology than is Stephen, though he may be more sophisticated in his grasp of its workings. By almost any standard *Portrait* is a great work of literature, but its greatness does not remove it from history, situate it beyond the play of ideology, or distinguish it in *kind* from, say, *A Modern Daedalus*. Its distinction, and Joyce's, is that it is the sort of text that invites us to examine critically the network of popular and formal, institutional ideologies that contribute to it—not, assuredly, from a privileged critical vantage beyond ideology, but as best we can, given our own horizons and blind spots.

It has been a contention of this study that an important element in Joyce's literary genius is his appreciation of the importance of popular literature in the society of his time. Ireland was already remarkably literate in 1841, when it claimed a 47 percent literacy rate, but by 1911 the figure had climbed to 88 percent. The number of different newspapers and periodicals more than doubled in a similar period.³ These figures represent a qualitative shift in the influence of popular literature from marginality, in a basically rural society whose popular consciousness was still significantly influenced by folklore, to centrality. As a result the characters of Joyce's fiction are all *bovaristes*, and Joyce provides the textual evidence of their possession by their reading. As should be evident, the bulk of this material in the period between 1840 and 1914 participated in an ideology that could be termed "degenerate romantic," from the Wild West tales of Joyce's youth to the *Count of Monte Cristo*, from Bulwer-Lytton to Grant Allen or James Lane Allen—or at least this seems to be Joyce's understanding of the situation. Unlike most cultural spokesmen of the period Joyce does not decry the pernicious influence of the new mass literature—he leaves that to Stephen—but he does raise the question of its role in the most suggestive way possible to a novelist, by highlighting its dialogical participation in the thoughts and speech of his protagonists.

Among the competing voices of this study those of Joyce and of Bakhtin have been dominant, although in the case of Bakhtin the voice is already highly mediated by translation and by the critical context of postmodernism within which his writings first became widely known in the West. Of these two, Bakhtin's voice has no doubt at times appeared to be the more authoritative one, simply because critical discourse assumes a position of mastery over literary discourse. But the object of this study, on the contrary, has been to set up a dialogue between these two figures, in which the language of each would enrich that of the other, without any ascription of dominance to either. Since the critical dicta of the mature Joyce are for the most part gnomic or elusively epigrammatic, Bakhtin's language has tended to predominate in analytic moments. But the agenda of our study has been set by Joyce—by his reading in the first place, but predominantly by the texture and scope of his writing. Often Joyce's work has encouraged or even demanded a modification of Bakhtin's methods: in reading the later stories of *Dubliners*, for instance, we have been drawn to practice a kind of small-group discourse analysis that has no obvious precedent in Bakhtin's writings. Throughout that volume, so sedulously does Joyce's text invoke strictly rhetorical figures that we have been drawn toward a kind of analysis more properly structuralist than Bakhtinian.

Similarly, popular literature is not a major concern of Bakhtin's published work; his interest is in the folkloric element, and then only as it intersects his concept of carnival. He does note the participation of popular novelistic genres in Dostoevsky's work (*PDP*, 102–6), but this is mainly to emphasize the polyphony of genres that contribute to the Dostoevskian novel. Yet most of Bakhtin's methods of analysis are readily adaptable to the examination of popular literary genres, and in his analysis of time and space in what he terms the "adventure novel," for instance, he demonstrates this. Bakhtin has little concern for literary hierarchies, except to invert them where possible. But his major criterion for novelistic greatness is a writer's sensitivity to all the dominant and marginalized voices of his culture, which in Joyce's time as in ours most emphatically includes the voices of the popular genres. The immense impact of Joyce's portrayal of popular consciousness issues from his appreciation of its contingent nature, its dependence upon the languages that surround it and of which it is constituted. Bakhtin noted, late in his life, "I live in a world of others' words. And my entire life is an orientation in this world, a reaction to others' words . . . , beginning with my assimilation of them . . . and ending with assimilation of the wealth of human culture (expressed in the word or in other semantic materials). The other's word sets for a person the special task of understanding this word" (SG, 143). Preeminently among modern writers, Joyce attempted this; creating nothing, he heard with unrivaled acuity the voices of his culture and reinscribed in the matrix of fiction its "chronicles of disorder." Our task is to listen.

NOTES

Chapter 1

1. See Brantlinger, *Bread and Circuses*, for an excellent survey of negative critical approaches to popular culture.

2. Herr, *Joyce's Anatomy of Culture*, 2.

3. From Sheehy's *May It Please the Court*, quoted in Scholes and Kain, *The Workshop of Daedalus*, 175.

4. *Willing's Press Guide*.

5. Leslie, *End of a Chapter*, 191.

6. Ellmann, *James Joyce*, 50.

7. Joyce, *Letters*, 2:82.

8. Ibid., 85.

9. See Jameson, *Political Unconscious*, 207.

10. Joyce, *Letters*, 2:153, 159, 167, 182, 188, 189; 1:208.

11. Ibid., 2:88–89, 86; 1:288.

12. These and other perspectives appear in the extensive collection of essays on the problem of popular culture, Davison, Meyersohn, and Shils, *Culture and Mass Culture*.

13. Bradbury, *Social Context*, 251–52.

14. Neuburg, *Popular Literature*, 15.

15. See Kershner, "Joyce and Stephen Phillips' *Ulysses*," 194–201.

16. See, e.g., Horkheimer and Adorno, "The Culture Industry: Enlightenment as Mass Deception," in *Dialectic of Enlightenment*.

17. See "The Death of the Author," in Barthes's *Image/Music/Text*, 142–48.

18. Althusser, *Lenin and Philosophy*, 142–45.

19. Ibid., 222–23.

20. Jameson, *Political Unconscious*, 76.

21. Ibid., 207.

22. Morson, "Preface: Perhaps Bakhtin," in Morson, *Bakhtin: Essays and Dialogues*, vii.

23. Todorov, *Mikhail Bakhtin*, ix.

24. See the opening chapters of *FMLS* on "translinguistics" and the limitations of linguistics; see also "Language, Speech, and Utterance" in *MPL*, 65–82.

25. "Take a dialogue and remove the voices ..., remove the intonations ..., carve out abstract concepts and judgments from living words and responses, cram everything into one abstract consciousness—and that's how you get dialectics." "From Notes Made in 1970–71," in *SG*, 147.

26. "The Study of Ideologies and Philosophy of Language," in *MPL*, 9–16.

27. "Bakhtin, Marxism, and the Carnivalesque," in LaCapra, *Rethinking Intellectual History*, 315.

28. See "Characteristics of Genre and Plot Composition in Dostoevsky's Work," *PDP*, 101–80, where the genre of the serio-comic, or *spoudogeloion*, is traced, as well as "Rabelais in the History of Laughter," *RW*, 59–144.

29. See especially "Discourse in the Novel," *DI*, 259–422.

30. Clark and Holquist, *Mikhail Bakhtin*, 293.

31. Cited by Orr, "Dialogism and Heteroglossia."

32. Clark and Holquist, *Mikhail Bakhtin*, 317.

33. De Man, *Resistance to Theory*, 109.

34. For an analysis of the term in recent discourse, see "Ideology" in Geuss, *Idea of a Critical Theory*, 4–25; see also "Mutations of a Critical Ideology" in Eagleton, *Criticism and Ideology*, 11–43; for a historical perspective, see McGann, *Romantic Ideology*, 10–14.

Chapter 2

1. Rabaté, "Silence in Dubliners," 48. Cf. Herring, "Structure and Meaning in Joyce's 'The Sisters,'" 134: "Upon reflection, a reader might first be struck with the gnomonic nature of the story's language: it is elliptical, evasive, sometimes mysterious. A mystery is there to be uncovered, but boy and reader will be frustrated by language in their attempts to solve it."

2. Hélène Cixous notes that the window the boy watches "is also the mirror that reflects the candles lighted for the dead." *Exile of James Joyce*, 378. This entire discussion in Cixous's book, "The Magic of Signal and Silence," 371–88, is relevant.

3. Kenner, *Ulysses*, 70.

4. Rabaté, "Silence in Dubliners," 53.

5. Terdiman, *Discourse/Counter-Discourse*, 60, 61.

6. Herring, "Structure and Meaning in Joyce's 'The Sisters,'" 135.

7. Jameson, *Political Unconscious*, 84.

8. Connolly, *Personal Library of James Joyce*, 27–28.

9. *New Catholic Encyclopedia*, quoted in Bremen, "'He Was Too Scrupulous Always,'" 63.

10. Egoff, *Children's Periodicals*, 3, 16.

11. Ibid., 25.

12. *British Library Catalogue*.

13. Cited in Magalaner, *Time of Apprenticeship*, 149.

14. Turner, *Boys Will Be Boys*, 104.

15. Ibid., 108, 122.

16. Ibid., 145. The varying titles of these magazines are no doubt responsible for some confusion among Joyce's annotators regarding them. Gifford (*Joyce Annotated*, 34) agrees with Magalaner, *Time of Apprenticeship*, 149) that the *Halfpenny Marvel* began in 1893 and the other two in 1894, while in their edition of *Dubliners* (p. 465) Scholes and Litz have the *Marvel* in 1893, *Union Jack* in 1894, and *Pluck* in 1895. None of these seem aware of the earlier *Union Jack*.

17. *British Library Catalogue*.

18. Magalaner, *Time of Apprenticeship*, 149.

19. Turner, *Boys Will Be Boys*, 108.

20. Ibid., 112.

21. "Boys' Weeklies," in Orwell, *Collected Essays*, 1:460–85.

22. Turner, *Boys Will Be Boys*, 143–44.

23. In a novel of which Joyce was fond, *At Swim-Two-Birds* (1939), Flann O'Brien

features an Irish writer of cowboy stories and indeed has the writer's characters come to life, staging cattle drives and roundups on the outskirts of Dublin.

24. Williams, *Keywords*, 90–92.

25. Hart, *Joyce's "Dubliners,"* 171.

26. Cawelti, *Adventure, Mystery, and Romance*, 212–14.

27. Turner, *Boys Will Be Boys*, 80. Note that boys' magazines typically sent a double message. Jack Harkaway's running away to sea is clearly presented as a sign of his heroic character, while the narrator warns, "We are no advocates for running away; boys who run away from school generally turn out scamps in after life. They show an independence of action and a strong self-will, in which it is very injurious for the young to indulge"; cited in Turner, 88.

28. Bulwer-Lytton, *Last Days of Pompeii*, 13.

29. Ibid., 369.

30. Magalaner, *Time of Apprenticeship*, 46.

31. Bulwer-Lytton, *Last Days of Pompeii*, 140.

32. Ibid., 143.

33. Ibid., 144.

34. Ibid., 124–25.

35. Ibid., 128.

36. Marcus, *The Other Victorians*, 253.

37. Ibid., 257.

38. Ibid., 255.

39. Kaye, "The Wings of Dedalus," 37.

40. Feshbach, "Death in 'An Encounter,'" 85.

41. Quoted in Gifford, *Joyce Annotated*, 43.

42. *British Library Catalogue.*

43. Stone, "'Araby' and the Writings of James Joyce," 350.

44. *British Library Catalogue.*

45. Stone, "'Araby' and the Writings of James Joyce," 350.

46. W. Scott, *The Abbott*, xvi.

47. Ibid., 67 (chap. 8).

48. Ibid., 116 (chap. 13).

49. Ibid., 292 (chap. 27).

50. Ibid., 293 (chap. 27).

51. Ibid., 372–73 (chap. 34).

52. Ibid., 162 (chap. 17).

53. Ibid., 223 (chap. 21).

54. Ibid., 78 (chap. 9).

55. Harry Stone suggests in "'Araby' and the Writings of James Joyce," 354, that Mangan's anonymous sister, the "Madonna of the Silver Bracelet," is another Mary, like the "Mary Sheehy Joyce regarded as his original 'temptress' and 'betrayer.'" Insofar as the boy identifies with Roland, this is even more likely than Stone realizes: the women who rule Roland's life include Magdalen (one of the most significant Catholic Marys), Lady Mary of Avenel, and of course Mary Queen of Scots. Joyce's target is Mariolatry, the sentimental conflation of chivalric and religious impulses.

56. W. Scott, *The Abbot*, 121 (chap. 14).

57. Ibid., 296–97 (chap. 28).

58. Ibid., 426 (chap. 38).

59. Edwards, *Vidocq Dossier*, 10–13.

60. Vidocq, *Memoirs*, xiv–xv.

61. Stone, "'Araby' and the Writings of James Joyce," 350–51.

62. Vidocq, *Memoirs*, 136 (1:chap. 8).

63. Ibid., 221 (1:chap. 14).

64. Ibid., 220 (1:chap. 14).

65. Edwards, *Vidocq Dossier*, 132.

66. Stone, "'Araby' and the Writings of James Joyce," 357–58.

67. Kenner, "Molly's Masterstroke," 20–21.

68. Goldman, *Joyce Paradox*, 20.

69. Somewhat less obvious is the unusual splitting of the romantic hero into two characters, Thaddeus and Devilshoof, a ploy which enables Thaddeus to act with Victorian irreproachability even while his dark twin Devilshoof performs the violent or underhanded acts that enable the plot to progress and that, incidentally, earn the audience's reluctant admiration.

70. Balfe, *Bohemian Girl*, 4.

71. Cited in Brandabur, *Scrupulous Meanness*, 62. More recently, Cóilín Owens has suggested that the mother's phrase is a corruption of "Deireadh fonn saor fhonn," "the end (or purpose) of free desires (or airs)." Owens observes that the phrase contains a version of "Buenos Aires." It might also be noted that the phrase points equally to the closing off of desire and the end of songs. Personal communication, 16 February 1988.

72. The father's hatred of the "Damned Italians" ironically applies by association to the Irishman Balfe, who began his career with the Italian Opera.

73. See Florence L. Walzl, "*Dubliners*: Women in Irish Society," 33.

74. Marcus, *The Other Victorians*, 245.

75. Miles, *Forbidden Fruit*, 6. For a more general treatment of the incest theme in nineteenth-century popular culture, see chap. 4 of Twitchell, *Forbidden Partners*, 127–84.

76. Gay, *Bourgeois Experience*, 373. Independently of the present author, at several conferences both Mary Power and Cóilín Owens have suggested that Joyce may mean to allude to this pornographic work. It might be noted that Fanny Burney's *Evelina, or The History of a Young Lady's Entry into the World* (1778) involves a disguised incest theme. The original Eve was after all the first participant in an incestuous relationship, in that she was consubstantial with her mate; possibly the "Eveline" diminutive during the nineteenth century became a coded reference to incest.

77. *Eveline*, 3.

78. Ibid., 3.

79. Ibid., 88.

80. Joyce, *Letters*, 1:171.

81. Cleland, *Fanny Hill*, 157.

82. Ibid., 161.

83. Miles, *Forbidden Fruit*, 9.

84. Joyce, *Letters*, 2:151.

85. Huppé, cited in Bowen, "After the Race," 56, n. 1.

86. Dumas, *Three Musketeers*, 21 (1:chap. 2).

87. Ibid., 88 (1:chap. 7).

88. Ibid., 292 (1:chap. 25).

89. Ibid., 330–31 (1:chap. 27).

90. See Davenson, *Livre de Chanson*, 569–72.

91. Young, *Sands of Pleasure*, 398. Ellmann in *Consciousness of Joyce*, 134, lists the date of Joyce's edition as 1908; both Boston and London (Richards) editions are dated 1905, and the only later edition listed in the *British Library Catalogue* is 1919. I have been unable to locate a 1908 edition.

92. Ellmann lists Joyce's edition as London: Macmillan, 1896; *Consciousness of Joyce*, 119.

93. Mason, *Courtship of Morrice Buckler*, 24.

94. Joyce, *Letters*, 2:212

95. Stanislaus Joyce, "Background to *Dubliners*," 526.

96. Joyce, *Letters*, 2:132–33.

97. Humphries, "Ferrero Etc.," 239–43.

98. Ferrero, *Militarism*, 166; Humphries, "Ferrero Etc.," 244.

99. Ferrero, *Militarism*, 56–57.

100. Ibid., 82.

101. Ibid., 196–97.

102. Ibid., 218.

103. Ibid., 287.

104. Manganiello, *Joyce's Politics*, 50; ref. to Ferrero, *L'Europa giovane* (Milan, 1897), 163–70.

105. Eagleton, "Text, Ideology, Realism," 160 (italics in original).

106. Dumas, *Three Musketeers*, 121–22 (1:chap. 11).

107. Ibid., 360 (1:chap. 29).

108. Hart, *Joyce's Dubliners*, 71.

109. Halper, " 'The Boarding House,' " 74, has noted that the language of gallantry continues in "The Boarding House": Mrs. Mooney tries not to receive her daughter's confession in "too cavalier a fashion," Bob Doran is a "man of honour," and so forth.

110. Beck, *"Dubliners": Substance, Vision, and Art*, 153.

111. Cheryl Herr analyzes this genre of song within the context of music-hall performance, commenting, "The simple themes and easy stylizations of such numbers show us cultural operations of dichotomizing, repeating, socializing, and mediating in almost pure form"; *Joyce's Anatomy of Culture*, 192.

112. Ibid., 87.

113. Cf. here Richard Terdiman's discussion of the critical move beyond binarism in *Discourse/Counter-Discourse*, 25–40.

114. De Man, *Resistance to Theory*, 89.

115. De Man's observation, "What we call ideology is precisely the confusion of linguistic with natural reality, of reference with phenomenalism" (ibid., 11), carries the unfortunate and surely mistaken implication that the thoroughly deconstructive mind escapes the hegemony of ideology. Eagleton's critique of the deconstructionists' "confrontation of *ideology* with *textuality*" is also to the point here: "There is no single structure known as 'logocentricity' that we can point to as the secret of ideology" (Eagleton, "Text, Ideology, Realism," 149, 151).

Chapter 3

1. Kenner, *Dublin's Joyce*, 9. Robert Boyle, S.J., analyzes Gallaher's varieties of cliché in " 'A Little Cloud,' " 88.

2. Robert Scholes has enumerated some of the multiple ways in which the story and its characters have counterparts elsewhere in *Dubliners* in " 'Counterparts,' " 93–95.

3. *L'ordre du discours* (Paris: Gallimard, 1971), 12, cited in Terdiman, *Discourse/Counter-Discourse*, 55.

4. "The Possessed," in Sacks, *Man Who Mistook His Wife*, 115–18.

5. Scholes, " 'Counterparts,' " 97.

6. Barthes, *S/Z*, 74.

7. Norris, "Narration under a Blindfold," 207.

8. Ibid., 207.

9. Ibid., 213.

10. West and Hendricks, "Genesis and Significance," 714.

11. Ibid., 713, 714.

12. Heumann, "Writing—and Not Writing," 96.

13. Cited in Bayley, *Romantic Survival*, 13.

14. Yeats, *Memoirs*, 139.

15. Boyle, " 'Two Gallants' and 'Ivy Day in the Committee Room,' " 104–5.

16. Spivak, "Marx after Derrida," 243.

17. Boles, *Interaction Process Analysis*.

18. Bormann, "Fantasy and Rhetorical Vision," 406.

19. See O'Brien, *Dear, Dirty Dublin*, 45–48.

20. Hayman, " 'A Mother,' " 127.

21. Ibid., 128–29.

22. Ibid., 131–32.

23. On the allusive significance of her name, see Power, "Naming of Kathleen Kearney," 532–34.

24. Joyce, *Letters*, 2:124.

25. Cf. Kain, " 'Grace,' " 141.

26. Senn, "Rhetorical Analysis," 121–28.

27. Derrida, *Of Grammatology*, 7–9.

28. Ibid., 11–12.

29. Ong, *Interfaces of the Word*, 22.

30. See, for example, Adams, *Surface and Symbol*, 177–81; Beck, *"Dubliners,"* 289–96.

31. Beck, *"Dubliners,"* 286.

32. Ibid., 279.

33. Herr, *Joyce's Anatomy of Culture*, 236, 39.

34. Ibid., 239–45; cf. Torchiana, *Backgrounds for Joyce's "Dubliners,"* 212–16.

35. Kain, " 'Grace,' " 140.

36. Tindall, *Reader's Guide*, 39.

37. Senn, "Rhetorical Analysis," 122.

38. See 1 Cor. 12:30; see also *New Catholic Encyclopedia*, 6:673, 670.

39. Gerhard Friedrich first pointed out the striking resemblance between this final passage and the opening passage of Bret Harte's *Gabriel Conroy* in "Bret Harte as a Source for James Joyce's 'The Dead.' " It might further be noted that such descriptions of weather and landscape open many of the chapters of Harte's novel, although there is an apparent appropriateness to this in a tale of adventure set in the American West, which is totally lacking in Joyce's urban story. Thus the passages where Joyce's Gabriel imagines the outdoors acquire a suggestive force, a suspicion of the uncanny, which is absent from Harte's novel.

40. Brandabur, *Scrupulous Meanness*, 116–18. Florence L. Walzl in *"Dubliners*: Women in Irish Society,"* 50–51, also notes that "the plot progresses by a series of confrontations Gabriel has with women," but other than remarking that his "enlightenment . . . has come about through a woman," she makes little of the fact. In "What Is a Woman . . . A Symbol of?" Tilly Eggers treats the issue more fully.

41. Torchiana, *Backgrounds for Joyce's "Dubliners,"* 240–41.

42. See *PDP*, 195–96. Gabriel's outburst, "I'm sick of my country, sick of it!" may

well represent his deeper feelings but is unconnected to any set of ideas he is able to articulate; the less clichéd parts of his after-dinner speech are, of course, a reply to Miss Ivors in the form of hidden polemic.

43. Scott, *Joyce and Feminism*, 137.

44. See Booth, "Freedom of Interpretation: Bakhtin and the Challenge of Feminist Criticism," 154.

45. Mary Jacobus, for example, discusses the difficulties of theoreticians who assume that the writing of a woman is different *in se* from that of a man and the "essentialist" position that that assumption implies. She also discusses the suggestive dead end of postmodernist approaches like that of Irigaray, for whom woman is a space beyond the play of linguistic differences. She claims that the only solution to this impasse is to begin from ideology; feminist criticism "ultimately has to invoke as its starting-point this underlying political assumption." See "The Question of Language," 39.

46. See below, chap. 4, "Romantic Image," on the use of tableau in popular romance.

47. Reed in *Victorian Conventions* discusses the Victorian taste for "interpreting existence in emblematic terms," and observes that "whole novels might appear emblematic" (22, 23), although he fails to note the prevalence of the emblematic tableau.

48. Mitchell and Rose, *Jacques Lacan*, 137. The quotation is from Mitchell and Rose's synopsis.

49. Ibid., 140–41, 146–47.

50. See, e.g., Moseley, " 'Two Sights for Ever a Picture,' " 426–33, which rather confusedly invokes the pictures discussed above, the *Divine Comedy*, women in their Neoplatonic role, and Gabriel as Christ. Florence L. Walzl's "Gabriel and Michael: The Conclusion of 'The Dead' " is the classical essay on the subject.

51. "Ici il s'agit des choses qui sont d'autant plus surprenantes à voir surgir, qu'elles surgissent dans une époque dont les coordonnées historiques nous montrent qu'au contraire rien semblait, bien loin de là, y répondre à ce qu'on pourrait appeler une promotion, voire une libération de la femme. . . . Néanmoins ces idéaux, au premier plan desquels est l'idéal de la dame comme telle . . . sont ceux qui se retrouvent dans des époques ultérieures, et jusqu'à la nôtre, voient leur incidences tout à fait concrètes dans l'organisation sentimentale de l'homme contemporain." From the seminar "L'Ethique de la psychanalyse," 10 February 1960, typescript. Translation courtesy of Henry Sullivan and Elly Ragland-Sullivan.

52. Pecora, " 'The Dead' and the Generosity of the Word," 243.

53. Harte, *Gabriel Conroy*, 1:22–23.

54. Ibid., 1:284.

Chapter 4

1. See Terdiman, *Discourse/Counter-Discourse*.

2. Hayman, "*A Portrait of the Artist as a Young Man* and *L'Education sentimentale*"; Lind, "*The Way of All Flesh* and *A Portrait of the Artist as a a Young Man*."

3. Veeder, *Henry James*, 1–9.

4. On chiasmic structure see Kenner, *Ulysses*, 7–8 and passim. See also Gose, "Destruction and Creation."

5. Although the present discussion is restricted to the special case of the dialogiza-

tion of Stephen's own language as embodied in indirect inner monologue, the more "objective" sections of *Portrait* elegantly demonstrate the heteroglossia of Joyce's voice in Bakhtin's character zones, "the field of action of a character's voice, encroaching in one way or another upon the author's voice" (*DI*, 36). This corresponds closely to what Hugh Kenner has analyzed as the "Uncle Charles Principle" in *Joyce's Voices*, 15–38.

6. Emerson, "The Outer Word and Inner Speech," 25.

7. In "Work in Progress," Frank O'Connor first pointed out—rather scornfully—the crucial role of repetition in Joyce's lyrical mode.

8. The perception of consciousness as narrative has recently emerged in circles far removed from Bakhtinian criticism or indeed postmodern criticism in general. For example, the neurologist Oliver Sacks observes in *The Man Who Mistook His Wife for a Hat*, "Each of us *is* a singular narrative, which is constructed, continually, unconsciously, by, through, and in us—through our perceptions, our feelings, our thoughts, our actions; and, not least, our discourse, our spoken narrations" (105). Sacks feels this is clinically manifest in Rorsakov's syndrome.

9. See Kershner, "Time and Language," 604–19.

10. Kenner, *Joyce's Voices*, 68.

11. Frank, "Spatial Form in Modern Literature," *Sewanee Review* 8 (Spring–Autumn 1945), adapted in *Widening Gyre*.

12. Naremore, "Consciousness and Society in *A Portrait of the Artist*," 128–29.

13. Gifford, *Joyce Annotated*, 10. Sidney Feshbach in " 'Writ Our Bit as Intermidgets' " (379), argues that Joyce's early style, like Stephen's, is "based directly on some of the most traditional European conventions."

14. Kristeva, "Word, Dialogue, and Novel," in *Desire in Language*, 64–66. The essay was originally published in 1969. See also André Topia's discussion, "The Matrix and the Echo," which provocatively links intertextuality to the *style indirect libre*.

15. Kristeva, "Word, Dialogue, and Novel," 66.

16. See, for example, Hodgart, *James Joyce: A Student's Guide*, 61.

17. Avery, *Nineteenth Century Children*, 140–41.

18. Charlotte Yonge, *What Books to Lend and What to Give* (1887), quoted in ibid., 138.

19. Meigs, *Critical History*, 192.

20. Avery, *Nineteenth Century Children*, 147.

21. Hughes, *Tom Brown's School-Days*, 59 (1:chap. 3).

22. Ibid., 70 (1:chap. 4).

23. Ibid., 60 (1:chap. 3).

24. Ibid., 324 (2:chap. 7).

25. Ibid., 358 (2:chap. 8).

26. Ibid., 121 (1:chap. 6).

27. Bradley, *Joyce's Schooldays*, 49.

28. Hughes, *Tom Brown's School-Days*, 96–97 (1:chap. 5).

29. Bradley, *Joyce's Schooldays*, 49.

30. Hughes, *Tom Brown's School-Days*, 277 (2:chap. 5).

31. Ibid., 168 (1:chap. 8).

32. Ibid., 70 (1:chap. 4).

33. Ibid., 92 (1:chap. 5).

34. Ibid., 61 (1:chap. 3).

35. Ibid., 313 (2:chap. 6).

36. Ibid., 331 (2:chap. 7).

37. Bradley, *Joyce's Schooldays*, 82.

38. Ibid., 50, 22.

39. David Newsome, *Godliness and Good Learning* (London: John Murray, 1961), quoted in Avery, *Nineteenth Century Children*, 146–47.

40. Farrar, *Eric*, 13.

41. Ibid., 52.

42. Ibid., 100, 101.

43. Lunn, *The Harrovians*, 2.

44. Ibid., 7.

45. Turner, *Boys Will Be Boys*, 79–80, 90.

46. Bradley, *Joyce's Schooldays*, 149, n. 39.

47. Lunn, *The Harrovians*, 14.

48. Ellmann, *James Joyce*, 56; Gifford, *Joyce Annotated*, 164, 166.

49. For example, see *P*, 505. The play has been the basis for at least two recent films.

50. Eugene Sheehy, *May It Please the Court* (Dublin, 1951), 8–10, quoted in Gifford, *Joyce Annotated*, 166.

51. Bloom also played in Anstey's farce while at school (*U*, 438/536) and confesses that his friend Gerald, who impersonated a girl in the play, first gave him a taste for corsets. In *Joyce's Anatomy of Culture*, Herr briefly discusses the play in the context of theatrical cross-dressing (153).

52. Anstey, *Vice-Versa*, 50.

53. Ibid., 64.

54. Ibid., 110–11.

55. Ibid., 88.

56. Ibid., 147.

57. In a note to his edition of *Portrait* (507, n. 77.06), Anderson points out that Heron imitates British schoolboy slang from the play; *Portrait* contains a number of verbal echoes of it.

58. Stephen's emphasis upon the element of futurity closely parallels Bakhtin's observation that consciousness is actually "consciousness of the fact that I, in my most fundamental aspect of myself, still am not. I live in an 'absolute future.'" Cited by Clark and Holquist, *Mikhail Bakhtin*, 72.

59. For a fuller exposition of this idea see Kershner, "Wilde and Joyce on Shakespeare."

60. Cf. Bakhtin, as paraphrased by Clark and Holquist, *Mikhail Bakhtin*, 92: "The author-creator is thus to the text as the self is to consciousness. This means that the author-creator's residual presence in the text is that point, in absentia, from which the structure of all the text's space/time distinctions are calibrated *in praesentia.*"

61. See, for example, Goldberg, *Classical Temper*.

62. It should be noted that although most of his discussions of consciousness stress its constitution by formal languages, Bakhtin allows that consciousness is semiotic in a broader sense: "Consciousness can harbor only in the image, the word, the meaningful gesture, and so forth" (*MPL*, 13).

63. Althusser, "Freud and Lacan," in *Lenin and Philosophy*, 218–19

64. Althusser, *For Marx*, 232–33.

65. Greer, *Modern Daedalus*, xiii, xii.

66. Ibid., 5.

67. Ibid., 16.

68. Ibid., 26.

69. Ibid., 35.

70. Ibid., 37.
71. Ibid., 65.
72. Ibid., 93.
73. Ibid., 104.
74. Ibid., 120.
75. Ibid., 131.
76. Ibid., 259–60.
77. Ibid., 43.
78. Dumas, *Count of Monte Cristo*, 612 (1:chap. 48).
79. Ellmann, *James Joyce*, 75.
80. Ibid., 94.
81. There is a more extensive discussion of the imagery of subhuman and superhuman in *Portrait* in Kershner, "Degeneration."
82. Dumas, *Count of Monte Cristo*, 43 (1:chap. 6).
83. Ibid., 378 (1:chap. 33).
84. Ibid., 329 (1:chap. 30).
85. Ibid., 613 (1:chap. 48).
86. Ibid., 1315, 1314 (2:chap. 113).
87. Ibid., 138 (1:chap. 15).
88. Ibid., 233 (1:chap. 15).
89. Ibid., 234 (1:chap. 15).
90. Ibid., 329 (1:chap. 30).
91. Ibid., 717 (2:chap. 56).
92. Ibid., 613 (1:chap. 47).
93. Ibid., 501 (1:chap. 40).
94. Ibid., 612 (1:chap. 48).
95. Ibid., 520 (1:chap. 41).
96. Ibid., 612 (1:chap. 48).
97. Ibid., 494 (1:chap. 40).
98. Kenner in *Dublin's Joyce*, 158–78, discusses Stephen as an analytical machine like Sherlock Holmes. Much of Kenner's argument equally well establishes a parallel to the Count.
99. Dumas, *Count of Monte Cristo*, 858 (2:chap. 70).
100. On the dandy figure, see Moers, *The Dandy*. See also William Veeder's excellent discussion of the dandy as variant of the Byronic hero, an interpretation which draws upon Camus and Mario Praz, *Henry James*, 132–45.
101. Joyce, "A Portrait of the Artist," 258–59.
102. Ibid., 265.
103. Ibid., 262.
104. Eugene Sheehy, quoted in Scholes and Kain, *Workshop of Daedalus*, 141.
105. Ibid., 152.
106. Colum, *Our Friend James Joyce*, 73.
107. Ibid., 38.
108. Ibid. Jerrold Seigel explores the aesthetic and ideological ramifications of the bohemian image which Joyce and Stephen approximate in *Bohemian Paris*. See especially chaps. 4 and 10.
109. Dumas, *Count of Monte Cristo*, 347 (1:chap. 31).
110. Ibid., 351 (1:chap. 31).
111. Ibid., 247 (1:chap. 24).
112. Ibid., 1315 (2:chap. 113).
113. Thorslev, *Byronic Hero*, 24.

114. Twitchell, *Living Dead*, 108.
115. Quoted in D. Stone, *Romantic Impulse*, 14.
116. Thorslev, 66–70.
117. Ibid., 88.
118. Kroeber, *Romantic Narrative Art*, 112.
119. Bayley, *Romantic Survival*, 15.
120. Schug, *Romantic Genesis*, xiv.

Chapter 5

1. Cited in *P*, 497, n. 43.18.
2. Susan Stewart in *Nonsense: Aspects of Intertextuality in Folklore and Literature* argues that nonsense is perceived and defined strictly contextually.
3. Egoff, *Children's Periodicals*, 6, 13.
4. *Peter Parley's Tales about Ancient and Modern Greece*, 5.
5. Ibid., 9.
6. Ibid., 5.
7. Ibid., 59.
8. Ibid., 199. It seems odd that the Clongowes Jesuits should adopt a textbook containing this assertion. In any case, Parley's statement casts a different light on Stephen's championing Byron, which in *Portrait* is made to appear an act of heroic defiance made without the suggestion or support of any external authority.
9. *Peter Parley's Travels about Ancient Rome with some account of Modern Italy*, 87.
10. *Peter Parley's Tales about Ancient and Modern Greece*, 172.
11. O'Brien, *Dear, Dirty Dublin*, 44–45.
12. Magalaner and Kain, *Joyce: The Man, the Work, the Reputation*, 125–28.
13. Hynes, *Edwardian Turn of Mind*, 157.
14. Brown, *James Joyce and Sexuality*, 29–35, 95, 137.
15. Brome, *Havelock Ellis*, 55.
16. Grosskurth, *Havelock Ellis*, 61.
17. Quoted in ibid., 167.
18. Ellis, *New Spirit*, v.
19. Quoted in Brome, *Havelock Ellis*, 68.
20. Ellis, *New Spirit*, 27–28.
21. Ibid., 148.
22. Ibid.
23. Ibid., 156.
24. Ibid., 157–58.
25. Ibid., 277.
26. Ibid., 279–80.
27. Ibid., 246.
28. For a different perspective, see Bonnie Kime Scott, "Emma Clery in *Stephen Hero*," 57; see also her *Joyce and Feminism* and *James Joyce*.
29. Allen, *Increasing Purpose*, 7–8.
30. Ibid., 66.
31. Ibid., 86.
32. Ibid., 85.
33. Ibid., 87.
34. Ibid., 112.

35. Ibid., 139.
36. Ibid.
37. Ibid., 146.
38. Ibid., 140.
39. Ibid., 141.
40. Ibid., 153.
41. Ibid., 127.
42. Ibid., 155.
43. Ibid., 210.
44. Ibid., 296.
45. Ibid., 297.
46. Allen, *Mettle of the Pasture*, 345.
47. Ibid., 448.
48. Ibid., 343.
49. Ibid., 124–25.
50. See Mercier, "Justice for Edouard Dujardin"; Staley, "James Joyce and One of his Ghosts"; Ellmann, *James Joyce*, 95, 126, 358, 411, 520, 615.
51. Brown, *James Joyce and Sexuality*, 100.
52. McKilligan, *Edouard Dujardin*, 99.
53. Barthes, *S/Z*, 19.
54. Dujardin, *L'Initiation*, 3. The passages quoted read, "le dévouement à quelque rêve de bonté," "l'oeuvre d'égoïsme, noble ou vil . . . qui est le contraire du sacrifice." Translation by the present author.
55. Ibid., 200. "Un jour je me suis demandé . . . si je ne devais pas me faire prêtre."
56. "Sommaire biographique" in Dujardin, *Les Lauriers*, 76.
57. Quoted by Carmen Licari, "Introduction" to Dujardin, *Les Lauriers*, 17. "Il avait gardé un souvenir émerveillé de l'apparition, à Rouen, au moment de sa première communion, de l'archevêque de la ville pour lequel il avait composé et lu le compliment d'acceuil. Il m'avouait qu'il aurait aimé être un prélat qui bénit les fidèles et leur donne son anneau à baiser dans un geste plein de dignité et d'onction; son côté 'cabotin' s'y complaisait."
58. Dujardin, *L'Initiation*, 43–44. "Il me semble que je regrette un coeur où me confier, des bras à qui m'offrir, un esprit qui me prenne, et ne plus être pour moi seul et être ami et dire et entendre des paroles."
59. Ibid., 204–5.
60. Ibid., 206–7. "Leurs lyrismes remplirent le vide de mon coeur et, à l'automne, quand je vins m'établir à Paris, j'avais comme oublié la crise religieuse"; "C'est-à-dire . . . que la religion ne fut plus à tes yeux la forme de l'amour."
61. Ibid., 89. "Marcelin connut . . . l'horreur après le désir satisfait. . . . Il n'avait plus eu dans ses bras que le cadavre de la créature, veuve de toute charme."
62. Ibid., 108–9. "Ils dansait pourtant plus sagement. Ils parlaient de choses et d'autres. Il invita quelques autres jeunes filles; une fois il aperçut Amélie qui dansait avec Paul. Il était donc revenu? Amélie était rouge. Que lui disait-il? Marcelin se sentit furieux."
63. Ibid., 132. "Vous m'avez joué, très ordinairement. Vous n'avez pas entrevu la vie qui vous était offert. . . . Mon âme, toute de tendresse, mon âme de printemps et aux neuves sèves, si vous l'aviez eue, cette âme que nulle femme n'eut encore et qui vous était promise, ô folle compagne d'un soir!"
64. Ibid., 161. "Uniquement occupés de leur vice, aveugles et sourds à quoi que ce fût hormis la chair."
65. Ibid., 194–95. "Hais, sache haïr fortement le christianisme conciliateur qui

s'habille à la moderne et s'embarque sur le dernier bateau des philosophes à la mode."

66. Quoted by Licari in Dujardin, *Les Lauriers*, 23. "Le christianisme, pour moi, c'est une révolution, une très importante révolution—comme, de nos jours, et *mutatis mutandis*, l'avènement du léninisme."

67. McKilligan, *Edouard Dujardin*, 12.

68. Dujardin, *L'Initiation*, 225. "Ô joie d'entrer dans la vie! joie, ô joie de vivre!"

69. Ibid., 241. "Puis, peu à peu, les termes de la question s'ennuageaient; il se répétait des mots dont le sens de plus en plus s'enveloppait dans un brouillard; et, maintenant, il allait, presque sans pensée, dans un grouillement d'idées confuses."

70. Ibid., 244. "Que veux-tu? . . . Pas la taille d'un ascète, encore que bien dégoûté d'être un jouisseur. . . . Comme les autres, tout simplement, un pauvre bougre qui vit la vie."

71. Olivier de Magny suggested that it is useful to view Daniel Prince as a symbolist aesthete (quoted by Licari in Dujardin, *Les Lauriers*, 54); Desruyssarts is a far more likely candidate.

72. Cited by McKilligan, *Edouard Dujardin*, 4.

73. Ibid., 43. "Ô visions des temps, choses qui furent en les siècles de mes années, joies enfantines très suaves, fausses amours, pleurs des rêves, cris des aspirations, pitiés vers Dieu, ô piétés très profondes et anciennes, vie passée, ô ce qui fut mes jours, rochers nus et frémissements des vents obscurs. . . ."

74. Cf. Curran, [From "Memoirs of University College, Dublin"], 147; Magalaner and Kain, *Joyce: The Man, the Work, the Reputation*, 43, 79–80.

75. Dujardin, *Les Lauriers*, 225–28.

76. Ibid., 257.

77. Hayman, "*A Portrait of the Artist as a Young Man* and *L'Education sentimentale*," 161–62.

78. Ellmann, *Consciousness of Joyce. Mercure de France* published the novel's original edition in 1898; it was reprinted by Albert Messein in 1920 and again, with a new introduction by Dujardin, in 1925. I have been unable to locate any other reference to a 1912 edition.

79. Gabler, "The Seven Lost Years of *A Portrait of the Artist as a Young Man*," 53.

Chapter 6

1. Foucault, *History of Sexuality*, 12.

2. Ibid., 106, 127–28.

3. Tanner, *Adultery in the Novel*, 13.

4. Ibid., 14.

5. Quoted in Hynes, *Edwardian Turn of Mind*, 160.

6. Joyce was aware, at least indirectly, of Carpenter's work. In an edition of Tolstoy's *Essays and Letters* that Joyce owned, several quotations from and references to Carpenter's attacks on the materialism of modern science are set off with Joyce's pencil markings in the margin. From the passages marked it would appear that Joyce was sympathetic to Tolstoy's and Carpenter's attempt to reinterpret science from a more spiritual perspective. See Connolly, *Personal Library of James Joyce*, 38. Richard Brown in *James Joyce and Sexuality*, 106–7, has suggested that Joyce was probably aware of Carpenter's work.

7. O'Brien, *Dear, Dirty Dublin*, 191–92.

8. Several critics have stressed his extreme disorientation in sections of *Portrait*;

see, for example, McKnight, "Unlocking the Word-Hoard." It should also be noted that in the late nineteenth century some physicians postulated a hereditary disposition to syphilis occurring in "degenerate" families.

9. Garvin, *Joyce's Disunited Kingdom*, 42–46; cf. Waisbren and Walzl, "Paresis and the Priest."

10. Money, *Destroying Angel*, passim.

11. See Trilling, *Sincerity and Authenticity*.

12. Brown observes that the preface to this play discusses the contemporary debate on marriage; *James Joyce and Sexuality*, 28.

13. Joyce's edition of the first was dated 1906; Brown briefly discusses *La Porta chiusa* in *James Joyce and Sexuality*, 24.

14. Hynes, *Edwardian Turn of Mind*, 174–85.

15. Although Ellmann, *Consciousness of Joyce*, lists the date of publication of this book as 1908, it was originally published in 1905; the *British Library Catalogue* lists only one later edition, in 1919.

16. Brown discusses Albert from a somewhat different perspective; *James Joyce and Sexuality*, 28–35.

17. Albert, *L'Amour libre*, 36. "Nous retrouvons dans les limites de l'espèce humaine cette évolution des relations sexuelles vers l'amour que nous avons vu se dessiner à travers la série entière des êtres vivants." Translation by the present author.

18. Ibid., 86.

19. Ibid., 108. "Nous pouvons dire qu'il y a, dans la société bourgeoise, comme une force tendant à maintenir l'instinct sexuel au niveau du simple accouplement brutal et l'arrêtant dans son évolution naturelle vers sa forme supérieure."

20. Ibid., 118. "Les prostituées sont les amoureuses types du régime capitaliste," 118. The analogy between prostitution and bourgeois capitalism has by no means been abandoned by contemporary Marxists: cf. Jean-François Lyotard, *Economie libidinale* (Paris: Minuit, 1974), 169.

21. Albert, *L'Amour libre*, 182. "Vous honissez de pauvres créatures qui se vendent pour quelques écus à un homme qui passe,—la faim et le besoin absolvent les unions éphemères; tandis que la société tolère, encourage l'union immédiate bien autrement terrible d'une jeune fille candide et un homme qu'elle n'a pas vu trois mois durant; elle est vendue pour toute sa vie. Il est vrai que le prix est élevé!"

22. Ibid., 200. "Nombre de couples, en effet, ont opéré déjà la réforme urgente. Ils vivent en union libre en dehors et au-dessus de la loi méprisable. Et cette rébellion n'est pas inutile, certes! au progrès de notre idéal. Elle est un acte de bonne volonté et un acte de révolte grandement profitable à la cause de l'amour libre. Mais elle ne suffit pas."

23. Ibid., 205.

24. Ellmann, *Consciousness of Joyce*, chap. 3; Manganiello, *Joyce's Politics*, chap. 3.

25. Brown, *James Joyce and Sexuality*, 35.

26. Joyce, *Letters*, 2:89, 99.

27. From Joyce, "A Portrait of the Artist," in *P*, 265–66.

28. Kenner, "Rhetoric of Silence," and Wellington's note, "A Missing Conversation," in the same issue; see also Kenner, "Molly's Masterstroke."

29. For representative discussions of the play as failure, see Gorman, *James Joyce*, 226; Farrell, "*Exiles* and Ibsen," 122; or Levin, *James Joyce*, 38.

30. Simon, "James Joyce's *Exiles*," 22–23.

31. Williams, "*Exiles*," 108.

32. It should be noted that a response to Allen's book, *The Woman Who Did Not*

by "Victoria Crosse," was published by John Lane in 1895. This extended short story is narrated by a man returning from Indian service who encounters a mysterious, beautiful woman named Eurydice aboard ship. He falls in love with her, as she does with him, but she tells him she is married; although her husband is unfaithful and does not love her, she regards marriage as inviolate. "As a sacrament, married life is holy; as a theory it is perfect. In practice, perhaps, it is not always either, for humanity is neither holy nor perfect, but blame Humanity for that, not Marriage" (77–78). Despite a good deal of sighing, "pallid, suffering" faces, and stolen kisses, the book fails to develop any tension or any real interest; virtue, after all, is especially boring in a romance.

33. Allen, *Woman Who Did*, 9–10.
34. Ibid., 13.
35. Ibid., 43.
36. Ibid., 29.
37. Ibid., 37.
38. Ibid., 39.
39. Ibid., 88.
40. Ibid., 101.
41. Ibid., 97.
42. Ibid., 144.
43. Ibid., 180. See Kershner, "Degeneration," 416–48.
44. Joyce, *Letters*, 2:177.
45. Young, *Sands of Pleasure*, xiii.
46. Ibid., 124.
47. Ibid., 124–25.
48. Jameson, *Political Unconscious*, 56.
49. De Rougemont, *Love in the Western World*, 275.
50. Young, *Sands of Pleasure*, 398.
51. Barthes, *Mythologies*, 103–5.
52. Michaëlis, *Dangerous Age*, 8.
53. Ibid., 19, 20.
54. Ibid., 28.
55. Ibid., 61.
56. Ibid., 49.
57. Ibid., 56.
58. Ibid., 60.
59. Ibid., 93–94.
60. Ibid., 129–30.
61. Ibid., 84.
62. Ibid., 102.
63. Ibid., 147.
64. Ibid., 79.
65. Ibid., 214.
66. Ibid., 123–24.
67. Tinayre, *Maison du péché*, 318. Translations by the present author. Because Joyce read the book in translation, the original French passages have been omitted from these notes.
68. Ibid., 339.
69. Lasch, *Haven in a Heartless World*, 8.
70. See Gillis, *For Better, For Worse*, chap. 8, "Better a Bad Husband Than No Husband at All: The Compulsion to Marry, 1850–1914."

71. Barthes, *Roland Barthes*, 121.

72. Possibly Joyce means to imply something along the lines of Lasch's observation that the "emergence of the nuclear family as the principal form of family life reflected the high value modern society attached to privacy, and the glorification of privacy in turn reflected the devaluation of work"; Lasch, *Haven in a Heartless World*, 7.

73. Rose, *Parallel Lives*, 266.

74. Marcus, *The Other Victorians*, 132–33.

75. See Freud's "On the Universal Tendency to Debasement in the Sphere of Love," 173–86.

76. Rose, *Parallel Lives*, 8.

77. Lawrence, *Women in Love*, 144.

Chapter 7

1. Barthes, "Style and Its Image," 99.

2. It should be noted that, as Jerome J. McGann observes, the ideology of romanticism itself is characteristically packed with contradictions; see *Romantic Ideology*, 2.

3. Lee, *Modernisation of Irish Society*, 13.

BIBLIOGRAPHY

Adams, Robert M. *Surface and Symbol: The Consistency of James Joyce's "Ulysses."* New York: Oxford University Press, 1967.

Albert, Charles. *L'Amour libre.* Paris: P.-V. Stock, 1899.

Allen, Grant. *The Woman Who Did.* London: John Lane, 1895.

Allen, James Lane. *The Increasing Purpose.* London: Macmillan and Co, 1900.

———. *The Mettle of the Pasture.* London: Macmillan and Co., 1903.

Althusser, Louis. *For Marx.* Trans. Ben Brewster. London: New Left Books, 1979.

———. *Lenin and Philosophy and Other Essays.* Trans. Ben Brewster. New York: Monthly Review Press, 1971.

Anstey, F. [Thomas Anstey Guthrie]. *Vice-Versa: A Farcical Fantastic Play.* London: Smith, Elder and Co., 1910.

Attridge, Derek, and Daniel Ferrer, eds. *Post-structuralist Joyce: Essays from the French.* Cambridge: Cambridge University Press, 1984.

Avery, Gillian. *Nineteenth Century Children: Heroes and Heroines in English Children's Stories, 1780–1900.* London: Hodder and Stoughton, 1965.

Bakhtin, M. M. *The Dialogic Imagination: Four Essays.* Ed. Michael Holquist, trans. Caryl Emerson and Michael Holquist. Austin: University of Texas Press, 1981.

———. *The Formal Method in Literary Scholarship.* [As by Bakhtin/P. N. Medvedev.] Trans. Albert J. Werle. Baltimore, Md.: Johns Hopkins University Press, 1978. Reprint. [With new introduction by Wlad Godzich.] Cambridge: Harvard University Press, 1985.

———. *Freudianism: A Marxist Critique.* [As by V. N. Volosinov]. Trans. I. R. Titunik. New York: Academic Press, 1973.

———. *Marxism and the Philosophy of Language.* [As by V. N. Volosinov.] Trans. Ladislav Matejka and I. R. Titunik. New York: Seminar Press, 1973. Reprint. Cambridge: Harvard University Press, 1986.

———. *Problems of Dostoevsky's Poetics.* Trans. Caryl Emerson. Minneapolis: University of Minnesota Press, 1984.

———. *Rabelais and His World.* Trans. Helene Iswolsky. Cambridge: MIT Press, 1968. Reprint. Bloomington: Indiana University Press, 1984.

———. *Speech Genres and Other Late Essays.* Ed. Michael Holquist, trans. Vern McGee. Austin: University of Texas Press, 1986.

Balfe, M. W. *The Bohemian Girl: Grand Opera in Three Acts*. New York: Charles E. Burden, n.d.

Barthes, Roland. *Image/Music/Text*. Trans. Stephen Heath. New York: Hill and Wang, 1977.

———. *Mythologies*. Trans. Annette Lavers. New York: Hill and Wang, 1979.

———. *Roland Barthes*. Trans. Richard Howard. New York: Hill and Wang, 1977.

———. "Style and Its Image." In Barthes, *The Rustle of Language*, 90–99. Trans. Richard Howard. New York: Hill and Wang, 1986.

———. *S/Z*. Trans. Richard Miller. New York: Hill and Wang, 1974.

Bayley, John. *The Romantic Survival: A Study in Poetic Evolution*. London: Constable, 1957.

Beck, Warren. *"Dubliners": Substance, Vision, and Art*. Durham, N.C.: Duke University Press, 1969.

Benstock, Bernard, ed. *The Seventh of Joyce*. Bloomington: Indiana University Press, 1982.

Berger, Peter L., and Thomas Luckmann. *The Social Construction of Reality: A Treatise in Sociology of Knowledge*. New York: Doubleday and Co., 1966.

Boles, Robert F. *Interaction Process Analysis: A Method for the Study of Small Groups*. Cambridge, Mass.: Addison-Wesley, 1950.

Booth, Wayne. "Freedom of Interpretation: Bakhtin and the Challenge of Feminist Criticism." In Gary Saul Morson, ed., *Bakhtin: Essays and Dialogues on His Work*, 145–76. Chicago: University of Chicago Press, 1986.

Bormann, Ernest G. "Fantasy and Rhetorical Vision: The Rhetorical Criticism of Social Reality." *Quarterly Journal of Speech* 58 (December 1972): 396–407.

Bowen, Zack. " 'After the Race.' " In Clive Hart, ed., *James Joyce's "Dubliners": Critical Essays*, 53-61. New York: Viking, 1969.

Boyle, Robert, S.J. " 'A Little Cloud.' " In Clive Hart, ed., *James Joyce's "Dubliners": Critical Essays*, 84-92. New York: Viking, 1969.

———. " 'Two Gallants' and 'Ivy Day in the Committee Room.' " In Peter K. Garrett, ed., *Twentieth-Century Interpretations of "Dubliners,"* 100–106. Englewood Cliffs, N.J.: Prentice-Hall, 1968.

Bradbury, Malcolm. *The Social Context of Modern English Literature*. New York: Schocken Books, 1971.

Bradley, Bruce, S.J. *James Joyce's Schooldays*. New York: St. Martin's Press, 1982.

Brandabur, Edward. *A Scrupulous Meanness: A Study of Joyce's Early Work*. Urbana: University of Illinois Press, 1971.

Brantlinger, Patrick. *Bread and Circuses: Theories of Mass Culture as Social Decay*. Ithaca, N.Y.: Cornell University Press, 1983.

Bremen, Brian A. " 'He Was Too Scrupulous Always': A Re-examination of Joyce's 'The Sisters.' " *James Joyce Quarterly* 22 (Fall 1984): 55–66.

British Library General Catalogue of Printed Books to 1975. 360 vols. London:

Clive Bingley and K. G. Saur, 1979.

Brome, Vincent. *Havelock Ellis, Philosopher of Sex: A Biography.* London: Routledge and Kegan Paul, 1979.

Brown, Richard. *James Joyce and Sexuality.* Cambridge: Cambridge University Press, 1985.

Bulwer-Lytton, Edward. *The Last Days of Pompeii.* New York: Charles Scribner's Sons, 1903.

Cawelti, John. *Adventure, Mystery, and Romance: Formula Stories as Art and Popular Culture.* Chicago: University of Chicago Press, 1976.

Cixous, Hélène. *The Exile of James Joyce.* Trans. Sally A. J. Purcell. New York: David Lewis, 1972.

Clark, Katerina, and Michael Holquist. *Mikhail Bakhtin.* Cambridge: Harvard University Press, 1984.

Cleland, John. *Fanny Hill: Memoirs of a Woman of Pleasure.* New York: Dell/Putnam, 1982.

Colum, Mary and Padraic. *Our Friend James Joyce.* New York: Doubleday and Co., 1958.

Connolly, Thomas E. *The Personal Library of James Joyce: A Descriptive Bibliography.* University of Buffalo Monographs in English, no. 6. Buffalo, N.Y., 1955.

Curran, Constantine P. [From "Memoirs of University College, Dublin—The Jesuit Tenure, 1883–1908."] In Robert Scholes and Richard M. Kain, eds., *The Workshop of Daedalus: James Joyce and the Raw Materials for "A Portrait of the Artist as a Young Man,"* 146–48. Evanston, Ill.: Northwestern University Press, 1965.

Davenson, Henri. *Livre de Chanson: Introduction à la chanson française.* Rev. ed. Paris: Cahiers du Rhône, 1955.

Davison, Peter; Rolf Meyersohn; and Edward Shils, eds. *Culture and Mass Culture.* 9 vols. Teaneck, N.J.: Somerset House; Cambridge: Chadwyck-Healey, 1978.

De Man, Paul. *The Resistance to Theory.* Minneapolis: University of Minnesota Press, 1986.

De Rougemont, Denis. *Love in the Western World.* Rev. ed. New York: Harper and Row, 1974.

Derrida, Jacques. *Of Grammatology.* Trans. Gayatri Chakravorty Spivak. Baltimore, Md.: Johns Hopkins University Press, 1976.

Dujardin, Edouard. *L'Initiation au péché et à l'amour.* Paris: Albert Messein, 1925.

_____. *Les Lauriers sont coupés suivi de Le Monologue intérieur.* Rome: Bulzoni Editore, 1977.

Dumas, Alexandre. *The Count of Monte Cristo.* [Trans. anon.] New York: McGraw-Hill, 1946.

_____. *The Three Musketeers.* Trans. William Robson. New York: Heritage Press, 1950.

Eagleton, Terry. *Criticism and Ideology*. London: Verso, 1978.
_____. "Text, Ideology, Realism." In Edward Said, ed., *Literature and Society*, 149–73. Baltimore, Md.: Johns Hopkins University Press, 1980.
Edwards, Samuel. *The Vidocq Dossier*. Boston: Houghton Mifflin, 1977.
Eggers, Tilly. "What Is a Woman . . . A Symbol of?" *James Joyce Quarterly* 18 (Summer 1981): 377-95.
Egoff, Sheila A. *Children's Periodicals of the Nineteenth Century*. London: The Library Association, 1951.
Ellis, Havelock. *The New Spirit*. 3d ed. New York: Boni and Liveright, 1920.
Ellmann, Richard. *The Consciousness of Joyce*. New York: Oxford University Press, 1977.
_____. *James Joyce*. Rev. ed. New York: Oxford University Press, 1982.
Emerson, Caryl. "The Outer Word and Inner Speech: Bakhtin, Vygotsky, and the Internalization of Language." In Gary Saul Morson, ed., *Bakhtin: Essays and Dialogues on His Work*, 21–40. Chicago: University of Chicago Press, 1986.
Eveline: The Amorous Adventures of a Victorian Lady. Paris, 1904. Reprint. New York: Grove Press, 1970.
Farrar, Frederic W., D.D. *Eric, or Little by Little: A Tale of Roslyn School*. New York: Dutton, 1887.
Farrell, James T. "*Exiles* and Ibsen." In Seon Givens, ed., *James Joyce: Two Decades of Criticism*, 95–131. New York: Vanguard Press, 1948.
Ferrero, Guglielmo. *Militarism*. London, 1902. Reprint. New York: Benjamin Blom, 1971.
Feshbach, Sidney. "Death in 'An Encounter.' " *James Joyce Quarterly* 2 (Winter 1965): 82–89.
_____. " 'Writ Our Bit as Intermidgets': Classical Rhetoric in the Early Writings of James Joyce." *James Joyce Quarterly* 17 (Summer 1980): 379–87.
Foucault, Michel. *The History of Sexuality*. Trans. Robert Hurley. Vol. 1. New York: Random House, 1980.
Frank, Joseph. *The Widening Gyre: Crisis and Mastery in Modern Literature*. New Brunswick, N.J.: Rutgers University Press, 1963.
Freud, Sigmund. "On the Universal Tendency to Debasement in the Sphere of Love." In James Strachey and Anna Freud, eds., *The Standard Edition of the Complete Psychological Works of Sigmund Freud*, vol. 11, 179–90. London: Hogarth Press, 1966.
Friedrich, Gerhard. "Bret Harte as a Source for James Joyce's 'The Dead.' " *Philological Quarterly* 33 (October 1954): 442–44.
Gabler, Hans Walter. "The Seven Lost Years of *A Portrait of the Artist as a Young Man*." In Thomas F. Staley and Bernard Benstock, eds., *Approaches to Joyce's "Portrait": Ten Essays*, 25–60. Pittsburgh, Pa.: University of Pittsburgh Press, 1976.
Garrett, Peter K., ed. *Twentieth-Century Interpretations of "Dubliners."* Englewood Cliffs, N.J.: Prentice-Hall, 1968.

Garvin, John. *James Joyce's Disunited Kingdom and the Irish Dimension.* Dublin: Gill and Macmillan, 1976.

Gay, Peter. *The Bourgeois Experience: Victoria to Freud.* Vol. 1. New York: Oxford University Press, 1984.

Geuss, Raymond. *The Idea of a Critical Theory: Habermas and the Frankfurt School.* Cambridge: Cambridge University Press, 1981.

Gifford, Don. *Joyce Annotated: Notes for "Dubliners" and "A Portrait of the Artist as a Young Man."* Rev. ed. Berkeley and Los Angeles: University of California Press, 1982.

Gillis, John R. *For Better, For Worse: British Marriages, 1600 to the Present.* New York: Oxford University Press, 1985.

Givens, Seon, ed. *James Joyce: Two Decades of Criticism.* New York: Vanguard Press, 1948.

Goldberg, S. L. *The Classical Temper: A Study of Joyce's "Ulysses."* London: Chatto and Windus, 1961.

Goldman, Arnold. *The Joyce Paradox: Form and Freedom in His Fiction.* Evanston, Ill.: Northwestern University Press, 1966.

Gorman, Herbert. *James Joyce.* New York: Rinehart, 1940.

Gose, Elliott B., Jr. "Destruction and Creation in *A Portrait of the Artist as a Young Man.*" *James Joyce Quarterly* 22 (Spring 1985): 259–70.

Greer, Tom. *A Modern Daedalus.* London: Griffith, Farron, Okeden and Walsh, 1885.

Grosskurth, Phyllis. *Havelock Ellis: A Biography.* New York: Knopf, 1980.

Halper, Nathan. " 'The Boarding House.' " In Clive Hart, ed., *James Joyce's "Dubliners": Critical Essays,* 72–83. New York: Viking, 1969.

Hart, Clive, ed. *James Joyce's "Dubliners": Critical Essays.* New York: Viking, 1969.

Harte, Bret. *Gabriel Conroy, Bohemian Papers, Stories of and for the Young.* 2 vols. Boston and New York: Houghton Mifflin, 1903.

Hayman, David. " 'A Mother.' " In Clive Hart, ed., *James Joyce's "Dubliners": Critical Essays,* 122–33. New York: Viking, 1969.

––––––. "*A Portrait of the Artist as a Young Man* and *L'Education sentimentale*: The Structural Affinities." *Orbis Litterarum* 19 (1964): 161–75.

Henke, Suzette, and Elaine Unkeless, eds. *Women in Joyce.* Urbana: University of Illinois Press, 1982.

Herr, Cheryl. *Joyce's Anatomy of Culture.* Urbana: University of Illinois Press, 1986.

Herring, Phillip. "Structure and Meaning in Joyce's 'The Sisters.' " In Bernard Benstock, ed., *The Seventh of Joyce,* 131–44. Bloomington: Indiana University Press, 1982.

Heumann, J. Mark. "Writing—and Not Writing—in Joyce's 'A Painful Case.' " *Eire-Ireland* 16 (Fall 1981): 81–97.

Hodgart, Matthew. *James Joyce: A Student's Guide.* London: John Lane-Bodley Head, 1978.

Horkheimer, Max, and Theodor W. Adorno. *The Dialectic of Enlightenment.*
    New York: Continuum, 1985.
Hughes, Thomas. *Tom Brown's School-Days: By an Old Boy.* New York: Harp-
    er and Bros., 1911.
Humphries, Susan L. "Ferrero Etc.: James Joyce's Debt to Guglielmo Ferrero."
    James Joyce Quarterly 16 (Spring 1979): 239–51.
Hynes, Samuel. *The Edwardian Turn of Mind.* Princeton, N.J.: Princeton Uni-
    versity Press, 1968.
Jacobus, Mary. "The Question of Language." In Elizabeth Abel, ed., *Writing
    and Sexual Difference*, 37–52. Chicago: University of Chicago Press, 1982.
Jameson, Fredric. *The Political Unconscious: Narrative as a Socially Symbolic
    Act.* Ithaca, N.Y.: Cornell University Press, 1981.
Joyce, James. *The Critical Writings of James Joyce.* Ed. Ellsworth Mason and
    Richard Ellmann. New York: Viking Press, 1959.
———. *"Dubliners": Text, Criticism, and Notes.* Ed. Robert Scholes and A.
    Walton Litz. New York: Viking Press, 1969.
———. *"Exiles": A Play in Three Acts, Including Hitherto Unpublished Notes
    by the Author, Discovered after his Death, and an Introduction by Padraic
    Colum.* New York: Viking Press, 1951.
———. *Letters.* Vol. 1. Ed. Stuart Gilbert. New York: Viking Press, 1957. Vols.
    2 and 3. Ed. Richard Ellmann. New York: Viking Press, 1966.
———. *"A Portrait of the Artist as a Young Man": Text, Criticism, and Notes.*
    Ed. Chester G. Anderson. New York: Viking Press, 1968.
———. "A Portrait of the Artist." In James Joyce, *"A Portrait of the Artist as a
    Young Man": Text, Criticism, and Notes*, ed. Chester G. Anderson, 257–
    66. New York: Viking Press, 1968.
———. *Stephen Hero.* Ed. John J. Slocum and Herbert Cahoon. New York:
    New Directions, 1963.
———. *"Ulysses": The Corrected Text.* Ed. Hans Walter Gabler with Wolfhard
    Steppe and Claus Melchior. New York: Random House, 1986. Second page
    citations are to the 1961 Random House edition.
Joyce, Stanislaus. "The Background to *Dubliners*." *The Listener* 51 (25 March
    1954): 526–27.
Kain, Richard M. " 'Grace.' " In Clive Hart, ed., *James Joyce's "Dubliners":
    Critical Essays*, 134–52. New York: Viking, 1969.
Kaye, Julian. "The Wings of Dedalus: Two Stories in Dubliners." *Modern Fic-
    tion Studies* 4 (Spring 1958): 31–41.
Kenner, Hugh. *Dublin's Joyce.* Bloomington: Indiana University Press, 1956.
    Reprint. Boston: Beacon Press, 1962.
———. *Joyce's Voices.* Berkeley and Los Angeles: University of California Press,
    1978.
———. "Molly's Masterstroke." *James Joyce Quarterly* 10 (Fall 1972): 19–28.
———. "The Rhetoric of Silence." *James Joyce Quarterly* 14 (Summer 1977):
    382–94.

_____. *Ulysses*. London: George Allen and Unwin, 1980.

Kershner, R. B., Jr. "Degeneration: The Explanatory Nightmare." *Georgia Review* 40 (Summer 1986): 416–44.

_____. "Joyce and Stephen Phillips' *Ulysses*." *James Joyce Quarterly* 13 (Winter 1976): 194–201.

_____. "Time and Language in Joyce's *Portrait*." *ELH* 43 (1976): 604–19.

_____. "Wilde and Joyce on Shakespeare." *Texas Studies in Language and Literature* 20 (Summer 1978): 216–29.

Kristeva, Julia. *Desire in Language: A Semiotic Approach to Literature and Art*. Trans. Thomas Gora, Alice Jardine, and Leon D. Roudiez. New York: Columbia University Press, 1980.

Kroeber, Karl. *Romantic Narrative Art*. Madison: University of Wisconsin Press, 1960.

Lacan, Jacques. "L'Ethique de la psychanalyse." Seminar at L'Hôpital Ste.-Anne, Paris, 10 February 1960. Typescript.

LaCapra, Dominic. *Rethinking Intellectual History: Texts Contexts Language*. Ithaca, N.Y.: Cornell University Press, 1983.

Lasch, Christopher. *Haven in a Heartless World: The Family Besieged*. New York: Basic Books, 1977.

Lawrence, D. H. *Women in Love*. New York: Viking, 1976.

Lee, Joseph. *The Modernisation of Irish Society, 1848–1918*. Dublin: Gill and Macmillan, 1973.

Leslie, Shane. *The End of a Chapter*. New York: Charles Scribner's Sons, 1917.

Levin, Harry. *James Joyce*. New York: New Directions, 1941.

Lind, Ilse Dusoir. "*The Way of All Flesh* and *A Portrait of the Artist as a a Young Man*: A Comparison." *Victorian Newsletter* 9 (Spring 1956): 7–10.

Lunn, Arnold. *The Harrovians*. London: Methuen, 1913.

MacCabe, Colin, ed. *James Joyce: New Perspectives*. Bloomington: Indiana University Press, 1982.

McGann, Jerome J. *The Romantic Ideology: A Critical Investigation*. Chicago: University of Chicago Press, 1983.

McKilligan, Kathleen. *Edouard Dujardin: "Les Lauriers sont coupés" and the Interior Monologue*. Leeds: University of Hull Publications, 1977.

McKnight, Jeanne. "Unlocking the Word-Hoard: Madness, Identity and Creativity in James Joyce." *James Joyce Quarterly* 14 (Summer 1977): 420–35.

Magalaner, Marvin. *Time of Apprenticeship: The Fiction of Young James Joyce*. London: Abelard-Schuman, 1959.

Magalaner, Marvin, and Richard M. Kain. *Joyce: The Man, the Work, the Reputation*. New York: New York University Press, 1956. Reprint. New York: Collier Books, 1962.

Manganiello, Dominic. *Joyce's Politics*. London: Routledge and Kegan Paul, 1980.

Marcus, Steven. *The Other Victorians: A Study of Sexuality and Pornography in Mid-Nineteenth-Century England*. New York: Basic Books, 1974.

Mason, A. E. W. *The Courtship of Morrice Buckler: A Romance*. London: Grayson and Grayson, 1900.

Meigs, Cornelia, ed. *A Critical History of Children's Literature: A Survey of Children's Books in English from the Earliest Times to the Present*. New York: Macmillan, 1953.

Mercier, Vivian. "Justice for Edouard Dujardin." *James Joyce Quarterly* 4 (Spring 1967): 209–13.

Michaëlis, Karin. *The Dangerous Age: Letters and Fragments from a Woman's Diary*. [Trans. anon.] London: John Lane, 1912.

Miles, Henry. *Forbidden Fruit: A Study of the Incest Theme in Erotic Literature*. London: Luxor Press, n.d.

Miller, J. Hillis. *Fiction and Repetition: Seven English Novels*. Cambridge: Harvard University Press, 1982.

Mitchell, Juliet, and Jacqueline Rose, eds. *Jacques Lacan, Feminine Sexuality*. New York: Pantheon, 1986.

Moers, Ellen. *The Dandy, Brummell to Beerbohm*. New York: Viking Press, 1960.

Money, John. *The Destroying Angel*. Buffalo, N.Y.: Prometheus Books, 1985.

Morson, Gary Saul, ed. *Bakhtin: Essays and Dialogues on His Work*. Chicago: University of Chicago Press, 1986.

Moseley, Virginia. " 'Two Sights for Ever a Picture' in Joyce's 'The Dead.' " *College English* 26 (March 1965): 426–33.

Naremore, James. "Consciousness and Society in *A Portrait of the Artist*." In Thomas F. Staley and Bernard Benstock, eds., *Approaches to Joyce's "Portrait": Ten Essays*, 113–34. Pittsburgh: University of Pittsburgh Press, 1976.

Neuburg, Victor. *Popular Literature: A History and Guide*. London: Woburn Press, 1977.

Norris, Margot. "Narration under a Blindfold: Reading Joyce's 'Clay.' " *PMLA* 102 (March 1987): 206–15.

O'Brien, Joseph V. *Dear, Dirty Dublin: A City in Distress, 1899–1916*. Berkeley and Los Angeles: University of California Press, 1982.

O'Connor, Frank. "Work in Progress." In James Joyce, *"A Portrait of the Artist as a Young Man": Text, Criticism, and Notes*, ed. Chester G. Anderson, 371–77. New York: Viking Press, 1968.

Ong, Walter J., S.J. *Interfaces of the Word*. Ithaca, N.Y.: Cornell University Press, 1977.

Orr, Leonard. "Dialogism and Heteroglossia: A Bakhtinian Approach to Joyce's *Portrait*." Paper presented at the conference "Joyce in Milwaukee," Marquette University/University of Wisconsin–Milwaukee, 11–16 June 1987.

Orwell, George. *The Collected Essays, Journalism and Letters of George Orwell*. Ed. Sonia Orwell and Ian Angus. 4 vols. New York: Harcourt, Brace, and World, 1968.

Pecora, Vincent P. " 'The Dead' and the Generosity of the Word." *PMLA* 101 (March 1986): 233–45.

Peter Parley's Tales about Ancient and Modern Greece. Philadelphia: Thomas, Cowperthwait and Co., 1839.

Peter Parley's Travels about Ancient Rome with some account of Modern Italy. Philadelphia: Desilver, Thomas and Co., 1836.

Power, Mary. "The Naming of Kathleen Kearney." *Journal of Modern Literature* 5 (September 1976): 532–34.

Rabaté, Jean-Michel. "Silence in *Dubliners*." In Colin MacCabe, ed., *James Joyce: New Perspectives*, 45–72. Bloomington: Indiana University Press, 1982.

Reed, John R. *Victorian Conventions*. Athens: Ohio University Press, 1975.

Rose, Phyllis. *Parallel Lives: Five Victorian Marriages*. New York: Knopf, 1984.

Sacks, Oliver. *The Man Who Mistook His Wife for a Hat*. New York: Simon and Schuster, 1985.

Said, Edward, ed. *Literature and Society*. Baltimore, Md.: Johns Hopkins University Press, 1980.

Scholes, Robert. " 'Counterparts.' " In Clive Hart, ed., *James Joyce's "Dubliners": Critical Essays*, 93-99. New York: Viking, 1969.

Scholes, Robert, and Richard M. Kain, eds. *The Workshop of Daedalus: James Joyce and the Raw Materials for "A Portrait of the Artist as a Young Man."* Evanston, Ill.: Northwestern University Press, 1965.

Schug, Charles. *The Romantic Genesis of the Modern Novel*. Pittsburgh: University of Pittsburgh Press, 1978.

Scott, Bonnie Kime. "Emma Clery in *Stephen Hero*: A Young Woman Walking Proudly through the Decayed City." In Suzette Henke and Elaine Unkeless, eds., *Women in Joyce*, 57–81. Urbana: University of Illinois Press, 1982.

_____. *James Joyce*. Feminist Perspectives series. Atlantic Highlands, N.J.: Humanities Press International, 1987.

_____. *Joyce and Feminism*. Bloomington: Indiana University Press, 1984.

Scott, Walter. *The Abbott*. London: Adam and Charles Black, 1913.

Senn, Fritz. "A Rhetorical Analysis of James Joyce's 'Grace.' " *Moderna Sprak* 74 (1980): 121–28.

Siegel, Jerrold. *Bohemian Paris: Culture, Politics and the Boundaries of Bourgeois Life, 1830–1930*. New York: Viking, 1986.

Simon, Elliott M. "James Joyce's *Exiles* and the Tradition of the Edwardian Problem Play." *Modern Drama* 20 (March 1977): 21–35.

Spivak, Gayatri Chakravorty. "Marx after Derrida." In William E. Cain, ed., *Philosophical Approaches to Literature*, 227–46. Canbury, N.J.: Bucknell University Press, 1984.

Staley, Thomas F. "James Joyce and One of His Ghosts: Edouard Dujardin." *Renascence* 35 (Winter 1983): 85–95.

Staley, Thomas F., and Bernard Benstock, eds. *Approaches to Joyce's "Portrait":*

Ten Essays. Pittsburgh: University of Pittsburgh Press, 1976.

Stewart, Susan. *Nonsense: Aspects of Intertextuality in Folklore and Literature.* Baltimore, Md.: Johns Hopkins University Press, 1979.

Stone, Donald. *The Romantic Impulse in Victorian Fiction.* Cambridge: Harvard University Press, 1980.

Stone, Harry. " 'Araby' and the Writings of James Joyce." In James Joyce, *"Dubliners": Text, Criticism, and Notes*, ed. Robert Scholes and A. Walton Litz, 344–67. New York: Viking Press, 1969.

Tanner, Tony. *Adultery in the Novel.* Baltimore, Md.: Johns Hopkins University Press, 1979.

Terdiman, Richard. *Discourse/Counter-Discourse: The Theory and Practice of Symbolic Resistance in Nineteenth-Century France.* Ithaca, N.Y.: Cornell University Press, 1985.

Thorslev, Peter. *The Byronic Hero: Types and Prototypes.* Minneapolis: University of Minnesota Press, 1962.

Tinayre, Marcelle. *La Maison du péché.* Paris: Calmann-Levy, 1917.

Tindall, William York. *A Reader's Guide to James Joyce.* New York: Farrar, Straus and Giroux, 1959.

Todorov, Tzvetan. *Mikhail Bakhtin: The Dialogical Principle.* Trans. Wlad Godzich. Minneapolis: University of Minnesota Press, 1984.

Topia, André. "The Matrix and the Echo: Intertextuality in *Ulysses*." In Derek Attridge and Daniel Ferrer, eds., *Post-structuralist Joyce: Essays from the French*, 103–26. Cambridge: Cambridge University Press, 1984.

Torchiana, Donald. *Backgrounds for Joyce's "Dubliners."* Boston: Allen and Unwin, 1986.

Trilling, Lionel. *Sincerity and Authenticity.* Cambridge: Harvard University Press, 1971.

Turner, E. S. *Boys Will Be Boys.* London: Michael Joseph, 1948.

Twitchell, James B. *Forbidden Partners: The Incest Taboo in Modern Culture.* New York: Columbia University Press, 1987.

———. *The Living Dead: A Study of the Vampire in Romantic Literature.* Durham, N.C.: Duke University Press, 1981.

Veeder, William. *Henry James: The Lessons of the Master.* Chicago: University of Chicago Press, 1975.

Vidocq, Eugène. *Memoirs of Vidocq.* 2 vols. New York: Arno Press, 1976. Reprints vols. 25–28 of the 1828–29 London edition, *Autobiography: A Collection of the most Instructing and Amusing Lives. . . .*

Waisbren, Burton A., and Florence L. Walzl. "Paresis and the Priest: James Joyce's Symbolic Use of Syphilis in 'The Sisters.' " *Annals of Internal Medicine* 80 (June 1974): 758–62.

Walzl, Florence L. "*Dubliners*: Women in Irish Society." In Suzette Henke and Elaine Unkeless, eds., *Women in Joyce*, 31–56. Urbana: University of Illinois Press, 1982.

———. "Gabriel and Michael: The Conclusion of 'The Dead.' " In James Joyce,

"Dubliners": Text, Criticism, and Notes, ed. Robert Scholes and A. Walton Litz, 423–43. New York: Viking Press, 1969.

Wellington, Frederick V. "A Missing Conversation in *Ulysses*." *James Joyce Quarterly* 14 (Summer 1977): 476–79.

West, Michael, and William Hendricks. "The Genesis and Significance of Joyce's Irony in 'A Painful Case.'" *ELH* 44 (1977): 701–27.

Williams, Raymond. "'Exiles.'" In Colin MacCabe, ed., *James Joyce: New Perspectives*, 105–10. Bloomington: Indiana University Press, 1982.

————. *Keywords: A Vocabulary of Culture and Society*. 2d ed. New York: Oxford University Press, 1985.

Willing's Press Guide and Advertisers' Directory and Handbook. East Grinstead: Thomas Skinner Directories, 1904.

Yeats, W. B. *Memoirs*. Ed. Denis Donoghue. New York: Macmillan, 1972.

Young, Filson. *The Sands of Pleasure*. Boston: Dana Estes and Co., 1905.

INDEX